VISIT US AT

www.syngress.com

Syngress is committed to publishing high-quality books for IT Professionals and delivering those books in media and formats that fit the demands of our customers. We are also committed to extending the utility of the book you purchase via additional materials available from our Web site.

SOLUTIONS WEB SITE

To register your book, visit www.syngress.com/solutions. Once registered, you can access our solutions@syngress.com Web pages. There you will find an assortment of value-added features such as free e-booklets related to the topic of this book, URLs of related Web site, FAQs from the book, corrections, and any updates from the author(s).

ULTIMATE CDs

Our Ultimate CD product line offers our readers budget-conscious compilations of some of our best-selling backlist titles in Adobe PDF form. These CDs are the perfect way to extend your reference library on key topics pertaining to your area of expertise, including Cisco Engineering, Microsoft Windows System Administration, CyberCrime Investigation, Open Source Security, and Firewall Configuration, to name a few.

DOWNLOADABLE EBOOKS

For readers who can't wait for hard copy, we offer most of our titles in downloadable Adobe PDF form. These eBooks are often available weeks before hard copies, and are priced affordably.

SYNGRESS OUTLET

Our outlet store at syngress.com features overstocked, out-of-print, or slightly hurt books at significant savings.

SITE LICENSING

Syngress has a well-established program for site licensing our ebooks onto servers in corporations, educational institutions, and large organizations. Contact us at sales@syngress.com for more information.

CUSTOM PUBLISHING

Many organizations welcome the ability to combine parts of multiple Syngress books, as well as their own content, into a single volume for their own internal use. Contact us at sales@syngress.com for more information.

SYNGRESS®

Syngress

IT Security Project Management

Handbook

Susan Snedaker

Russ Rogers   Technical Editor

KEY	SERIAL NUMBER
001	HJIRTCV764
002	PO9873D5FG
003	829KM8NJH2
004	BC1289MPQV
005	CVPLQ6WQ23
006	VBP965T5T5
007	HJJJ863WD3E
008	2987GVTWMK
009	629MP5SDJT
010	IMWQ295T6T

PUBLISHED BY
Syngress Publishing, Inc.
800 Hingham Street
Rockland, MA 02370

Syngress IT Security Project Management

Printed in Canada.
1 2 3 4 5 6 7 8 9 0
ISBN: 1-59749-076-8

Publisher: Andrew Williams
Acquisitions Editor: Jaime Quigley, Erin Heffernan
Technical Editor: Russ Rogers
Cover Designer: Michael Kavish

Page Layout and Art: Patricia Lupien
Copy Editor: Judy Eby
Indexer: Odessa&Cie

Distributed by O'Reilly Media, Inc. in the United States and Canada.
For information on rights, translations, and bulk sales, contact Matt Pedersen, Director of Sales and Rights, at Syngress Publishing; email matt@syngress.com or fax to 781-681-3585.

Acknowledgments

Syngress would like to acknowledge the following people for their kindness and support in making this book possible.

Syngress books are now distributed in the United States and Canada by O'Reilly Media, Inc. The enthusiasm and work ethic at O'Reilly are incredible, and we would like to thank everyone there for their time and efforts to bring Syngress books to market: Tim O'Reilly, Laura Baldwin, Mark Brokering, Mike Leonard, Donna Selenko, Bonnie Sheehan, Cindy Davis, Grant Kikkert, Opol Matsutaro, Steve Hazelwood, Mark Wilson, Rick Brown, Tim Hinton, Kyle Hart, Sara Winge, Peter Pardo, Leslie Crandell, Regina Aggio Wilkinson, Pascal Honscher, Preston Paull, Susan Thompson, Bruce Stewart, Laura Schmier, Sue Willing, Mark Jacobsen, Betsy Waliszewski, Kathryn Barrett, John Chodacki, Rob Bullington, Kerry Beck, Karen Montgomery, and Patrick Dirden.

The incredibly hardworking team at Elsevier Science, including Jonathan Bunkell, Ian Seager, Duncan Enright, David Burton, Rosanna Ramacciotti, Robert Fairbrother, Miguel Sanchez, Klaus Beran, Emma Wyatt, Krista Leppiko, Marcel Koppes, Judy Chappell, Radek Janousek, Rosie Moss, David Lockley, Nicola Haden, Bill Kennedy, Martina Morris, Kai Wuerfl-Davidek, Christiane Leipersberger, Yvonne Grueneklee, Nadia Balavoine, and Chris Reinders for making certain that our vision remains worldwide in scope.

David Buckland, Marie Chieng, Lucy Chong, Leslie Lim, Audrey Gan, Pang Ai Hua, Joseph Chan, June Lim, and Siti Zuraidah Ahmad of Pansing Distributors for the enthusiasm with which they receive our books.

David Scott, Tricia Wilden, Marilla Burgess, Annette Scott, Andrew Swaffer, Stephen O'Donoghue, Bec Lowe, Mark Langley, and Anyo Geddes of Woodslane for distributing our books throughout Australia, New Zealand, Papua New Guinea, Fiji, Tonga, Solomon Islands, and the Cook Islands.

# Author

Susan Snedaker (MBA, BA, MCSE, MCT, CPM) is Principal Consultant and founder of VirtualTeam Consulting, LLC (www.virtualteam.com), a consulting firm specializing in business and technology consulting. The company works with companies of all sizes to develop and implement strategic plans, operational improvements and technology platforms that drive profitability and growth. Prior to founding VirtualTeam in 2000, Susan held various executive and technical positions with companies including Microsoft, Honeywell, Keane, and Apta Software. As Director of Service Delivery for Keane, she managed 1200+ technical support staff delivering phone and email support for various Microsoft products including Windows Server operating systems. She is author of *How to Cheat at IT Project Management* (Syngress Publishing, ISBN: 1-597490-37-7) *The Best Damn Windows Server 2003 Book Period* (Syngress, ISBN: 1-931836-12-4) and *How to Cheat at Managing Windows Small Business Server 2003* (Syngress, ISBN: 1-932266-80-1). She has also written numerous technical chapters for a variety of Syngress Publishing books on Microsoft Windows and security technologies and has written and edited technical content for various publications. Susan has developed and delivered technical content from security to telephony, TCP/IP to WiFi, CIW to IT project management and just about everything in between (she admits a particular fondness for anything related to TCP/IP).

Susan holds a master's degree in business administration and a bachelor's degree in management from the University of Phoenix. She also holds a certificate in advanced project management from Stanford University. She holds Microsoft Certified Systems Engineer (MSCE) and Microsoft Certified Trainer (MCT) certifications. Susan is a member of the Information Technology Association of Southern Arizona (ITASA) and the Project Management Institute (PMI).

Technical Editor

Russ Rogers (CISSP, CISM, IAM, IEM, HonScD), author of the popular *Hacking a Terror Network* (Syngress Publishing, ISBN 1-928994-98-9), co-author on multiple other books including the best selling *Stealing the Network: How to Own a Continent*(Syngress, ISBN 1-931836-05-1), *Network Security Evaluation Using the NSA IEM* (Syngress, 1-597490-35-0) and Editor in Chief of *The Security Journal;* is Co-Founder, Chief Executive Officer, and Chief Technology Officer of Security Horizon; a veteran-owned small business based in Colorado Springs, CO. Russ has been involved in information technology since 1980 and has spent the last 15 years working professionally as both an IT and INFOSEC consultant. Russ has worked with the United States Air Force (USAF), National Security Agency (NSA), and the Defense Information Systems Agency (DISA). He is a globally renowned security expert, speaker, and author who has presented at conferences around the world including Amsterdam, Tokyo, Singapore, Sao Paulo, and cities all around the United States.

Russ has an Honorary Doctorate of Science in Information Technology from the University of Advancing Technology, a Masters Degree in Computer Systems Management from the University of Maryland, a Bachelor of Science in Computer Information Systems from the University of Maryland, and an Associate Degree in Applied Communications Technology from the Community College of the Air Force. He is a member of both ISSA and ISACA and co-founded the Global Security Syndicate (gssyndicate.org), the Security Tribe (securitytribe.com), and acts in the role of professor of network security for the University of Advancing Technology (uat.edu).

Russ would like to thank his father for his lifetime of guidance, his kids (Kynda and Brenden) for their understanding, and Michele for her constant support. A great deal of thanks goes to Andrew Williams and Jaime Quigley from Syngress Publishing for the abundant opportunities and trust they give me. Shouts go out to UAT, Security Tribe, the GSS, the Defcon Groups, and the DC Forums. I'd like to also thank my friends, Chris, Greg, Michele, Ping, Pyr0, and everyone in #dc-forums that I don't have room to list here.

Special Contributors

A special thank you to the following authors for contributing their expertise to various sections of this book: Bryan Cunningham, Principal at the Denver law firm of Morgan & Cunningham LLC, Norris Johnson, Mike Rash, Frank Thornton, Chris Hurley, and Mike O'Dea.

Contents

Foreword

Not everything that counts can be counted and not everything that can be counted counts.

—Albert Einstein

As the late management guru Peter Drucker once said, "Plans are only good intentions unless they immediately degenerate into hard work." The intent of this book is not to lead you through long, arduous planning processes while hackers are stealing your network out from under you. The intent is to provide you with effective network security planning tools so that you can "degenerate into hard work" as quickly as possible to keep your network secure with the least amount of effort.

Rather than losing sleep at night wondering who's wandering around your network in the dark, you can create a comprehensive security solution for your company that will meet your security needs today and will allow you to address new security requirements in the future. This book is designed to help you do exactly that.

—Susan Snedaker
Principal Consultant and Founder
VirtualTeam Consulting, LLC

Acknowledgments

Thanks to all the hardworking folks at Syngress for all the front- and back-end work they do. Chris and Andrew, thanks for suggesting this book and making this project a reality; Jaime, thanks for staying around to get this project completed and keeping me sane along the way; Erin, thanks for bringing this project across the finish line. Many thanks to my ace technical editor, Russ Rogers, who contributed his superlative security expertise to this book. And last but not least, thank you to Lisa, my family, friends, and clients who supported (and put up with) me during this project.

Chapter 1

IT Security Project Management Building Blocks

Solutions in this chapter:

- Corporate Security Project Plan Components
- The True Cost of IT Security
- IT Security Project Success Factors
- Project Constraints
- Corporate Strategy and IT Security
- How Corporate Culture and Policies Impact IT Security

☑ Summary

☑ Solutions Fast Track

Introduction

Let's start by stating two assumptions we're making in this book. First, we're assuming you have a solid understanding of IT project management. If not, we have provided you with a free download of the book *How to Cheat at IT Project Management* (visit www.syngress.com/solutions to register this book and download the PDF) so you can fill in any gaps you may have. Second, we'll assume that you have a fairly good understanding of network security. This book is not intended to teach you basic IT project management nor is it intended to teach you how to implement specific network security solutions for your particular situation. What this book *will* do is provide an operational framework for you to use in designing your own IT security project plan.

Now that we've gotten those details out of the way, let's talk about network security. It's a massive subject and an enormous undertaking for any network administrator out there in the real world right now. By creating a project plan for addressing network security, you can approach this sometimes onerous task with a well thought-out plan. By creating a comprehensive plan for network security, you can be confident your network is as secure as humanly possible. There is no magic bullet and network security is a never-ending task, but using a consistent methodology will reduce your errors and omissions. In network security, it's often what you overlook that intruders exploit.

In this chapter, we're going to look at project management from a security planning perspective. We're not going to specifically cover IT project management, but we will use that framework to develop our IT security project plan. This will help reinforce your IT project management skills while providing you with a roadmap for implementing IT security in your organization.

Corporate Security Project Plan Components

Before discussing the specifics of IT security project planning, let's set the stage. Every company has a wide variety of diverse network components that have an effect on security (e.g., users, firewalls, and network topologies). As such, every company usually ends up with one overarching corporate security project plan, and many individual security project plans, each covering a specific area (see Figure 1.1). In formal project management language, the corporate security project plan is considered a "program," which by definition is a related set of project plans that are managed across the enterprise to enable optimal use of resources and to reduce project conflict (i.e., time, cost, resources). To keep it simple, we refer to the "corporate IT security project plan" as the "master plan" and to the sub-level plans as "individual focus areas" or "individual security area project plans." The larger the project, the more difficult it is to manage successfully; therefore, you are more likely to be successful if your corporate security is broken down into small project areas. We'll refer back to this model throughout the book as we explore how to create successful IT security project plans.

One important note at this juncture is that the topic areas included in Figure 1.1 may not be the topic areas you need for your corporate security project plan. You may not need all of these or there may be one or more additional security areas you need to include. The areas listed in Figure 1.1 are commonly used in many organizations but this is not considered an exhaustive list by any means.

Figure 1.1 Corporate Security Project Plan Components

Corporate IT Security Project Plan						
Individual Security Area Project Plans						
General Security	Infrastructure Security	Communication Security	Wireless Security	Web Security	Cryptography	Operational Security
Access Control	Devices & Media	Remote Access	Access Control	Access Control	Encryption	Incident Response
Authentication	Topologies	Email	Authentication	Authentication	Public Key (PKI)	Policies
Auditing	Intrusion Prevention/ Detection	Instant Messaging	Auditing	Auditing		Disaster Recover
Attacks	System Hardening	Voice over IP (VoIP)	Attacks	Attacks		Regulatory Issues
				System Hardening		Configuration Management

The True Cost of Security

Let's begin with a brief overview of why we even care about network security. If our networks and data didn't need to be secured, we could just leave the gates open and allow anyone in. The reality is obviously far from that. Data needs to be secured because it provides your company with a competitive edge or because it's confidential personal information such as credit card data or social security numbers. There are thousands of reasons why networks and data need to be secured and the unfortunate truth is that there is always someone out there looking for a new way in. That said, it's also true that the majority of security breaches are internal. Whether permissions are incorrectly set allowing a user to access an important file or whether a sophisticated user manages to get a hold of his boss's password in order to look at pay rates or performance reviews; malicious or inadvertent security breaches are most often an inside job.

According to the FBI, nearly 80 percent of security violations are caused by authorized users with legitimate access (i.e., "insiders"). Security threats include disgruntled employees, unsuspecting users, and outside contractors with insider access. U.S. companies spend over $6 billion annually on computer security hardware and software, but the best firewalls and security tools cannot prevent internal security breaches caused by internal issues (e.g., poor end-user security practices, inadvertent mistakes, lax attitudes, employee exploitation of security holes and intentional attacks or hacks).

How much is security worth? Network administrators are constantly under pressure to reduce costs and expand services. A recent study shows that as a percentage of revenues, IT budgets have gone down over the past few years. So, while the actual dollar amount of the corporate budget has risen, the percentage allocated to IT from corporate revenues has dropped (i.e., your company is growing but is not giving you the financial resources you need to do your job). For the sake of argument, let's assume that you have trimmed all the fat from your budget. You are running lean and mean and have no more "give" in your budget. What do you do when push comes to shove? Whatever your answer, it probably directly or indirectly impacts network security (e.g., not having enough IT staff to maintain systems; fewer upgrades to secure operating systems; fewer purchases or upgrades of intrusion detection systems; less time to plan and implement a comprehensive security solution).

So, rather than fall victim to decreasing IT budgets, let's discuss a proactive stance. As discussed in *How to Cheat at IT Project Management* , one of the keys to success in the IT world is understanding the company's business plan. No one is going to hand you a blank check; you have to be savvy. To that end, we look at some quantifiable and verifiable numbers that can be used to develop a strategy for getting your IT security budget approved.

Business Intelligence...

How IT Budgets Are Actually Spent

The February 2006 issue of "CIO Insight Magazine" discusses a research study on IT spending. The conclusions? Many IT professionals agree that their companies do not spend enough on IT (i.e., IT departments are handling an ever-increasing number of projects while IT spending is moving away from hardware and software to staffing and services). The study also surveyed how IT budgets are spent. Interestingly, security software was eighth on the list of technology spending. Disaster recovery and business continuity was first on the list of initiatives. According to Ken Goldstein, an economist with the Conference Board (a business research organization), part of the reason companies are reluctant to spend more on IT is that businesses "haven't gotten full utilization out of what they've already spent, and they need to. They will not necessarily cut back their spending, but what we will get is this cautious, conservative spending." (CIO Insight, February 2006, p. 69.) Making the effort to align IT projects with corporate strategies and to develop and present a business case for key IT projects, continues to be one of the best ways to ensure that your IT department has the tools and resources it needs. Security spending should be a discrete line item in your IT budget. You should prepare the business case for security separately (though in an integrated manner), otherwise it may get lost in the larger IT budget.

Prevention vs. Remediation

One of the best ways to support an increase in IT spending for security, is to clearly delineate the cost of preventing a security breach versus the cost of fixing a security breach. Most corporate executives appreciate a rational approach to the business end of IT, and find a risk analysis and financial overview helpful tools in justifying additional expenditures. A recent study by Computer Economics shows that spending on security is approximately 3 percent of all IT expenditures, which has remained fairly constant for the past three years. Most telling is that security spending has remained constant while other areas of IT spending have fallen over the same period of time. In addition, spending on security has shifted. Many of the efforts made in the past several years to harden networks against attack are paying off in lower remediation efforts.

This is the key take away for IT professionals today in making the business case for security. Security spending in the past has reduced the cost of remediation efforts today. Sometimes it's hard to make the case for something that's absent, but this is an opportunity to tout how successful past efforts have been. If you don't have specific data you can point to, you can generate some realistic estimates. Determine how much you've spent on hardening the network and calculate about how much time that has saved in both IT staff time and in productivity on the network. When the network is attacked, you have three expenses: the IT staff time, the productivity of people trying to use the network and the often more intangible cost to the company's reputation (which sometimes becomes a legal issue with financial implications). If you're hard pressed to figure out how much your company has saved by not having security breaches, do some research and find industry averages applicable to your industry or company size. To assist in that, we've provided a few numbers, courtesy of research by the Computer Economics group. While this data may be generic, it's a good starting point to help you make the business case for the return on investment for past security spending and why it's a good idea to keep spending that money. Here's another hint: Sit down with your company's financial expert and have a few financial metrics generated based on your findings. If you can show a positive return on investment (ROI) or an internal rate of return (IRR), your company's management will have to sit up and pay attention. Along the way, you'll help secure your reputation as someone who understands the *business* of IT.

The independent research firm, Computer Economics, suggests using the following four steps to create a generic ROI for computer security:

1. Analyze the potential economic impact of a security breach (you may want to delineate the potential impact of several different categories of security issues such as virus, phishing, DoS, etc.).

2. Determine the business exposure (network, Internet connectivity, e-commerce intensity, and so on).

3. Examine and delineate the cost of security.

4. Calculate the ROI of security.

For example, if a virus invades your network, you can track how many IT staff hours were required to remediate the situation, by calculating how long you spent fixing the problem (e.g., 60 minutes × 48 users × an average hourly rate based on overall salary levels in the organization). Sometimes, you can determine how much revenue was lost during that time (e.g., if you had to shut down an e-commerce server for four hours, what were the average hourly sales for that particular day and time?) Can you calculate how many of those customers will not return or will spend less in the future? Probably not, but you know the four-hour outage will have a ripple effect that is larger than the calculated hourly loss. In general, some quantifiable data is better than none, and you can use it to begin tracking and analyzing the true cost of security breaches. Some executives only understand the value of security spending when they understand the actual cost of such a breach to the organization.

Potential Economic Impact

In order to understand the potential economic impact of a security breach, you have to look at the cost of remediation and the short- and long-term impact to the organization. The immediate impact of remediation includes the cost of labor and parts to repair damaged systems, the loss of organizational productivity during the repair phase, and the impact these repairs have on the cash flow and financial transactions of the company. If your company is e-commerce-intensive, this impact will likely be even more significant. The loss of security around credit card data or the destruction of a month's worth of e-commerce transaction data clearly has an economic impact beyond the cost of repairing the security breach. Look at all areas of your business where the network and the Internet are factors. (A specific plan to assess the risk to your network is discussed later in this book.) At this point, your goal is to look at the cost of security so that you can make a business case to corporate to gain the necessary organizational, political, and financial support you need for your security projects.

The short-term impact of a security breach (e.g., if your e-commerce site experiences a DOS attack) includes the potential loss of sales and the potential loss of contracts and relationships with suppliers, vendors, and key customers. If your organization has suffered a serious and very public security breach, your sales team might have more difficulty closing a big deal. Clearly, the reputation of the organization suffers and, while it might be difficult to quantify, it reduces the company's reputation and associated "goodwill."

The long-term impact of a security breach includes the loss of key customers, the loss of market confidence, and the erosion of share price if the company is publicly held. The public perception of a company in the marketplace is not built overnight, but it can be destroyed overnight by an avoidable security breach. The news is full of recent examples of companies that inappropriately managed data security and ultimately paid the price. It is hard to recover from that kind of major security lapse, both in the real terms of remediation and in the less tangible terms in the minds of suppliers, customers, shareholders, and the community.

The bottom line is: the more devices attached to your network and the more reliant your company is on the Internet for doing business, the more a security breach will cost. The Computer Economics group estimates that if you are highly reliant on the network and the Internet for your business activities and you have 100 attached devices, the cost of a security breach is approximately $250,000. If you have 250 devices, the cost is approximately $500,000. These costs include cleaning infected systems, recovery from hacks and intrusions, a loss of revenue, and a loss of employee productivity. As you can see, it becomes much easier to justify security-related spending when you clearly delineate the cost of not doing so.

Business Intelligence...

The Real Cost of Remediation

A quick scan of the headlines will tell you that security breaches are on the rise. It takes time and effort to stay one step ahead of hackers. However, a recent report reveals that many companies would rather spend money cleaning up the aftermath of an attack on their network security, than deal with it proactively. Security spending is still seen by some as a giant black hole where money goes in and nothing comes out. However, a glance at the headlines shows that companies that experience massive public security breaches end up in trouble with their customers, their employees, their shareholders, and often the government.

A well-publicized incident in June 2005, involved a serious security breach by CardSystems, a credit card processing company. The company was holding on to credit card data it was not supposed to have in order to "analyze" it. However, the data was not properly secured and 40 million credit card holders' personal data was compromised. Credit card companies had to re-issue millions of credit cards. (MasterCard alone had to re-issue 13.9 million cards.) CardSystems was sold to another company in what appeared to be a "fire sale" in September 2005. After reviewing the incident, the Federal Trade Commission determined there were clear security problems and required the company to have an independent security audit every other year for the next 20 years. This is a classic example of a security breach that could have been avoided. It started on the inside from apparently "benign" behavior (i.e., no one initially attempted to hack the data). The data was stolen because internal procedures violated two areas: their agreement with credit card companies on how they would handle customer data, and their decision not to follow appropriate protocols for monitoring and managing data to ensure its security. (For additional information, go to *www.consumeraffairs.com/news04/2006/02/ftc_cardsystems.html*.)

A Vermont college system employee on vacation in Canada, had her laptop stolen from a locked car. The laptop contained personal and financial data for over 20,000 Vermont college system employees and students. The data was not encrypted. Details about the theft were not

Continued

disclosed for three weeks, even though the data at risk included people's social security numbers, birth dates, bank account numbers, and payroll information. A second security breach involved a hacker using an IT staff person's e-mail address to send a system-wide message regarding the stolen laptop. (For additional information, go to *http://www.burlington-freepress.com/apps/pbcs.dll/article?AID=/20060409/NEWS01/60409031 6/1009/NEWS05.*

A security breach in Spokane, Washington left hundreds of bank and credit union debit card customers in a tight spot when they were informed their debit cards had been compromised. New cards and PIN numbers were issued. The breach cost banks, credit unions, and customers thousands of hours for canceling and re-issuing debit cards. The cost to banks, credit unions, and customers ran into the hundreds of thousands of dollars. (For additional information, go to *http://www.kxly.com/news/index.php?sect_rank=1&story_id=1253.*)

Security spending is time and money well spent. Your job as the network administrator is to make the business case for security spending. One way is to align security goals with business goals. When you tie security to business objectives, senior executives are more likely to understand, value, support, and fund security initiatives.

Business Exposure

This section discusses the relative exposure of your business, which will help you present your business case for security-related spending, and help you gain critical support for your IT security project. Some business exposure can be assessed by looking at the following categories and determining what percentage of your business they comprise:

1. **E-commerce Retail Sales** If your company sells product via the Internet, there are numerous security issues that must be addressed. From Web site security to transaction security, and from credit card processing to identifiable user information, your company has a legal and ethical obligation to maintain a certain level of security.

2. **Business-to-business (B2B) Transactions** Some companies only deal with other businesses (i.e., not the general public). These B2B transactions are vulnerable to outside and inside attacks. Disruption of this revenue stream can be devastating, because it can damage a

company's cash flow and its relationship with key business partners (i.e., eroding trust and confidence reduces the value of the business transaction).

3. **Internet Connectivity and Reliance** Some companies rely heavily on the Internet. If your company uses the Internet to connect with customers, vendors, regulatory authorities, employees, or shareholders, you must assess the risk of loss or disruption in each of those categories. The more you rely on the Internet as a business tool, the greater your need for tight security and additional security funds.

4. **Dispersed Workforce.** If your company's employees work from home, work on the road, connect from airports, coffee shops or vendor's locations, your network security needs to take this workforce model into account. The risks to the network obviously increase when users are roaming around out in the wild unsecured world of coffee shop (or hotel) wireless networks and your network security plan has to account for these types of arrangements.

5. **Electronic Data Interchange with Businesses and Consumers** You risk a security breach whenever you exchange data directly across the Internet. There are numerous technologies that will secure those exchanges.

6. **Data Sensitivity** Legislation regarding the privacy of medical history and other personal data (e.g., social security numbers, credit card numbers, household income, credit scores, and so on) has expanded. Any company dealing with confidential personal information must have strong security processes in place to ensure that the data is handled properly at all stages (i.e., from collection to storage, retrieval, and analysis). Disruptions in this area can result in serious financial and legal consequences.

Cost of Security

The amount of money spent on security should match the risks associated with a potential breach of security (e.g., a financial firm has a higher risk profile than a paper supply company). However, both companies must assess their risk and decide on a reasonable level of protection. You can spend a lot of money on security, but at some point your ROI diminishes because you are outspending your risk.

When planning for the cost of security, evaluate the following:

- Company size

- Nature of company business

- Government regulations

- Reliance on e-commerce, Internet, and network connectivity

- Nature of business transactions

- Business structure (centralized, multiple locations, mobile workforce, and so on)

- The tangible and intangible value of the information and company data

- The potential impact of a security breach on the company's reputation and bottom line

One point that can be easy to miss in all of this is that your security really should be calibrated to the value of your company's data. To use an analogy, there's no point on putting a $5,000 alarm system on a 1979 Chevrolet Cavalier that has a rusted out frame and 150,000 miles on it. It's probably pretty low on the list of cars that get stolen (no offense intended toward anyone who owns such a vehicle, but chances are you don't worry about it getting hot wired in your driveway). On the other hand, if you own a $250,000 custom sports car, a $5,000 alarm system might not be enough. You might also add a low-jack system that disables the engine when the car is reported stolen and you might also install a GPS tracking device so you can locate the vehicle if it is stolen. The point is that your security measures need to really take into account the value of the data and the potential impact if that data (or network services) are disrupted. However, since you will have defend your budget, you also need to make sure your security solution is commensurate with the value of the data and network services and the relative cost of business disruption.

ROI of Security

Once you have delineated the cost of security threats and security spending, you can calculate a ROI or do a break-even analysis. The Computer Economics group determined that for a company with high exposure to risk factors (e.g., e-commerce companies), the break-even point for security per device is approximately $375 for a company with 100 devices. The per-device cost is approximately $400 for a company with 500 devices, or about $250,000. For the following example, we use a 100-device network. The cost for security hardware, software, implementation, management, and personnel is estimated to be $196,000 for a high risk company. The cost of a single security breach is estimated at $233,000. While this appears to be a $37,000 savings, it may not adequately address the loss of productivity, opportunity costs (e.g., What else could we have done with our time if we were not remediating a security breach?) and the cost of the black mark on your business's reputation. The numbers show that the cost of avoiding a problem is less than the cost of fixing a problem. Put some numbers together for your organization that show the net positive result of problem avoidance. (For more information on the economics of computer security, go to *www.computereconomics.com*.)

Business Intelligence...

The Ultimate Cost of Security

A recently released survey by CompTIA sheds light on the cost of security. (See The Channel Insider, "Poll: IT Security Training Not a Priority" by Pedro Periera at *http://www.thechannelinsider.com/article2/0,1895, 1934496,00.asp*).

According to CompTIA Chief Operating Officer (COO) Brian McCarthy, employers do not invest in enough training; fewer than 25 percent of employees receive any type of security training. While the investment in security hardware and software has increased in recent years, the investment in training has not kept pace, which is alarming when you consider

Continued

that 80 percent of all security breaches are caused internally, many due to simple human error. Much of that error can be directly attributed to a lack of security training. Companies have a false sense of security when they look at the capital investments they make in hardware and software solutions, but without adequate training on the proper configuration, use, and maintenance of the security solutions, those capital investments are wasted. The survey also found that, on average, IT departments spend 2 percent of their time and 5 percent of their budgets on security. That is pretty low when you consider that the average security breach typically costs a company approximately 1.5× what they spend on security solutions.

Now for the cold hard truth. According to the Gartner Group, 50 percent of all businesses that suffer a data loss due to an attack or system failure, go out of business within three years of the attack if they fail to restore the lost data within 24 hours.

Project Success Factors

In ITPM, we discussed the factors that contribute to project success. These factors bear repeating because they are significant when it comes to IT security. As we step through these success factors, we will look at them with an eye toward IT security. As you are reading, you may find there are additional nuances to these elements that are unique to your company or organization. If so, make a note for future reference. Understanding project success factors will make your job easier as you plan and implement your project.

Success Factor 1: Executive Support

The number one success factor of any project is executive support. If company executives do not understand or care about a project, they will not allocate the time, money, or resources needed to make it successful. Most corporate executives are aware of the need for IT security; however, if management is still not taking IT security seriously enough, you will have to embark on an education campaign to help them understand the importance of sound IT security planning. Like an insurance policy, the cost of having a sound IT security plan it is almost always less than the cost of not having one.

IT security is not inexpensive. The cost of labor to assess, plan, implement, manage, monitor, and respond is expensive. Add to that the layers of hardware and software components needed to keep IT secure, and you start seeing IT dollars disappear. Without executive support for IT security planning and implementation, it will be hard to get IT security budgets approved.

Business Intelligence...

Executive Support 101

In most companies, the easiest way to gain executive support for IT security spending is to make the business case for the expenditures. Tying IT security in with the corporate strategy, mission, values, and goals can help executives understand and approve needed expenditures. A little aversive therapy also goes a long way (e.g., get examples of companies, ideally in your industry or segment, that have had security breaches. Highlight not only what the ultimate cost of remediation was, but also how embarrassing it was to the company. It only takes one or two good examples to help executives understand that they do not want to pay the clean up cost when the prevention cost is lower.

Without executive support, IT security initiatives will ultimately fail because the organization will allocate time and resources to other projects. There are numerous competing demands and priorities in every company. If your executive team does not understand or value security initiatives, you will have an uphill battle. Organizations need to develop a corporate culture that supports security from the ground up; however, this can only be created when there is support and active involvement at the top. Most security breaches happen inside the organization; therefore, developing a security culture is critical to maintaining IT security. Do your homework, make the business case, and give your corporate leaders the tools they need to make informed decisions that support IT security.

Success Factor 2: User Involvement

Most security breaches occur from inside an organization. Some breaches are intentional and some are completely innocent, but the net result is the same—security is compromised and the company is put at risk. Users often view security differently than IT employees, which is why there is poor communication between the two groups. The user's view is, "I need to access everything at the same time." The IT perspective is, "You need as little access to as few resources as possible." Neither perspective in the extreme is useful; there has to be a balance between the two. By involving key users in your security planning process, you will have the "real world" perspective at the table. Hearing user's objections to security measures will allow you to modify them accordingly.

A good example of that balance is *password policies*. If you require a 10-digit minimum length password that must be changed every two days, there is a high likelihood that users will write the passwords down at their desks so that they do not forget them. This type of security circumvention occurs because the users were not consulted when the security policies were created. In most cases, however, if you can find a balance between the user's needs and the security needs of the organization, you are more likely to see higher user compliance. When you involve key users in the process, you avoid having them circumvent policies that are too stringent and you avoid having to revise your policy after it fails.

Success Factor 3: Experienced Project Manager

In the case of IT security, it is critical that the project manager have experience successfully managing projects, since any errors or omissions in a security plan can have serious consequences. A project manager using a proven, consistent project management methodology is more likely to generate a solid IT security project plan than one who has no consistent method for approaching an IT project. If you are the project manager for

The Power of Clarity

In my consulting work, I often see people launch into projects without a clear sense of direction, whether the project is self-initiated or handed to them by a client, boss, or co-worker. Stepping back and asking what outcome you are trying to achieve and what the major objectives are will bring clarity to your project. When defining your IT security project, you want to define three to five major objectives that will drive IT security for your firm. Be very clear about what you are trying to achieve and you will have a much better chance of achieving it.

Success Factor 5:
Clearly Defined (and Smaller) Scope

Studies consistently show that projects that are clearly defined and smaller in scope are more successful than those that are not. Whenever you start a project, you should always begin with the project objectives. The planning process should develop your top three to five high-level objectives into smaller tasks that eventually define your entire project from start to finish. When a project is clearly defined, it is easier to see if it is missing any elements or if it is hitting the mark.

Another success element is having a smaller scope. A scope is defined as the total amount of work to be accomplished for a project. The smaller the scope, the more likely that the project will be successful. The bigger the project, the more elements there are, resulting in the likelihood that one or more of them will be overlooked. In recognition of this important success factor, this book approaches IT security as a series of project plans, not one big plan. The overarching IT security plan includes sub-plans for each IT security area. To some extent, each of those sub-plans can be managed as separate plans. By defining sub-plans for each individual security area, you can accomplish two important goals: 1) you can assign the right people to the project based on their areas of expertise, and 2) you can focus intently on that aspect of security so that all of the key elements are addressed.

Success Factor 6:
Shorter Schedules, Multiple Milestones

With a smaller scope come shorter schedules. Again, this is fairly intuitive. It is hard to plan far into the future because so many intervening factors can arise over the course of 6, 9, or 12 months. Keeping shorter schedules means reducing project scope. One of the ways to do this with IT security is to divide your security planning into segments (as we have done for this book.)

Another interesting statistic is that projects with multiple milestones are far more successful than those with few milestones. By definition, a milestone is a marker in a project plan that indicates a significant event. It can be a checkpoint to ensure everything is on track, or it can be a checkpoint that indicates that some external event must be completed before the project can proceed. It is like directions to a location you have never been to before. If you read them once before heading out, you are likely to get lost along the way. On the other hand, if you read the directions along the way, you are more likely to turn left when you should turn left and right when you should turn right. Multiple milestones help you navigate time and schedules more effectively.

Success Factor 7: Clearly Defined Project Management Process

If you use a consistent process for defining, implementing, and managing projects, you are more likely to produce successful projects. Again, it is a process that should be implemented to help ensure that you include key elements in the right order at the right time. If you do not have a consistent project management process, you should develop one. (ITPM provides a methodology that you can use to cover the key elements of project planning.)

Success Factor 8: Standard Infrastructure

When developing your IT security project plan, look for opportunities to use standardized components, from software and hardware infrastructure elements to templates and off-the-shelf solutions. Carefully analyze the cost of purchasing infrastructure versus creating your own. Small- and medium-sized companies often fall victim to the "it costs too much" mentality when looking at off-the-shelf solutions to incorporate into their products or projects. However, if you add in the cost of errors, omissions, re-work, and cost and schedule overruns, you will probably find that purchasing these components or elements is a better business decision, even if it costs more than you expected. In addition, re-using standard templates and sections of IT project plans for your IT security plan enables you to avoid reinventing the wheel and will yield more consistent results over time.

Project Constraints

This section covers project constraints as they pertain to IT security project planning. If this is not a concept you are familiar with, refer to Chapter 1 in ITPM for a more detailed explanation.

Every project has four constraints: scope, time, cost, and quality. The relationship between these elements is described by different people in different ways, but the essential understanding is that there is a relationship between these elements. The total amount of work that can be accomplished (scope) is determined by how much time you have, how much you are willing to spend, and what level of quality is required. Conversely, the amount of time you need to complete a project is related to what you are willing to spend, what level of quality is required, and how much work you need to accomplish. The relationship is often shown in this manner:

Scope = Time x Cost x Quality

Let's look at the reverse of this. If you define a project and your division manager says that it is fine except you have to reduce the cost by 30 percent, you are forced to make some hard decisions. You can reduce the scope of work to reduce the cost, or you can reduce the quality to reduce the cost. If you change one of the constraints you also have to change another one. Changing one constraint without revisiting the others sets the project up for failure.

The scope of an IT security project can be defined by the IT security master plan or sub-plans. Reducing the scope allows you to reduce the time and cost of the project while still delivering high quality. Ideally, you should create an IT security project plan overview and then create separate sub-plans, which will allow you to manage the scope, time, cost, and quality more effectively.

In addition to understanding the interaction of the four constraints in a project, it is also important to understand how to prioritize those constraints. In every project, one constraint is typically "etched in stone" (e.g., the executive team tells you that your project cannot exceed $100,000 or that it must be completed within 6 months maximum). When you have this type of constraint, you have to make the other constraints more flexible. For example, suppose that in 12 months your company is going public through an Initial Public Offering (IPO). As part of the rigorous process, your company wants to make sure its network security is firmly in place at least 6 months prior to the IPO. Therefore, you are given 6 months to put your network security plan in place. Depending on a number of factors (e.g., how large your network is, what security is already in place), you may determine that 6 months is manageable only if you hire outside security consultants for assistance. That means that because time is the top priority and least flexible constraint in this project, you have to be more flexible with the other constraints. In this case, the cost will probably increase to accommodate the constraint. If the company executives are inflexible on all four constraints, the project will probably fail.

There is a saying in project management that states, "Things are more likely to go wrong than they are to go right." If the four project constraints are etched in stone, you have little chance for success. Increase your odds by negotiating with the executive team for one or more flexible constraints. That doesn't mean they open the checkbook and let you spend without limit. It does mean that they will need to understand that with a hard deadline that is fairly aggressive, they will have to give on the cost or the scope. If they refuse, the result will be what typically happens in many organizations. The team agrees to unrealistic targets because it really has no choice and then it fails to meet those targets because they were unrealistic. The plan changes in the middle of the project because something has to give way. Saying that it's not allowed to happen doesn't prevent it from happening. Negotiate up front for realistic parameters and priorities so that everyone benefits.

Corporate Strategy and IT Security

What does corporate strategy have to do with IT security? Suppose that over the next three to five years, your firm's strategy is to gain market share through the strategic acquisition of targeted companies in select geographic regions of the U.S. As network administrator, you must ensure that your corporate IT assets are protected today, while also making sure that new locations can be incorporated in the future. Each company acquired has its own network infrastructure, security policies, and tools for managing security. How you seamlessly integrate these acquisitions into your company and still keep all IT assets secure should be part of your IT security project plan.

Let's look at another example. Your company manufactures several products that are sold by mass merchandisers around the world. To remain competitive against the influx of low-cost alternatives to your products, your company decides it needs to improve its supply chain and distribution channel management. Part of that initiative involves providing suppliers and customers with real-time access to production and shipping data. This initiative would impact IT security by opening your network to vendors on one side and customers on the other, thereby exposing your network to a host of new, potential security problems.

It is critical that you are intimately aware of your company's short- and long-term strategies in order to effectively plan, implement, and manage IT security. If you do not understand how IT resources are used today and how they will be used tomorrow, you will not be able to create and manage a successful IT security project. Reworking a plan is expensive and results in a lot of wasted time and effort. Rework can be reduced by looking ahead at corporate strategies, at where your company is headed. If you align your IT security project with corporate goals at the project outset, you avoid some rework. That said, the business world is a dynamic environment and it is guaranteed that plans will change. If you start out closely aligned, you may be able to make minor modifications rather than wholesale changes to your security plan.

How Corporate Culture and Policies Impact IT Security

In addition to clearly understanding and aligning with your company's strategies, you also need to understand its culture and policies. Every company has a unique culture. Some companies have a very lax "we are all friends here" culture, where rules are few and seldom enforced. Others have very formal "buttoned down" cultures, where managers are addressed as "Mr. Brown" or "Ms. Black," and where rules are many and conscientiously enforced and obeyed. If your IT security policy does not address the reality of your corporate culture, it will not be effective. If you establish 52 rules of network security in a company where things run rather fast and loose, 51 of those rules will be disregarded whenever possible. You cannot single-handedly change your corporate culture, but you can influence it greatly when it comes to IT security. If you educate executives and users about the importance of IT security and how it affects them, you are more likely to gain their support and compliance. The reverse is also true. If you work in an environment where rules and regulations sometimes overwhelm even the simplest business process, you may need to make a case for having a more relaxed environment. Again, the complex password scenario is the one that consistently comes to mind. If you require passwords that look like *x%v93P!2m5>6*, users are going to write them down even if it is against the rules.

Company policies also come into play when creating an IT security plan. Does your company require a background check on employees who handle money, manage confidential personnel files, or who have full administrative rights on the network? Does your company have policies in place that address current regulatory requirements such as Health Insurance Portability and Accountability Act (HIPAA) or Sarbanes-Oxley (SOX)? If so, your IT security plans should also address these policies. Reviewing corporate policies will help you align your IT security with the requirements and realities of your company. Make sure you include legal, financial, and human resources representatives on the IT security project team, which will help ensure policies related to network security are properly addressed.

And finally, if you include users (Success Factor #2) in your security planning project, you are much more likely to strike a balance between the need for tight network security and the need for users to easily access the necessary resources. If you neglect to bring users into the mix until you are ready to implement the security solution, you will probably find that users are more resistant because you are simply "laying down the law." A collaborative approach, while taking more time in the planning stages, generates a better result and reduces problems in the implementation stage. The cost of making changes to a project in the planning stage is significantly less than making changes in the implementation stage; therefore, including users early in the process will save you time and money in the long run.

Summary

In this chapter, we looked at the underlying rationale for why it is important to have a sound IT security project plan prior to implementing IT security solutions. Every IT initiative must be funded, and IT security is no exception. While most executives understand the risks in today's connected world, many are still reluctant to authorize IT budget increases or to wholeheartedly support security initiatives. Your job is to make a business case for IT security spending through developing a sound analysis of the economic impact of a potential security breach, the risk profile of your company, and the cost of prevention. With this data, you can develop an approximate ROI calculation that will make sense to any corporate executive.

We also looked at the success factors of security projects. Executive support is key for two primary reasons. First, they have to authorize the financial expenditures. Second, without their support, the project is likely to fall off the list of key initiatives or corporate priorities, which means you will eventually be scrambling to find the time and resources needed to complete the project. User involvement is the second success factor. Involving users early in the planning process may seem like a major inconvenience; however, their involvement will help ensure that the implementation phase of your project goes more smoothly. Ultimately, user involvement will help you create a better project plan. Other success factors include having an experienced project manager who can ensure that the project scope, time, and processes are well-managed.

Each project has four constraints, which must be balanced and prioritized. It is important to understand that if you increase the scope, you also have to change one or more of the project's other constraints. Conversely, if you reduce the budget, you also have to change one or more of the project's constraints. It is also helpful to understand the priorities of these constraints. If there is a hard budget or a hard deadline, the other project constraints must be flexible to accommodate the inevitable problems and changes that occur during the implementation phase of the project.

Mandating all four constraints results in project failure on one or more fronts.

Another critical element to the success of your IT security project is understanding where your company is headed to in the future. If you craft an IT security plan that fails to account for possible future activities of your company, you will have to continually change your plan or you will have gaping security holes. Rather than continually reworking your plan, try to determine where your company is headed in the next three years and then plan accordingly. While this will not eliminate change to your IT security plan, it should help reduce it to a minimum.

As you develop your IT security policy, look at your company's culture. While you may have to implement new rules and regulations where none exist, you should try to align your security planning with the corporate culture to the greatest degree possible. When you do, you increase the likelihood that users will comply with IT security requirements. You may also need to work collaboratively with various stakeholders within the organization (e.g., Human Resources, Finance, Legal and so on) to ensure that the IT security policies match the corporate culture and the existing company rules, regulations, policies, and legal requirements. Creating an IT security policy in a vacuum will yield less than optimal results, if not outright failure.

Solutions Fast Track

The True Cost of IT Security

☑ According to FBI statistics, 80 percent of corporate security breaches occur from within the organization.

☑ Despite the initial cost of security hardware, software, and planning, prevention is usually less expensive than remediation.

☑ Many firms fail to take into account the "soft" costs of security breaches, including opportunity costs, cost to the reputation of the firm, and residual costs in the marketplace.

☑ When making a business case for IT security spending, assess the economic impact of a security breach, determine your company's level of risk, determine the cost of prevention and the value of the data, and calculate the ROI.

☑ Many companies fail to provide adequate training; errors account for a majority of security breaches. Training is key to the successful implementation of a security plan.

☑ Fifty percent of all businesses that suffer an attack or data loss go out of business within three years if they fail to recover from the data loss within 24 hours.

IT Security Project Success Factors

☑ Executive support is key to the success of all projects, but even more so to IT projects that require capital expenditures and cultural and political support.

☑ If users are not involved with the decisions regarding security implementation, there is a high likelihood that they will fail to comply or will actively seek ways to circumvent security.

☑ An experienced project manager contributes to IT security project success in many ways. Among them, he or she helps to clearly define project objectives, manage the scope of the project, create meaningful milestones, and develop project processes that foster success.

☑ Whenever possible, standardizing project infrastructure reduces the cost and time of the project. If you can reuse tools, processes, or methods from other projects, or if you can implement standardized tools or equipment, your projects will typically generate better results by reducing the learning curve and ramp-up time (which often leads to errors and omissions).

Project Constraints

☑ All projects have four constraints that must be balanced throughout the project. The scope (total amount of work to be done), the cost (budget), the time (schedule), and the quality.

☑ If you increase or reduce any element, one or more of the other constraints must change. If you reduce the cost of the project, you must increase the time or reduce the scope or quality of the project.

☑ Studies have consistently shown that projects that are shorter in length and smaller in scope tend to be more successful. One useful strategy is dividing your total IT security plan into multiple sub-plans. You can keep an eye on the overall IT security picture through a master IT security plan with multiple sub-plans incorporated.

☑ Gain agreement as to project priorities prior to the start of the project. Negotiate for one or more flexible constraints, since mandating all four constraints almost always results in the project failing to meet those parameters.

Corporate Strategy and IT Security

☑ While developing your IT security plan, you must take into account your company's strategy.

☑ Understanding where your company is headed and how it plans on getting there will enable you to develop an IT security plan that will meet the current and future needs of the organization.

☑ Developing an IT security plan that addresses the company's short- and long-term goals is important, but keep in mind that companies have to remain flexible and nimble to survive in today's global economy. Your IT security plans should be equally nimble to address the constant change your firm is experiencing.

How Corporate Culture and Policies Impact IT Security

☑ Companies all have very unique cultures. It would be imprudent to disregard the corporate culture when developing an IT security project plan.

☑ When developing security policies, look at your corporate culture and determine the most effective ways to implement security. Including users and key stakeholders from various parts of the organization in the security planning process, will help ensure that you implement policies consistent with user behavior.

Chapter 2

Defining the Security Project

Solutions in this chapter:

- Defining the Security Problem
- Defining the Security Mission or Outcome
- Defining Potential Security Project Solutions
- Defining the Optimal Security Project Solution
- Applying Security Project Constraints
- Developing the Security Project Proposal
- Identifying the Security Project Sponsor

☑ Summary

☑ Solutions Fast Track

Introduction

This chapter discusses the initial steps for creating an Information Technology (IT) security project plan using standard project management methods. This chapter introduces the concepts you need to create both the overall corporate IT security project plan and the individual plans (ISAPs) that you'll find toward the end of this book beginning in Chapter 9. As we step through the project management elements in this chapter, we're going to keep it short and sweet because each of these elements will be repeated again in each of the security project plans included starting in Chapter 9.

Defining the Security Problem

The first step in developing a solid IT security project plan is to define the problem. We can easily state that the problem is that "our networks are not secure or that there are assets in the organization that need to be protected from intentional and unintentional attack." Those statements are true on the macro level, meaning that these general statements apply to almost every organization (and computer) in the world. However, every company is different and every organization has its own unique set of security vulnerabilities to consider. Applying a one-size-fits-all approach to network security will simply not work.

As discussed in Chapter 1, an effective way to approach IT security is to create a corporate security plan that includes the individual focus areas of security (e.g., infrastructure, wireless). Breaking down each of the segments into smaller, individual focus areas allows you to better manage each aspect of security. Another challenge you will encounter is that there are many areas that overlap (i.e., does physical access fall under operational security, infrastructure security, or general security?) Creating a corporate IT security plan and individual plans gives you the opportunity to review your overall security project plan to ensure that all critical security elements are addressed.

Let's begin with a review of some of the industry's standard definitions and focus areas of security that you can use to create your security project plan.

Network Security and the CIA

An easy way to begin looking at network security is via the well-known acronym *"CIA"* which stands for *confidentiality, integrity* and *availability*. These are the three overarching areas of network security that touch upon every network component from firewalls to user passwords. Let's look at these in detail so you can begin formulating your network security problem statement.

Confidentiality

Confidentiality refers to preventing the unauthorized access, disclosure, and use of information, and is part of the broader concept of privacy. Every company has different confidentiality needs (e.g., a hotel must keep guest room and credit card numbers and home addresses private; a beverage company must keep its product formula secret; an online retailer must keep customers' shopping data private; and an online search company must keep the user search data private).

Confidentiality is maintained through user authentication and access control. User authentication ensures that the person trying to access the data is authorized. Access control is the process of defining which users and groups should have access to the data. In combination, these mechanisms help ensure the confidentiality of data; however, there is little you can do to guarantee confidentiality without the users' participation, agreement, and compliance. User awareness, training, and education are vital components of any security solution, and typically part of a company-wide awareness, training, and education initiative. In the larger scheme of things, confidentiality has to do with how users handle and utilize confidential data and these are often elements of regulatory issues such as the Health Insurance Portability and Accountability Act of 1996 (HIPAA). These are typically part of a company-wide awareness, training and education initiative in which the IT department should participate.

Integrity

In the IT world, *integrity* refers to the reliability and trustworthiness of the information. *Data integrity* refers to the need to retain or preserve the information (without alteration or corruption) from source to destination. *Source integrity* refers to the verification process that is involved in ensuring that the data came from the correct source rather than from an imposter or a "man-in-the-middle (MITM)." Finally, integrity also refers to whether or not the correct data was initially entered, and whether the calculation or action will yield the same result each time.

While there is a "user" component to integrity, securing the network so that data and the sources of data cannot be altered is an IT function.

Availability

Most companies rely heavily on computers and networks, and the data that resides there. *Availability* is a critical function for companies that rely on electronic data and communications. Like data and network integrity, availability is an IT function (e.g., making sure the network is up and running, the data is available to the right users at the right time, the Web sites and Internet resources are available to the appropriate parties). Your IT security plan must also account for when users inadvertently lock up records in a database, server hard drives crash, routers fail, or hackers hack.

CIA in Context

How much security is enough to ensure CIA? To answer this question, we use this analogy: "How much security do you need in your personal life?" A lot of people that live in the country know their neighbors and do not lock their cars or homes. Contrast that with people who live in urban settings where cars are stolen and homes are burglarized. The amount of security the city dweller needs is different than what the country resident needs. The point is, you cannot decide how much security is enough without first putting everything in context. The same holds true for companies. We all expect our bank to have extremely tight security not only because of the risk of financial loss but the potential for identity theft as well. A manufacturer of screen doors may have a fairly low need for security because they may not handle data much more complex and confidential than last year's sales numbers. Granted, you may not want these publicly divulged (if you're a privately held firm), but you wouldn't implement the same types of security systems your bank should. In Chapter 3, we'll discuss developing project objectives and we'll specifically talk about the security assessment. A security assessment (or audit) will help clarify the specific problem areas in your organization so that you can fine-tune your security project plan to address any shortfalls.

Business Intelligence...

One Size Fits None

It is very important that you to take the time to clearly define your organization's unique security profile before implementing any plans or solutions. There are thousands of companies selling all kinds of security solutions. Clearly, some are better than others, but more importantly, some are more appropriate for your company than others. You need to determine how much time, money, and effort should be expended to develop the appropriate security solution. If you do not have a clear idea of your security needs before you start shopping for hardware, software, or a security consultant, you may be talked into a solution that is too big, too small (rarely), too expensive, or not appropriate for your firm.

Define the Problem

Now that you have an overview of the major security elements to be considered, you can begin to define your IT security project plan problem statement. The information you considered as you read the previous section should have helped you begin to see how you can define your problem statement. While yours will be unique, we've provided a few samples for you to use as starting points. Be sure the problem statement matches your organization's real needs. Be sure you're focusing on the overarching corporate IT security plan. We'll work on problem statements in the smaller, more focused security plans later in the book. The sample statements below are just starting points. You don't need to spend days thinking up your problem statement, but you should hit the major points. As we continue to refine our project plan, we'll continue to add detail to the plan that should help you address all needed areas of IT security for your firm. Don't add the "laundry list" here, try to create a clear, concise overview of the corporate IT security situation that is causing you to take on this project. While your security project plan will be unique to your organization, the following are good starting points:

- My company works with highly confidential data that is currently exposed to potentially inappropriate internal and external access, use, and distribution.

- My company lacks a comprehensive approach to IT security, and the network assets are at risk. There is no system in place to ensure that only authorized users can access confidential data. We also lack a consistent method for monitoring network access to certain resources.

- My company's security measures were put in place on an "as needed" basis; we have never done a comprehensive review of the security measures. Since the company has both internal and external employees that access confidential data while working remotely, we need to ensure that our security policies and practices protect the corporate assets.

As you can see, it doesn't take a rocket scientist to write a problem statement that will get you going. If you're a detail-oriented person, you might want to define your problem more specifically. However, at this point, we're really just taking a high-level look at the problem. Later, we'll dig into the detail because part of every IT security project plan is making an assessment of the current network and current security measures. Rather than repeat that, we'll mention it here and return to it later.

Defining the Outcome

If you know what the problem is, you can identify the desired outcome. This is where you begin defining how much security is appropriate for your organization. If your security meets the highest level of government security standards, you are setting the bar extremely high. However, if your company is a regional retailer of shoes, it is probably too much security. Taking the time to clearly identify your desired outcome can help you define the right level of security for your organization. Your security project plan should incorporate elements specific to your network and to your company. The mission statement defines what the overall end result should look like. The following are good starting points.

- Our security solution should take into account the need to secure all network data. We must be compliant with the Health Insurance Portability and Accountability Act (HIPAA) standards. Our security solution should prevent unauthorized access at all branch locations, and monitor access to confidential data files. Our auditing systems should be able to spot unusual access or traffic patterns.

- Our security project plan should secure corporate network resources while providing customers with fast and easy access to the Internet through our wireless network connections.

- Our firm requires extremely high data security to prevent unauthorized access, use, retrieval, sharing, forwarding, removal, or modification of confidential research and development data. If this data were stolen by competitors, the financial losses would be staggering and could potentially put the company out of business.

■ The desired outcome is to provide a reasonable level of security for the network while keeping administration and day-to-day monitoring tasks to a minimum. In addition, we want to prevent unauthorized network access, virus infection, and malicious software (malware) installation.

As you can see, these statements vary greatly. The last one indicates that a less rigorous security solution would probably be just fine. The first item indicates there are potential legal ramifications (HIPAA) of a security breach. This would indicate a need for a stronger security solution. Matching the value (tangible and intangible) of your company's data and the severity of the impact of a potential breach or outage with the proposed solution will help you define the optimal solution for your company.

Defining Potential Security Project Solutions

In traditional project management, once you have defined the problem and the desired outcome, you begin thinking about potential security project solutions, which is done by brainstorming ideas and narrowing the resulting list down to the solutions that fit both the problem and the outcome. The list of choices is further narrowed by looking at which potential solution is the most viable for your specific circumstances. In this case, you cannot identify potential solutions until you identify the required components of security. The objective at this stage is to identify (at the corporate IT security project level) the relative scope of your project. Another potential solution might be to hire a security expert, or you might decide to send one or more IT staff to security training programs. The reason you're spending time looking at this is to help you develop an idea of the scope of your project and the possible solutions you could employ. If you don't spend time reviewing all potential options, you might miss finding the most optimal solution possible. Don't start from a limited point of view, start from the position that "all things are possible" and we'll narrow down the choices later.

Keep in mind that your security solutions will be modular. What is appropriate for your overall corporate IT security solution may not be appropriate for individual security project plans. A good solution may be to hire a security consultant to do an extensive security audit and make recommendations. However, your optimal solution for the wireless security plan will be different. If you have no expertise, you should hire a consultant to implement your wireless security plan and train your IT staff. If you have a lot of experience, you might hire an outside consultant just to review your staff's plan.

The key here is understanding that different segments of the plan, while interrelated, should be addressed individually. The optimal solution for one security area might not be right for another. Your optimal solutions should be based on your company's business, industry, current infrastructure, and risk profile, as well as your IT team's proven expertise. Take an unbiased look at the optimal solutions so that you can develop the best solution for your company.

Defining the Optimal Security Project Solution

At this point, you understand your overall security problem and the desired outcome. You've looked at all possible security solutions and made a list. Now, you need to review your list of possible solutions and narrow it down to the most optimal solution. Notice we still haven't identified or considered constraints such as time or money. If we start with limited options, we might miss finding the best option, so we start with all possible solutions and look for the very best one given what we know about our company. For example, your company may have a culture that supports hiring the best and the brightest, then your best solution might be to go find the best IT security person on the planet. If your company is always running on a shoestring or has a culture that supports "homegrown" initiatives, you may choose to hire or train IT security staff.

You may not be able to identify the optional security solution until you do an assessment. IT project management is an iterative process; as you receive new information, you have to make modifications to previous definitions.

The good news here is that once you've done all this high level work for your corporate IT security project, it will be easier to do these same steps for your smaller, individual security area project plans.

Applying Security Project Constraints

You have looked at optimal options, and now you have to adjust your plans accordingly. Every project has four constraints: scope, time, cost, and quality. If your IT security budget is slashed by 25 percent, you will have to adjust your budget accordingly. If you reduce cost, you will typically have to reduce the scope, quality, or increase time. Quality is often sacrificed, which can have serious consequences in the security arena. You will have to make some hard decisions. The following sections review the security project plan constraints and how they apply to your corporate IT security master plan and your individual security project plans.

Scope (Amount of Work)

The *scope* is the total amount of work to be accomplished. If you have a tight budget, you may decide to focus on the three major security areas that will be the foundation of your security project plan (i.e., identification and authentication, auditing, and malicious code protection). You may also decide to define several phases so that you can cover the most pressing security needs first, and then add additional elements in smaller security project plans. Choose your scope carefully to ensure that the corporate assets are covered. If your scope does not cover the most important and vulnerable assets, you may have to request a larger budget (see Chapter 1). One of the worst mistakes you can make is defining, planning, and implementing a security plan that does not cover the key areas. If you cannot implement the security project plan necessary for your company, document the risks and bring it to your manager's attention. Make sure the decision makers know what the impact of their decision will be on the IT department. They rely on your expertise; if you silently accept budget or timeline cuts, you are doing your company a disservice. Be professional but clear about the implications of failing to implement the full scope of a security project plan.

Time (Schedule)

Everyone always wants projects completed as quickly as possible. Every project requires a certain amount of *time* to complete. A schedule is developed after you define the work to be accomplished and compile the necessary resources. If you have to shorten your schedule, you might have to reduce the project's scope and quality, or increase the budget to allow you to purchase additional time-saving tools or hire additional staff. In traditional project management, there is the concept of "crashing the schedule," which means running things in parallel. In security project plans, the danger is in leaving a gap or making an error. As you go through the project planning process in this book, assume that "crashing the schedule" is not an option. In addition, make sure you allow plenty of time for testing, which is one of the best quality control tools you can use. You may also choose to hire additional staff to test your security solutions and to purposely look for ways to break your security.

Cost

IT departments are being asked to do more with less money, even as IT budgets have increased. The amount of spending on security is, on average, approximately 5 to 10 percent of IT budgets, which is not much when you consider the cost of a security breach. If you are forced to reduce your budget, you will have to find creative ways to address the shortfall (e.g., "borrow" staff from other departments, re-use or re-purpose tools you already own). If your budget is cut, you will have to reduce the scope or the quality of your project. Also, the amount of time the project takes might have to be reduced to address the budget issues, or you might have to increase the amount of time needed to complete the project in order to avoid overtime costs.

At the risk of repetition, be very careful about agreeing to implement a security plan that lacks sufficient scope, time or money. At the end of the day, everyone will forget what the agreed upon scope, budget or schedule was and they'll come looking for you when that security breach occurs. No one will remember the discussion you had six months ago about the risk of implementing a lower cost security plan. What they'll remember is that you and your team implemented the plan and it didn't work. Of course on the flip side, if you successfully implement a plan and no security problems ever occur, don't expect a pat on the back or a letter of congratulations. The absence of a problem is rarely rewarded, but at least you and your team will sleep better at night knowing your network and corporate data are as secure as they reasonably can be.

Quality

The quality of an IT security project plan often comes down to the amount of testing and review that is done prior to, during, and after project implementation.

Now that you have reviewed the project constraints for your IT security project plan, you can compare them to your optimal solution and revise it as needed. If your optimal solution is too expensive or will take too long, you will have to modify your solution to fit within the project constraints. Conversely, if you feel strongly that your optimal solution is exactly what your company needs, prepare a brief document outlining why this security solution is the right one for your company and why the resources should be expended to implement it. Be clear, concise, and factual. Document the risks associated with *not* implementing the optimal solution, so that your manager or the company's executive team can make an informed decision. Clearly delineate the risks of not implementing the best solution for your company.

Finally, it is important to note that you may not know exactly what your security project plan constraints are at this juncture in the security project planning process. Some companies require a proposal, the assumption being that the more impressive the proposal the bigger the budget. In some cases, you cannot write an intelligent proposal until you understand the constraints. If you do not have specific data regarding your IT security project's constraints, list your assumptions. That way when you submit your proposal, you have a starting point with which to negotiate.

Business Intelligence...

Setting Security Priorities Based on Constraints

In a perfect world, we would have all the time, money, and resources needed for our projects. The reality is that there are always limitations to contend with. As you begin defining your security project plan and understanding the project constraints, you will get a better idea of the project's constraint priorities (e.g., if you are told you need to implement a security plan quickly, you might believe that the highest priority is time (schedule). If that is the case, you either have to reduce the scope to finish the security project plan quickly, or you have to increase the

Continued

budget to hire additional staff to help plan and implement the project. However, don't assume that because you keep hearing how quickly this project needs to happen that time is the highest priority. In fact, cost might still be your highest priority in terms of what to focus on even though everyone's harping on time.

To verify your assumptions you can test the waters by asking, "If we need to get this done quickly, I'm assuming we'll have a budget that supports overtime and hiring outside help. Is that correct?" If you believe budget is the priority, test the waters by stating, "Since we are working with a limited budget, the amount of work we can get done will also be limited. I'm assuming that is acceptable." These kinds of tests help you push the boundaries to find out where the real limitations are. You need to understand the priorities so that when push comes to shove, you will know on what basis to make decisions. To run a successful project, you need to know how to allocate resources and how to make decisions based on priorities. If cost is the primary constraint, you might increase the length of the security project plan or decrease the scope. If time is the primary constraint and you incorrectly assume that cost is the constraint, your decisions will create problems for all concerned.

Developing the Security Project Proposal

Once the preliminary work is done, you can develop a security project proposal and use it to negotiate a bigger budget or a longer timeline, or to discuss security project constraints. In either case, develop a security project proposal that will be the basis of your overall security project planning. This document should contain the following elements, at minimum:

- Project name
- Proposal date
- Project manager
- Problem statement

- Mission or outcome statement

- Proposed solution

- Project constraints (if known)

- Desired security project completion date

- Initial proposed Budget (if known)

- Other relevant information

Once this proposal is developed, bring it to your security project plan sponsor for approval. The format of the proposal depends largely on what is generally accepted in your firm. Some companies have a formal culture that requires a printed, bound document be provided to the security project plan sponsor. Other companies have an informal culture where a quick e-mail might suffice. Regardless of how the proposal is captured, be sure that two things occur:

- The proposal is written clearly and concisely.

- The proposal is discussed in real time (face-to-face is best; phone is acceptable).

If you don't write the proposal down, you have no record of your starting point. If you simply submit the proposal without also talking with your project sponsor about it, you risk having misunderstanding right from the start. Let's talk about the role of the security project sponsor in this type of project.

Identifying the Security Project Sponsor

A security project sponsor is the person who champions the security project plan within the organization. He or she is typically high enough in the organization to have the authority to help remove or reduce the roadblocks that your security project plan will invariably run into. The security project sponsor can be your direct supervisor or the president of your company. The role of the security project sponsor is to approve the security project plans, budget, and schedule, and help provide resources for the project. If he or she is not motivated to help ensure the project's success, your project will probably run into problems down the line. If you suspect this is the case, find someone else to be your security project sponsor who will partner with you for success (and who has the political pull in your company to get things done).

Once you have identified a security project sponsor, start off by sitting down with him or her and discussing your initial security project proposal, including your assumptions regarding security project constraints. This is also a great opportunity to develop a better relationship and a clear and mutual understanding of the proposed project. If everything is in sync, you are ready to write your security project proposal. If things are not in sync, determine if you need to clarify it, incorporate feedback from your security project sponsor, or go back to the drawing board. Whatever the outcome, if your security project sponsor does not make time to talk with you at this early stage, it should be a warning flag and you should re-think your approach (e.g., find a new sponsor, find a new method for scheduling meetings with your sponsor).

This is also a good time to clarify how you and your security project sponsor will interact and work together. Some people prefer quick e-mail updates, while others prefer a regularly scheduled, face-to-face meeting. Your job as IT security project manager is to ensure the project's ultimate success, which means that you may have to bend a little to achieve your objectives. If your security project sponsor wants an in-depth, detailed, blow-by-blow update on a weekly basis, you will either have to provide it or suggest a suitable alternative. Take time at this juncture to determine how you can best collaborate with your security project sponsor to achieve your ultimate goal—a successful project.

Summary

All security project plans should begin with a clear definition of the problem, the outcome, the possible solutions, and the optimal solution, which will set the foundation for success. Remember, smaller projects with smaller scopes, shorter timelines, and more milestones are typically more successful. This method works well because it helps you focus on the overall needs of the company first, and then provides a method for looking closely at the individual security areas.

Solutions Fast Track

Defining the Security Problem

- ☑ All projects should start by defining the problem to be solved. If you cannot state the problem to be solved, you need to give additional thought to the subject before proceeding.

- ☑ Confidentiality, integrity, and availability (CIA) are the three areas that security must address.

- ☑ Additional security data regarding known security problems are addressed in the security assessment performed later in the process.

Defining the Security Mission or Outcome

- ☑ The mission or outcome statement should state the desired or required result of your security project plan.

- ☑ At this stage in the planning process, the statement should describe the outcome desired (or required) for your corporate IT security project plan. Individual security topic areas will be defined later.

☑ If you cannot state the desired outcome clearly and concisely, you may not have a clear idea of what you are trying to achieve. Clarity at this stage of the planning process is critical to success.

☑ Defining the problem and mission should take a relatively short time.

Defining Potential Security Project Solutions

☑ Your planning process should include a brainstorming session to identify all possible security solutions.

☑ Do not filter solutions because they initially seem to be too expensive or too innovative. List all solutions at the outset.

Defining the Optimal Security Project Solution

☑ Look at all potential solutions and decide which one appears to be the optimal solution. It is not always the first solution you think of.

☑ Be sure the optimal solution fits the problem and mission statements.

Applying Security Project Constraints

☑ Every security project has four constraints: scope, time, cost, and quality.

☑ Review your optimal solution in light of the known security project constraints.

☑ Since constraints are not always known at this juncture, list any assumptions you have made about security project constraints so that you can verify them later.

☑ Be prepared to discuss the security project constraints based on your security project proposal. If you state the business case clearly, your higher budget or longer schedule may be approved with little push back.

Developing the Security Project Proposal

☑ Be sure to capture the key elements of the security project proposal. This includes security project name, project manager, date, problem, mission, potential solutions, optimal solution, and constraints (known or assumed).

☑ The proposal can be formal or informal, depending on your company's culture.

☑ Be sure to have the proposal approved by your sponsor before proceeding.

Identifying the Security Project Sponsor

☑ The security project sponsor can be your supervisor, manager, or a company executive.

☑ The security project sponsor approves the security project plan, budget, and schedule, and helps clear roadblocks to the project's success.

☑ The security project proposal is the first opportunity you have to check and align expectations with the security project sponsor.

☑ Schedule a meeting with the security project sponsor to discuss the initial proposal.

☑ If your security project sponsor is too busy or unwilling to participate, try to find a new security project sponsor. A good security project sponsor can pave the way to success; a poor security project sponsor can create roadblocks and delays.

☑ Take time at this juncture to understand the best way to communicate with your security project sponsor. Setting clear expectations now will save time later.

Chapter 3

Organizing the IT Security Project

Solutions in this chapter:

- Identifying the IT Security Project Team
- Identifying IT Security Project Stakeholders
- Defining IT Security Project Requirements
- Defining IT Security Project Objectives
- Defining IT Security Project Processes

☑ Summary

☑ Solutions Fast Track

Introduction

All projects require organization before they can be fully planned and implemented. This chapter looks at some of the most common methods used for organizing Information Technology (IT) security project plans. Once the organizing phase for the corporate IT security plan is complete, we will begin identifying the details of the project.

Project planning and management are iterative processes. This chapter steps through the numerous processes that are part of organizing an IT security project plan. However, that being said, you may not be able to clearly articulate some of these elements until you have done additional work (e.g., you cannot clearly define all of your IT security project requirements until you have performed a network risk assessment or thorough audit). Sometimes in the planning phase, you cannot define certain elements until you have gone a few steps further in the process. If there are elements you cannot define, create a placeholder and go back to them when you have more detail. Also, you may need to complete one or more individual security area project plans before you can finalize your overall corporate IT security plan.

Identifying the IT Security Project Team

There are often two distinct groups within a project team: one helps with the definition phase and the other one implements the project. Typically, the definition phase of an IT project requires outside input, which is where many IT projects start to go bad. A lot of these phases are planned in the back of the server room by IT staff, which is fine if you are discussing something purely technical; however, IT projects impact many others beyond the IT staff.

A successful project, as you'll recall, involves users and appropriate stakeholders (see next section) early. One of the best ways to make sure you avoid re-doing a lot of planning work is to include users on the initial project team. Just because they are part of the initial team doesn't mean they have to be on the implementation team, though it's often a good idea to include a few users/stakeholders on that team as well. During the planning phases, key users should be selected for their ability to add value to the process, not for political purposes (though we all know you sometimes have to accept the 'political appointee' graciously). Getting users involved can create critical mass for your project and if well-managed, it might even generate user commitment because you'll have key staff championing the IT project to others in the organization. Participating in creating something usually creates that all-important "buy in" and you'll need your users to be on board with any security project so this is as good a place as any to start. Keep in mind that IT staff often misunderstand the needs of the users and users almost always misunderstand the IT function, so be prepared to do a bit of educating (and a lot of listening) along the way. The more opportunities you have to educate users on how things in the IT world work, the more effective you can be in meeting user's needs. The more opportunities you can take to really understand what users need, the more effective your IT projects will be.

Some projects benefit from users being involved in the process. You may decide to have subject matter experts from key user areas participate in the entire project. In a security project, there will be pieces a user does not understand (e.g., encryption). On the other hand, a user can provide a great reality check when you are deciding between smart cards or a 10-step logon procedure.

Create clear criteria for selecting the right people for the project. Avoid inviting people that are not critical to a successful project. Also, keep the project team as lean and mean as possible to make it easier to manage.

Identifying IT Security Project Stakeholders

Stakeholders are the people who are impacted by a project or who impact projects. It is always a good idea to find out who may be impacted before going too far into the planning stage. If you overlook this step, you will invariably receive additional information later in the planning cycle that will cost more time, money, and effort. Consider this: Suppose you are well into your security project (you may have even begun implementing it), and you find out from Human Resources that there is a new government regulation that your company must comply with. You also find out that Human Resources knew about it three months ago but did not know that it would have an impact on the IT group. Now you have to go back and redesign part of your authentication project plan, because it does not take the new regulation into account.

At the outset of the IT security project planning process, have a meeting with key members of every department that is present. Create a brief presentation using your project proposal (see Chapter 2). Explain what you are trying to accomplish and find out who should be involved in the project planning. There are often key people outside of a project implementation team that should be included in both the planning and testing phases. Once everyone knows about your project, follow up with an e-mail to those same parties asking them to respond to some short questions. The questions should be designed to ask if there are any department-level considerations that should be included in the planning process (e.g., finance might indicate they do not need to participate; however, you want someone to help you understand what types of data the finance department works with, how sensitive it is, where it is stored, and so on).

One way to categorize stakeholders for an IT security project is to determine who must be *involved*, who might be *influential*, and who must be *informed*. Those who should be involved are those who will either provide critical input to the project, or be directly affected by the results of the project. Influential stakeholders should not be overlooked because they can be key to gaining support for the project and keeping corporate resources focused on achieving the project's objectives. Influential stakeholders are often project champions within an organization; therefore, utilize them whenever possible. Finally, there is a group of stakeholders that should remain informed, which includes the executive team, and may also include key stakeholders who were part of the initial planning and who may need periodic updates to fulfill corporate or government reporting requirements. This is especially true if your IT security project plan touches on industry or governmental requirements such as SOX or the Health Insurance Portability and Accountability Act of 1996 (HIPAA).

The following is an initial list of potential project stakeholders who should be represented on your IT security planning team:

- IT staff
- User representatives
- Human Resources
- Finance
- Legal
- Departmental managers
- Regional or site managers

Defining IT Security Project Requirements

Security project plan requirements are not defined until the stakeholders are identified; however, a preliminary set of project plan requirements can be created. The key is making sure you get the stakeholders' input before finalizing your security project plan. If you fail to involve the stakeholders, you will end up with a security project plan that is missing key requirements, or is difficult or impossible to implement or maintain.

Project requirements are those elements that your security project plan must incorporate. There are four categories of requirements: *user, business, functional*, and *technical*. Requirements can also be analyzed in the following way:

- **User Requirements** What do end users need to help maintain a secure network environment?

- **Departmental Requirements** What do the various departments need for security? Human Resources needs tight security on personnel files; Accounting needs tight security on credit card numbers and company financials; and Business Development may have specialized security needs related to staff that travels frequently.

- **External User Requirements** Are there vendors that need to connect to the network? If so, what are their needs? Do you provide customers the ability to get real-time data online, and if so, what are their requirements? Does your company allow employees to connect to the corporate network from home or on the road? How should these external connections be protected?

- **Corporate Policy Requirements** Are there any corporate policies that can be interpreted as requirements for an IT security project plan? If so, put them in your security project plan.

- **Governmental Regulation Requirements** Is your organization subject to Sarbanes-Oxley (SOX) regulations, Health Insurance Portability and Accountability Act (HIPAA), or any other governmental regulations that could impact your IT security project plan?

You may have other requirements relevant to your industry, business activities, location and more. This is not an exhaustive list but just a starter to get you thinking about all the requirements. As you can see, this is where having representatives from different parts of the organization can really help you out since there may be numerous requirements that should be addressed.

In addition, consider the project constraints (scope, time, cost, and quality) as project requirements (e.g., some IT project managers include the initial project constraints if there are specific requirements). If your budget for the security project plan is $25,000, you might include it as a requirement. In the early stages, it is better to include elements that you may later determine you do not need, than to inadvertently overlook an important requirement.

Requirements are the elements that a security project plan must provide. If you do not involve your stakeholders in defining the IT security project plan requirements, you may end up with a project that fails to meet stakeholder requirements, which can result in project failure. When you put up firewall security so secure it is impenetrable, you think your project is a success, until you begin receiving user complaints such as they cannot utilize the Internet or share files with customers or vendors. The perception of the success of the project has just plummeted. You have met IT's security requirements, but failed to take user requirements into consideration.

To effectively gather stakeholder requirements, hold an initial project meeting. Invite all potential stakeholders and work with them to identify as many potential requirements as possible. Once you have compiled an extensive list, pare it down and circulate it for approval. When you state the requirements that the security project plan must achieve, you have identified the scope of the project. If your list of requirements is too long or varied, consider breaking it down into several smaller security project plans. You will probably have to reduce the requirements to a manageable subset before proceeding to the formal planning stages. Reducing requirements is a way of managing the scope; if you do not define and manage your requirements throughout the project, you will have a bad case of *scope creep*, a term used often to describe uncontrolled changes in a project's scope. To help avoid (or minimize) scope creep, create a clear set of the requirements necessary to create a secure environment.

The reverse situation can be equally challenging. Suppose you invite a number of key stakeholders to a meeting to gather IT security project plan requirements, and no one comes? Or, suppose a number of people come that have no meaningful input? At that point, you would need to explain the necessary requirements before continuing the meeting. For example, you might distribute a list of possible requirements via email and ask them to respond. You may have to get creative but don't simply accept that the users have no requirements if they fail to deliver them. They have requirements and it's up to you to ferret them out prior to finalizing your project plan.

Business Intelligence...

Taking the Pain Out of Meetings

People hate boring meetings, and the truth of the matter is, many IT-related meetings are boring. Some IT staff are more comfortable interacting with computers than with users. Following are some tips to help facilitate communication at the meeting:

1. Decide what you want out of the meeting.

2. Plan the meeting from the user's perspective; try to anticipate how he or she will respond to the meeting and plan accordingly.

3. Have a Human Resources manager or a facilitator moderate the meeting. A facilitator can help keep the meeting on track, on time, and on topic. If your team does not have a facilitator, use company resources.

4. Be sure the users understand why they have been invited to the meeting.

5. Avoid "planning by PowerPoint." PowerPoint presentations should not be considered security project plans. However, PowerPoint presentations are an effective communication tool that can be used to explain the project overview.

6. Publish a meeting agenda and stick to it. Having an agenda helps participants understand the preferred objective and can help keep the meeting on track. An agenda will also help ensure that the meeting's objective is achieved.

7. Assign owners for follow-up items. If your meeting requires follow up, list the tasks, the due dates and the owners, and then follow up with them.

Defining IT Security Project Objectives

Once you have identified the stakeholders and compiled your requirements, you are ready to sit down with your team and begin developing the security project objectives.

After identifying the requirements, create three to five major objectives. The corporate IT security project plans and the individual security project plans each have different objectives. For ease of reference, they are referred to as the Corporate IT Security Project (CISP) and the Individual Security Area Project (ISAP). In Figure 3.1, the two levels of objectives are marked by the numbers 1 and 2. Number 1 indicates the CISP-level objectives and Number 2 indicates the ISAP-level objectives. You will create a distinct set of objectives for each of your ISAP plans; however, those objectives may overlap from one project to another.

Figure 3.1 IT Security Master and Sub-project Plan Objectives

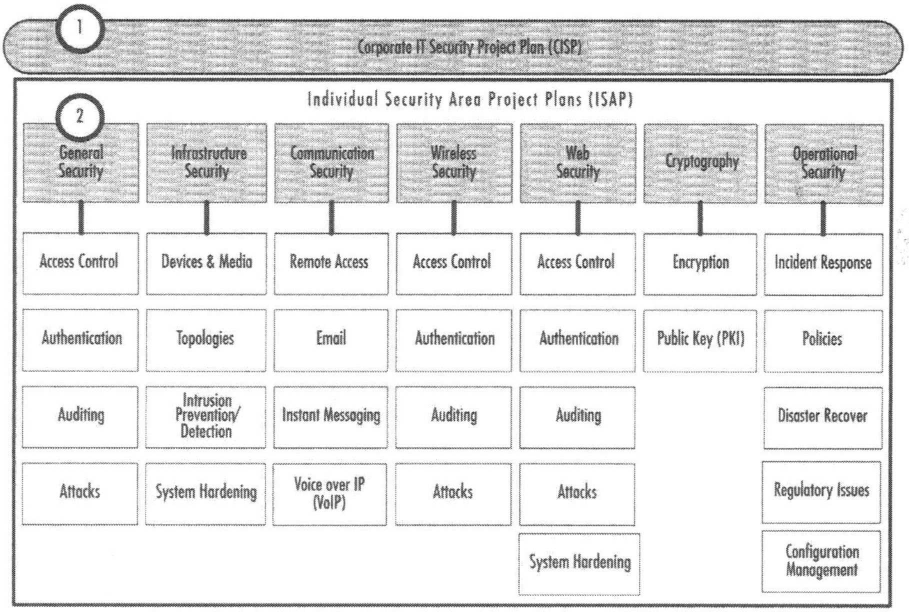

The following is a sample list of CISP objectives:

- Provide a comprehensive security management framework for the organization.

- Provide a clear and consistent set of corporate security policies.

- Identify specific security areas to be reviewed and managed.

- Create specific ISAP plans to manage the appropriate security elements within the company.

ISAP-level objectives go into a deeper level of detail within the various security topic areas. Use the sub-items listed below each header in the ISAP section as the starting point of your objectives (e.g., under "General Security" in Figure 3.1, the following topics are listed: Access Control, Authentication, Auditing, and Attacks). These objectives can be stated as follows:

- Review, define, and implement access controls on the network.

- Review, define, and implement user and computer authentication.

- Define and implement auditing policies and procedures.

- Review vulnerabilities and develop prevention and countermeasures against attacks.

Everyone approaches things a bit differently, which is fine as long as everyone adheres to the underlying methodology. You want to define three to five major objectives that take into account your chosen project solution and requirements. If you find yourself defining 10 objectives, you are going into detail too early. Look at your list of objectives to see if one or more can be rolled up into a higher-level objective. On the other hand, if you only come up with two objectives, you may need to spend more time defining your project. Sometimes, if you only have one or two objectives, you need to break them down into more specific objectives. Three to five is a general guideline; some successful projects have three objectives, and some have eight. Make sure you double-check your objectives for your project plan. If your list of objectives is too long, you should consider breaking it into smaller sub-projects.

Defining IT Security Project Processes

Now we come to one of the large chunks of project definition that many people would rather skip. Let's face it – once the project is underway, processes will be used. They will be defined on the fly, they will be made up in the face of an emergency and they will almost certainly be less than optimal. As much as you probably don't want to do this (unless you're a real detail-oriented person), it really does help to define your project processes ahead of time. We're not going to delve too deeply into this topic but we will provide some helpful reminders to get you on track. Refer to your IT project management notes or references if you need a more in-depth refresher. The following is a list of project processes you should consider implementing for your project. If you aren't familiar with these concepts, you can review the IT Project Management material (see Chapter 1 for details on how to access this material). Your IT security plans should use fairly rigorous processes to ensure that your IT security project plan is airtight. We'll review each of these topics briefly with an eye toward IT security projects.

- Acceptance Criteria
- Risk Management Plan
- Change Management Plan
- Communication Plan
- Quality Management Plan
- Status Reporting
- Defect, Error, and Issue Tracking
- Escalation Procedures
- Documentation Procedures
- Approval Procedures
- Deployment Plan

- Operations Plan
- Training Plan

Acceptance Criteria

Acceptance criteria (sometimes called "success criteria)" are the criteria by which someone *accepts* results. Success criteria are the criteria by which someone deems the project a *success*. Though acceptance and success go hand-in-hand, it is possible that some projects may meet the acceptance criteria and still not be deemed successful. Numerous studies show that an IT project can come in on scope, on time, on budget, and with the required level of quality, and still not be deemed successful. Why? The most common reason is failure to communicate project status and progress. For our discussion, we use the term "acceptance criteria" to help keep focused on those tangible elements that can be measured and reported. Acceptance criteria such as, "users are able to log onto the network using the new required password format" is not a measurable statement. "100% of existing users are able to log onto the network using the new required password format on the first attempt," is both specific and measurable. Acceptance criteria typically address a project's requirements and are written in clear, concise, and specific ways to measure and quantify the project's delivery of the requirements.

Risk Management

There are numerous risks involved in developing an IT security project plan; therefore, it is important to spend as much time planning your project as necessary to avoid additional problems later in the process. Again, it helps to include key stakeholders so that you have an understanding of the risks of the project, which can run the gamut from, "What happens if we fail to implement?" to "What happens if we get bogged down in phase 2 of the project?" to "What are the financial and legal consequences of a failure in ISAP-level project 1, 2, or 3?" To help identify the potential risks, identify the following:

- What project risks must be managed?

- How much project risk is acceptable?

- How should those risks be managed (avoid, reduce, respond)?

- How will I know if those project risks are occurring?

- When should I implement my contingency plan?

- Who is responsible for implementing and managing the contingency plans?

You may need to create a security project plan for your network risk and threat assessment before developing a larger corporate IT strategy. You need to understand the unique threats to your network and corporate resources before you can create specific requirements for your security project plan. An audit can be a discrete project plan, or it can be incorporated into each IT security project plan.

Remember, too, that when we discuss risk management here, we're specifically discussing risks to the IT security project itself. Risk assessment from a network or data perspective is part of a threat assessment or security audit and is a separate process. In this phase, you need to understand what can go wrong with your project and how to deal with it. As with many other aspects of project management, risk assessment and planning ahead of project implementation can help save time, effort, and stress once the project is underway. By looking at what could go wrong before getting into the planning and implementation stages, you can find ways to avoid some risks and minimize others. Also, sometimes you will discover that your project plan is actually improved by the innovative ideas used to mitigate project risk.

Change Management

Errors and omissions in the IT security world create gaping holes that can be exploited, either unintentionally by users, or intentionally through internal or external attacks. Errors and omissions happen because changes to the security project plan are not managed well.

Managing change in an IT security project plan is a two-fold process. First, you have to identify the necessary changes and assess the impact these changes will have on your overall security project plan (e.g., will it impact your e-commerce application if you change how you configure your firewall). The second aspect of change management is keeping track of the changes. Changes should be incorporated and clearly documented into your security project plan (i.e., how, when, where, and why the change was made).

Successfully managing changes to a security project plan can mean the difference between success and failure. If you do not thoroughly assess and document those changes, you may not know which project plan elements were implemented, which will create security holes.

Business Intelligence...

Avoiding Endless Decision Loops

Some companies have a culture that encourages decisions be re-visited repeatedly. This is particularly true with project changes. For example: A team meets to discuss an unanticipated problem, brainstorm possible solutions, decide on a solution, analyze the potential risks of that solution, and determine how to incorporate that change into the security project plan. Two months later, someone encounters a problem that is related to the change, and the decision has to be re-hashed. No decision is reached and subsequent meetings are called to discuss the problem, which puts the project at risk. The project is endlessly delayed and rogue decisions are being made and implemented that are outside the formal security project planning process, which leads to "unspecified" results.

To avoid endless decision loops, document your change management process and use it faithfully. If you document everything you do, including the changes and the reasons for those changes, you can avoid the endless decision loops that delay projects indefinitely.

Communication

Communication is critical when you are planning your IT security project plan. Users can help secure the network by following the security policies and reporting suspicious activity. Your communication plan should address the communication needs of each stakeholder group. The communication plan is also an opportunity to distribute a positive message about the project and its progress.

Assess each stakeholder group individually and develop the appropriate communication plans (e.g., executives may want a high-level "dashboard" report on a quarterly or monthly basis, while users may want a more detailed understanding of how the project is going. If you are sending out long weekly e-mail updates, chances are good that most people will not read them. If you are printing out memos in a company that relies on e-mail, you are also missing your audience. The frequency of communication, the content of the communication, and the medium for communication are all important aspects of developing a successful communication plan for your IT security project plan.

Quality

In many cases, the quality of an IT security project plan can be measured, monitored, and controlled through testing. Your quality processes might include the level of testing required for each major security area in your security project plan. Moderate testing yields moderate quality, and extensive testing yields higher quality. The Federal Reserve Bank's banking system requires a higher level of security than a used book store; therefore, the cost to implement that security should be reflected. Lower quality is not necessarily a bad thing; however, it must be appropriate to the needs of your company.

Status Reporting

IT security projects have a unique set of demands for status reporting. As you begin implementing various security measures, you need to keep key stakeholders up to date (e.g., how much the project has cost to date, how the project is progressing against schedule). They may also want to know if particular parts of security have been modified or upgraded for governmental or corporate reporting purposes. Keeping key stakeholders in the loop is a bit of an art form. You need to ensure that you share important information regularly, supply the needed information in a clear and concise manner, and send updates on a regular schedule.

One successful method you can incorporate is to talk with the various stakeholders when you are defining project requirements, to help determine what type and frequency of update will be most useful to them. Information that is short, clear, concise, and well-organized is far more likely to be read and absorbed than long, rambling missives.

Defect, Error, and Issue Tracking

As with change management, defect, error, and issue tracking are important in IT security project plans. You can use whatever terminology makes the most sense to you in your organization (defect, error or issue), for clarity we'll simply call it issue tracking. Closely track issues related to your IT security project plan; not doing so may create huge security holes and gaps. Managing project issues is an important part of the project manager's job. Be sure you have a solid issue-tracking process defined in your IT security project plan.

Issues should be tracked to capture the source, the description, the owner of the issue, the agreed-upon resolution, and the timeline for resolution. Issues should also be assigned a unique identifier so that they can be found quickly.

Escalation Procedures

Escalation procedures are important for IT security project plans. If an issue cannot be resolved through normal channels, you need to have a pre-defined process for escalating it. This is where working with your sponsor and key stakeholders can be helpful, because they can lend you their organizational authority and help you create appropriate escalation procedures.

Define the parameters for an escalation well in advance of beginning the project. An escalation raises the awareness and visibility of problems. Having well-defined parameters will help your team decide what issues should be escalated and how to do so. The sooner you know about a problem, the better chance you have of resolving it successfully. If a team member fails to recognize that an issue should be escalated, your project's budget, timeline, or deliverables can be put at risk.

In addition, by clearly defining escalation parameters and procedures, you are less likely to have to defend your decisions later. When you define your escalation procedures and the project sponsor and key stakeholders sign off on them, you minimize the finger pointing that often happens when problems occur.

Documentation Procedures

IT security project plans require a rigorous level of documentation. As you develop your individual security project plan, define the documentation requirements and procedures in detail. It is important to find a balance between the need for documentation and the need to get work accomplished. If you require more paperwork than is reasonable and necessary, the IT staff will likely provide incomplete or inadequate documentation in an effort to get through the tasks quickly. There is nothing more frustrating than performing a 5-minute task and then spending 25 minutes on the paperwork. Be sure you provide IT staff with templates, forms, and easy-to-use procedures to create the necessary project documentation. The easier it is for staff to document the needed data, the more likely they will comply.

One of the real dangers is having staff provide false information because the documentation requirements were too onerous. This could lead to significant security holes, but more importantly, there could be serious legal implications.

You may have more stringent or specific documentation requirements if your organization is trying to become certified or is subject to governmental or industry regulation. Locate the in-house experts on those regulations and be sure to get their input on the documentation needs for the security project plan.

Approval Procedures

Approval procedures should include who approves changes to the security project plan, who approves increases in expenditures, and who approves final deliverables. Create approval procedures that document exactly what is being approved, when it is being approved, and by whom. Keep it clean and simple to ensure that you get the approvals your project needs in order to continue moving forward in a timely manner.

In most companies, the project sponsor is the person who provides the needed approval for most of the changes. Therefore, your approval procedures should specify that all approval points and changes to the budget or schedule must be reviewed by your project sponsor. You should also identify subject matter experts in various areas of security that can be consulted, or you may need to have Human Resources or Legal review certain project parameters before moving forward. Take the time to identify the needed project approval points and identify the person or persons needed to grant approval. When your project is at a critical juncture, you do not want to be running around trying to determine whose signature is needed.

In addition, there are often political and organizational issues surrounding certain types of approvals. For example, if your security project requires a change in the way users access information or in the availability of certain resources (e.g., prohibiting access to secure data outside of normal business hours), you need to determine who has the authority to grant approval for those changes. If you do not go through the proper channels, you may run into an organizational dead end or face unexpected backlash.

Deployment

In the case of IT security plans, there may not be specific deployments or deployment plans required. On the other hand, if you are installing additional security devices such as smart card readers, fingerprint readers, or additional routers, firewalls, or other network hardware/software, you have to develop a deployment plan as part of your security project plan.

The deployment plan should also take into account key stakeholder input; you do not want to interrupt network services during a key client visit or during a major project deliverable. Make sure your deployment plans and associated schedule are known to those that will be impacted by it, so that they can log off. You want to avoid surprise or unplanned disruptions to company operations to the greatest degree possible. The deployment plan should be coupled with pro-active communication plan so that everyone is on the same page (see the "Communication" section earlier in this chapter).

Operations

Another key area in IT security plans is how security will be maintained on a day-to-day basis once you have completed your projects and tightened security. To use an analogy, it does not matter how many locks you have if you leave the door open. As part of your IT security project planning, you should know what is required on an ongoing basis to keep your security measures in place. This includes on-going monitoring, and making necessary changes to ongoing operational activities that reflect the new security policies and procedures. As your business grows and changes, you will have to reassess the impact of that change on your security project plan. If you create a security project plan specifically for performing a security audit, you can use that plan each year (after updating it) to reflect the current status of your company, network, and data resources.

Training

Training runs the gamut from training IT staff on new security software and hardware tools, to learning how to use new tools and techniques for monitoring and responding to attacks, training users how to avoid installing malicious software (malware) on their systems, and so forth. Training also includes training IT staff on new security procedures for ongoing operations. Users often need to be trained, which is another area that your key stakeholder's can help by identifying training needs so that security is maintained throughout the security project plan.

Involve your company's training team in the planning phases and in status reports so they can coordinate their training efforts with your project's progress. Users should be trained as close to actual need for those skills as possible. If you do not have a training department or if this type of training typically falls to someone in the IT department, make sure that identifying training needs, developing training materials, and delivering training programs are all tasks incorporated into your security project plan. Also make sure that the person or persons assigned to these tasks are in the loop regarding project progress so they can plan accordingly.

Finally, there may be training needs along the way. You may think that your team has the skills needed to implement your security project plan, and then find out later that a key member of the team has left the company or is otherwise unavailable. While you cannot plan for these types of possibilities, keep them in the back of your mind as you develop your training outline and your costs for associated training.

Summary

As seen in this chapter, there are some elements of IT security project plans that are different from other projects. Errors and omissions in this area could have a serious impact on your security and, therefore, on your business. Your project team can help you organize your project appropriately, especially if you include key stakeholders in the project organizing process. You may find that you will have different members of the project team on different phases of the project. Identifying and including key stakeholders will help support the project's success. Additionally, stakeholders can provide vital input as to the project's requirements so that the final project plan reflects user, functional, technical, organizational, and regulatory requirements. Once you have identified your requirements, you can create the project's objectives, which describe the project's scope. Finally, organize your project and identify any needed procedures for your security project plan. The necessary planning takes a lot of time on the front end doing, but is a wise investment that will pay dividends on the back end.

Solutions Fast Track

Identifying the IT Security Project Team

☑ A project will be more successful if you involve those outside the IT staff early in the process.

☑ Your IT security project plan team may have different members for the various phases of the project.

☑ Some members of the team may be needed to define and organize the project, a different subset of team members may be needed to test and implement the project, and another team may be responsible for the ongoing maintenance of security after the project is complete.

Identifying IT Security Project Stakeholders

☑ Stakeholders are categorized as involved, influential, and informed.

☑ Involved stakeholders are the people who must be closely involved with the project in order for it to be successful.

☑ Influential stakeholders are those who influence the project. They may not be closely involved in the day-to-day elements of the project, but they will have an influence over the outcome.

☑ Some stakeholders need to be informed. Stakeholders can include the executive team, regional or departmental managers, or the training staff.

Defining IT Security Project Requirements

☑ Taking time to clearly identify the requirements for your IT security project helps you define the scope of your project.

☑ There can be user, Financial, Legal, Accounting, corporate, industry, and governmental requirements.

☑ Stakeholders can be excellent resources for identifying project requirements.

☑ Project planning is an iterative process. You may have to come back to the requirements definition phase after you have done some initial assessments.

Defining IT Security Project Objectives

☑ Projects that are limited in scope have a better chance of success; therefore, defining three to five key objectives per project is optimal.

☑ If you have 10 or 20 objectives, you are probably going into the detail too soon. See if you have any related objectives that can be rolled up into higher-level objectives.

☑ If you can only define one or two objectives, your project scope may be too small or you may not clearly understand the problem. If you skipped the problem definition steps (see Chapter 2) or if you short-circuited them, you may want to re-visit them to make sure that you have a clear understanding of your project.

Defining IT Security Project Processes

☑ IT security projects require and use defined processes, because omissions and errors can create huge security holes.

☑ Keep your procedures simple. Only require as much time, effort, and documentation as is necessary. Unnecessary or cumbersome processes and procedures are almost always circumvented, thus creating potential for error.

☑ Each IT security project has different procedure and reporting requirements. Stakeholders can be another source of feedback when looking for checks and balances in this arena.

Chapter 4

Building Quality Into IT Security Projects

Solutions in this chapter:

- **Planning IT Security Project Quality**
- **Monitoring IT Security Project Quality**
- **Testing IT Security Project Quality**

☑ Summary

☑ Solutions Fast Track

Introduction

We often think of quality as something to check for in workmanship (e.g., whether a chair or a car is well-made). Quality in software projects is also easy to spot. A program that has few bugs and works as advertised is considered a higher quality product than one that keeps crashing or one that generates errors. When we think of Information Technology (IT) security, we typically think of secure versus vulnerable, protected versus unprotected, and safe versus at-risk. None of these really evoke thoughts of quality, but if you think about what will make a network secure, protected, and safe, it is the quality of several processes.

How well you perform your risk assessment will result in how well-protected your network ultimately is. How well you delineate the steps necessary to harden your servers or your network infrastructure ultimately leads to how secure your network is. Quality should be at the forefront of your mind as you define, organize, plan, and manage your IT security project plans. In this chapter, we look at some of the elements you should address in your IT security project plans.

Quality and security have a lot of common traits. Just as with quality, security is difficult to quantify or recognize, because the measure of its success is the absence of failure. Much like insurance, you never want to have to use it, but unlike insurance, if you have your security systems in place, the expectation is zero failure, not 98 percent success. The quality of a security project plan seems more difficult to quantify, but if you do so, adding these measurements to your project will help you maintain the highest possible security standards.

Planning IT Security Project Quality

Just as with standard project management, quality begins in the planning phases. Errors and omissions in the planning stage are amplified throughout the security project plan, and typically become very serious issues at the other end of the project lifecycle, in the implementation or maintenance phases. Planning is the first place quality is "built" into the security project plan, but as with all project management, it's a continuous cycle (see Figure 4.1). The security project plan is created, implemented, monitored, and tested. Any changes are typically brought back through the project lifecycle as revisions through the change management process. Revisions are almost always necessary, as more detail becomes known through the planning process. As we plan, we understand the security project plan better and may revise the security project plan based on new data or a deeper understanding. In addition, we typically test our assumptions, create workflow models, and develop lab protocols. The results of these should feed back into the security project plan in a logical and thoughtful manner. This continuous loop helps create continuous improvement.

One word of caution: Don't get caught up in the loop, and never deliver final results. You will have to draw a line at some point and deliver the final security project plan. One indication that you need to stop looping and start delivering is when you find that the revisions are becoming smaller and of less importance, or that you've refined the data to about an 80 to 90 percent level of accuracy or acceptability. You'll most likely never reach 100 percent; shooting for it is one of the reasons people get locked in a feedback loop. You might also have key metrics that you define that indicate when it's time to move forward, or you might have a hard deadline that drives you to finalize your security project plan. Keep in mind that achieving higher and higher levels of quality when you're nearing 100 percent becomes more difficult. It's not a straight line increase between 95 percent and 96 percent, it's an exponential increase. The time, effort, and cost associated with perfection is rarely practical, and you'll need to assess your level of quality against your level of risk and determine when to stop revising and when to start working.

Figure 4.1 Quality Assurance Process

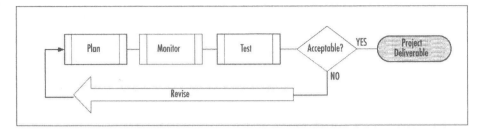

The following are specific areas of the planning process that directly impact quality:

- User requirements
- Functional requirements
- Technical requirements
- Acceptance criteria
- Quality metrics
- Change management procedures
- Standard operating procedures
- Federal or state laws, industry regulations, and certifications

User Requirements

If a security project plan fails to meet key *user requirements*, the project is essentially a failure. It's sometimes easy to forget the fact that IT is a service provided to the company to facilitate, enable, and enhance its ability to get the job done. Business activities are performed by various company users, so it's important to find a balance between pure IT security objectives and what users actually need. As discussed in Chapter 3, including key users into your IT planning process early in the lifecycle will help ensure that user needs are considered throughout. It's easier to negotiate and find solutions to user objections or issues early on, than it is to go back through your security project planning steps and re-work a "perfect" IT security solution. The net result might not be the optimal one from an IT security standpoint, but if it meets corporate, IT, and user needs, you have a much better chance of successfully implementing and maintaining security.

Functional Requirements

Functional requirements are often derived directly from user requirements. Functional requirements describe how a system should perform, often from the user's perspective. The system can be described or defined as any part of your IT security solution, such as user logon requirements or firewall functional requirements. Functional requirements are typically delineated as the services, tasks, or functions required of the system. To use a more concrete example, suppose you are defining the user logon process. The functional requirements might include the requirement that the user only has to log on once to access all information, or it might state that the user be required to logon additional times as they move across domains or into more confidential data. The functional requirements would define how that logon function should work, so that when the security solution is being developed, the IT staff can create the solution that fits these requirements.

Functional requirements are often tied to federal, state, or industry regulations, as well as certifications. For example, if you are working on a security project plan that includes the student health services on a local college campus, you must be compliant with a variety of regulations including the Health Insurance Portability and Accountability Act of 1996 (HIPAA). (See Chapter 9 for more detailed information on some of the common regulations that might impact your IT security project plan.) Requirements that are part of governmental or industry regulation

www.syngress.com

typically have a precise and detailed list of specifications that your staff, processes, and technology must comply with in order to meet standards. Where available, these should be included as functional requirements. If the requirements are not clear or do not provide the set of detailed specifications necessary to meet certification or regulatory requirements, you'll need to do a bit more research. In some cases, you may need to consult with industry or regulatory experts for clarification, or you may need to seek appropriate legal advice in order to ensure your IT security project plans deliver the requirements for federal, state, industry regulation, or certification.

Business Intelligence...

Functional Requirements Can Help Reduce Complex Security Challenges

Storage Area Networks (SAN) are complex devices that are used by many network entities, from servers to users to applications, and beyond. Using functional requirements can help you reduce the complexity so that rather than trying to wrap your arms around the entire universe of users, you can look at the required functionality. In this way, you can look at the functional areas to determine how the SAN security system should work. An article that appeared on the Search Security Web site in December 2005, describes the five A's of SAN security as authentication, access, auditing, alarms, and availability. Approaching SAN security from these functional areas allows you to work through your security project plan in a methodical manner. Once your functional requirements are defined, you can move into defining the technical requirements. (For more information on the five A's article, go to http://searchsecurity. techtarget.com/tip/1,289483,sid14_gci1152494,00.html.)

Technical Requirements

The *technical requirements* are usually created after the functional requirements. Technical requirements are statements of parameters or measurements (e.g., the Transmission Control Protocol [TCP]/Internet Protocol [IP] ports that are required for various applications so that the firewall can be properly configured, the number of users a solution must support and the maximum amount of time it takes a user to login can be defined; and the minimum amount of disk space required for an Intrusion Detection System (IDS) can be configured.) These are all examples of technical requirements that should be included in your security project plan. As you can see, it usually makes sense to create your functional requirements to describe how your security systems should work, and then create your technical requirements. However, there may be times where you start with technical specifications because your system needs to meet very specific technical parameters. Keep in mind that most legal, financial, regulatory, and industry requirements begin as functional requirements, and must be translated into technical requirements in order to be incorporated into the security project plan (e.g., if you are required to protect personal information due to HIPAA, you should build those requirements into your functional and technical requirements as well as into your acceptance criteria).

Acceptance Criteria

It's always a good idea to define the criteria by which a security project plan as a whole or an individual project deliverable will be accepted. In some project management situations, acceptance criteria are the measurements by which the security project plan is accepted and paid for; therefore, these metrics can literally mean the difference between profit and loss. With internal projects, there usually isn't the issue of whether or not you'll get paid; the issue is whether or not the security project plan will be deemed completed and successful. At some point in our careers, most of us have been in a situation where it almost feels like a pair of six-year-olds quipping back and forth, "Did too!" and "Did not!" This is the kind of situation you would always prefer to avoid rather than repair, and the best way to do that is through *acceptance criteria*.

By definition, acceptance criteria are "pre-established standards or requirements that a project must meet." When you define these at the outset of the security project plan, you can get all of the relevant stakeholders on the same page and agreeing to the same results. Referring back to the user example: Suppose the Accounting department wants users to have to login a second time to examine specific documents, but the Sales department wants one fast, easy way for its remote sales people to login to the network and retrieve accounting documents, sometimes over intermittent or slow connections. If you appease one group, you'll likely frustrate the other. In this case, you'll end up with a security project plan that is deemed a failure (or at least, less than successful) by one group or the other. To avoid this kind of push-pull, define requirements and acceptance criteria for each of your individual security area project plans, as well as for your security project plan as a whole. Make special note of any legal, financial, regulatory, or industry requirements that must be met, and build them into your acceptance criteria.

Quality Metrics

Specific *quality metrics* may be difficult to define for your security project plan because, as stated at the outset of this chapter, the definition of quality is "the complete absence of incidents." If your network is targeted by hackers and they fail to get in, you have achieved a quality result. While you and your IT staff understand the enormity of that result, it's entirely possible that those outside of the IT world see it as a non-event. In reality, it is the compilation of non-events that proves that your security solution delivered the requisite level of quality.

Still, there are ways to define quality. For instance, when implementing intrusion prevention and intrusion detection systems, you want 100 percent prevention and zero percent intrusion. Is this a reasonable and achievable metric? It would seem so since even one intrusion could cost your company millions of dollars, thousands of hours, and untold cost to the company's reputation. However, let's remember that quality has to do with errors and defects. Even if you have zero errors or defects, a network intrusion can still occur for other reasons; therefore, you need to define the level of errors or defects that are acceptable. While most everyone would agree that zero is the best, it's usually not an achievable metric. You will have to balance your time and budget against your quality metrics to make sure you're delivering a reasonable solution. If you wait until it's perfect, you will never implement anything. Be clear about where you're drawing the line and why. Document what exposure these choices might create, and the decision-making process that you used to balance the time and cost against results, so that you have a clear record of this process that you can refer back to later, or that you can provide to management should you be asked.

As discussed previously, quality needs to be balanced against the constraints of the security project plan. For example, to meet the requirement of 100 percent prevention of intrusion, you might have to spend twice as much as is in your budget. On the other hand, you might be able to achieve 95 percent prevention within your budget. The cost also has to be counterbalanced with the amount of risk your company is willing to accept, as well as the value of the data being protected. This equation is critical to understanding and addressing the cost of security. The acceptable level of risk and the value of the data being protected should be kept in mind throughout your IT security project planning process.

In many cases, quality is not a discrete deliverable, but rather a mindset and a cultural attitude. When you focus on quality in your IT security project plan, you are sending a message to the team and the company that quality is critical to the success of the project. Defining and quantifying it in ways appropriate to your specific security project plan is a worthwhile endeavor. You might be surprised at how you and your team can define quality within the framework of an IT security project plan.

Change Management Procedures

We talk more about *change management* procedures later in the book, so we'll just touch on them in this chapter. Changes to the security project plan are made throughout the project lifecycle. While changes are inevitable, it doesn't mean that you shouldn't strive to reduce the number of required changes with thorough and thoughtful up-front planning. That said, change will always happen for a variety of reasons; therefore, having a well thought-out plan for managing change is crucial to both project quality and project success. As you know, when you change a setting in one place, it can have a ripple effect throughout the network. The same is true of any change you make to your security project plan; it can (and usually will) ripple throughout your security project plan. In addition, because you're specifically focusing on security, you also have to recognize that changes to a security project plan can have both intended and unintended results. The unintended results are those unexpected things that occur as a result of inserting change into an already thought-out security project plan.

Create, implement, and manage your change management process for your security project plan to ensure that the final result meets quality and security standards. If change is allowed to run rampant throughout your security project plans, you will deliver a patchwork project that will more than likely leave you exposed on several fronts. While change management won't prevent all errors, omissions, or gaps, it will certainly help reduce them.

Standard Operating Procedures

Standard operating procedures (SOPs) are sometimes outside the scope of a security project plan, but in the world of network security, they must tie in very tightly to the project. Once the security measures have been implemented and tested, someone has to take ownership of maintaining security throughout the organization. This is done through a number of measures including training, the defining and adherence to SOPs, and the designation and training of an incident response team (also called a

Computer Security Incident Response Team [CSIRT]). Therefore, it's advisable to include the definition of SOPs in the IT security project plan itself.

Think about it. Your security project plan team will include representatives from many key areas of your organization. What better time to develop procedures for maintaining security than when you have the key people responsible for doing so participating in the planning? While you may need to circle back to this team toward the end of the project life-cycle (since you probably cannot define SOPs until you've defined and implemented your specific security solutions), these key people should be involved in defining the SOPs that will help maintain security. If you implement a security solution that is virtually impossible to monitor and maintain, have you delivered a quality project? You may have delivered a top quality security project plan result, but users and management are not likely to perceive the project as high-quality if it leaves them completely overwhelmed or confused about how to maintain security on a day-to-day basis. Therefore, keeping an eye on SOPs, not just for the IT team, but for users, department leads, and others, will help make sure your security project plan not only delivers a quality result, but will also help ensure that the result is maintained over time.

Monitoring IT Security Project Quality

Another element of planning *IT security project quality* is defining how you'll monitor the quality of your security project plan. Suppose one of your projects is to harden network servers? Each server will be audited to determine the server role, the types of connections, the criticality of the server's data (or role), and the types of security measures that will be applied. Next, the servers will be hardened one-by-one based on the audit results and the relevant security standards.

Let's look at a brief example. Suppose Max is assigned to harden the database server. On the day that Max is changing some of the server settings, he's distracted by a personal problem he's having and he's been on the phone throughout the day trying to sort it out. He's not paying close attention and he accidentally skips over three critical steps. He mistakenly reports that he's completed the task and everything is set. That evening, the servers are taken down for routine maintenance and the database server fails to come back online properly. Another member of the IT staff, Jill, knows that Max worked on the server earlier that day, so she calls him at home and asks him what changes he made. He says that he made the changes indicated in the security project plan for the database server. Jill thanks him and hangs up, and goes to work troubleshooting the server, without success. Frustrated, she pulls the security project plan out, looks at the list of steps to be taken, and walks through them again. She discovers that three key steps were missed. She makes the necessary changes, makes some notes, reboots the server, and it comes back online as expected.

This is the most benign scenario—several hours of Jill's time were wasted due to an error on Max's part. We might chalk it up to "these things happen," except that this was completely avoidable. In addition, while it was just a waste of a few hours' time, suppose this database was the backend on an e-commerce server and a database error exposed critical data to users over the Internet? Suppose credit card data were exposed and hackers managed to grab some of that data before the server was finally locked down. Max's error could have been very costly to the company, and all because he was simply not paying attention.

So, given that these kinds of things do happen, how can you devise a security project plan to monitor the quality of your project as you move forward? One very easy way to implement the method is to create "completion criteria," which are checklists with a bit more muscle. Completion criteria are requirements that define the successful completion of a task. (When we look at defining IT security project plan tasks later in this book, we'll revisit completion criteria and look at them in a bit more detail.) However, if Max had used a checklist that described the steps needed to successfully harden the database server, he would have been less likely to miss three critical steps. Depending on how your company works and what its culture is like, you may choose to print out tasks with completion criteria on them and require the IT staff person (in this case, Max) to initial them after each step is completed. This gives you a paper trail to follow should things go wrong.

Completion criteria can also be used by a second person, whose primary responsibility is project quality. For instance, while all security tasks are important, you and your team may designate 10 or 20 tasks as being absolutely critical to a sound security project plan. You may have a second person check the results of these tasks as a backup (or insurance) plan. While no one likes having their work checked, most people understand that when security is at stake, the more eyes the better. Having work double-checked can help protect the company, the network, and the IT staff. Avoiding errors is always better than repairing errors. Therefore, using completion criteria as a checklist for quality assurance is a simple, easy-to-implement tool to help maintain the highest level of quality (and security) possible.

This is just one example of how you can monitor quality in your security project plan. By making quality a constant focus and part of your team's culture, you can find ways to monitor it throughout the project lifecycle that are meaningful and appropriate to your IT security project plan.

Another reminder: If your company is subject to industry or governmental regulations, you may have very specific monitoring requirements that your security project plan must conform to. Even if those regulations do not have specific monitoring requirements, you can review the regulations and develop meaningful monitoring requirements for your project.

Testing IT Security Project Quality

As part of your IT security project planning process, you should develop thorough testing security project plans for each of your Individual Security Area Projects (ISAPS). You can do this in any number of logical ways, depending both on the nature of the project and the culture (and sometimes budget) of the company. For example, your test security project plans should test each area secured during the project, and an overall quality security project plan should also run a more comprehensive test on the entire network. That comprehensive security project plan would be designed and developed in tandem with your ISAPs so that there are no gaps in between the various ISAPs. Since network components work together in an integrated way, it doesn't make sense to create testing silos that don't test security as data or users moving across physical and logical boundaries. In other words, your test security project plans have to mimic real life scenarios, likely attacks, and normal (and abnormal) usage.

Based on your risk analysis, your testing should accommodate those identified risks. However, you might also consider creating tests that don't follow normal rules. Hackers are pretty creative and users can do weird things, so while specifically addressing known risks is vital, so too is addressing the potential problems you can foresee.

How much testing is enough? Again, the answer depends on how confident you want to be in your security solutions. You'll need to strike a balance, but you should err on the side of more, not less, testing, to ensure your security solutions are working as intended. If you have very serious security needs, you may choose to work with an external security consulting firm to help test your solutions to make sure you're not falling victim to "group think." While an external firm could be used for an end-to-end security project plan (from assessment to implementation to testing), it might make sense for some companies to hire a firm simply to test the results of the project. Human nature is such that if we devise the security project plan, we're also likely to test the security project plan and perhaps not test the actual security. Therefore, you might want to have a different IT group test the security than those who implemented it. This also helps ensure there is no collusion among IT staff in terms of leaving back doors open or creating security holes for their work convenience. Since most security breaches occur from within the organization, you have to build in safeguards against potential collusion, whether among IT staff or among others. In a perfect world, we could simply trust everyone, but we know that in this world, we have to take reasonable safeguards. Your testing security project plans should cover every angle, not just the ones you cover in your IT security project plan.

Summary

In this chapter, we included a section on quality for the simple reason that a high-quality security project plan is clearly preferable to a low-quality security project plan. There are numerous ways you can ensure you deliver a high-quality security project plan and result. Quality is delivered through developing a thoughtful and thorough IT security project plan. This is accomplished first through planning activities. User requirements are a great place to start, because if users' requirements are not addressed, they will circumvent security in order to get their jobs done. Technical requirements are developed after functional requirements so that you make sure your security systems have all the required functionality to deliver a strong security solution before specifying the technical elements for the project. It's easy to get distracted by defining how many failed attempts to access a resource should be allowed before an administrator is notified (technical requirements), and the failure to list administrator notification of failed attempts as a functional requirement. While they go hand-in-hand, it's a good practice to first define functional requirements so there are no gaps in your security project plan. Acceptance criteria are typically tied to user, functional, and technical requirements. These criteria should be specified and agreed to at the outset of the planning phase to ensure that all stakeholders are on the same page with regard to expected deliverables. When acceptance criteria are defined in advance, it gives everyone a stationary target to shoot for when developing and delivering a security project plan.

Your IT security project plan should also include thorough plans for monitoring and testing IT security project plan results. Remember, there are two separate entities here—the IT security project(s) itself and the ongoing IT security maintenance. We're primarily focused on the IT security project plans themselves, although you may create a security project plan that defines how ongoing security will be maintained, monitored, and tested.

Solutions Fast Track

Planning IT Security Project Quality

☑ Planning quality in an IT security project plan means that quality must be a mindset, not just a specific set of deliverables.

☑ Quality can be managed through several planning mechanisms, including well-defined user requirements, functional requirements, technical requirements, acceptance criteria, and quality metrics.

☑ Including user requirements helps the IT security project plan meet the end-user's needs, and will ultimately yield higher quality and better security.

☑ Defining functional requirements helps ensure all functionality required by the various systems is included in the security project plan.

☑ Defining technical requirements typically follows defining functional requirements.

☑ Quality metrics can sometimes be difficult to define for a security project, but looking for opportunities to quantify this data will improve quality and security.

☑ Change management procedures ensure that when changes are needed to the security project plan, they are evaluated, implemented, tested, and integrated in a manner that maintains or increases security.

☑ Standard operating procedures are used to ensure that the security solutions that are implemented are maintained on a day-to-day basis. Involving key stakeholders in defining SOPs at the appropriate time can improve the actual and perceived quality of your project.

www.syngress.com

Monitoring IT Security Project Quality

☑ Quality begins in the planning stages, but is implemented throughout the security project plan lifecycle. Monitoring the quality of project results is critical to a successful project.

☑ How you monitor quality throughout your IT security project plan will depend, in part, upon the nature of the project. Work with your team to identify ways to monitor quality as you complete project work.

☑ One way to manage and monitor quality is to use completion criteria for each task. This is a list of steps that must be completed before a task is considered complete.

☑ Completion criteria can be used by the person performing the task to ensure all steps are done in the proper sequence.

☑ Completion criteria can be used by someone monitoring quality to perform "spot checks." In some situations, it might be appropriate to have someone step through the most critical security tasks a second time to double-check results.

Testing IT Security Project Quality

☑ Testing IT security project plan results is the third element of delivering a quality IT security project plan. If you don't test the solutions you put in place, you have no idea if an attacker would be successful or not.

☑ Develop a test security project plan for each area of security you will be working on. Also develop an overall security project test plan so that you don't focus solely on the areas you've worked on.

☑ You might choose to hire an outside consulting firm to test your security to uncover blind spots you and your team may have.

☑ If you choose to design, implement, and test your own security solutions, make sure you get a broad representation of people together who can help think of all the things that could go wrong.

☑ Errors and omissions are the biggest holes in security and are the ones attackers are most likely to find and exploit.

☑ There is no single right answer to the question, "How much testing is enough?" You and your team will need to assess the risk of attack and the consequences of a successful intrusion or attack, and determine at what point you feel comfortable that your systems are a secure as they can be within your company's budgetary constraints.

Chapter 5

Forming the IT Security Project Team

Solutions in this chapter:

- **Identifying IT Security Project Team Requirements**
- **Identifying Staffing Requirements and Constraints**
- **Acquiring the Needed Staff**
- **Forming the IT Security Project Team**

☑ **Summary**

☑ **Solutions Fast Track**

Introduction

If you're an experienced project manager, you've learned that a security project team makes or breaks a project. A security project plan is nothing but a "to do" list until you have a security project team compiled of competent people who can actually do the work and deliver the results. Therefore, if you don't spend time planning and organizing your security project team, you're missing a huge opportunity, and simultaneously creating a big problem for yourself as project manager. In this chapter, we're going to talk about how to go about forming a security project team for an Information Technology (IT) security project. The material in this chapter intersects with much of the other data presented throughout the book, because the security project team touches all aspects of the project. Even if you're an experienced project manager (which we're assuming you are), you'll gain valuable insight and knowledge from looking at your security project team through the security perspective presented in this chapter.

Identifying IT Security Project Team Requirements

An IT security project team is not a static group of people; its membership should shift and change as you move through the various stages of a project. There will be some people who need to be involved in the initial planning stages to ensure various stakeholder needs are met. However, that same group may not be needed again until the project is in its final stages and you're ready to define standard operating procedures to maintain security in daily operations. Therefore, your first task should be to gather your core IT security project team and define the requirements for that team. There are a number of things that should be considered beyond just who should be involved. Outside of the staffing issue, you should give some consideration to the following areas when forming your IT security project team:

- **Organizational** Which departments, divisions, or sections of the company should be represented on the security project team? Is there a budget issue (e.g., hiring freeze, cutbacks, and so forth) that could impact your project? What about unions or collective bargaining issues that will impact team membership (or the project itself)? Are layoffs imminent or is your company in a hiring mode?

- **Technical** What are the different technical specialties that should be represented on the security project team? Are there different types of technologies (e.g., engineering approaches, software languages, equipment) that should be represented or that will have to be coordinated? What are the technical interfaces that require special knowledge (e.g., database, network, wireless, Web, Virtual Private Network (VPN), e-commerce, and so forth)?

- **Logistical** Where are security project team members located? Are they local, remote, overseas? How will you coordinate their activities? What technologies will you use to facilitate team and project work?

- **Interpersonal** What types of formal and informal relationships exist among team members (or potential team members)? Are there known relationships you can leverage or known issues you can avoid?

- **Political** What alliances exist among various stakeholders and how will these influence your project (for better or for worse)? Are there any people on the IT security project team with political clout, or any members on the team that seem to be out of favor politically? How will this affect your IT project?

Roles and Responsibilities

Once you've reviewed the environmental elements, you should identify the key roles and responsibilities needed for the IT security project team. Do this without regard to the people in your IT department or in your

www.syngress.com

organization. You need to define an optimal environment first, then you can pare it down to meet both budget and personnel constraints. If you start with a limited view of your staffing needs, you're almost certain to develop a short-sighted plan. Also, if you start thinking of who can fill which role, you may inadvertently have a bias toward (or against) particular people who are currently in certain roles. This, too, would be a mistake. The flip side, however, is that if there is someone in a certain role that you know from past experience (or political savvy) will be a "required" member of your security project team, you'll have to plan around that fact. Sometimes that's a good thing, other times it's a hindrance, but as the security project team manager, you have to deal with these issues.

Roles and responsibilities within your IT security project team are not the same as competencies and staff. Defining roles and responsibilities is independent of who should take them on. People are far more productive when they know what is expected of them and how they fit into the team, so spend time defining these roles. If you need to "borrow" four database administrators for your project, make sure they all understand the role they are expected to play as part of your IT security project team, and that they understand their various roles among themselves. Resist the urge to let them sort it out by themselves, since how they define roles and responsibilities may not map to your needs or your approach. Also, resist the urge to let the person with the biggest title win. One best practice you might want to incorporate into your project management skills is to avoid using organizational titles. If one person comes in as Senior Database Analyst and another comes is as Associate Database Analyst, don't just let the pecking order rule the day. Clearly define how you want these folks to interact, who their lead is, and to whom they all report to in your project structure.

Defining responsibilities typically includes defining deliverables or what each security project team member will be responsible for accomplishing. Again, the more clarity you start with, the better the result.

Working with each member of the team to establish clear, well-defined responsibilities also helps ask and answer questions about conflicting roles, responsibilities, and deliverables. Avoid overlapping responsibilities, and work with the security project team to clarify any issues before getting started on the project work itself. These responsibilities and deliverables also become part of the security project team members' performance review process at project closeout.

To aid in your thinking, we've included a list of roles that might be appropriate to your IT security project. It's not an exhaustive list, but it should help get you started:

- Manager or team lead
- Assistant managers, supervisors, team or group leaders
- Help Desk staff
- Platform specialists
- Trainers
- Support staff
- Technical writers
- Network, System Administrator, and Infrastructure staff
- Programmers and developers
- Web developers and Web staff
- Media and Public Relations
- Marketing and Sales staff
- Legal staff
- Human Resources staff
- Auditors or Quality Assurance staff

Business Intelligence...

Evenly Distributing the Opportunities

We all know that some projects are more interesting to work on than others. Some projects are exciting because they are cutting edge, they use brand new technology, and they have high impact and high visibility. Those are the projects on which reputations can be made. Then there are the mundane, utility projects that have little excitement or interest, but must be done.

As IT manager, you should strive to ensure that even your best performers have to work on some of the boring projects. The only way someone becomes a star performer is to be given opportunities to shine by working on projects with some challenge, visibility, and so on. If you keep allowing your best staff to monopolize the best projects, your junior staff may never get a chance to grow, learn, and show what they're capable of. One way to mitigate the risk of assigning junior members to a high visibility or critical project is to assign a senior team member to oversee the junior team member's work. This accomplishes two key objectives: it mitigates your risk with the junior team member, and it helps develop leadership and management skills in senior team members. Providing these kinds of growth opportunities in a controlled and manageable manner is part of what makes people enjoy their work. Most people are far more satisfied working in an environment that leverages their talents and provides opportunities for growth.

Competencies

In addition to identifying roles and responsibilities, your IT security project plan will undoubtedly require very specific sets of competencies. Again, avoid thinking about specific people at this point, and work to identify the competencies required. This is one area that will probably require some revision down the road (e.g., your corporate IT security project plan will include several Individual Security Area Projects (ISAPs), and those ISAP's may each contain very specialized competencies. You want someone very familiar with Intrusion Prevention Systems and Intrusion Detection Systems (IPS/IDS) to implement your IPS/IDS solution, and you want someone very familiar with your database structure and use to help design and implement a database security solution). These are competencies you can identify generically as you go through your planning process and develop additional detail as it becomes available.

Keep in mind that competencies are not confined to technical competencies. You should consider including competencies from other areas such as:

- Technical
- Communication (verbal and written)
- Training
- Negotiation
- Translating technical language into user language
- Reporting
- Legal, financial, regulatory

Technical

Obviously, your competencies list would not be complete without a full list of the required technical competencies as a starting point. Though you've probably got this covered, it is wise to sit down and review which technical competencies are required for all of your IT security projects (i.e., the corporate IT security plan and the ISAPs). This may be a list you have to re-visit a few times as your IT security project plans come into focus. Creating this list of required technical competencies can help you determine if you have the expertise in-house, if you need to train internal staff, if you need to hire additional staff, or if you need to hire an external vendor. Knowing where your technical competencies are and where your gaps are will help you create a viable staffing plan. Having untrained or unknowledgeable (or outright incompetent) staff performing critical or complex technical security tasks can leave gaping holes in your security systems.

Communication

Let's face it. IT departments are not known for their wonderful communications skills. Unfortunately, many IT departments do a terrible job communicating, probably because the IT staff are so busy working on technical issues that they forget (or try to forget) there are users out there awaiting information, responses, and updates. When putting together your IT security project team, look for one or more people who are good at communicating and enjoy it. You may have to look for someone outside your department to help, by having them attend key meetings and write up brief status updates and announcements on behalf of your security project team. That's fine, as long as you make communicating with key stakeholders a deliverable in your security project plan. Remember, project success is as dependent on *perceived* success as it is on *actual* success (perceived success, in fact, trumps actual results). Therefore, it is very important to find someone who is good at communicating, who can add communication tasks to the security project plan and be the task owner and implement those plans.

Training

Training is another competency you should have represented on your security project team. Someone with a training background or perspective can help identify areas that will require IT staff training and user training. Including this competency also creates awareness of the need for training, and can help ensure that training tasks are either included in the security project plan or are appropriately tied in with the security project plan through the Training and Development department.

Negotiation

You may not think that negotiation is a necessary competency for an IT security project team, but it can be helpful to have, especially when you have to negotiate a bigger budget, the loan of several key staff people for a months-long security project team, or with a vendor for a large security-related purchase. Negotiation is how business gets done, and if you have someone on your security project team that is comfortable (and successful) at negotiating, it can help your project tremendously. Keep in mind, however, that not everyone approaches negotiating in a similar manner. In some respects, it's very cultural (country-to-country, company-to-company, department-to-department, individual-to-individual). Ensure that if you bring someone to the security project team to help negotiate, that he or she has similar values to you and your team. If the negotiator believes in "winning at any cost" and your attitude is "create a win-win outcome," you're likely to get a result from your negotiator that you don't like. Set clear rules and boundaries if you have someone else negotiate on your (or your team's) behalf.

Translating Technical Language

IT people sometimes forget how to say things in plain English. Rather than explain that the server requires Simple Mail Transfer Protocol (SMTP) server authentication and that you'll be implementing Secure Password Authentication (SPA), they simply tell the user that they'd be securing outgoing email. The ability to translate technical language and jargon into plain English (or some other language) is a competency that is sometimes under-represented on IT teams. By explaining things simply and clearly, and in an appropriate (e.g., not condescending or simple-minded) manner, you can help users and executives become more comfortable with what's going on behind the scenes. Remember that most executives and users think IT is spooky, secret stuff. By translating it for "normal" people, your IT project details can be more accessible and therefore less threatening.

Reporting

Have you ever noticed how some people have a knack for coming up with perfect report formats? They seem to instinctively know what data belongs together, how it should be organized, and how one piece of data relates to another. These folks can be valuable assets to a security project team, so you may want to include reporting as a competency. Having one or more security project team members with this ability can help you develop meaningful reporting procedures. Various stakeholders require different types and frequencies of reporting. You could have a security project team member with a strength in reporting plan the various types of reports. This can contribute significantly to perceived project success, since most people are satisfied with accurate, timely information.

Legal, Financial, and Regulatory

When you're dealing with an IT security project plan, you have to make sure that your legal, financial, and regulatory bases are covered. Identifying the competencies needed for your IT security project(s) and including them in your security project plan, will help ensure that you pull in the right professionals at the right time, and that you leave no gaps in your security project plan.

Once you've created the list of competencies (some may be required, and some may be optional that could enhance the project), you can begin laying out a rough timeline for when those competencies will be needed (e.g., you might find that you'll need the Legal department to review the regulatory requirements and translate them into plain language at the outset of the project.) You may not need the Legal department again for your security project plan, or you may need it to advise the Human Resources department on the implications of performing employee background checks on all employees who will have access to Research & Development (R&D) data. If you can identify when during the project lifecycle you're likely to require these various competencies, you will have a head start on your staffing requirements and staffing plan.

There may be additional competencies not listed here that your IT security project plan will require. This is a good time to give it some serious thought, and to get your security project team to think the project through to help identify needed competencies. The more thought you give to it now, the less it will keep you up at night.

Identifying Staffing Requirements and Constraints

Once you've identified your required competencies, you have to begin looking at your staffing requirements, which match competencies with actual people in (or outside of) your organization. Look for the optimal candidates for each competency first, and then make note of the second, third, and fourth choices. Devise strategies for filling gaps, either through training, hiring, or contracting. In some cases, it may be appropriate to divide your IT security project plans into phases and shift your competencies accordingly. Sometimes you can reasonably delay hiring or training until a later phase.

Reality usually sets in once you've created your "dream team" (e.g., Jill is temporarily on assignment in Madrid, Spain; Craig is your best IPS/IDS guy, but he's out with a family situation for another month; John is your go-to guy for all Internet-related work, but he's already working overtime to get the new Web site up and running; Lisa is absolutely your best security administrator [users, access controls, auditing, log file management, and so forth], but she's recently been promoted and will be heading off to a new position at a regional office within the month.) You know the drill; your best people are not always available and yet you have a project to plan, implement, manage, and complete. Determining your staffing constraints is where you insert a bit of organizational reality into your "perfect world" security project plan, so that you can actually get your project work done.

Sometimes your staffing constraints are financial. You may need four database administrators to help design and implement database security, but you'd have to temporarily transfer them to your IT payroll and your budget doesn't have the room. Other times you may need to hire a contractor with a specific skill set or hire a new position or bring in a security consultant—all while you're being tasked with improving security for about 5 percent of your overall IT budget. While life and budgets aren't always fair, your job as IT security project manager is to find creative solutions to these problems. Brainstorm with your security project team or make a strong business case to your security project plan sponsor. Whatever you do, you'll have to live with staffing constraints and negotiate your way through the process.

This might also be a milestone or checkpoint that you can use to sit down with your security project plan sponsor and discuss your staffing needs. Since most company's budgets are not unlimited, you're probably going to have to make a few tough decisions. Best practices include going to your security project plan sponsor prepared with your staffing needs, costs, and alternatives. Don't march in with a list of demands, and don't expect your sponsor to solve your problems for you. Be prepared, and come in with various alternatives along with the risks and rewards of those alternatives. Work cooperatively and proactively with your security project plan sponsor to find acceptable solutions to the staffing and budget limitations that you might encounter.

Also keep in mind that if you cannot gather the people you need to fill critical (or required) roles or to provide required competencies, your project is at risk of failing. Though you haven't moved beyond the planning stage yet, you will be positioning your project to fail if you take off without adequate resources and simply hope that something will change down the line. As much as you might not like being the bearer of bad news, you have to work hard with your security project plan sponsor to find a reasonable solution. If your sponsor "orders" you to proceed despite your lack of critical resources, you will have a serious problem on your hands for two reasons. First, it will spell disaster for most projects and, second, you will have a serious security problem in the making. If you can't find someone competent enough to install or configure a new IDS system, you could potentially open the floodgates for hackers—not a good situation and one that will absolutely come back and fall on your shoulders. This can be a difficult situation, but unless you're going to get fired for saying, "I don't want to proceed until I have the needed resources for success," hold firm and negotiate for what you need. Don't hold a hard line—get creative, be flexible, and find the necessary middle ground to get your security project plan work accomplished successfully. The goal is to increase security from its existing state and to find out whether or not you have the right resources to help you get there.

Acquiring the Needed Staff

Once you've determined who you need and when, you'll need to put some thought into how you will actually "acquire" those people for your security project plan. Some companies have very formal procedures that must be followed, that track time, expense, department, and project numbers. In other companies, it's a negotiated process (e.g., "You need Justin? You can have him two hours a day for the next month. I can't afford to have him away from his other work any more than that."). Be sure to talk with the person's direct supervisor or manager to get the okay first. No one likes their staff yanked out from under them (or enticed onto a project with promises of fame and glory), so be sure to use common courtesy when gathering your security project team. In addition, there may be something about Justin's performance that you don't know. Suppose Justin has just been put on a performance improvement plan because he's been spending most of his days surfing the Internet, and not getting much work done? Suppose Justin really is an incredibly bright guy, but doesn't get along well with others? Do you really want him on your security project team? The flip side is that you should try to ensure that the people you think you want on the team will actually be valuable members. You can ask others who they'd recommend for a particular role or to provide a particular competency, to see whose name keeps popping up. If Justin's name never comes up, it should make you wonder if he has trouble working well with others, doesn't carry his weight, talks incessantly, or has some other behavior that causes people to avoid working with him.

www.syngress.com

Beyond that, you'll need to think about some of the routine aspects of managing a team, including:

- Where will the team meet and work?

- What procedure is needed to formally pull someone onto the project?

- What cost accounting procedures are required to track personnel costs?

- How are external staff (vendors, contractors, other departmental staff) acquired and managed?

- How you will handle staffing if project timelines slip?

At this stage of your IT security project plan, you may not have enough detail to answer these questions; however, they should be answered at some point. Project management is an iterative process, so you will likely have to review these questions periodically as you plan and implement your security project plans.

Forming the IT Security Project Team

Your IT security project team will likely require a rotating or changing cast of characters, so you may want to name your various teams (e.g., a "project definition" team, a "requirements" team, a "communications" team, a "training team," and so forth). There may be some people who are members of several teams and others who are members of only one team. If you want to get creative and have fun, you can let the teams name themselves around a common theme (so there's some relation and they can be easily remembered). Once your teams are formed, your first step is to create team rosters. This will help the team members know who's on the team and how to contact other team members. It will also help you as you move through your various projects, since some teams won't fire up until later in the project lifecycle.

Identify Training Needs

At this point, you'll also need to identify your initial training needs. You have already identified your project's required competencies and the people needed to provide those competencies. However, if your company is like most, you have a few gaps between the needed competencies and the available staff. Determine if you need to provide training to fill those gaps.

Whether you provide training or hire external consultants, contractors, or vendors, you'll need to make sure there's room in your project budget for these additional costs. These are the kinds of costs that often sneak up on you and cause you to blow your project budget even before the project has gotten underway. This is another checkpoint between you and your security project plan sponsor that you can use to perhaps shift some of the training costs to the Training department or the Human Resources department (if appropriate), or to ask for additional funds specifically earmarked for training.

Team Processes and Procedures

If you're an experienced IT project manager, you probably have a hard drive folder or notebook full of project processes and procedures that you've developed over time. If so, this is the time to pull them out and review which ones you'll need, and which ones that may need to be modified to meet the needs of this particular project. We've provided a refresher list for you, but if you need a more thorough review, go back through your IT project management documents to make sure you've covered all the bases.

- How often will security project team meetings occur?
- Where will they be held?
- Who must attend?
- How long will they last?
- How should team members prepare for these meetings?

- How will the meetings be facilitated and what is expected of the participants?

- How will status be reported to you? How often and in what format?

- How will project status be reported to executives, users, and other stakeholders?

- How will project performance be tracked, measured, and assessed?

- How will project team members' performance be tracked, measured, and assessed?

- How will problems be handled?

- When will problems be escalated and resolved?

- How are project changes made?

- How are project change requests evaluated, implemented, and tracked?

- What type of documentation are team members expected to keep?

- How and where is project data captured and archived?

- *How will security checkpoints or milestones be identified, verified, and documented?*

Though this list is fairly long, it covers the essentials. The last bullet point is in italics to specifically highlight that particular issue. Project processes for standard IT projects work fine to a point. However, you also need to look at processes and procedures that will document your security improvements, especially if you are subject to various regulatory or legal requirements. The problem with some of these requirements is that they are vague or unclear, and they leave organizations with a lot of questions about exactly how to implement them. While the legal authorities are sorting it all out, you can attempt to make sure your bases are covered by developing processes and procedures for documenting everything (including your documentation) so that you have the needed data at hand.

Your security project may require other very specific processes. However, make sure that any and all processes and procedures you introduce actually help drive the project forward. Some people mistake *process* for *product*, meaning they think that all of the busy work associated with developing processes and ensuring people comply with the processes actually accomplishes security project plan work. In fact, processes and procedures that are overly burdensome will grind your project to a halt. Check with your security project team about what processes and procedures will help them get their jobs done. If you believe additional processes are required, check with the team to ensure they'll actually help. Process for process's sake is just a waste of time.

Team Kick-off Meeting

At the beginning of the project, you should schedule a security project team kick-off meeting that includes all members of the team. You may choose to include those who will participate in the project in later phases, in order to create a cohesive team and to provide a sense of starting off together. Planning this meeting (and subsequent team meetings) will help it be both interesting and productive. The security project team kick-off meeting is the first and best opportunity to get people excited about the project, and to assist them in forming the necessary team relationships that will help the project move forward. A solid foundation for the security project team will weather any bumps in the road that may occur later on.

Keep in mind that an effective meeting is one that has a specific purpose. We have all attended meetings that wandered around and at the end of the allotted time, nothing was accomplished. If you want people to attend your meetings, make them so action-packed and useful that no one wants to *miss* one. Clearly state the purpose of the meeting in the invitation. Attach or later forward a meeting agenda with clearly defined objectives and outcomes. Start and end the meeting on time, actively manage the meeting, move it along, and keep the conversation on topic.

Assign action items for follow up along with due dates and owners. If meetings are productive, your team will attend. If meetings are a waste of their time, they'll find excuses not to attend and security project work will often begin to fall behind schedule.

The team kick-off meeting sets the tone. You can start your project off on the right foot by holding an effective meeting with your new team.

Business Intelligence…

Geography and Project Teams

We all know that IT security project teams can be (and often are) geographically dispersed around a country or around the globe. If you're managing a security project team that is not centrally located, your communication skills are even more important. If you're managing a global team, you have your work cut out for you, especially if you don't have existing relationships with some of your team members. Keep in mind that people in different countries and cultures communicate differently, they approach work differently, they interact differently, and they respond differently to feedback, criticism, and debate. If you are managing a global team for the first time, you should make a concerted effort to understand the culture from which your team members come and how they view work and their participation on the team. Remember, too, that security may be viewed very differently from one country to the next. Finally, keep in mind that terminology should be well-defined; you should check for understanding before assuming everyone is on the same page. While technological terms are somewhat "universal" in nature, be sure that everyone has the same understanding—whether they're across town or across the globe.

If you're looking for a few communication tools that work with worldwide teams, consider instant messaging, email, Skype, Voice Over Internet Protocol (VoIP), and any one of the variety of online collaboration tools such as *GoToMeeting.com*, *WebEx.com*, *LiveMeeting.com*, or *Windows NetMeeting* (or many others) in order to collaborate in as near real-time as possible.

Summary

Forming the security project team is one of the most important planning tasks, because projects don't just run themselves and project tasks don't just magically get done—they rely on people to do them. Therefore, the people you surround yourself with on this project will be the key to success. Taking time to start at the top and define the roles, responsibilities, and competencies needed will help you avoid narrowing your focus too early. Often if we like or dislike someone with a particular skill or competency, our decision making can be influenced. Starting with the impersonal data will help ensure you create a solid list before focusing in on the specific people you need.

Since there are few companies where people are just sitting around waiting for their next assignment, you will have to contend with a variety of staffing issues and constraints. How they manifest will vary from company to company; you're probably well aware of the issues you're likely to face. This is a good time to sit down and talk with your project sponsor to make sure you have his or her support and to help you gain the resources you need to ensure a successful project. If you are unable to secure the necessary people (skills, competencies, roles) for your project, you're headed for a very rocky road ahead. Be flexible and creative when looking for ways to resolve staffing constraints, but don't launch a project with glaring staffing holes either.

Define project processes and procedures from A to Z so your team can get its work done quickly and efficiently. They should know how, when, and to whom to submit a status report and what data should be in that report. They should know how to notify the team or you of a problem, and how to escalate and resolve problems. They should understand what constitutes a change, how to submit a change request, and what the procedures are for managing change requests throughout the project lifecycle. Processes and procedures help the project run smoothly and they help you avoid having to reinvent the wheel from project to project.

www.syngress.com

Solutions Fast Track

Identifying IT Security Project Team Requirements

☑ Organizational, technical, logistical, interpersonal, and political requirements should be considered when forming your security project team.

☑ Roles and responsibilities should be identified for the security project team, to help everyone form a clear picture of where and how they fit in.

☑ Competencies should be defined without regard to which specific person or people will provide those competencies. Start with your ideal "wish list" and pare it down, as needed.

☑ Competencies can include (but are not limited to) technical, communication (verbal and written), training, negotiation, translating technical language into user language, reporting, legal, financial, and regulatory.

Identifying Staffing Requirements and Constraints

☑ Once you've identified the skills and competencies you need for your security project team, you can begin identifying people to fill roles or to provide specific competencies.

☑ You may find that you have roles or competencies required for the project that you cannot fill with company resources. You'll have to devise a plan for obtaining the necessary resources you need, and check with your security project plan sponsor.

☑ Staffing is always influenced by various constraints, from vacation time to other company obligations, to politics and beyond. Your job as project manager is to make sure you have the resources you need to deliver a quality IT security project.

☑ If the quality of your project will be significantly impacted by staffing constraints, you should work closely with your security project plan sponsor to address those deficiencies. Moving forward as if resources will magically appear or problems will disappear is unwise.

Acquiring Needed Staff

☑ Give some thought to how you will actually "acquire" the staff you need for your security project team. Consider your company's culture, organizational style, and staffing levels.

☑ Make a practice of talking to a person's supervisor or manager before talking directly to a staff person you'd like to join your security project team. It's polite and may save you problems later on.

☑ Ask around to find out who other people would recommend for a particular role or to provide a specific competency. This gives you a clue as to how others view individuals within the organization. If someone is very smart but impossible to work with, you might think twice about inviting him or her to the security project team if you have other options.

Forming The IT Security Project Team

☑ As soon as you know who the members of your security project team are, create a team roster. This provides everyone a list of team members and contact information and begins to create a sense of belonging to a team.

☑ You may create several sub-teams and provide sub-team rosters for those participating later in the project lifecycle or those participating on a particular section of the project.

www.syngress.com

☑ Once you've put your security project team together, you should look at their training needs. It's more common than not that you were unable to get your "dream team" and some skills gaps may exist. Addressing training needs at the outset will help you plan and budget appropriately.

☑ This is also a good point to define security project team processes and procedures. You may have a fairly standard list of these that you can reuse, or you may have to define new ones just for this project. A thorough set of processes and procedures helps team members be more productive with less effort.

☑ Remember that security-related processes and procedures, especially those required by law or other regulation, should be built into your security project planning process.

☑ Be sure to plan a security project team kick-off meeting, so that you can begin to create a sense of the team and let everyone know that the project is underway.

Chapter 6

Planning The IT Security Project

Solutions in this chapter:

- Creating the IT Security Project Work Breakdown Structure
- Defining Project Tasks and Sub-tasks
- Checking Project Scope
- Developing Task Details
- Identifying and Working With the Critical Path
- Testing IT Security Project Results
- Budget, Schedule, Risks, and Communications

☑ Summary

☑ Solutions Fast Track

Introduction

We've arrived at what many consider the heart of the project management planning stage. Each of the other activities described in earlier chapters of this book is vital to the success of the project, but some of what is required in those other steps can't be fully completed until the work described in this chapter is complete. Once you complete this chapter, you should go back and review the first five chapters to revisit and revise your data.

In this chapter, we define the specific tasks that make up the project work package or "deliverables." Keep in mind that we're discussing two different project types in this book: the overarching master security project plan, and the smaller, individual security area project plans. Together, you have a total security project plan that incorporates the specific security elements relevant to your company. In later chapters, we show you Work Breakdown Structures (WBS) for various individual security area project plans. If you're familiar with WBS, this chapter provides details related to security that will be helpful to you. If you're a bit rusty on your project management skills, this chapter will also provide a quick refresher.

Creating the IT Security Project Work Breakdown Structure

The WBS is like a "to do" list only with more muscle. It is a list of all the major and minor tasks that need to be accomplished in a project. It is most easily created by starting with the three to five project objectives you created in Chapter 3. Those three to five major objectives can each be broken down into major tasks that, when completed, would achieve that particular objective. Be sure that your WBS tasks are at the same level. Many people have a tendency to dig down into the detail on some tasks, but not on others, so keep this in mind. Some people find it helpful to use a standard outline form to ensure their WBS makes sense. For example, suppose your project was to secure your home wireless network. The major steps would be:

1. Configure what router to use unique to Service Set Identifier (SSID).

    1.1 Log into the Wireless Application Protocol (WAP) or router administrator account.

    1.2 Locate the access point name and modify the default name to a unique name.

    1.3 Locate the SSID and change the default name to a unique name.

    1.4 Log out of the WAP or router administrator account.

2. Disable the SSID broadcast.

3. Enable security (Wireless Encryption Protocol [WEP] or Wi-Fi Protected Access [WPA]).

4. Configure Media Access Control (MAC) address filtering.

If 1.1, 1.2, 1.3, or 1.4 were at the same level as 2, 3 or 4, you would not have good construction (e.g., because 1c is at a deeper level of detail than items 2 or 3). By using this outline form, you can insert detail as you think of it, while keeping track of the levels. There are many different ways people create the WBS. Some advocate simply listing out all the tasks you can possibly think of and ordering them later. However, most people think through tasks in a fairly linear way, so creating an outline and then popping in details that may come to mind out of order is also an acceptable way of approaching the WBS.

The key is not to get sidetracked by trying to place your tasks in order at the same time you're thinking of them. If you're working on this with your initial project team (a recommended approach), you should try to use a white board and simply list all the tasks you can collectively think of and then organize them. If you do it this way, you will find that tasks at all levels of the WBS pop out in random order, and that's fine. Capture them and order them later. If you try to approach this too methodically, you're likely to overlook or omit something, because you'll be too busy trying to keep everything in order rather than making sure you're covering all your bases.

A sample security WBS for an Information Technology (IT) security project plan might look something like that shown in Figure 6.1. Notice that we've stayed at a fairly high level at this point. We're assuming we've already audited network security and identified security needs, though these can be part of a master security project plan. (Chapter 10 walks you through a security assessment and auditing project plan.) We've got a bit of detail under task 2, but we've indented those subtasks and used a sub-numbering system to indicate the relationship of those tasks to the top-level task. Later, we can refer just to task 2.4 or 2.4.1 (a subtask of that task), and readily understand the relationship among these tasks. In later chapters, we walk through more specific WBS structures for Individual Security Area Projects (ISAPs). The structure shown in Figure 6.1 is not the only structure your WBS can take, but it is commonly used and is probably familiar to you.

Figure 6.1 Sample WBS (Top Level)

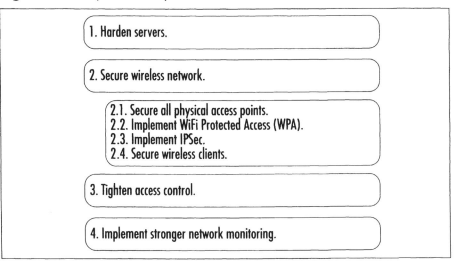

In any security-related project, there's a good chance you'll find tasks that span the boundaries between two different projects. We've talked about the corporate IT security project as separate from the individual security area projects (ISAPs), but in reality, there are all interrelated. When you're creating your security project plan, you're well aware of the fact that you can't look at security in silos. What you do in one area often impacts another, which is why we describe the corporate IT security project plan as the glue that binds the ISAPs together, and ensures you have a comprehensive approach to security. As you develop your WBS for any security-related project, be sure to capture tasks that either fall completely outside the scope of your project, or that span the boundaries. You can capture them as un-numbered tasks, or you can place them in a "parking lot" file. Just be sure to capture them, and make sure they're addressed at some point.

Defining Project Tasks and Sub-tasks

As shown in Figure 6.1, Task 2 has four sub-tasks defined. Typically, you would define the major tasks and go back and identify the sub-tasks (in this case 2.1, 2.2, and so forth) afterward. For each major task, you will then develop sub-tasks. Some IT project managers find it helpful to assign each major task to a subset of the project team and have them work through the details. For example, you might have your wireless experts develop the tasks for Task 2, so that they bring their expertise to bear on the development of those related tasks. Who better to recommend tasks for securing your wireless network than your wireless experts? While it may sound obvious, you'd be surprised how many times in the frenzy of planning a project that these things get overlooked. While planning is almost always improved by the input of subject matter experts, it is doubly so with IT security. An error or omission in security can mean you've left the door open for the bad guys.

Though we're assuming you have strong project management skills, a quick refresher never hurts. Keep these things in mind while you create your WBS:

1. Don't worry about the order in which you define your tasks (or sub-tasks). You can reorder them later.

2. Tasks should use a verb/noun format. Avoid using "Access control" as a task name. Instead, use "Tighten access control" or "Test access control" so the intent of the task is clear.

3. Use a numbering system that makes sense to you. One commonly used one is shown in Figure 6.2.

4. You can go down any number of levels, depending on the level of detail you want to define for each task. There is a point of diminishing returns, so define a reasonable amount of detail. Additional detail can be defined and captured in the task's details.

5. Once you believe your WBS is complete, review it thoroughly when you're alert, refreshed, and focused. Have your security project plan team review it for errors or gaps, as well.

Figure 6.2 Sample Work Breakdown Numbering System

```
1. Task
2. Task
    2 .1 Subtask
    2 .2 Subtask
        2 .2.1 Sub-sub task
        2 .2.2 Sub-sub task
3. Task
4. Task
5. Task
    5 .1 Subtask
    5 .2 Subtask
        5 .2.1 Sub-sub task
        5 .2.2 Sub-sub task
            5 .2.2.1 Sub-sub-sub task
```

Checking Project Scope

Once you've identified your project's tasks, sub-tasks, and so on, you should have a very clear idea of what the project looks like. If not, you need to do more work on defining your tasks. If your task list is a thousand miles long and filled with tasks like, "Sharpen all red pencils," your task list is too detailed and you need to scale it back a bit. Then, look at all the tasks and see if they fit within your defined project scope. This is your first real opportunity to do a "scope check" and ensure that all the work you've defined fits within your stated scope. More often than not, a good WBS will detail more work than was included in the initial scope. That's natural, because we tend to be able to better define the project the further into it we get. However, the problem it creates is rather obvious—you have approval to do "X" amount of work and your project plan has delineated "2X" work.

You have several choices at this point, but the most obvious are to either scale back your WBS or increase your scope. Now for your spot quiz: If you increase the scope of your project, what else must change? If you answered time, budget, or quality, then you know your project management well. If you increase your scope at this point, you'll have to renegotiate the amount of time you'll have to complete the project (more), the amount of money you'll need to complete the project (more), or the quality (less) you'll be able to deliver if time and cost cannot change.

Your second choice is to look at your security project plan and your WBS and decide if there are any elements that are not crucial to the successful completion of the project. Sometimes when people get into WBS mode, they start defining their "wish list," or they include everything they can think of. Sometimes this can be an effective way to accomplish things in the organization that has been looking for a project, but most of the time it just clouds the issue. Clean out your WBS if you can't change your scope, time, schedule, or budget. Pare it down to the bare minimum and re-check your scope.

IT security projects are tricky to the extent that if your WBS defines a scope of work that is larger than the initial discussion or agreement about the scope, you need to really ask yourself what should "give." Should it be the scope or some of the tasks in the WBS? How can you decide when you're talking about network security? While our tendency is usually to say "It's all important!" the truth is that if you carefully review your WBS, you may actually find tasks that can either be put into a different security project plan or that may truly be redundant or optional. Finally, this situation may force you and your team to get a bit creative and think of ways you can scale things back and actually improve your security or your security project plan (or both). The old expression "Necessity is the mother of invention" sometimes holds true, and if you and your team put your collective minds to it, you may be able to find ways to increase security while scaling back the project scope.

This is also a great time to check in with your security project plan sponsor. Run the WBS by him or her and gain approval for your WBS and your scope. If there are problems, now is the time to find them and fix them. If you find yourself in the position of having to go to bat for a larger budget or longer schedule, you should be prepared to make the business case for this. Remember, it's natural that you would have a better idea of the project's scope once you've created your WBS, because the act of creating the WBS drives clarity. With that clarity should come an understanding of the areas in which the project has grown. If you believe these are important areas to include, then clearly link each of these areas to the business objectives, the risks of not addressing these areas, and potential alternatives to addressing these areas (e.g., you might prioritize several of the items and agree to make them part of a Phase II project, because you and your team believe that, while important, these items may not be pressing or critical in the near-term). Finding creative solutions and bringing alternatives to the table is always preferable to saying, in essence, "We need a bigger budget. Period." Sometimes that works, especially if the items are critical areas to address, but often the answer is, "Find something else to cut out of it then." It may be a negotiation, but if your network security is at risk, it's worth putting some effort into discovering ways to get it done. If you need some fuel for your fire, check out Chapter 9 where we discuss some of the legal ramifications of not securing your network. Better yet, do a bit of Internet research and look for recent articles pointing out the cost or ramifications of a security breach. If you can find a company like yours or in the same kind of business, it might really drive the point home. There's nothing like a little reality check from time to time.

Business Intelligence...

Smaller is Better When it Comes to Scope

As we discussed in Chapter 1, studies have consistently shown that smaller projects are more successful. That makes sense when you think about it; it's easier to get your arms wrapped around a project, it's easier to keep staff motivated and focused, it's easier to monitor progress, and so on. One of the first places you'll begin to get a sense of the scope of your project is once you've made the first or second pass through your WBS. As you define the tasks and sub-tasks, you'll see the scope of the project more clearly. Sometimes in the process of delineating your WBS, you see that your scope has expanded significantly. Other times, your WBS may indicate the project isn't as large and complex as you'd first thought (a somewhat rare occurrence). Using your WBS to gauge your scope can help you decide whether you need to break your project down into smaller projects, or whether your scope managed to creep up during the definition phase of the project lifecycle. Whatever the case, your WBS will define your scope, and this is an excellent time to check your scope and make the necessary adjustments. If the scope is out of control at this point, your project is not likely to succeed.

Developing Task Details

There are numerous *task details* you can include in your IT security project plan, but we're going to focus on two types of details—the most commonly used task details and the details that specifically relate to IT security. We're taking a two-pronged approach, because people often skip over defining even basic task details, and these details (both basic and security-related) are extremely helpful project management tools.

How you develop your task details is somewhat a matter of personal project management style, but there are some guidelines that will help you develop really solid task details. First, the person or group that will be performing the task is typically the best resource for helping to define task details. To go back to our wireless example, you're better off having your wireless expert define the wireless security task details, than having your database administrator define them. The experts can usually define the task detail more quickly and effectively than the project manager can; therefore, rather than sitting down one late night and trying to define all these task details, begin delegating at this point. It's an obvious but sometimes overlooked piece of the puzzle.

Owner

The first task detail that comes to mind is the *task owner*. In an IT security project, you may choose to have security area experts head up the ISAPs; therefore, they may be considered the owners for tasks related to his or her individual security area. You may choose to assign ownership of tasks to those who will oversee the work or to those who will actually do the work. It depends largely on how your IT organization is structured. In any case, there is a rule about task ownership that you should heed: "A task with no owners won't get done; a task with two owners won't get done." In other words, a task should have only one owner. That owner may or may not complete the work itself, but he or she is responsible for the work getting done. If you have two or more task owners, no one takes responsibility for the task, and you, as the IT project manager, won't know who to hold accountable (e.g., Jose says it was Keiko's responsibility; Keiko says she thought Manish had it under control; Manish says he thought Larry was heading it up; and Larry says he thought Jose said (in a meeting last week) that he had completed the task. Assign one owner per task to maintain accountability and responsibility for task completion.

Resources

The term *resources* can be used to indicate anything needed for a security project plan's completion, whether that's people, money, tools, equipment, software, or supplies. For each task, you should have the task owner (or a subject matter expert) define the resources needed for that task. While they may not know exactly which resources they need, they should define (at a minimum) the people or skills required and any known tools, software, or equipment they can think of. These two types of resources—people and supplies—are used both in scheduling and in budgeting, so defining these elements at this stage will be very helpful in developing your initial project schedule and budget. Remember, project management is an iterative process, so you'll probably have to go back to this a few times to hone the details as the picture becomes clearer.

With an IT security project, you're likely to need resources that you, as the project manager, may not know about or even understand. Do you know what AirSnort is, how it's used, or what it might cost? Would you think to include the cost or even require the use of these tools in your wireless security project plan? (Ironically, many hacker tools are available as standard tools built right into operating systems, or as free shareware programs widely available on the Internet). If you're a wireless security expert, you might. If you're an IT manager or an IT project manager that might not be your strength, therefore, relying on your subject matter experts to help define the needed resources for tasks is critical. Otherwise, you may lack the tools or expertise needed to secure your network, or you may find yourself at the short end of your budget quicker than anticipated.

Also, because IT security project plans require specific expertise in key areas, you should also require your subject matter experts to define the type of expertise required to perform a particular security task. If the task is to review Access Control Lists (ACLs) on several key network objects, anyone on your IT staff could probably complete that task. However, if the task is to test the database so that script errors won't provide an opening to hackers, there's a good chance you need a database expert to help you with that. So, be sure to define required expertise within your task resources. This will help ensure you have the expertise needed for the task, and will also help you better estimate what skills and knowledge you'll need to complete your IT security project plan. That might mean training internal staff or contracting out, but you need to know this going into the project so that you can properly allocate time, money, and resources.

Completion Criteria

We briefly discussed *completion criteria* earlier, so we'll quickly revisit it here. Completion criteria are the criteria by which you or anyone else can determine if a task was completed properly. Completion criteria can be a simple checklist or a more comprehensive set of standards or protocols. Whatever will be used to determine if the task was successfully completed should be defined in advance, in the completion criteria for the task. Often, the task owner or the subject matter expert is the best person to create these completion criteria; however, sometimes additional research may be required. It's also possible that you won't be able to define the completion criteria for some of the tasks until later in the project cycle, when you have a better understanding of the project. Defining completion criteria for a security project is absolutely crucial. The number of errors and omissions drops significantly when you define the completion criteria for each task. In addition, when you define these criteria at the beginning of the security project plan lifecycle (when things are relatively calm), you reduce your chance of missing something important once the project is in full swing.

Also keep in mind that if you have specific requirements—whether functional, technical, legal, or regulatory—they should be addressed via the completion criteria in the tasks. Quality is built into a project through task details, and one of the most important task details are the completion criteria. If you need to meet specific requirements, build this into your task detail via the completion criteria, to ensure the requirements actually are met. Otherwise, it's a bit of a crap shoot.

Schedule

Best practices in project management include the use of the 8/80 rule when defining the *schedule*. This rule states that you should not define any task that takes less than 8 hours, and no single task should take more than 80 hours. This is a very broad guideline, but it helps on both ends of the scheduling spectrum. Obviously, if you schedule tasks that are less than 8 hours, you're headed for an absolute scheduling nightmare. On the other hand, if you have a task that takes more than 80 hours, there's a good chance it can be broken down into smaller tasks that are more manageable.

Once you've created your IT security project plan's WBS (for the corporate IT security project plan or any of the ISAPs), you can begin estimating task duration. Let's take a moment to distinguish between *duration* and *effort*. You're probably familiar with these two terms, but it's important to understand the difference. *Duration* is the amount of time you allot for the task to be completed. *Effort* is the actual amount of time it takes to complete the task (e.g., you may schedule two weeks (duration) to implement network server auditing, but the actual task of setting up that auditing might take a total of 4 hours (effort). Successful security project plans schedule around duration, not effort. Most of the people (probably all of them) on your project team have other duties, responsibilities, and deliverables. By scheduling the duration, you're defining in what time period the task needs to be completed. One person might complete the task on Day 1 of the two-week duration, another might not be able to complete it until Day 14. It's 4 hours worth of work that has to be scheduled in among other conflicting priorities. Using the duration will give your security project plan team members the flexibility needed to complete their tasks in a manner that fits their workload.

Once you've defined task duration, you can begin to get a sense of how long your project will take to complete. We haven't yet discussed dependencies, which can push your schedule out further, nor have we talked about scheduling resources, which can expand or contract your schedule, but duration will give you a high-level sense of your project's overall schedule length.

www.syngress.com

Budget

If you've defined all of your tasks and identified the needed resources, it stands to reason you should be able to develop your preliminary budget at this point, right? Well, yes and no. You can go through your tasks and identify the resources needed—both in terms of people and supplies—but that doesn't necessarily account for all of your IT security costs. It doesn't include training (e.g., hiring outside contractors to fill in for three team members that will be in China starting up a new corporate division for six weeks during your project). These are the kinds of things that can break a budget and they often sneak up on you. So, once you've defined your tasks, needed resources, and required expertise, you may want to get the team together to talk about what you might be missing from your budget. In an IT security project plan, you almost certainly will require tools, training, and equipment. Some of those resources will be specific to an ISAP, and others will be useful across several ISAPs or in your corporate IT security project plan. Look for areas where you can leverage resources to reduce the overall cost of your security project plan budget. When you can show executives they're getting more "bang for the buck'" with some of their IT security expenditures, they may be less reluctant to approve the purchase.

You may need assistance in creating a budget from your Finance department. If that type of resource is available, take advantage of it. Having someone well-versed in creating a line item budget can help speed the process and make sure you don't overlook important budget components.

Dependencies

If you've created even one project plan, you know that defining *dependencies* is a key task in your planning process, because it ultimately determines the length of your schedule. If you fail to identify dependencies, you will end up with excessive idle time in the project, or you'll end up crashing your schedule to get it completed in time. If your dependencies are linked to external events, you have additional challenges to consider.

In an IT security project, there are numerous interconnected elements that can impact your schedule that should be listed as dependencies. Hardening your servers may be dependent upon upgrading several of the operating systems or some other task. The order in which you perform these tasks may be vitally important, and identifying the dependencies properly, and therefore performing the tasks in the requisite order, can literally mean the difference between having or not having a secure network.

Different people use different methods of identifying and recording dependencies. Some people like to use sticky notes, placing them on a whiteboard, drawing lines to define dependencies, and then loading all of that data into a project management software program. Others prefer to identify dependencies within the project management software program right from the start. Your subject matter experts are a good source of data about dependencies, because they can tell you that if you do Task 7.2.3 before Task 4.1.9 you will generate errors and Task 3.3.5 will fail. Finally, if you are developing your dependencies for your ISAP, you should note all of the dependencies that link to or rely on external tasks, activities, or events. Be sure to mark these dependencies in the relevant tasks, and create milestones in your security project plan schedule to indicate the need to link to external data, tasks, or events.

Constraints

Constraints impact projects by limiting the approach or methods the team can use to complete the project. Constraints can be internal or external to your department, division, or company. What are the kinds of constraints you're likely to find in an IT security project plan? Some are the same as any other project, and some are unique to security. While your list of constraints might be longer, shorter, or contain different items, the following are five elements that are likely found on many lists:

1. Expertise
2. Tools
3. Budget
4. Organizational change
5. Governmental or regulatory requirements

Expertise

As mentioned earlier, the lack of specific security expertise is a constraint that should be carefully considered. If you lack the depth and breadth of expertise on a particular aspect of security that is vital to your security project plan, you will need to figure out the best way to address that gap. These constraints can cause difficulty in your project planning and execution, because, unlike standard IT projects, security project plans can be less forgiving (i.e., someone is often waiting for you to make a mistake so they can exploit it).

If you find your security project plan needs specific expertise, and if you believe this expertise is in short supply, difficult to locate, or very expensive, this is a significant constraint on your project that should be noted and addressed with your security project plan sponsor.

Tools

Sometimes tools can be a constraint, especially if one of your subject matter experts recommends (or requires) a particular tool and your budget can't accommodate it. If there's a piece of equipment that you share with another department, or a piece of equipment you need to rent or lease, list this as a constraint as well, since it could impact the ability of your project team to move on to specific tasks that require the use of this tool or equipment.

Budget

Is a *budget* ever large enough? Probably not, but in the world of IT security, a skimpy budget may translate into network vulnerability or, even more importantly, legal liability. Don't let your corporate executives tell you to be "penny wise and pound foolish." You might be able to shave a few thousand dollars off the budget, but you need to assess the risks of doing so. If your budget has a bit of fat that can be trimmed, great. If not, then you're starting to cut into the muscle of your project and need to clearly delineate the risks to your boss, security project plan sponsor, or corporate executives.

Sometimes the issue isn't the total amount of money, but the timing of the funds (e.g., smaller companies often track [and manage] their cash flows very tightly). It's possible that your budget for this project was approved, but you're later told that you can't spend that $10,000 on x, y, or z until June, because the company doesn't have the cash. Clearly, this is a constraint that impacts your team's ability to get the security project plan completed on time; therefore, it should be listed as a constraint. If you're really on top of your game, you will prepare a cash flow model for your project so that you can define when you'll need which amounts of capital. If this is beyond your skill set, see if you can offer one of the Finance people a free lunch or a pair of movie tickets to help you project your cash expenditures during the lifecycle of the security project plan. Your executives will be impressed and your Finance folks will probably be relieved to have an idea of when these expenditures might come in.

Organizational Change

Sometimes *changes to the organization* can create project constraints that we don't immediately recognize. If your company is in the process of evaluating another company for acquisition, this might be a constraint on your security project. You might not be able to conclude your project in a timely manner if your project resources are reallocated to another project, or are unavailable due to this acquisition. While this scenario may not be relevant to your organization, take a look around your company and see if there are any upcoming changes that could constrain on your project.

Governmental or Regulatory Requirements

Governmental or regulatory requirements have an impact on an IT security project plan. Are these constraints? It depends on the nature of the requirements. In some cases, these might simply be included in the functional and technical requirements. In other cases, these regulations might be constraints on the project as a whole. Any governmental or regulatory requirement that limits the way your team approaches the project should be considered a constraint and should be listed.

Along with constraints, you may also want to make a note of how that constraint impacts your security project plan, the approach to your plan, or methods the plan can use. Typically, constraints are risks or challenges you must live with, but any planning you can do to mitigate these constraints is usually worth the effort.

Business Intelligence...

Compliance Confusion

The ever-changing landscape of compliance clearly impacts IT security project plans, especially in the planning stages. While you should certainly utilize standard IT project methodologies, you also have to implement whatever additional tools and techniques are needed to become or remain compliant. We've stressed the importance of involving executives and users throughout the process, because at the end of the day, you're only as secure or compliant as your users allow you to be. All the access controls in the world won't help when an authorized user prints out a patient's medical file for review and accidentally leaves it at a coffee shop after a hectic morning. We'll talk about security policies and procedures later in this book, but you may want to add some additional planning steps to your IT security project plan to ensure that your organization can become and remain compliant with whatever regulations apply to your firm. The document called "8 Steps to Compliance Readiness" on Gantthead.com is helpful, and can be found at www.gantthead.com/article.cfm?ID=228710.

Lessons Learned

You may want to define and capture *lessons learned* as tasks are being completed. It's very common for these key findings to get lost as people move onto new tasks or new projects. Trying to sit down at the end of a project and gather lessons learned is like sifting through sand; most of it falls through the cracks. Although a particular task may not lead to a major "a ha" moment, it could certainly lead to a new or refined best practice, or just a slight modification to a test procedure that lends itself to improved productivity, better security, or less user frustration. Whatever is learned, the task work should be captured as part of the task detail. As part of your project processes and procedures, you can convene a "lessons learned" meeting each month or each quarter and have everyone compile the lessons learned from their tasks. Discussing these frequently and regularly can save other IT security project plan team members time and effort on later tasks, it can streamline and improve your project, and it can help everyone avoid common pitfalls or share better methods. If you wait to gather these at the end of your project, you not only risk having these innovations be forgotten, but you miss the opportunity for team members to benefit from this knowledge earlier in the project lifecycle.

Identifying and Working With the Critical Path

Sometimes people use an incorrect definition for *critical path*; therefore, let's start by defining it so that we all start from the same baseline. By definition, the critical path is the longest, least flexible path through your project. If any task that is on the critical path slips (e.g., is late), the project will not be finished on time. Most project management software programs will graphically show you the critical path after you've loaded in your task dependencies and duration.

The critical take-away here is that you should be clear about which tasks are on your critical path and which are not, especially within your ISAPs. It will help you make better decisions about how to allocate resources to your project. If one ISAP is delayed, it might ripple through your corporate IT security project plan and delay the start or completion of other ISAPs. Ultimately, this impacts your overall network security because the longer it takes you to complete various elements of your corporate IT security plan, the longer the bad guys have to work on weak targets.

Testing IT Security Project Results

How you approach testing your *security project plan results* and security is up to you. You may choose to develop a wholly independent testing plan. You may also choose to develop testing criteria within tasks or phases of your project. Because you're dealing with network security, it's important to decide how you will test project results before you launch into your project. If you choose to develop an independent testing plan, you should tie in key tests or test points to your task details (e.g., if a task is defined as "Harden Server 123," completion criteria should be localized tests on Server 123 to ensure the hardening tasks were successful). However, since Server 123 doesn't live in isolation, a more expansive test will also need to be performed to ensure that the cross-boundary issues are addressed (e.g., what protocols, applications, or users are connecting to Server 123, and are all of those areas secure as well.). If a user is accessing confidential data located on Server 123, and Server 123 is secure, that's great. But what about the fact that the user is in the Dallas airport using an unsecured wireless connection? Now how secure it that data? Even if the user is connecting to a secure Web site requiring a user login, that data is still traveling from the laptop through the unsecured wireless connection to a hardwired Internet connection before traveling on to the secure site. Since security is defined by the weakest link, this particular scenario describes a secure server and unsecured confidential data. Do your testing procedures for Server 123 account for this? Probably not, because it's outside the scope of the task, "Harden Server 123." Therefore, your project planning should include testing procedures that test down (ISAPs) and across (corporate) the enterprise. (Figure 7.1 represents the cross-boundary issues.) However, be sure your security project plan includes testing procedures.

As a reminder, it's often helpful to look at testing in terms of *people*, *process*, and *technology*. The *people* aspect has to do with testing how people can (and do) interact with network resources. *Process* has to do with testing various security processes, whether through settings, automation, or interactive testing. *Technology* has to do with verifying configuration, hardware, and software settings. If you look at these three areas in your testing plan, you're more likely to develop a comprehensive test plan.

While you've probably looked at your enterprise and decided what's included, now's a good time to review your project and what it encompasses. Is there something you've thought of that you want to test that is *not* included in the project plan or the WBS? If so, this is a good indication that there is an omission that should be addressed. (For your review, we've included a list in Chapter 9 of potential areas that might need to be included in your security project plan or might need to be part of your test plan [see Table 9.1].). While this list is long, it is not exhaustive, and you should take a close look at your organization to see what else might need to be included.

Testing plans vary significantly from one type of project to another, but a common set of steps for testing include the:

1. Testing stage
2. Schedule of the test
3. Location of the test
4. Participants in the test
5. Environment; general IT and equipment
6. Data to be used for testing
7. Backup and restore procedures
8. Testing procedure
9. Issue, problem, and error reporting procedure
10. Issue resolution procedure

11. Retesting procedure

12. Signoff procedure

We've also included a list of test types that will provide a reminder as to how you want to develop your testing plans. These will be very specific to both your organization, the risks, the threats, and the types of technology you have (ISAPs), but here's a refresher to get you started:

1. Unit testing

2. Integration testing

3. Usability testing

4. Acceptance testing

5. Beta testing

6. Regression testing

7. Performance testing (stress and load testing, stability testing, and reliability testing)

8. Benchmark testing

Budget, Schedule, Risks, and Communications

Once you have the details generated via your WBS, you can create a more detailed budget and schedule. You can also step back and look at various project risks and develop mitigation strategies. Finally, you can develop your communication plans because you'll now have sufficient information to allow you to determine who needs to be in the loop with regard to your project.

Budget

If you're working on your corporate IT security plan, it will have to encompass the underlying budgets for all the ISAPs. If you don't have those project plans developed, be sure your budget contains placeholders for those amounts. Also be sure to communicate this information to the appropriate parties. Clearly, you want to avoid a situation where the budget that is approved contains only a portion of your overall IT security project plan costs. You can create your high level corporate IT security project plan with ISAP budget placeholders, or you can delineate the cost of each ISAP and add to it the corporate IT security project plan piece. It's just two different approaches that will lead you to the same result. Either way, remember that your corporate IT security project budget is a sum of the underlying ISAP budgets and the costs of the discrete components of the corporate IT security project itself. When it comes to budget approval, you want to have all the projects included and not have to go back for a second round of budget approvals after your projects are underway.

Schedule

For the most part, the comments just made about the budget preparation hold true for the *schedule*, with a few minor exceptions. First, some portions of the project work can be run in parallel; therefore, the overall corporate IT security project plan schedule is not exactly the sum of all underlying schedules. However, as you look across your ISAPs and the corporate IT security project plan, you may discover scheduling conflicts that didn't come into play until you looked at all of the projects in a holistic manner. The scheduling component becomes more complex when you're juggling resources across multiple projects, so if you are tackling more than one ISAP project at a time (i.e., running in overlapping or parallel modes), you'll need to map out your resource requirements across all projects. This moves your corporate IT security project into the realm of *program* management. (A program is a collection of related projects.) If you need to schedule a number of projects, you will want to rely on a good project management software program to help you with resource load balancing.

Risks

Each project carries its own set of *risks*. As you know from your project management experience, the risks are both internal and external to the project. As with your budget and schedule, you have individual ISAP risks as well as risks to the overall corporate IT security project plan. It's possible that as you evaluate your projects, you'll see risks that span several ISAPs that were not present when looking at your projects one by one. One example of that kind of risk is that the resources you need won't be available at the right time. If several of your team members are working on one ISAP security project plan that gets delayed, it might have an impact on one or more of the other ISAPs. Looking holistically at your risks across the entire range of projects (ISAPs and corporate IT security project plan) will allow you to see the big picture and plan your risk mitigation strategies accordingly.

Communications

Communicating in the IT security project plan is really no different from other projects. It's included here because some IT project managers aren't great communicators, and this is a huge missed opportunity. An interesting statistic about security project plan success is that the *perception* of success is just as important as the actual results when people are asked to assess the project's success. So, you can knock yourself out to deliver the absolute best results only to find that, because you didn't do a good job communicating during the project, it's deemed "acceptable" at best.

Create communication plans and implement them. Remember the four C's: Communicate clearly, concisely, and consistently. Most people just want information, but many people in IT seem to think that if they don't know the answer, they should wait until they do know the answer before saying anything. Just the opposite is true. If you don't know, say you don't know, and then communicate what you're doing to find out when you'll next communicate. When you fail to communicate, your project falls into the corporate black hole and you lose the opportunity to maintain a positive attitude about the project and its results.

Business Intelligence...

Users Are the Key to Compliance and Security

IT security has become a major issue in the compliance arena, though that pointed focus is a bit misplaced. In some ways, IT security is the "low hanging fruit"—easy to point to and grab as the solution to this challenging problem. Computer and information technology is still an evolving field. Fifty years ago, no one had to worry about managing electronic information, so the answers we're seeking today have to be developed based on the ever-changing technological landscape. IT technologies must contribute to security, but in the end, people within the organization must be engaged in helping create and maintain security. There are different ways to do this, but continued visibility is an important aspect. Whether you have your Human Resources department or your Training department involved, be sure to consider creating a regular communication channel to educate and engage users in the security process. The Computer Security Institute has developed two regular newsletters, one focused on users and the other focused on top-level executives, that you can sign up to receive. They can be customized to your organization (i.e., you can add your logo, street address, and a small section for company-specific information) for regular distribution to your users and executives. This fee-based newsletter is just one solution, but it's a good idea to implement a system for keeping IT security and security practices in the forefront of your users' minds. You can take a look at sample newsletters at www.gocsi.com/awareness/publications.jhtml. Keeping users up-to-date about changing IT threats and security best practices is a great way to help bolster your IT security project plan results.

Summary

Planning an IT security project plan isn't dramatically different from planning any other kind of IT project, it just has a few nuances that are good to know about going in. We reviewed the basics of planning your IT security project plan and discussed those differences. The WBS is where the proverbial rubber hits the road, where the project details begin to take shape. Within your tasks, you can include the data that provides guidance on the successful completion of the tasks as it relates to your security requirements. Functional and technical requirements should be translated into completion criteria. Ultimately, these ensure that your security project plan provides the requisite level of security and complies, where necessary, with laws and regulations such as Sarbanes-Oxley and others.

After completing your WBS, you should perform your first scope check. It's here that you discover whether your scope and the tasks defined in your WBS are aligned. In most cases, there is some sort of mismatch and, therefore, you have an opportunity to work through these disconnects fairly early in the planning stages.

We discussed the importance of developing task details and how these details can be used to enhance security and ensure your project delivers the quality results you require. It's important to have subject matter experts participate in developing the WBS and the task details, since they are closest to the technical details and are the ones best suited to developing meaningful task details and metrics.

Project constraints in an IT security project plan are slightly different because legal, regulatory, or industry requirements are constraints not always found in other kinds of IT projects. Be sure to include all legal, regulatory or industry requirements not only in your task details, but also in your constraints. These are likely to shape the way your project proceeds, and should be addressed at the outset of the project planning phase.

Testing is an important element in IT security and it's vital that your project plan include test procedures. In some cases, this can be accomplished via task details and completion criteria. In many cases, however, it also requires you to test down through the ISAP and across the enterprise to ensure there are no gaps in security. Some organizations and projects require a separate IT security test project plan, others simply require that discrete testing tasks be built into the project WBS.

We looked at the areas where the ISAPs and the corporate IT security project plan come together. In later chapters of this book, we'll look at some individual security area project plans and step through them. However, it's important to understand that there may be two discrete types of plans you're working with; the corporate IT security project plan, which addresses the entirety of corporate IT security, and the individual security areas like wireless security or operational security. These areas are sometimes implemented as individual projects, but must also be viewed as part of the larger whole. We looked at aspects related to both the corporate IT security project plan and the individual security project plans as it pertains to the critical path, budget, schedule, and risks. We finished the chapter with the four C's discussion, reiterating the importance of communicating clearly, concisely, and consistently.

Solutions Fast Track

Creating the IT Security Project Work Breakdown Structure

☑ The WBS is developed from the three to five major objectives identified in the definition phase of the project.

☑ Use a numbering system to help manage tasks. You can later refer to them by number rather than name to lend clarity to your communications.

☑ Your WBS may include the tasks from your sub-projects, or it may include just the corporate IT security project plan tasks.

Defining Project Tasks and Sub-tasks

☑ Tasks should follow the 8/80 rule. If they are shorter than 8 hours, roll them up into another task (if possible). If they are longer than 80 hours, split them into smaller tasks.

☑ Tasks and sub-tasks are often identified in a linear manner, but should not be placed in a formal order. The final order for tasks will be based on the logical flow of the tasks as well as the dependencies and constraints.

Checking Project Scope

☑ Once you've identified all of the project's tasks, you can check the scope of the project.

☑ It's common to find that the WBS defines work that is larger than the defined (or desired) scope of the project. Either you'll need to reduce your WBS task list, or you'll need to adjust your scope statements.

☑ This is typically the genesis of scope creep, so this is your first and best place to address potential scope creep.

☑ Often the process of creating the WBS causes you to discover additional information germane to the project planning process. This often causes you to have to reevaluate your scope.

☑ If your scope has legitimately changed based on the information you've discovered, discuss the proposed changes with your project sponsor.

Developing Task Details

☑ The task details can include all kinds of data. For an IT security project, it should include functional and technical requirements, as well as any legal, regulatory, or industry requirements.

☑ Your completion criteria should include legal, regulatory, or industry requirements. When each task is completed according to specifications, there is a much higher likelihood that the project results will also be compliant.

☑ Gather lessons learned as part of the task detail. This may help team members avoid common pitfalls or leverage new streamlined methods.

☑ Regularly reviewing lessons learned helps share knowledge earlier in the project lifecycle. Waiting until the end of the project to gather lessons learned, misses an opportunity to improve the project and risks missing the opportunity to capture organizational knowledge.

Identifying and Working With the Critical Path

☑ By definition, the critical path is the longest, least flexible path through the project.

☑ When dealing with tasks from both the ISAPs and the corporate IT security project plan, you may have more than one critical path to deal with.

Testing IT Security Project Results

☑ Testing plans should be developed in the planning phase of the project.

☑ Tests should include testing the security or the result of individual security tasks.

☑ Tests should include testing the security in an individual security area plan (ISAP) as well as across the enterprise.

☑ Test plans may be implemented as separate projects or as part of the project's existing WBS.

☑ Test plans can include unit testing; integration testing; usability testing; acceptance testing; beta testing; regression testing;

performance testing; stress and load testing; stability and reliability testing; and benchmark testing.

Budget, Schedule, Risks, and Communications

☑ The budget for ISAPs and the corporate IT security project plan must be addressed individually and as a whole. Gaps or omissions in your budget can be difficult to resolve later.

☑ The schedule for ISAPs and the corporate IT security project plan can be challenging to manage since you have several potentially conflicting demands for resources.

☑ Some tasks can be run in parallel, but be sure to look for resource constraints and conflicts if you do so.

☑ Risks to your project involve the risks to the ISAPs and the combined risks of the projects. Some risks span ISAPs and should be addressed and managed as such.

☑ Remember the four C's: communicate clearly, concisely, and consistently. Successful projects are as dependent on the perception of success as on the actual outcomes.

Chapter 7

Managing the IT Security Project

Solutions in this chapter:

- Initiating the IT Security Project
- Monitoring and Managing IT Security Project Progress
- Managing IT Security Project Risk
- Managing IT Security Project Change
- Testing IT Security Project Results

☑ Summary

☑ Solutions Fast Track

Introduction

After you've thoroughly planned your project and circled back once or twice through various areas to develop additional clarity, it's time to begin the project. Whether you're working on the corporate IT security project or one of the individual security area projects, you need to get everyone moving in the same direction and you need to monitor the results as you go. In this chapter, we review these project management steps with a focus on IT security. Security is developed through the planning stages to make sure all bases are covered, but is implemented through the project tasks. It's later maintained through policies and operational procedures. In this chapter, we cover the implementation. In a later chapter, we look at the policies and operational procedures needed to maintain security in your network environment.

Initiating the IT Security Project

The best place to start your Information Technology (IT) security project is to make sure that all of your prior definition and planning tasks have been completed. At this point, you should have the following:

- Problem statement
- Mission statement
- Selected solution
- Project constraints and priorities
- Project requirements (functional, technical, legal)
- Work breakdown structure (WBS) with all tasks and task details defined
- Project risks and mitigation strategies
- Project budget and schedule
- Required competencies identified
- Project team formed
- Project processes defined

After making sure that all of the necessary elements are in place, check in with your project sponsor. Make sure that all systems are still "go" and that nothing has changed that will cause you to have to rework parts of your plan. This is also a good opportunity for one final "scope check" to ensure that the scope of work hasn't increased before the project work has begun.

When you're ready to begin the project work, start with a formal announcement and a team meeting. The formal announcement serves two purposes: it notifies the organization that the project resources are now required for the IT security project, and it gives your project some visibility. Sometimes IT projects are planned and implemented in the back of the server room, and no one outside of the IT department knows what's going on. In many cases that's fine; however, in the case of IT security projects, more visibility is needed. It's important that users, managers, division heads, and executives all understand that these initiatives are underway and that they are important. This is your opportunity for a bit of a "marketing blitz": let the company know how important this project is to the future of the organization and how individuals can contribute to its success.

Also take this opportunity to reiterate the importance of quality in your project. Participants must be committed to doing a good job because without quality in this project, your network security will be at risk. Attention to detail, following defined processes and procedures, and addressing issues and changes according to plan parameters is vitally important to a successful project outcome. Your kick-off meeting is the first and best chance to set the stage for this mindset, and can have a huge impact on the final result.

Monitoring and Managing IT Security Project Progress

The biggest challenge in an IT security project is managing the compliance issues. Often, there are so many conflicting requirements that even the most savvy IT security expert has difficulty discerning what's required or, in some cases, how to reconcile conflicting requirements. Even when these compliance requirements are straightforward, you have to be confident that the activities undertaken during the project work phase are generating compliant results.

As mentioned in Chapter 6, you need to establish processes and procedures that ensure that your results are compliant with whatever regulations apply to your firm. There are often stringent documentation requirements, and in some cases, you'll need to document your documentation.

Business Intelligence...

Focus, Simplicity, and Enforceability

Compliance was on the minds of many IT professionals who attended the April 2006 InfoSec World conference. Focus, simplicity, and enforceability are the keys to crafting corporate information security policies, according to conference attendees. "Pick your battles," Anish Bhimani, chief information security officer at JPMorgan Chase & Co. advised. He added that instead of having a laundry list of compliance items, companies should be "crystal clear" on what their security objectives are and spell them out in a policy that workers can easily understand and that is high level enough to remain relevant over an extended period of time. One thing to keep in mind is how many controls you're asking people to comply with. Focusing on the elements that matter the most and that will drive compliance is important. Keeping the requirements simple will help ensure compliance across the organization. Finally, focus on what can be enforced.

Using a consistent IT security project management methodology will help you in your quest for compliance, but you must also look at how your project plan interacts with your organization. As you implement your IT security project plan, keep an eye on the focus, simplicity, and enforceability of your processes and procedures. We'll look at policies that support compliance later in this book. For now, keep an eye on compliance requirements as you implement your IT security project plan.

Continued

www.syngress.com

because you may need to modify policies and procedures as you progress through the project to address user concerns or issues.

For more information on the InfoSec World conference article, go to http://www.computerworld.com/industrytopics/financial/story/0, 10801,110342,00.html

Task Progress

Your IT security project should be broken down into tasks with very clear, specific deliverables, which should be identified through the use of well-crafted completion criteria. If you are dealing with compliance issues, you should also make sure that the appropriate documentation is included in the mix. Different compliance requirements will have diverse reporting and documentation requirements, so be sure these are in place prior to initiating security project work. This is a good checkpoint to make sure you're comfortable with the documentation defined in each phase or task of your project. It's much easier to document the work you perform and what is required to maintain the requisite level of security, than it is to go back and try to ascertain what was done when and by whom.

Below is an example of completion criteria, which help ensure tasks are completed correctly. While the example uses a fairly simple task that would not normally need to be tracked across time, it shows you a concrete model of how completion criteria can be included in a task to help monitor results. In this example, the task is to set the network password policy to require the use of strong passwords. Previous tasks, upon which this task is dependent, have included activities to notify users that this will be required starting on a particular date, and to train users as to what constitutes a strong password. The language in this example is fairly generic; your completion criteria should include the specific steps (e.g., clicks, menu options, responses, and so forth) you would take (e.g., in a Windows Server 2003 environment or a Linux environment).

Completion Criteria Example – Strong Passwords

This task is complete when the following steps have been completed in order:

[Initial each step when complete.]

1. _____Log in on the administrator account to Server 123.

2. _____ Access password policies.

3. _____ Configure passwords to require at least 7 characters.

4. _____ Configure passwords to require at least one lower case letter, one upper case letter, one number and one special character.

5. _____ Configure passwords to disallow the use of any part of the username.

6. _____ Configure passwords to be different from the previous three passwords used.

7. _____ Configure passwords to require they be changed no less than every four weeks.

8. _____ Modify the Failed Login Notification box to include only this text (remove any pre-existing text and substitute it with this text): "You must change your password to conform to new password requirements. If you have trouble logging on, please contact Jaime at extension 1234 for assistance."

9. _____ Log off the administrator account.

10. _____ Log in on your own user account.

11. _____ Test password requirements by trying to set your password using these passwords. Note result as "Pass" or "Fail." Pass indicates you were able to login using that password; Fail indicates you were unable to successfully login using that password:

    a. AndrewW2006 [insert your own first name, last initial and year] Result: _____

    b. Password Result: _____

    c. [blank] Result: _____

    d. Monkey business Result: _____

    e. Pr9#Nsm44 Result: _____

12. _____ Reset your password to a password that is not on this list and that meets the requirements set above.

13. _____ Contact three users from the user contact list and verify that strong passwords are required and that users can log on. List users and results:

    i. User 1: _____ Result: _____

    ii. User 2: _____ Result: _____

    iii. User 3: _____ Result: _____

14. Note time and date you completed these steps in order:

    Name: _____ Date: _____

    Time: _____

    Additional Notes:

The success of a security project plan is built on the successful completion of tasks, and progress can be measured against the completion criteria

In addition to managing the compliance and documentation issues, you'll be managing standard project management issues related to tasks. Are the needed resources ready to begin their tasks? Are tasks starting and ending on time? Are tasks being completed successfully? If tasks are slipping, how does it affect dependent tasks? How are tasks on your critical path going? Is funding available when needed, and are tasks being impacted as a result? These are the kinds of normal project management issues you face on a regular basis and which you're skilled at, especially using project management software to help track any progress against your security project plan. There are two additional factors to keep in mind within the scope of an IT security project plan. The first is whether there are any external factors that must be addressed with respect to hard deadlines for compliance or changes to laws or regulations that occur during the work cycle of the project. The second is whether any issues arise that could jeopardize your overall security. Sometimes security and compliance requirements don't align, so you need to be sure that nothing will jeopardize your network security.

Project Progress

As stated earlier, a project with multiple milestones is usually more successful than a project with few milestones. Milestones are checkpoints in a security project plan: the more often you step back and take a look at where you are, the more successful your project will be. Milestones in your IT security project plan should include, among others, checkpoints on required activities and documentation related to compliance issues. As you move through your project work, keeping an eye on these two key elements will be crucial. It's very difficult to go back and create documentation, and it takes much less time and effort to create it concurrent with the security activity. Be sure you have milestones in your project plan for these key tasks. Also be sure to include milestones related to any external events or activities including hard deadlines for compliance, timelines for external audits (if any), and checkpoints to determine if there have been any relevant changes to the laws or regulations to which your IT security project might be subject.

In addition to regulatory issues, you want to ensure that your project is progressing as planned. In today's IT environment, it's easy to find multiple, conflicting demands pulling on your IT staff or security project plan team. It's easy to get off track under these conditions; therefore, it's critical that you, as the project manager, actively manage this situation. You'll have to use your best management skills to keep people focused and motivated on the tasks at hand while recognizing the conflicting demands staff face.

We're not going to get into a discussion of various methods of evaluating project progress other than to say that there are numerous methods you can use, including percent complete and earned value analysis (EVA), to name two common ones. Percent complete is really a ballpark estimate unless you use real metrics (e.g., if your entire project is scheduled for 60 days and you've hit the 30-day mark, are you actually 50 percent complete?) It depends on whether or not the tasks scheduled to be started, in progress, and complete by the 30th day are all on track. Percent complete can be deceiving (intentionally or unintentionally). EVA can also be an excellent tool but again, is subject to various kinds of intentional or unintentional manipulation and is not always accurate. Many people are intimidated or confused by EVA and choose not to use this method. Other people feel that for some projects, EVA takes more time to calculate than the actual work it is calculating. Whatever method(s) you use, be sure you apply it consistently as you move through your security project plan, so that you can keep yourself, your project team, your project sponsor, and the organization apprised of your progress.

While you're managing the project, be sure to keep your project sponsor in the loop using the agreed-upon timelines and deliverables for project status reporting. The project sponsor rarely needs to know all the gritty project details, but he or she should know the current status and issues well enough to help support (and possibly defend) the project to upper management should the need arise. Key check-in points should also be identified via project milestones.

Issues Reporting and Resolution

Issue management is very important in IT security projects. Issues may arise that impact your overall network security, and managing these effectively will be fundamental to delivering a successful project result. As issues arise, they need to be evaluated as to criticality—is the issue an emergency or is it simply something to be addressed before project completion? The criticality of an issue is an assessment of what impact it will have on the task, the schedule, the budget, or the overall project. As you're evaluating criticality, keep an eye on your risks and mitigation strategies, which should include specific triggers that indicate when a risk is occurring. Keeping these front and center will help as issues arise, because you can quickly determine if an issue is part of a defined risk or not. If it is part of a defined risk, the issue has been thought through and can be addressed in a systematic manner. If it is not part of a defined risk, the issue has to be looked at in more detail. Resolving project issues can be complex in some cases and the resolutions may have unintended effects, especially on the overall security of the network. Be sure your issue resolution process includes steps to evaluate the risk of implementing the solution as well as any potential unintended consequences you can think of (unfortunately, some may not be evident until later). Carefully thinking through issue resolution in a security project is very important, because each change brings with it the potential for creating an unintended security hole that may be exploited.

Documentation

Your standard issue reporting and resolution processes and procedures will work well for a security project plan with one notable exception: documentation. As we've continually stressed, documentation in a security project plan is important, because it provides you with an audit trail so that you can go back and see what's been done. It is also important, because it forms the basis of ongoing security operations procedures. Finally, documentation is critical because it is typically required (often in triplicate) for compliance audits. It can't be stressed enough that your documentation should be well-defined and completed in as near real-time as possible. It's also very important to understand that any and all documentation you generate, including the issue reports, could become legal documents should a security breach occur that results in litigation. In most cases, the best approach is to have a consistent approach to document project results and a track record for taking action on issues that arise. If you have well-documented problems but fail to adequately address or resolve them, you're leaving yourself wide open for security problems and potential litigation. Documentation combined with appropriate action is your best bet when it comes to managing an IT security project.

Monitoring IT Security Project Risk

In the planning phase of your project, you identified potential risks (internal or external) to your IT security project. Your planning process should include risk assessment, mitigation strategies, evaluation of the risk of mitigation plans, and triggers. As you move through your security project plan, it's important to continually check your list of known risks. If you have identified triggers, you should quickly spot the risks and take immediate action to address them. In some IT projects, failure to spot these risks early may be a "non-event," but in a security project they usually have more serious implications.

In addition, as your security project plan progresses, you may identify new risks that could not be anticipated until the project was underway. These risks might be related to project work or they might be new risks from the outside world. You can't know everything in advance of performing project work; sometimes new risks crop up. Actively managing these new risks using the same evaluation and planning methodology you used in the planning stages will generate the best results. Sometimes new external threats show up that throw a wrench in the works (e.g., during your project work, you might discover that a new network intrusion method has cropped up.) This might be a risk to security that was never considered because it wasn't known at the time. Should it be included in your project plan? It's hard to say until you and your team take the time to evaluate the risk of such an intrusion, evaluate the steps required to address the new threat, and determine whether or not it can safely be incorporated into your project plan. When you're dealing with security, it's rarely a good idea to respond without doing your homework. Sometimes such action exposes you to a whole new set of risks.

Be aware of potential new threats or regulations. Address these risks by assessing the likelihood of occurrence, the criticality of such an occurrence, and the cost or impact of such an occurrence, and then create your mitigation strategy accordingly.

Managing IT Security Project Change

Change is an absolute certainty in projects, which is why all projects have (or should have) project managers. Someone has to ensure that the project continues to make steady progress and that any new information is incorporated in a logical, consistent manner. What kinds of changes can occur in your project? If you're an experienced project manager, you've probably seen it all. Key stakeholders making new requests (demands) of the project, key staff not being available, new corporate plans that were under wraps are suddenly unveiled—these are the kinds of changes that happen to all projects, including IT security projects. Let's look at a few of the high-level categories and discuss these kinds of changes within the realm of IT security.

Key Stakeholder Change

It's very common for stakeholders to submit change requests for a project (e.g., a departmental manager asks for a change to the logon procedure for his staff or a vice president requests that a particular portion of the network be secured in a different manner than was specified). A director demands that some procedure be changed or an executive demands that particular security tasks be delayed until after a certain time or event. All of these kinds of changes have to be managed by the IT project team.

Your standard change management procedures should be employed consistently throughout the project lifecycle. These procedures should include evaluating the requested change, assigning it a level of criticality, and assessing what actions might be taken to address the change. Once it's decided that a change is desirable or acceptable, it must go through the risk evaluation process. By definition, change is a project risk because you're deviating from the project plan. Therefore, you should view all major change as a risk and evaluate it using the same methodologies you use to evaluate other kinds of risk. Be especially aware of unintended consequences of change. Think through these situations very carefully to determine if these changes will support, enhance, or erode security. If they will not support or enhance security, they should probably not be implemented. However, we all know that in the real world, things are rarely perfect and you may be forced by circumstances to implement a change that does not support or enhance security. You'll have to evaluate the pro's and con's before making a final decision. This might be a good time to check in with your security project plan sponsor if you have conflicting demands that cannot be easily resolved.

Also, use your functional and technical requirements documents to address major stakeholder change requests. Sometimes stakeholders simply fail to understand the implications of their change requests and once they are discussed in light of the original specifications and the risks of the requested change, they may rescind those requests. If not, your job is to negotiate a reasonable solution to the problem. Look over the original specifications and determine whether the stakeholder's change request:

1. Falls under the original specifications (i.e. you and your team may have missed something).
2. Falls outside of the original specifications, but is a desirable modification that will support or enhance security.
3. Falls outside of the original specifications, is a reasonable modification, but does not support or enhance security.
4. Falls outside the original specifications, is not a reasonable modification, and may or may not support security.

Clearly, having had key stakeholder input from the start of the project should reduce these kinds of change requests, but change always pops up in one form or another. As you evaluate these potential changes using these four criteria, you can take a logical approach toward incorporating the requested change or explaining the reasons for rejecting the requested change. Be sure to effectively communicate with key stakeholders and take time to explain the rationale for the decision. While the stakeholder might not be pleased with the final outcome, he or she should at least understand why the decision was made. If you can defend your position, be sure you're being reasonable. Sometimes in the midst of project work, we want to reject change just because it's inconvenient, not because it's undesirable. Make sure you don't fall into that trap.

Key Staff Change

We've all experienced staff changes in project work. We've spent time identifying core competencies and skills needed for a successful project, we've identified the key people we needed, and were assured they'd be available for the project. However, when the time comes, that person is unavailable. Sometimes this happens because the project timeline has slipped and that person's window of availability has closed. Other times, the project is on target but the person has been pulled to a higher priority task or is simply no longer available (promotion, left the company, out on family leave, and so forth). The key is how you handle it as the project manager.

    If these key staff are critical to project success, their lack of availability should have been identified as a project risk and mitigation strategies should have been identified at the outset of the project. This might include identifying your second and third choices for the work, or sending someone through training to be the backup. It may also mean that you've identified an outside contractor who could fill that role, if needed. In rare cases, you may have to put that aspect of project work on hold until the key person becomes available. This would clearly not be an optimal solution but one of last resort.

Key Environmental Change

Things change within organizations every day. There are times when upper management have plans they're working on that they cannot divulge to anyone, even though they will impact other organizational plans and projects. It's the nature of business. If an executive team is discussing a hostile takeover of a competitor or an acquisition of another firm, they may not be able to disclose this information (legally, ethically or strategically) to you. However, you may later find yourself in the midst of running your IT security project when plans are announced and suddenly your environment shifts dramatically.

Another example of an environmental change that could impact your project is if laws or regulations regarding data security in your industry or segment change. It is a common occurrence these days that changes are discussed for months or even years without resolution. It's impossible to adequately plan because the discussion regarding these regulations changes and shifts until it's finally just locked in one day. If you responded to every shift in approach before the regulation was enacted, you'd spend all of your time reacting to these changes and never end up with any meaningful plan. Most IT professionals keep an eye on these proposed changes but proceed with their project planning work anyway. If you waited for the "final" word, you'd almost never be able to actually plan and implement a project. Once the final decision is reached and enacted, you may have to make sure that your plan incorporates the latest aspects of the regulation. If you keep on top of potential changes that could be implemented, you probably won't be blindsided. That said, it's entirely possible that despite your best efforts to keep an eye on the regulatory environment, you may need to step back and figure out "Plan B."

Testing IT Security Project Results

Testing IT security project results is an important element of delivering a successful security project plan result. How should testing be performed to ensure the results are as expected? That's not an easy question to answer. You probably performed some level of testing as part of your assessment and audit process before launching into this project, so you may choose to re-use those testing procedures to test project results. However, as stated earlier, there is a tendency to test our plans, not test our results, so it's easy to fall into a trap whereby we think we're testing the security of our network but we're just testing the work we performed. Both types of testing are useful; the real key is in understanding the difference. Start by asking what you're actually testing, why you're testing it, and what you expect to find. Include metrics and measurements to the greatest extent possible. A general assessment of "it worked" is not as helpful as "the database scripting did not generate an error when it was tested with situation A, B, and C" (where each A, B and C is described in detail).

In addition, it's important to remember that regardless of the type of IT security project you're working on, you need to look across all boundaries. Figure 7.1 depicts the cross-boundary types of testing you should consider for your project. Each Individual Security Analysis Programs (ISAPs) results should be tested to ensure that your wireless network or server infrastructure (or whatever you defined as an ISAP) is secured as expected via the security project plan. However, this type of "silo testing" will only tell you how secure that individual area is. Clearly, there are interactions across ISAPs as well, and these are the areas your corporate IT security project plan should address. The horizontal arrows in Figure 7.1 show corporate IT security testing that spans all ISAPs at various levels. In addition, through your risk assessment and planning processes, you may have identified some especially high-risk areas that deserve special attention. The areas called out in stars labeled 1, 2, and 3 indicate areas that additional attention and testing will be applied to in order to be sure these critical areas are addressed within the ISAPs, across the ISAPs, and as part of the overall corporate IT security project.

Testing is not an isolated event that generates a yes/no response. It must be looked at across the enterprise and evaluated based on its horizontal and vertical aspects (horizontal = across the enterprise, vertical = into the ISAP).

Figure 7.1 Cross-boundary Testing

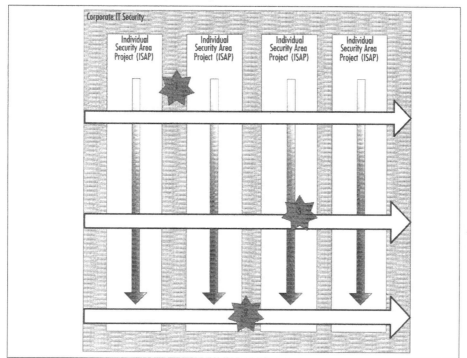

As mentioned in Chapter 6, testing should encompass many different elements. It may also be appropriate to create a separate security project plan devoted solely to testing. For example, there are network components, protocols, setups, user profiles, resource access control lists (and more) which need to be tested. Even if they are not part of the IT security project plan, the key elements related to securing your corporate network must be tested. This is different from ongoing monitoring in which these areas are watched, alerts are set, and log files are reviewed and analyzed. Testing requires an active "push" against security areas to ensure they don't collapse. A thorough testing plan is critical to solid results. You can use a variety of normal testing procedures including testing access controls (too much or too little access for various users and groups), as well as batch and interactive kinds of testing. (For a list of potential areas to look at for testing, refer to Table 9.1 in Chapter 9.)

Summary

Managing an IT security project is very similar to managing any other type of IT project in many respects. However, there are several unique characteristics that should be addressed as you move through the security project plan phase. Security is created and maintained by a consistent, well-thought out approach; all the planning in the world is useless if the implementation is sloppy.

Monitoring task progress is involves ensuring that tasks are being started and completed on time and being completed according to specifications and completion criteria. Project quality (and therefore network security) is built on the fundamental building blocks of successful task completion. If tasks are not completed according to specification, the project will most likely fail to deliver requisite levels of security. Compliance issues must also be addressed through adequate documentation. As you progress through your tasks, documentation about the work performed and other required data should be developed. Trying to go back and develop documentation and recall details is almost always more difficult than doing it in near real-time.

Keeping an eye on issues and changes is also another very important element of managing an IT security project plan. Issues that arise might be simple problems, but they might also be bigger issues that impact functional, technical, or legal requirements. Again, documenting the issues and actions taken in detail might be the difference between a compliant and non-compliant project result. Should a security issue arise in the future, these steps, actions, and resolutions might become legal issues, so be sure you carefully document your activities with regard to addressing project issues.

Change happens in all projects, but change to an IT security project plan can impact network security. Internal and external change must be monitored, evaluated, and responded to in a clear, concise, and methodical manner to ensure that security gaps are avoided.

Testing is an important part of project work and there are many different ways to approach it. It should be part of your project planning activities and comprehensive enough to ensure that your network is as secure as you've decided it can be. Testing also helps ensure that your project results meet functional, technical, regulatory, and/or legal requirements. Testing should be deep and broad so that various ISAPs are tested and security across boundaries is also tested.

Solutions Fast Track

Initiating the IT Security Project

- ☑ Your project plan should be comprehensive and complete before initiating project work. The areas that should be covered include: problem statement, mission statement, selected solution, project constraints and priorities, project requirements (functional, technical, legal), Work Breakdown Structure with all tasks and task details defined, project risks and mitigation strategies, project budget and schedule, required competencies identified, project team formed, project processes defined.

- ☑ Begin your project with a kick-off meeting to let everyone know the project is underway. This alerts the organization that it will need to provide the resources agreed upon during the planning phase.

- ☑ Take this opportunity to reiterate the importance of the project and of project quality. Without attention to detail, your network security will be put at risk.

Monitoring and Managing IT Security Project Progress

- ☑ A successful project is built on a series of successfully completed tasks.

- ☑ Task progress should be monitored as should the quality of task results.

- ☑ Project progress is monitored and managed through keeping an eye on individual task progress as well as the critical path tasks.

☑ Project issues should be addressed with an eye toward security and compliance. Document issues and resolutions and be sure they support or enhance security.

☑ In many IT security projects, documentation is a critical component to proving or verifying compliance. Be sure your documentation meets or exceeds minimum requirements.

☑ Be aware that project documentation of all kinds may become legal documents if there is a security breach down the road. Be cognizant of this potential when developing project documentation requirements and when writing the documentation itself.

Managing IT Security Project Risks

☑ Your security project plan should include identification of known or anticipated risks along with mitigation strategies.

☑ Once your project is underway, keep an eye on these risk factors as well as the triggers you've identified.

☑ Project risks are both internal and external and you may find new risks as you begin implementing your plan.

☑ Be aware of any potential new risks to your project such as a new threat or a new regulation. Address these risks by assessing the likelihood of occurrence, the criticality of such an occurrence, and the cost or impact of such an occurrence and then create your mitigation strategy accordingly.

Managing IT Security Project Change

☑ Change happens in every project, but change in an IT security project plan has the potential to create additional security challenges.

☑ It's not uncommon for stakeholders to request or demand change once a project is underway.

☑ Don't dismiss stakeholder change requests. Instead, review the requests and determine if you missed including them in your original project plan (IT error).

☑ Some change requests come up because more information is known once the project is underway. Changes should be evaluated to determine if they support, enhance, or detract from security.

☑ Changes that support or enhance security should be evaluated to determine what, if any, impact they will have on the existing project and on overall security.

Testing IT Security Project Results

☑ Test plans may be part of the project's WBS, or testing might be a separate project altogether.

☑ Test plans should test the security within the targeted area as well as across the enterprise.

☑ Testing is usually a combination of scenarios and interactive and scripted testing techniques.

☑ Be careful to avoid inadvertently "testing the plan." Instead, test the actual network security independent of the plan.

☑ Test plans should include people, process, and technology across the ISAPs and across the enterprise so that they are comprehensive, inclusive, and holistic.

Chapter 8

Closing Out the IT Security Project

Solutions in this chapter:

- Evaluating Project Completion

- Closing Issues Log, Change Requests, and Error Reports

- Preparing for Implementation, Deployment, and Operational Transfer

- Reviewing Lessons Learned

- Documentation and Compliance Reports

☑ Summary

☑ Solutions Fast Track

Introduction

In previous chapters, we focused on the elements of Information Technology (IT) project management that are particular to a security project plan. This chapter focuses on standard project management methods. (For the purposes of this chapter, we will assume that you have a solid IT project management background.)

Closing out a security project plan is different from closing out a standard IT project plan, because there are more serious ramifications for security projects. In a standard IT project, if you change the scope, decide to forego a few tasks, or are unable to resolve a problem, you can usually save those issues for a subsequent project or version. In the case of security, what you skip over or omit could be what hackers find and exploit; therefore, the project close-out process must be thorough and diligent. In this chapter, we look at determining when the project is complete, how to close out various issues, and how to prepare for implementation, deployment, and transfer. These elements are critical to maintaining security; thus, particular attention must be paid to this area. Finally, we look at capturing lessons learned and finalizing project documentation. This is another area that may require a different approach than that of a standard IT project, due to the potential for compliance with various laws, regulations, or standards related to network and data security.

Evaluating Project Completion

When is your IT security project complete and how will you know? The obvious answer is, "When all tasks are 100 percent complete," but a more accurate answer might be, "When all tasks on the critical path are 100 percent complete." Still, that's not a real-world answer, because the actual data vs. the planned data are often at odds with one another. As you near the conclusion of your IT security project plan, you should begin gathering data, status reports, and other information that will help you determine exactly when your security project plan will conclude.

There are numerous project tracking methods you can use for your IT security project to determine actual project completion. If your project parameters specify that the budget (cost) is the priority, you may have to terminate your project when you reach a specified budget amount, regardless of whether or not you've completed the project tasks. By the same measure, if you determine that schedule (time) is the highest priority, you may have to terminate your project when you reach a specified date or deadline, even if all of the project tasks have not been successfully completed.

The problem with this is that if you fail to complete all project tasks, you may be leaving yourself open to security breaches. As you manage the project, you need to keep these parameters in mind. You may have to make a few tough decisions (e.g., omitting a particular set of project tasks after determining they are not needed immediately or can be postponed with minimal risk). With security, you fall into a difficult situation where you can't reasonably reduce the scope, increase the budget, or lengthen the schedule without putting the security at risk. Some of the tasks that could potentially be omitted or delayed from the current project might include upgrading a particular technology that meets specifications today, but is not optimized for handling evolving threats. You might choose to delay this until a later phase when time, money, or resources are more available. This is not without risk to overall security and the project itself, but is an example of the kinds of situations where you might have to make a difficult trade off.

If you find yourself approaching the end of your schedule or the bottom of your budget and you haven't completed the security project plan, you have a problem. In Chapter 7, we recommended you keep your project parameters in the forefront of your decision-making, and that you actively manage the scope to avoid running into these problems. While problems will inevitably arise, managing them pro-actively will help you avoid running out of leeway on your project.

When all is said and done, it's a good idea to step back and look at the actual data vs. the planned data to determine what worked, what didn't work very well, what went horribly wrong, what snuck up on you, and what worked surprisingly well. In every project, there are all of these elements and looking at your project in retrospect will help you and your team learn a lot about many aspects of the project, the organization, and the team. A project summary report is often required (or desired), and the opportunity to look back through the report should be utilized in a positive, productive manner. Some company cultures seem to get locked on the negative aspects, and project reviews turn into blame-fests. Don't let this occur. Look at what worked, what didn't work, and what can be improved for next time. Be brutally honest in your review, but be professional and positive in your communication. Create a culture where people feel comfortable admitting their shortcomings, errors, or omissions so that a better system can be created to avoid those problems in the future. If you create a culture where people are reluctant to identify or own these issues, they'll keep cropping up. Remember the saying, "The definition of insanity is doing the same thing over and over and expecting different results."

Closing Issues Log, Change Requests, and Error Reports

As with any IT project, issues logs should be actively managed throughout the project lifecycle. If you've assigned an owner of the issues log (see Chapter 7), you should have little problem with outstanding issues at the end of the security project plan. If you have not been actively managing the issues log, you run the risk of ending up with open issues that prevent project closure or leave a huge security hole. Issues log items should be resolved and the resolution should be well-documented. Also, you may have legal liabilities that stem from the issues and resolutions (see Chapter 7). Addressing known issues in a reasonable manner and documenting those resolutions are important elements of reducing risk.

At this point in the process, change requests should be addressed and resolved. These change requests should be recorded, evaluated, incorporated (or rejected), and documented. As with issues, the key in an IT security project plan is to thoroughly document the changes made so you can update your documentation, operational procedures, and policies. At project close-out, you should not have any open change requests. Change requests should be evaluated and incorporated into the security project plan task plan or they should be rejected. If any are still open at the end of your project, it's usually because you have changes that need to be made to something that falls outside the scope of the project. If this is the case, be sure you find an appropriate method for transferring this knowledge to the appropriate parties (e.g., a change request deemed to be outside the scope of the project might be transferred to the training department so they can develop targeted training on this topic for users). Rather than changing the project itself, you might decide that changing a user procedure or policy makes more sense and delivers the same or more security.

Typically, error reports indicate a problem that should be resolved before a project is closed out. However, in some cases, error reports fall outside the scope of the IT security project plan. When this happens, the team decides whether the issues can be resolved in an alternate manner. An error report outside the scope of the project should be tracked as an "issue" that can be transferred outside the project during close out. If it's an actual error, it should be resolved within the scope of the project.

The net result is that all issues, change requests, and errors should be resolved or transferred at project close out. Whatever process you use, document all of it so you don't get caught short during an audit or in the aftermath of a subsequent security breach. Also, a security project has more legal and regulatory implications.

Preparing for Implementation, Deployment, and Operational Transfer

We've already covered closing out the issues, change requests, and error logs and transferring any open or outstanding items to the appropriate places. Beyond closing these items out, you should begin looking at the other elements of the IT security project that need to be documented and handed-off for implementation, deployment, or operations. Many of these are standard processes you've used countless times in other IT projects; however, when you move into the realm of IT security, there may be additional steps needed to complete the preparation for project completion. Remember, too, that since the perception of project success is as important as real deliverables in the minds of many stakeholders, how you handle closing the project and transferring operational knowledge can increase or decrease that perception. Users and others in the organization may only see the operational component, since much of the project plan may be done by subject matter experts including security analysts and high-end IT staff. Therefore, how you handle this aspect of the project may be the only part visible to the organization and may be the only thing upon which success is judged by a majority of stakeholders. Of course, at the end of the day, project success will be tied to what *doesn't* happen (e.g., the intrusion averted, the data secured, and so on). As we've discussed, it's often hard to tout success based on the absence of something, so your most tangible opportunity to tout project success may be through this operational transfer process. Make good use of it.

Preparing for Implementation

Implementing security elements is often part of the IT security project plan. However, there may be instances where certain portions of implementation fall outside the security project plan. This might include changes to policies and procedures that are recommended but not implemented, or changes to logons or other security methods that must be rolled out in a particular manner or in a particular timeline (e.g., some companies might choose to implement security measures in segments, such as first implementing security measures for all users in the Finance department). This is often done to find and resolve problems that may arise during the implementation phase without completely disrupting the organization. Your security project plan may have other kinds of implementation needs that will be completed outside the security project plan itself, or after project work is complete. If implementation happens outside the scope of your security project plan, be sure that the information required for implementation is well-developed by defining the implementation requirements and including tasks that address implementation needs. Also, be sure to include milestones in your security project plan so that internal (to the project) and external events remain in sync. Finally, be aware of the need to review your implementation plans from a security viewpoint. If you're implementing changes outside the scope of the project, are there risks to doing so? How will you test, monitor, and remediate implementation results? Who is responsible for the implementation work? Keep these issues in mind as you begin to close out the project, so that all of your hard work on the security project plan is supported throughout the implementation plans.

Preparing for Deployment

Deployment might also be part of the IT security project or it might fall outside the scope of the security project plan. Deployment might include installing new Intrusion Detection System (IDS)/Intrusion Prevention System (IPS) systems or upgrading servers based on recommendations from the security project plan. Security project plans often include the deployment of security solutions as a second phase of the project, but this varies from company to company and from one IT security project plan to another. Deployment includes installing hardware and software and documenting how they will be installed, tested, and turned over. In some cases, this is the same as an implementation plan. In other projects, there is a discrete deployment team whose job it is to take the recommendations and deploy them. As with an implementation plan, a deployment plan that is outside the scope of the security project needs to tie in closely. The deployment team needs to be aware of the security project plan timelines so they can plan accordingly. They also need to be aware of problems, issues, and questions that are still open so they can either participate in solving/closing those issues or so they can work around them.

All deployment plans should include a rollback plan that explains what you should do if things go wrong. Delineating the steps for backing out of a security implementation or deployment is important especially if the deployment causes significant network or resource access issues. If someone sets access control to critical files on a database server incorrectly and no one can access these files, what steps will you take to quickly resolve this? What if these changes have already been replicated across the enterprise? These are the kinds of things you should include in your deployment rollback plans for the major changes you're undertaking. Identifying how to roll back to the last known good state is an important part of the planning process, especially if these plans follow your IT security project plan.

Preparing for Operational Transfer

Operational transfer typically refers to the point at which a project is handed off to the users. However, in an IT security project plan, this may also be transferred to the IT staff responsible for the day-to-day operations. Since your security project plan(s) may have utilized subject matter experts to assess security and develop security solutions, your project may have developed information that needs to be documented and transferred to whoever is responsible for the day-to-day operations. In essence, the operational plan should include:

- The tasks for handing off the project deliverables
- The strategy to be used for the handoff (How will the handoff occur?)
- The key resources needed
- The task owners
- The timing of transfer tasks
- The cost of transfer tasks
- The schedule for transfers
- The risks and contingency plans for transfers
- The formal acceptance or closure methods for transfers

Your IT security project plan concludes with a successful transfer to operations. These operational plans form the keystone to maintaining security and, in particular, maintaining compliance after the project concludes. Therefore, it is critical that sound planning occurs at this juncture. These activities can be included in your IT security project plan itself, or they can be a separate implementation plan, whatever works best for your situation. Keep in mind that you should document operational issues throughout the project lifecycle, so that when it comes time to transfer operations you have well-documented data. Your operations data should include procedures for:

- Maintaining new security measures

- Monitoring security

- Reviewing and analyzing security audit and log files

- Taking action based on audit and log file analysis

- Alerting an emergency response team to a potential security problem

- Addressing user issues with new security policies and procedures

- Escalating emergency and ongoing issues

- Ongoing user security awareness and education

Be sure you identify the timelines for transfer and provide all necessary training, information, and documentation, so that the hard work undertaken during your security project plan lifecycle will be supported, maintained, and perhaps enhanced.

www.syngress.com

Business Intelligence...

Don't Just Lob It Over the Fence

Operational transfer is a critical component to maintaining IT security, even though some of these areas can fall outside the normal domain of the IT department. IT may not be involved with developing user policies beyond some basic IT issues like password complexity; however, in the world of IT security, paying close attention to operational transfer is very important. If you drop the ball here, all of that hard work you and your team did during the project lifecycle is put at risk, because all the best security measures in the world don't add up to anything without consistent operational security afterward. Operational transfer often hands over control from the project team to the user, but in the case of IT security, it might also include transferring operations from the project team to the IT staff who manage day-to-day operations. In either case, be sure that your project deliverables include the details and necessary information for the operations team. If necessary, create several working sessions where the project team can do a download to the operations group and provide the detailed information necessary for a successful hand off.

Reviewing Lessons Learned

As mentioned in Chapter 6, it's a good idea to document lessons learned during the course of the project itself, rather than wait until the last minute to gather this data. This should be included in the task details and the information should be shared with the team during the course of the security project plan. It's often the case that lessons learned can be used during the remaining project plan. At the end of the project, however, you should have a wrap-up meeting to review the lessons learned, the context of the lessons learned, the improvements that can be made, and the positive things that worked and should be repeated in the future. While it's important to discuss tough issues head on, it's also important to focus on what worked well or what you discovered that you could use in the future to make subsequent projects more successful.

Some of the things you should have captured during the project include:

- Problems resulting from incomplete or unclear project definitions (problem, mission, potential solutions, selected solution, project priorities).

    Example: The lesson learned might include spending more time defining the specific problem so that the project is more targeted or focused. It might also include spending more time with stakeholders in advance of project planning. Finally, it might involve asking someone from human resources to facilitate your planning meetings so they are more productive.

- Problems arising from lack of clarity or agreement regarding project parameters including scope, schedule, budget, and quality as well as the relative priority of each of these factors.

    Example: Users will be able to logon to access files. If a metric measures project success, it must be specific and measurable. Users will be able to logon to the system with a single username and password to access files across all domains. The logon should be completed by the server within 10 seconds of user data being submitted locally. Users logging in via remote connections should receive authentication within 20 seconds, depending on the user's connection speed.

- Problems arising from inaccurate or unrealistic scheduling or budgeting.

NOTE

Scheduling and budgeting are skills that are improved with practice and evaluation. Being honest about how well you and your team did in this area will help you find ways to improve for future projects).

Example: It is not possible to develop an accurate schedule until the requirements are clearly understood. One solution is to revise the high-level project plan and the high-level schedule in more detail as the project becomes more defined. This allows you to know if the project is getting too expensive. Too often, initial estimates are used as targets; learning to refine estimates and manage expectations is often a lesson learned in project management.

- Changes to the scope that caused problems including how changes were requested, evaluated, implemented, and documented.

  Example: Your current change management process may utilize a monthly change request meeting, but changes are occurring in the project that have not been discussed in the meeting. You may need to revise your process to include a more formal, written acceptance of changes so that stakeholders are not slipping changes in through back channels.

- Problems resulting from organizational challenges including lack of executive support, lack of organizational support, lack of reporting clarity, lack of resources stemming from organizational constraints, unanticipated organizational change, and so on.

  Example: You began implementing security changes for remote access, but the marketing department put an immediate halt to the security project plan because they were in the middle of a huge client project. Their plan was being disrupted in ways no one anticipated, and they could not afford the downtime. The lessons learned here might include bringing in a wider group of stakeholders during the planning process, and communicating more effectively about the expected outages and timelines once the security project plan begins, so that any mission-critical activities can be accommodated.

- Things that were unplanned and unanticipated that disrupted the project.

■ Anything that worked well (as opposed to a problem) from Items 1 through 6 above.

Example: Two Finance department employees and two subject matter experts assisted you in developing a more refined project budget.

Sometimes lessons learned are much simpler than that. It might be that someone discovers a faster, easier method of updating server settings or restoring a security template. It doesn't have to be a major, life-altering change to be worthy of mention. You may choose to create two cate-gories—one called "Best Practices" and the other one called "Lessons Learned." In this way, you can differentiate between the two and share the data accordingly.

Whatever you do, make sure you don't just gather the data, record it someplace, and move on. If you never incorporate the information, you've wasted your time capturing it. Find ways to make use of the data so that you and your team can continuously hone your project manage-ment skills and make continuous improvements. In this rapidly changing global business environment, organizations that don't learn often fail. This is a great opportunity for you to help ensure your organization continues to grow and learn and remain competitive in a highly competitive world.

Documentation and Compliance Reports

Documentation for your IT security project comes in two basic flavors: documentation you and your team need for departmental or organiza-tional reporting, and documentation you need for regulatory compliance reports. These are not necessarily one and the same, although to the extent that you can re-purpose material or generate one report that will serve two purposes, you'll be better off. Finding ways to streamline reporting and documentation from a compliance perspective is important, and you may choose to purchase a software solution that helps you maintain security and compliance. This may be part of your overall corporate IT security project plan or it may be a task or a sub-project.

The specific data needed to document your project at close out will vary depending on the details of the project. At minimum, you should have the following:

- Status reports from your team.

- Project status reports to your executive team.

- Project status reports to your project sponsor.

- Original project plan (including work breakdown structure [WBS], schedule, and budget).

- Revised project plan (including any change requests that were incorporated).

- Final project plan (including final schedule and budget).

- Lessons learned and best practices.

- Project team member performance reviews (some companies do this as part of project close out, some do not). Follow your company's practices regarding this or check with your Human Resources department).

- Suggested or implemented revisions to standard operating procedures.

- Suggested or implemented revisions to company and user policies and procedures.

- Documentation for user training (if applicable).

Let's look at these in more detail. The status reports from your IT project team should be collected and archived in some accessible location in the event there are any questions about what was done when. Again, these may end up as legal documents, so they should be handled in a manner appropriate to your company and the regulations under which it operates. If in doubt, seek the appropriate legal counsel. In some cases, these documents can raise more questions than they answer—especially if they are informal documents—so, be sure to either dispose of them or archive them in a manner appropriate to your situation. The same holds true of status reports to your executive team or project sponsor.

The original security project plan, including the WBS and all defined tasks, should be archived for two reasons. First, it's good to have a copy of the original plans for future reference. You will want a snapshot of the project in its original state for review and assessment. Second, the original project security plan details the scope of the project and may be used (or needed) later to assert that your firm took "reasonable care" to address security issues. This is a two-edged sword, however, since you may also find that your final project plan was scaled down and that one or more fairly important security areas were left out of the security project plan due to financial or scheduling constraints.

You should also review the original project documents against the final documents. In particular, review the actual data vs. the planned data for major tasks or deliverables, to see how well you're doing with planning and estimating. Accurately estimating the cost and duration of project tasks can be challenging, and the more you do it, the better you'll get if you spend time looking back at the original plan (e.g., if you thought that the assessment would take three weeks and cost $5,000, and it took seven weeks and cost $9,000, you need to understand why). There are essentially two things to look for: did things go wrong that you should have (or could have) anticipated (i.e., did you just miss something), or did things go wrong that you could not have anticipated. Be extremely honest in your assessment (it's not about blame, it's about understanding how to improve), and look for ways to enhance your overall project planning skills with the team. The better everyone becomes at project planning, especially with respect to identifying key tasks, creating a reasonable and achievable schedule, and developing a realistic budget, the better your project results will be.

Business Intelligence…

Compliance, Reporting and Security

The maze of compliance and reporting issues facing IT security projects can sometimes be daunting. More important, a company may be compliant and not secure or secure and not compliant. The problem is that many of these regulations are either still evolving or they are unclear because they were crafted by people who understood the intent but not the implementation of these measures. That leaves you, the IT security project manager, in the cross-fire. As you evaluate what documentation and compliance reports must be generated throughout the lifecycle of your project, keep in mind that you will have to find a balance. It will do you no good to claim you were fully compliant after a multi-million dollar security breach, nor will it do you any good to claim you had National Security Agency-grade security after a failed compliance audit. Make sure you discuss these challenges with your manager and with the project sponsor, so you don't end up being "thrown under the bus" if things get difficult later. Throughout this book, we've advocated documenting everything thoroughly, clearly, and accurately while being cognizant that these may become legal documents down the road. If you can present a compelling argument for the decisions you make, you may manage to successfully walk that fine line between security and compliance.

Ultimately, compliance is a business issue that must come from the top down in the organization. Much of the regulatory and compliance requirements had their genesis in corporate malfeasance. However unfortunate it is, the primary responsibility for taking "reasonable action" falls on the IT department, because it is the easiest, most clearly defined target. Whenever possible, bring this further into the organization and continue to educate executives and users that compliance is an organizational issue, not just an IT issue.

Summary

Closing out an IT security project includes many of the same tasks as closing out any other IT project. There are, however, a few notable differences. When evaluating security project plan completion, you need to be sure that you have completed all of the tasks in the project or you may subject your network to unexpected security risks. In a typical project, the ramifications of such an oversight are often not as serious as in a security project, so taking extra care to ensure the project is complete before closing it out, is always wise.

During the course of the project, you had issues, change requests, and error logs in which you tracked outstanding items. These should be reviewed and each item in the list should be properly dispatched. Leaving items open is messy and leaves your project exposed to risk. If an item cannot be properly closed, it should be transferred to some other mechanism or tracking system so the project can be closed and so the issue can still be addressed.

Another part of closing out the project is preparing for the implementation, deployment, and/or operational transfer. This is a very important part of the project, because it not only impacts the users' (and the organization's) perception of project success, it also helps ensure that the security measures you've worked so hard to develop are successfully implemented and maintained.

Project close-out is a good time to capture and summarize lessons learned, and to craft best practices based on those lessons. Though this information should be captured in task details throughout the project lifecycle and shared regularly during the security project plan, you should debrief with the IT project team at the end of the project to look at the bigger picture lessons learned and to develop plans for incorporating lessons learned into a future security project plan. Organizations that don't learn often fail. Knowing how to incorporate lessons learned into your processes and procedures will help you make continuous improvements to help your company remain highly competitive in the global marketplace.

Defining and developing project documentation should be part of your security project planning process and at project close-out, these documents should be gathered, summarized (if needed), and archived. Be aware that project documentation may end up in a courtroom some day, if a security breach occurs and litigation follows. While that's a scary thought for many IT professionals, you can (and should) seek legal counsel as to how and when to dispose of or archive project documentation for any security project. That said, normal project procedures included reviewing various project documents and closing or transferring issues. There may be additional documentation required for compliance-based reporting, and those should also be included in your project planning process. At the end of the project, you should have the required documentation for compliance reporting rather than having to step back through the project to define and develop that documentation.

Solutions Fast Track

Evaluating Project Completion

☑ Project completion typically occurs when all task work is completed.

☑ In security-related projects, ensuring all tasks are 100 percent complete is important to network security. Status reviews and task documentation can help ensure planned work is actually complete.

☑ If you've come to the end of your schedule or budget and you haven't yet completed your security project plan, you have a serious security risk that must be resolved.

Closing Issues Log, Change Requests, and Error Reports

☑ Closing out issues logs involves reviewing all open issues and determining the appropriate disposition. If an issue is open that needs to be resolved, you cannot close out the project.

☑ If an issue needs to be resolved outside the scope of the security project plan, be sure there is an appropriate transfer mechanism available so the issue remains visible and on someone's "to do" list.

☑ Change requests should be evaluated and either incorporated or rejected during the security project plan cycle. If there are open change requests, you may have a problem. As with open issues, a change may be needed outside the scope of your security project plan, and it may need to be transferred to the appropriate forum.

☑ Although error reports are likely to be hardware- and software-based and, therefore, resolved within the scope of the project, you should check that all open issues have been satisfactorily resolved and documented.

Preparing for Implementation, Deployment, and Operational Transfer

☑ All project documentation should be defined in the project definition phase and consistently collected and reviewed during the project plan phase.

☑ During project close out, documentation should be updated and finalized for review or archiving.

☑ Project documentation can be construed as legal documents related to the security project plan, and should be treated as such. Consult with legal counsel regarding the appropriate storage or disposition of these documents.

☑ Implementation, deployment, or operational transfer are all visible aspects of the security project. They present great opportunities to increase the perceived value and success of the security project through flawless execution.

☑ Operational transfer is an important connecting point between the IT security project team and those responsible for maintaining security on a day-to-day basis. Be sure to provide your operations staff with the tools and knowledge needed to successfully monitor, maintain, and improve security.

Reviewing Lessons Learned

☑ The lessons learned should be gathered as part of the tasks details and reviewed on a periodic basis with the team.

☑ A project close-out debriefing on the lessons learned and the best practices can help team members incorporate the findings and support organizational learning.

☑ Improving your project results through reviewing and incorporating lessons learned helps keep your company competitive in the worldwide market.

Documentation and Compliance Reports

■ Documentation needed for the project should be defined and developed during the project planning stage.

■ Documentation includes project status reports, original project plan, schedule, and budget; revised project plan, schedule, and budget; the actual data vs. the planned data analysis and more.

■ Compliance documentation should be defined in the project tasks and task details, so that at the end of the project you will have all of the data and documentation needed for compliance audits or reviews (to the degree possible).

■ Compliance documentation will vary depending on the laws and regulations your firm must comply with. Keep in mind that all project documentation related to a security project could become legal documents in the future; therefore, handle it accordingly.

Chapter 9

Corporate IT Security Project Plan

Solutions in this chapter:

- Defining Your Security Strategy
- Legal Standards Relevant to Corporate IT Security
- Corporate IT Security Project Plan Overview
- Corporate Security Auditing
- Corporate Security Project Parameters

- Project Work Breakdown Structure
- Project Risks
- Project Constraints
- Project Assumptions
- Project Schedule and Budget

WARNING: DO NOT PRACTICE LAW WITHOUT A LICENSE

In virtually every U.S. state, individuals are legally prohibited from practicing law without a license. For example, in Colorado, "practicing law" is defined, by law, to include, "counseling, advising and assisting [another] in connection with" legal rights and duties. Penalties for the unauthorized practice of law in Colorado can include fines or imprisonment. Information security consultants should not, under any circumstances, purport to advise customers as to the legal implications of statutes such as the HIPAA, Gramm-Leach-Bliley financial information privacy provisions, or other federal, state, or local laws or regulations. First, the consultants risk legal action against them by doing so. Second, they do their customers a grave disservice by leading them to believe that the customers can take any legal comfort from advice given them by non-lawyers.

Introduction

This chapter provides the framework for creating an overarching corporate Information Technology (IT) security project plan. In subsequent chapters, we'll step through Individual Security Area Projects (ISAPs). This and subsequent chapters are intended to be used as templates to guide you through your security project planning process. There is no one-size-fits-all approach to any security project planning process; thus, you will need to modify your security project plan to fit your organization's requirements. This chapter provides the basic building blocks to help you get started. As you read this chapter, keep in mind that the same principles apply, with some variation, to each of the ISAPs discussed later in this book. As you become familiar with the framework used in this chapter, you'll be able to see more clearly how this and subsequent ISAP plans should be modified to fit your own unique needs. This chapter also discusses a security audit.

Defining Your Security Strategy

Managing IT security across an enterprise is one of the most important business problems you'll face in your IT career. IT security impacts the ongoing viability and competitiveness of your company. Regardless of the assets and resources that need to be secured (information, technology, assets), you must have a clear strategy you can implement, monitor, and revise as the business and operational environments change. In the long run, the effectiveness of your overall IT security strategy depends on how well it is aligned with and supports the organization's business drivers. Your corporate IT security project plan must provide the strategic vision for how you address enterprise-wide IT security. Many organizations understand that IT security project success depends on gaining executive-level management support and aligning security goals with the mission, vision, and objectives of the organization. When IT security is aligned with business objectives, security becomes a tool to enable and support your company's strategy, rather than just a black hole for IT expenditures.

Your corporate IT security project essentially defines your security strategy for the organization. While it must include specific deliverables related to key areas of enterprise security, it also needs to address the higher level strategic security approach. Clearly, your security strategy should be aligned with organizational objectives in order to add value to the organization and gain key management support. Your security strategy should be defined prior to initiating your corporate IT security planning process so that you have a clear view of the required objectives. Your corporate IT security plans also have to align with the reality of your organization. You must live within the company's constraints, which may include budget, schedule, staffing, or other overarching organizational limitations. It doesn't matter if you create a masterful security strategy or project plan if it costs far more than your company can afford or requires resources your company doesn't have. Your goal should be to find an optimal solution that fits within the constraints of the organization.

A technical report, written by Richard Caralli at Carnegie Mellon entitled "The Critical Success Factor Method: Establishing A Foundation For Enterprise Security Management" (Technical Report, CMU/SEI-2004-TR-010, ESC-TR-2004-010, July 2004), identifies the following five key success factors in developing an enterprise security strategy:

- The skills, capabilities, and efforts of the entire organization must be utilized and mobilized.

- The key functions and processes in the organization must collaborate on shared security goals and strategy.

- The organization's security objectives or an articulation of its "desired state" must be developed and understood.

- Critical assets that are essential to achieving the organization's mission must be identified and protected.

- IT operations and support must enable security goals.

It should be evident that if you lack a strategic view of security in the enterprise, you'll have difficulty getting executive support for your initiatives. As you learned in Chapter 1, executive support for IT projects is the number one success factor. Developing a security strategy that supports and enhances organizational goals is the primary way to achieve your IT security mission-critical objectives. With that in mind, we'll dig into developing a corporate IT security plan that supports your organization's objectives. In addition, your strategy should take into account the pre-dominant legal issues your organization might have to contend with.

Legal Standards Relevant to Corporate IT Security

WARNING: THIS SECTION DOES NOT CONTAIN LEGAL ADVICE

This section provides an overview of a number of legal issues faced by infor-mation security professionals and their companies. Hopefully, it will alert you to the issues on which you should consult qualified legal counsel experienced in information security law. This chapter, however, does not, and cannot, pro-vide any legal advice or counsel to you. **You should not, under any circum-stances, purport to rely on anything in this book, chapter, or section "Legal Standards Relevant to Corporate IT Security," as legal advice.** Likewise, following any of the suggestions in this section does not create an "advice-of-counsel" defense to regulatory or law enforcement action or to civil legal claims. If you are involved in information security and have any questions regarding the law and IT security, you are strongly urged to retain qualified, experienced legal counsel.

The following sections discuss the legal standards relevant to IT security. The corporate IT security project plan is the appropriate place to discuss these elements, because you need to be cognizant of the legal issues sur-rounding IT as you formulate your comprehensive security project plan. As written in the above sidebar, nothing in this section (or book, for that matter) should be construed as legal advice in any manner. Instead, it is provided as an overview of some of the legal issues involved with IT security. Some IT professionals fail to understand the legal implications for IT security and put themselves and their companies at substantial legal risk. This section is intended to give you a jump start in understanding some of the issues so you can determine for yourself what additional resources and assistance you might need to ensure that you and your company are adequately protected.

We know that laws are made by politicians and that politicians are driven by public and media reaction to specific incidents. As is often the case, laws are made piecemeal to deal with individual incidents. At some point, a critical mass is reached and lawmakers may patch together a number of initiatives to address a growing concern. The result, however, is often a set of laws that are inconsistent, piecemeal, spotty, and sometimes contradictory.

This is the current situation in the law of information security. As discussed in "Selected Federal Laws" below, federal law regulates information security for, among other things, personally identifiable health care information, financial information of individuals, and, to an increasing degree, financial information in the hands of publicly traded companies. There currently is no "omnibus" federal statute governing all information security. Instead, the standards are pieced together in response to various perceived (and actual) problems found in the public and private sector.

For IT security professionals, this is a good news/bad news story. Often, attempts at "comprehensive" legislation turn out to be a jumbled mess, particularly when multiple economic sectors with differing operational environments and needs are being regulated, and lawmakers lack a clear understanding of the technological issues at hand. Such regulation can be particularly ineffective (or worse) when forced upon the private sector. On the other hand, a patchwork of different federal, state, and international laws and regulations (as is the current state of information security law) can be confusing and puts a premium on careful, case-specific legal analysis and advice from qualified and experienced counsel.

If you're reading this wondering how your small company can afford to address these legal issues, there is some good news. First, you can do your own research and become conversant with the various legal issues relevant to your company's IT security. First, you can do your own research and become conversant with the various legal issues relevant to your company's

IT security. You should be aware, however, that doing your own research provides you with no legal protection, unless you get a legal opinion from qualified outside legal counsel. At a minimum, you should take this information to a competent attorney that specializes in IT security and understands your business sector to get a legal opinion to protect your company's interests. If you do your homework, your legal bills will be far less than if you walk in the door unprepared. Have specific questions prepared and then ask "What else do I need to know?" It may not be your specific responsibility to do this, but as the IT security project manager for your company, you have the responsibility to bring these potential legal issues to the attention of senior management so they can make the determination as to the best way to address and mitigate legal risks.

Selected Federal Laws

To illustrate the array of laws that impact information security, the following provides a general survey of statutes, regulations, and other laws that may govern information security consultants and their customers. This list is not exhaustive, but may help identify issues and understand which "best practices" have actually been adopted in law. If any of these areas apply to your company, you can do additional research, consult your in-house counsel, or hire outside counsel to advise you on how to ensure your company's legal exposure is reduced to the greatest degree possible.

Gramm-Leach-Bliley Act

One of the earliest US government forays into mandating information security standards was the Gramm-Leach-Bliley Act (GLBA). Section 501(b) requires each covered financial institution to establish "appropriate safeguards" to: (1) ensure the security and confidentiality of customer records and information; (2) protect against anticipated threats or hazards to the security or integrity of those records; and (3) protect against unauthorized access to, or use of, such records or information which could result in substantial harm or inconvenience to any customer. GLBA required standards to be set by regulation for safeguarding customer information. This task was accomplished with the publishing of the

Interagency Guidelines Establishing Standards for Safeguarding Customer Information (the "Guidelines"). The Guidelines apply to customer information maintained by covered "financial institutions," both of which terms are broadly defined under applicable law and regulations. The Guidelines require a written security program specifically tailored to the size and complexity of each individual covered financial institution, and to the nature and scope of its activities. Under the Guidelines, covered institutions must conduct risk assessments to customer information and implement policies, procedures, training, and testing appropriate to manage reasonably foreseeable internal and external threats. Institutions must also ensure that their Board of Directors (or a committee thereof) oversees the institution's information security measures.

Further, institutions must exercise due diligence in selecting and over-seeing, on an ongoing basis, service providers (entities that maintain, process, or otherwise are permitted access to customer information through providing services to a covered institution). Institutions also must ensure, by written agreement, that service providers maintain appropriate security measures.

Health Insurance Portability and Accountability Act

The Health Insurance Portability and Accountability Act of 1996 (HIPAA) became law in August 1996. Section 1173(d) of HIPAA required the Secretary of Health and Human Services (HHS) to adopt security standards for protection of all Electronic Protected Health Information (EPHI). Development of these security standards was left to the HHS Secretary, who released the HIPAA Security Final Rule (the "Security Rule") in February 2003. All covered entities, with the exception of small health plans, must now comply with the Security Rule. Because HIPAA has, in some ways, the most elaborate and detailed guidance available in the realm of federal law and regulation with regard to information security, we focus more on the HIPAA Security Rule than any other single federal legal provision. In addition, many of the general principles articulated in the Security Rule are common to other legal procedures dealing with information security. In general, the HIPAA

Security Rule mandates specific outcomes and specifies process and procedural requirements, rather than specifically mandated technical standards. The mandated outcomes for covered entities are:

- Ensuring the confidentiality, integrity, and availability of EPHI created, received, maintained, or transmitted by a covered entity

- Protecting against reasonably anticipated threats or hazards to the security or integrity of such information

- Protecting against reasonably anticipated uses or disclosures of EPHI not permitted by the HIPAA Privacy Rule

- Ensuring compliance with the Security Rule by its employees.

Beyond these general, mandated outcomes, the Security Rule contains process and procedural requirements broken into several general categories:

- **Administrative Safeguards** Key required processes in this area include: conducting a comprehensive analysis of reasonably anticipated risks; matrixing identified risks against a covered entity's unique mix of information requiring safeguarding; employee training, awareness, testing, and sanctions; individual accountability for information security; access authorization, management, and monitoring controls; contingency and disaster recovery planning; and ongoing technical and non-technical evaluation of Security Rule compliance.

- **Physical Safeguards** Physical security safeguard measures include: mandated facilities access controls; workstation use and workstation security requirements; device and media controls; restricting access to sensitive information; and maintaining offsite computer backups.

- **Technical Safeguards** Without specifying technological mechanisms, the HIPAA Security Rule mandates automated technical processes intended to protect information and to control and record access to such information. Mandated processes include authentication controls for persons accessing EPHI, encryption/

decryption requirements, audit controls, and mechanisms for ensuring data integrity.

The Security Rule contains other requirements beyond these general categories, including: ensuring by written agreement that entities with whom a covered entity exchanges EPHI maintain reasonable and appropriate security measures, and holding those entities to the agreed-upon standards; developing written procedures and policies to implement the Security Rule's requirements, disseminating such procedures, and reviewing and updating them periodically in response to changing threats, vulnerabilities, and operational circumstances.

Sarbanes-Oxley Act

The Sarbanes-Oxley Act of 2002 (SOX) has gotten a lot of media attention in the past few years and came on the heels of some very well-publicized corporate scandals, most notably the collapse of Enron. SOX creates legal liability for senior executives of publicly traded companies, potentially including stiff prison sentences and fines of up to $5,000,000 per violation, for willfully certifying financial statements that do not meet the requirements of the statute. Section 404 of SOX requires senior management, pursuant to rules issued by the Securities and Exchange Commission (SEC), to attest to: "(1) the responsibility of management for establishing and maintaining an adequate internal control structure and procedures for financial reporting; and (2) …the effectiveness of the internal control structure and procedures of the issuer for financial reporting." (See Chapter 13 sidebar "SEC Announces Next Steps for Sarbanes-Oxley Implementation to Help Small Companies" for an update on recent changes related to Section 404). Section 302 also requires that pursuant to SEC regulations, officers signing company financial reports certify that they are "responsible for establishing and maintaining internal controls," and "have evaluated the effectiveness" of those controls and reported their conclusions as to the same.

Federal Information Security and Management Act

The Federal Information Security and Management Act of 2002, as amended, (FISMA) does not directly create liability for private sector IT security professionals or their companies. However, IT security professionals should be aware of this law, because it:

- Legally mandates the process by which information security requirements for federal government departments and agencies must be developed and implemented

- Directs the federal government to look to the private sector for applicable "best practices" and to provide assistance to the private sector (if requested) with regard to information security

- Contributes to the developing "standard of care" for information security by mandating a number of specific procedures and policies

If you work for the federal government or an organization that comes under federal auspices, your organization may be directly impacted by FISMA.

FERPA and the TEACH Act

The Family Educational Right to Privacy Act (FERPA) prohibits educational agencies and programs, at risk of losing federal funds, from having a policy or practice of "permitting the release of " specified educational records. FERPA does not state whether or not the prohibition places affirmative requirements on educational institutions to protect against unauthorized access to these records through the use of information security measures. It is certainly possible that a court could conclude in the future that an educational institution which fails to take reasonable information security measures to prevent unauthorized access to protected information is liable under FERPA for "permitting the release" of such information. The recent case of a Vermont college system employee having such data on a laptop that was later stolen (see Chapter 1 sidebar "The Real Cost of Remediation") might test this very statute. The 2002 Technology, Education, and Copyright Harmonization Act (the "TEACH Act") explicitly requires educational institutions to take "technologically feasible" measures to prevent unauthorized sharing of copyrighted information beyond the students specifically requiring the information for their studies, and, thus, may create newly enforceable legal duties on educational institutions with regard to information security.

Electronic Communications Privacy Act and Computer Fraud and Abuse Act

These two federal statutes, while not mandating information security procedures, create serious criminal penalties for any persons who gain unauthorized access to electronic records. Unlike laws such as HIPAA and GLBA, these two statues broadly apply, regardless of the type of electronic records that are involved. The Electronic Communications Privacy Act (ECPA) makes it a federal felony to use or intercept the contents of electronic communications without authorization. In addition, the Computer Fraud and Abuse Act of 1984 (CFAA) makes it a felony to gain unauthorized access to a very wide range of computer systems (including financial institutions, the federal government, and any protected computer system used in interstate commerce). As a result, IT security professionals, especially outside consultants who may test client security (i.e., try to hack into a system to gain unauthorized access) must take great care, and rely on qualified and experienced legal professionals to ensure they receive authorizations from their clients that are broad and specific enough to mitigate potential criminal liability under the ECPA and the CFAA.

Business Intelligence...

What to Look For in Your Attorneys

There are a number of obvious characteristics one should seek in any attorney retained for any purpose. These include integrity, a good repu-

Continued

www.syngress.com

tation in the legal community, and general competence. You also want
to consider an attorney with a strong background in corporate and business transactions who is familiar with the contracting process. One
useful tool for evaluating these qualities as you attempt to narrow your
list of potential attorneys to interview is a company called Martindale
Hubbell (www.martindale.com). Look for lawyers with an "AV" rating
(Martindale's highest).

(Note: Never hire any attorney without at least one face-to-face
meeting to learn what your gut tells you about whether you could work
with him or her.)

In the area of information security evaluation, you will want to look
for attorneys with deep and broad expertise in the field. The best way to
do so is to look for external, independently verifiable criteria demon-
strating an attorney or law firm's tested credentials (e.g., is the lawyer
you seek to retain listed on the National Security Agency Web site as
including individuals certified as having been trained in NSA's
Information Security Assurance Methodology (IAM)? If so, on the appropriate NSA Web page (e.g., www.iatrp.com/indivu2.cfm#C), you will
find a listing similar to this: Cunningham, Bryan, 03/15/05, (303) 743-
0003, bc@morgancunningham.net)

Has an attorney you are considering authored any published works
in the area of information security law? Has he or she held positions, in
the government or elsewhere, related to information security? Finally,
there's the gut check. How does your potential lawyer make you feel?
Are you comfortable working with him or her? Does he or she communicate clearly and concisely? Does he or she seem more interested in covering their own backside than in providing you with legal counsel to
protect your interests?

State Laws

In addition to federal statutes and regulations implicating information
security, there are numerous state laws that, depending on an entity's location and the places in which it does business (also known as *nexus*), can
also create legal requirements related to the work of information security
professionals.

Unauthorized Access

In Colorado (and in other states), it is a crime to access, use, or exceed authorized access to, or use of, a computer, computer network, or any part of a computer system. It is a crime to take action against a computer system to cause damage, to commit a theft, or for other nefarious purposes. However, it is particularly important for IT security professionals to be aware that it is also a crime to knowingly access a computer system without authorization or to exceed authorized access. This is one reason it is critical for IT security consultants, with the advice of qualified and experienced counsel, to negotiate a comprehensive, carefully worded, Letter of Authorization (LOA) with every client.

If you are hiring an outside consultant, they should insist on this type of authorization if they plan on testing your network's security. If they do not insist on this (or even mention it), you should seriously review the consultant's credentials to be sure they have the requisite skills and knowledge you're looking for. If they are not hired to actually test your system for vulnerabilities and will not be testing for the ability to gain unauthorized access, this type of LOA may not be needed. On the other hand, if a consultant asks for this type of authorization and it's not what you hired them to do, it should signal a serious disconnect that should be addressed before going any further. Be sure you're hiring a bona fide consultant and not a rogue hacker in a business suit.

Enforcement Actions

What constitutes the "reasonable standard of care" in IT security will continue to evolve, and not only through new statutes and regulations. Prosecutors and regulators will not be content to wait for such formal, legal developments. In lawsuits, prosecutors and regulators have demonstrated the clear intent to extend "reasonable" IT security measures even to those entities not clearly covered by specific existing laws. This is being done through legal actions leading to settlements, often including consent decrees (agreements entered into to end litigation or regulatory action) wherein a company agrees to "voluntarily" allow regulators to monitor (e.g., for 20 years) the company's IT security program. Such was the case with the company that ended up purchasing CardSystems, the credit card transaction processing company that was responsible for millions of credit card holders' information being compromised (described in Chapter 1).

Since these agreements are publicly available, they are adding to the "standard of care" to which organizations will be held. They also provide added support for similar enforcement actions in the future. Thus, even if your company is not specifically required by law to take certain security measures, it might still suffer rigorous legal consequences for its actions.

Three Fatal Fallacies

The saying goes, "A little knowledge is a dangerous thing." The same can be said of conventional wisdom. Unfortunately, many organizations and IT professionals, upon realizing they have legal and other requirements for IT security, have come to believe incorrect information regarding their security decisions. Let's take a look at a few of these common misunderstandings.

The "Single Law" Fallacy

Many IT security professionals, both within companies and those working as consultants, subscribe to the "single law" fallacy. That is, once they identify the laws, statutes, or set of regulations they think apply to them, they address just those issues under the belief they've got their legal bases covered. In fact, this may or may not be the case. Rather than blithely making these assumptions, you or your company should seek competent legal advice to mitigate the legal risks. Take, for example, a mid-sized college or university. IT security professionals may conclude that, since FERPA clearly applies to educational records, following guidance tailored to colleges and universities based on what they conclude are the appropriate Department of Education standards, is sufficient to mitigate any potential legal liability. This could be an expensive assumption to make, particularly if the educational institution does not ask itself the following questions:

- Does the school grant financial aid or extend other forms of credit? If so, it could be subject to GLBA.

- Does it operate hospitals, provide psychiatric counseling services, or run a student health service? If so, it could be subject to HIPAA.

- Does the school's Web site contain any representations about the security of the site and/or university-held information? If so, it could be subject to lawsuits under one or more (depending on whether it has campuses in multiple states) state deceptive trade practices laws.

The Private Entity Fallacy

Focusing on SOX and the resulting preoccupation with publicly traded companies, some institutions take solace in being private and in the fact that, so the argument goes, they are not subject to SOX and/or that they can somehow "fly under the radar" of federal regulators. Anyone who believes that lawyers for future plaintiffs (students, faculty, victims of attack, or identity theft) will be deterred by the literal terms of SOX is misguided. The argument will be that the appropriate "standard of care" for IT security was publicly available and well known. And, just because your company may not specifically be obligated under SOX, there are numerous other segments of the law that could apply such as HIPAA, GLBA, state statutes, and common law theories and, depending on where an entity does business, international and foreign law, such as the complex and burdensome European Union Privacy Directive.

The "Penetration Test Only" Fallacy

Some IT security professionals are so confident in their security solutions and implementations that they hire an outside security consultant just to try to break into the system. This can be the case when the company is strapped for funds and doesn't believe it can afford an outside security consultant, or when the organization has a fairly strong group of IT professionals in-house. The problem is, if you hire an outside consultant to do a penetration test (also called a "pen test"), you are exposing your company to potential legal liabilities. Think of it this way. An IT security consultant performs a penetration test and gets in. He or she exposes one or more weaknesses in your system. This exposes vulnerabilities that are now publicly (or at least with an outside entity) documented and open to the legal discovery process. While you may hire an outside firm to do a penetration test at some point, it should be as part of a holistic approach to IT security utilizing both internal and if desired, external, resources.

Do It Right or Bet the Company: Tools to Mitigate Legal Liability

In recent years, numerous articles have been written on how to protect your network from a technical perspective, but, at least throughout mid-2005, the headlines were full of examples of companies that have lost critical information due to inadequate security. ChoicePoint, DSW Shoes, several universities, financial institutions including Bank of America and Wachovia, MasterCard and other credit providers, and even the FBI have been named in recent news articles for having lost critical information. As one example, ChoicePoint was sued in 2005 in actions brought in states ranging from California to New York and in its home state of Georgia. Allegations in the lawsuits included that ChoicePoint failed to "secure and maintain confidential the personal, financial and other information entrusted to ChoicePoint by consumers"; failed to maintain adequate procedures to avoid disclosing some private credit and financial information to unauthorized third parties; and acted "willfully, recklessly, and/or in conscious disregard" of its customers rights to privacy.

It's not hard to imagine that if you work for a medium-to-large company that deals with consumer data of any kind, that one day you may be faced with an IT security-related lawsuit, frivolous or not. The question is, what can you as the IT security project manager do to help your company reduce its litigation "target profile?" Creating a thorough corporate IT security project plan helps, but there are a few additional tips we've provided below.

We Did our Best; What's the Problem?

Many companies feel that their internal IT technology and security staffs
are putting forth their best efforts to maintain and secure their networks.
They may know there have been no significant security breaches and that
the organization has well-defined procedures for handling important data.
They may even hire an outside security consultant for periodic penetration tests that result in no penetration occurring. All's well, right? Not
really. Simply doing one's best is not enough in today's litigious environment. Corporate efforts must also be grounded in complying with
existing, external legal standards. In ChoicePoint's case, at least based on
what has been made public, penetration tests would not have helped.
ChoicePoint appears to have fallen victim to individuals who fraudulently
posed as businessmen and conned people into giving them what may
have been otherwise secure information. This was a classic case of social
engineering at its best. Penetration testing would have shown that the
networks were secure, but as we know, no network is completely secure
and social engineering is a good example of that.

Addressing any one particular potential point of failure will almost never
be enough. Companies today must understand the potential sources of liability that apply to all companies, as well as those specific to their industry.
Companies can minimize their risk through understanding the legal environment and adopting and implementing policies to assure a high level of
compliance with current legal requirements. Of course, this approach
cannot be non-static, either. It requires an ongoing review and implementation to assure compliance in an ever-changing legal environment. As part of
your corporate IT security plan, you should be sure that your project plan
includes the ongoing security maintenance and monitoring activities
needed to continually assess and improve your organization's security measures. (This topic is addressed in more detail in Chapter 13.)

Negligence and the "Standard of Care"

Clearly, there are numerous variations to the ways IT security can be
breached and how those breaches can impact companies and individuals
(customers, employees, and so forth). Understanding the basis for liability

and conducting business in a manner designed to avoid liability is the best defense. In many cases, the claim of liability is based on a charge that the company and its officers and directors acted "negligently." In law, "negligence" arises when a party owes a legal duty to another, that duty is breached, and the breach causes damages to the injured party. Generally speaking, acting "reasonably" under the circumstances will prevent companies from being found "negligent." The problem is that the definition of "reasonable" can be tricky and changeable.

When a company maintains personal or confidential customer information, or has agreed to maintain as confidential the trade secret information of another business, its minimum duty is to use reasonable care in securing its computer systems to avoid theft or inadvertent disclosure of the information entrusted to it. Reasonable care may be an extremely high standard when trust and confidence are placed in a company to secure sensitive information. A reasonable "standard of care" is what the law defines as the minimum efforts a company must take not to have acted negligently (or, put another way, to have acted reasonably). A good starting point for all IT security is to implement security measures to the known standard of care required to avoid liability. While that sounds a bit like a circular statement, let's look at a very simple example. We all know that viruses make their way through e-mail systems all the time. Any company that does not have an enterprise-wide anti-virus software solution in place, that does not scan every incoming e-mail for viruses and other known attacks, has not implemented a reasonable level of care. If a new variant of a virus is released at midnight and your anti-virus vendor doesn't provide an updated signature file until 4:00AM, are you liable for private data being distributed by this new virus via an e-mail leaving your server at 2:00AM? Probably not. What about a case where that e-mail doesn't go out until 9:00AM? Now it's not so clear. Should your virus definition file be updated the instant the anti-virus company releases the update, or is there a "reasonable" window of time during which you cannot be held accountable? Unfortunately that question can sometimes only be answered by twelve people sitting in a jury box—not the ideal place to look for answers to corporate questions. Therefore, if you perform to a reasonable standard in your IT security practices, you will limit your liability to the greatest degree possible.

What Can Be Done?

Fully understanding the risks, as assessed by qualified and experienced counsel, is an essential first step. Taking action that either avoids liability or minimizes the consequences when things go wrong is the next step. The following are some suggestions that might help as you assess your risk and determine your optimal security solutions.

Understand Your Legal Environment

Mitigating legal liability begins with understanding the laws applicable to a company's business. Ignorance of the law is no excuse, and failure to keep pace with statutory requirements is a first source of liability. Working with professionals, whether inside or outside of the company, to track changes in legislation and tailor your IT security policies, is the first line of defense. Careful compliance with laws not only helps reduce the potential for criminal liability or administrative fines, but also demonstrates that all important "standard of care" that might mitigate civil liability as well.

Comprehensive and Ongoing Security Assessments, Evaluations, and Implementation

Working with qualified and experienced legal counsel and technical consultants, a company must identify and prioritize the information it controls that may require protection. That process should include cataloging the specific legal requirements applicable to such information and to the type of business you're in. Next, policies must be developed to ensure that information is properly maintained. As we've discussed, this has everything to do with end user and employee training on security policies, procedures, and security measures. Your corporate IT security plan is only as good as the implementation and maintenance of those security measures, so including the development and implementation of policies and procedures in your corporate IT security plan is vital.

The process of thorough and unbiased assessments, tests, evaluations, and implementation must be ongoing. A static one-shot assessment is almost worse than none at all. Almost equally bad is insufficiently training employees on appropriate policies and procedures for maintaining security measures, or never evaluating those employees on their understanding and implementation of security measures. (The need for employee awareness and training is discussed in Chapter 13.)

Use Contracts to Define Rights and Protect Information

Almost every company has trade secrets—from its customer lists to its business methodologies—that are what afford a competitive advantage. Any protection for these valuable assets will be lost if a company fails to make reasonable efforts to maintain the information as confidential. At a minimum, contracts must be developed that commit employees not to disclose the trade secrets or any information legally mandated to be protected (e.g., individual health care or financial information). These agreements are often most effective if entered into at the time of employment. While this clearly is not within the purview of the IT department, your understanding of the organizational mechanisms that support IT security will help you develop better IT security project plans. In addition, you may find it desirable to advise your Human Resources department, in conjunction with appropriate legal counsel, on what types of policies, procedures, and employee contracts are appropriate in your organization based on the nature and value of the company's data.

Employment policies should reinforce the employee's obligation to maintain confidentiality. These policies should also provide clear guidance on which procedures to use to maintain password security and to responsibly use the information secured on the network. Regular employee training should be implemented to reinforce the notion that these requirements are mandatory and taken seriously by management. Vendors and service providers that may need to review confidential information should only be permitted access to such information under an agreement limiting the use of that information and agreeing to maintain its confidentiality. In most cases, vendors or outsiders should be specifically required to sign confidentiality or non-disclosure agreements to mitigate liability. Hiring any outside consultant to perform a network security evaluation or to review other secret or confidential data without a proper confidentiality agreement in place, could later be found to be sufficient evidence that a company failed to make "reasonable efforts" to maintain information as confidential. In worst case scenarios, this can result in the information no longer being considered a trade secret and therefore no longer entitled to protection.

Use Qualified Third-party Professionals

A key requirement emerging as a critical part of the evolving IT security standards of care is the requirement to get an external review by qualified, neutral parties. These requirements are based on the theory that, no matter how qualified, expert, or well intentioned an organization's IT staff is, it is impossible for them to be truly objective. In addition, there is the ever-present risk of the "fox in the hen house," leaving senior management to wonder whether those charged with creating and maintaining IT security can and will fairly and impartially assess the effectiveness of such security. Finally, qualified and experienced outside legal counsel and technical consultants bring perspective, breadth of experience, and currency with the latest technical and legal developments that in-house staff normally cannot provide cost-effectively. This is not a pitch to get you to run out and hire an outside consultant, but the smart people know when to ask for help, and this might be a good place to start.

Making Sure Your Standards-of-Care Assessments Keep Up with Evolving Law

As suggested above, the legal definition of a "reasonable" standard of care is constantly evolving. Legislators are beginning to take seriously the threats and the substantial economic loss caused by cyber attacks, and to create laws to address these problems. New laws are continually being enacted to punish attackers and to shift liability to companies that have failed to take reasonable IT security measures. Contractual obligations can now be formed instantly and automatically simply by new customers accessing your company's Web site and using your services from anywhere in the world. As new vulnerabilities, attacks, and countermeasures come to public attention, new duties emerge. In short, what was "reasonable" last month may not be reasonable this month. IT security assessments and evaluations provide tools to evaluate and comply with best practices in protecting critical information. However, at best they are only snapshots unless they are performed on a consistent and ongoing basis. Best practices begin with understanding and complying with applicable laws, but security can only be maintained through tracking and implementing evolving statutory requirements. Working with qualified and experienced counsel to follow new legal developments in this fast-moving area of the law and provide advice on the proper interpretation and implementation of legislative requirements can be extremely helpful. In fact, it's becoming increasingly important for mid- to large-sized companies in this ever-changing legal landscape.

Plan for the Worst

Despite all best efforts, nothing can reduce a company's liability to zero (short of closing the doors permanently and even that's not a guarantee). One of the things smart companies have learned is that if (or when) a security breach occurs, the best thing a company can do is get out in front of it quickly. Clearly, part of your corporate IT security project planning work should include incident response to address any security breaches. It should also include your internal and external response plans, including updating security procedures, communicating with appropriate stakeholders, and possibly preparing public statements or press releases. Avoiding liability involves planning for problems (e.g., one class action filed against ChoicePoint alleges that shareholders were misled when the company failed to disclose [for several months] the existence of its security breach and the true extent of the information that was compromised.) Having policies in place to provide guidance to executives in communicating with customers and prospective shareholders may have helped ChoicePoint avoid these allegations.

California currently has a Notice of Security Breach law that was enacted in 2002. As of 2005, Arkansas, Georgia, Indiana, Montana, North Dakota, and Washington have followed suit by enacting some form of legislation requiring disclosure relating to breaches of security, and bills have been introduced in not less than 34 other states to regulate in this area. As of mid-2005, there was no similar federal regulation, although, several disclosure bills have been introduced in Congress. Again, though your job is not specifically to address the legal issues of a breach, your IT security plan should incorporate the development of policies and procedures to be implemented if a security incident takes place. By working with key stakeholders ahead of time, you can reduce the impact of a potential security breach by helping those outside the IT environment understand how you will respond, what steps you will take, and how you will communicate this information within the organization.

Insurance

As more information security breaches occur and are disclosed, the cost to businesses and individuals will continue to rise. In 2002, the Federal Trade Commission (FTC) estimated that 10 million people were victims of identity theft. According to Gartner, Inc., 9.4 million online users in the U.S. were victimized between April 2003 and April 2004, with losses amounting to $11.7 billion. Costs to business from these losses will likely grow to staggering levels in the coming years, and this trend is capturing the attention of some of the more sophisticated insurance companies. Some companies are developing products to provide coverage for losses resulting from breaches of information security. Companies should contact their carriers and do their own independent research to determine what coverage, if any, is or will become available. Again, this may fall outside the scope of your duties as IT security project manager, but is another opportunity for you to add value to your organization by recommending to your executives that they consider evaluating the need for such coverage. In many cases, executives may not be aware of the existence of this type of insurance and as an IT security expert, part of your job is to keep your company's executive team up to speed on this type of relevant information.

This rather exhaustive look at IT security from the legal perspective can cause many IT security professionals to start losing sleep at night. Clearly, there are risks in every aspect of business and IT security is no different. Your company must reduce its exposure to liability by taking reasonable measures, commensurate with best practices in the industry, to secure sensitive information. You can't provide a 100 percent guarantee that your network will never be breached or that your company won't face a lawsuit stemming from a breach. You can, however, develop a thorough IT security project plan, implement it flawlessly, maintain and review security on a regular basis, and train your company's staff on the latest security measures and attack countermeasures. With that in mind, let's return to your corporate IT security project plan.

Corporate IT Security Project Plan Overview

As discussed in the earlier chapters in this book, we're going to look at ISAPs. To that end, we're starting with the overarching plan, the corporate IT security project, which in most companies will include many of the ISAPs presented in subsequent chapters. The plans will all follow the same outline:

1. Define your overarching corporate security strategy.
2. Define the specific problem area (security audit, risk assessment).
3. Define the desired (required) outcome(s).
4. Identify potential solutions.
5. Define project constraints.
6. Define project requirements (functional, technical, legal).
7. Select optimal solution.
8. Define project team.
9. Define project procedures.
10. Define project work breakdown structure, tasks, owners, resources, budget, and schedule.
11. Monitor and manage project.
12. Hand off and close out project.

As mentioned in the previous section, you need to start from a clearly defined security strategy. It is outside the scope of this book to step you through developing that strategy, but you can find ample information in various resources, including *"How To Cheat At IT Project Management."* Defining your strategy in alignment with corporate goals should be the starting point for your corporate IT security project plan. This chapter assumes that you've done that work already. If you haven't, take a step back and define your strategy before developing your corporate IT security plan. You'll save yourself a lot of time and re-work by doing so.

Depending on how your organization works, it's usually advisable at this point to identify your core project team or at least those players you need at the outset to help you develop project parameters. If you work on this by yourself, you may inadvertently be creating two problems. First, you undermine your own ability to develop team buy-in for the project. When people work together to define a project, they are much more likely to feel a sense of ownership and will therefore work harder to make sure the project is successful. Second, you will probably overlook key elements because you can't reasonably expect to know everything that should be included in the project. Getting training, human resources, finance, operations, and legal representatives on the team early will help ensure that your project plan contains all the required elements to meet key stakeholder needs. If you miss this step, you will either deliver a project that falls short of organizational needs, or you'll have to go back and re-work a lot of your project plan. Change is always easier and less expensive to instigate at the outset of the project planning process.

In the IT security world, defining the problem is typically accomplished through a security audit. You may choose to perform a comprehensive security audit or you may choose to audit individual security areas first. Regardless of which way you approach the auditing function, be sure that at the end you have a comprehensive overview. If you work first on the individual areas, be sure you don't leave gaps "between" the individual security areas (i.e., the places where various security areas meet or intersect). If you look at your overall corporate security first, be sure to focus clearly on the individual security areas so you don't miss some area of detail in one of the ISAPs. Either way, you need to take a comprehensive look, but you can choose to go at it from either direction as long as you keep in mind that you need to look broadly and deeply at the current state of security in your organization.

Before we head into the details, let's quickly review the framework for our approach to corporate IT security. If you recall, we delineated numerous security areas in Chapter 1. We've included that same diagram here in Figure 9.1 for your reference.

Figure 9.1 Corporate IT Security Project Plan Components

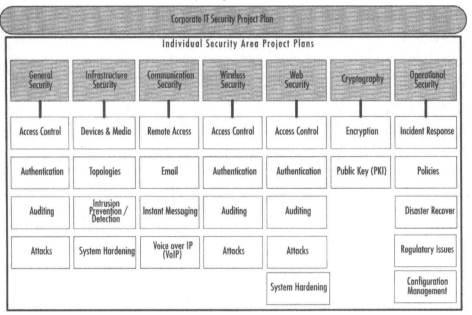

As we move through this chapter, keep in mind that we're focusing on the overall corporate IT security project plan, but that these same elements will also be used in subsequent individual security area project plans. You may have additional ISAPs defined for your organization and, if so, you can utilize this framework to develop project plans to address those specific areas.

Corporate Security Auditing

Before you can embark on any IT security project, you need to understand the current environment. As we've stated several times, in project
management, you should start with a problem statement. The problem
statement for corporate security can be as general as, "We currently have
no clear understanding of our network's vulnerabilities." However, the
more specific you get, the better your solution will be. If you say, "Our
network consists of servers, network storage devices, end user computers,
Web services, wireless access and sensitive corporate and customer data.
We do not have a detailed approach to securing these network resources."
You are getting closer to defining the real problem and closer to identifying the real need. One way to develop a solid security project plan
problem statement is by conducting a thorough security audit. Since
knowing your starting point is the logical genesis of any security plan,
we're going to delve into the details of conducting a security assessment
or audit. You can conduct your assessment as one of the first major objectives of your corporate IT security plan, or you can create a separate
security assessment and auditing project plan to be conducted and concluded prior to the development of your corporate IT security project
plan or any of your ISAPs. Either method is acceptable as long as your
projects build upon the results of your audit. In this chapter, we'll use the
terms *assessment* and *audit* interchangeably.

   Auditing means different things to different people but we'll use a
definition commonly used in the IT security world: a thorough and
methodical review of systems and technologies focused on finding vulnerabilities. Some companies hire outside security consultants to assist
with their security auditing. If you choose to perform your own network
security audit, you're going to need several tools and a lot of expertise to
do so effectively. You'll also need one or more people on your team to
volunteer to think like hackers so you can discover vulnerabilities hackers
would likely exploit.

Business Intelligence...

Ethical Hackers?

The term "ethical hackers" seems like a bit of an oxymoron, however, it's actually a growing field of interest these days. In order to effectively thwart hackers, you need to have the same or better skills as hackers. There are numerous companies that train people to hack systems so they can use their skills for the benefit, not detriment, of the company. Numerous organizations provide ethical hacker training and certification programs and you can find many listed using a quick online search. These courses teach participants to use the same tools, techniques, and thought processes that hackers use in order to exploit vulnerabilities and to force their way into computers, networks, and other electronic corporate resources. However, there's good news and bad news. The good news is that having these skills on your IT team can be valuable in keeping your corporate network safe. The bad news is that it's always a bit unnerving to teach your employees how to hack a network. However, if you look at the open source model for software development, you find a similar logic. Open the knowledge to many and you have a better chance of exposing and addressing vulnerabilities. And, while you can send your employees for training, you can also hire an outside consultant who is a certified ethical hacker to teach your IT staff how to hack. Remember, though, your employees may choose to learn on their own, so keep all of your options open and keep an eye on your network through various, independent methods.

Choosing A Target

Hackers, like robbers or car thieves, will attack the easiest targets first. For example, in the case of wireless networks, hackers will certainly take an unsecured wireless network over a protected one any day. Just like the car thief, the easiest cars to steal are ones that are (in this order):

1. Running with the key in the ignition
2. Unlocked
3. Locked
4. Locked and have a visible security device (e.g., a steering wheel lock),
5. Locked and have an alarm system
6. Locked and have an alarm system and an engine-disabling device

For a hacker, the easiest networks to hack are those that are unsecured. However, corporations can be rich targets for hackers, either because of the data on the network (financial, personal identification, and so forth) or because they can access trade secrets, Research & Development, and other confidential corporate data. The potential payoff makes it worth the effort. Finally, there is the "hacker of convenience" who hacks into a network just to see if he or she can; sometimes it just boils down to bragging rights. Therefore, your goal in network auditing is to find the vulnerabilities from easiest to hardest (just like a car thief). If you plug the obvious holes, you're better off than doing nothing, but you're not secure.

Business Intelligence...

The Best Defense is a Good Offense

What's the best way to secure your network? By taking both a defensive and offensive position. The defensive position consists of all the things you do to secure your network, from requiring strong passwords, to controlling and auditing access to key files, to hardening your servers. It's like locking the doors and windows on your house to make sure it's secure before heading off on vacation. However, that's not enough in network security. Hackers, like professional burglars, are scoping out your network just looking for an opening. In network security, you have to also take an offensive approach and attack your network from as many different angles as possible. Not only do you have to think like a

Continued

hacker, you have to be as creative as a hacker and think of different ways to attack your systems. This is one reason outside consultants can be helpful; they aren't well-versed in your systems and will come in with a fresh perspective and without any pre-conceived notions about how your system does (or does not) work. He or she will be able to examine elements of your network security you and your team may overlook.

Why Security Fails

An important aspect of understanding how to secure your network comes from understanding why network security fails in the first place. It's not just a matter of an unused port being left open on a server or a default setting being left in place. Security and security failure depends on a number of interrelated aspects including:

- Improper configuration
- Failure to update
- Faulty requirements
- Human factors
- Policy issues
- Incorrect assumptions

Improper Configuration

Improper configuration is one of the first areas IT managers think of when they think of how security can fail. Failing to change settings from the default or out-of-the-box settings is a major source of security risk, since every hacker in the world has access to the same data you do when it comes to default settings. Those of you familiar with Microsoft Windows Server operating system know that the major change to the 2000/2003 versions is that the default settings came locked down rather than fully open. In older versions, Microsoft assumed you'd lock down any functionality you didn't want to use or didn't want users to access. However, that left many open doors for attacks. In the latest versions, the out-of-the-box configuration comes locked down and you have to deliberately enable key functionality. This is clearly a better approach to security but it's not a cure-all. Other equipment including routers and wireless access points in particular, come with default settings that many companies fail to change during normal installation and configuration.

In addition to using default settings, there is also the chance for simple error when making changes to configuration settings. Other times, the settings are properly configured but the resulting configuration has unintended consequences elsewhere in the system. These are the kinds of issues a solid security assessment plan will try to locate and address.

Failure to Update

Anyone working in network security these days is well aware of the need, or rather the requirement, to keep systems up-to-date. The adage that "two heads are better than one" comes into play from both sides of this issue. Hackers are increasingly collaborating together and are getting smarter and more sophisticated. On the other side of the issue, various hardware and software vendors are also working harder to maintain security. Since attackers are never going to stop trying to improve their chances of getting into your system, you have to stay one step ahead through keeping systems up-to-date. If you don't have a comprehensive plan in place for keeping operating systems, applications, and security applications (anti-virus, anti-spyware, and so forth) up-to-date, your entire network is vulnerable. Part of your assessment should include your current update plans.

Faulty Requirements

Functional and technical requirements are the foundation of any technology project. Whether building a server, designing a rocket, or constructing a solar power generator, all require well-designed requirements. If the requirements are faulty in any way, you have a poorly designed system. In the case of network security, requirements tend to build one upon the next, creating a layered effect (e.g., the requirements for the server hardware, operating system, applications, communications protocols, network routers, and firewalls combine to create the security that impacts that one specific server. If anywhere along the line those requirements are poorly conceived, designed, or executed, you have a potential security gap. This was the case about ten years ago when some Department of Defense systems had serious security vulnerabilities. It wasn't that the vulnerabilities were new or unique, it was that the systems were poorly engineered and long-term plans for remediation were needed. If they had fixed the issues immediately, it would have had a dire impact on the mission. Faulty or poorly designed requirements can create a serious problem at many different levels of network security. Each of your ISAPs as well as your corporate IT security project plans should include functional, technical, and legal/compliance requirements to ensure that you are addressing security at the most basic level.

Human Factors

In network security, humans are the weakest link. Human behavior is fairly predictable. We don't remember complex passwords very well, so we write them down. If we don't have to use complex passwords, we use ones we can easily remember so we don't have to write them down. Unfortunately, these end up being passwords that can be easily guessed or found through a dictionary search. Using your pet's name or your wife's birthday helps if the attacker doesn't know you, but a large number of security breaches happen inside the organization. If your user account has administrative privileges and you use your wife's birthday as your password, how hard is it for someone in your organization to hack into your account? If you use a word found in the dictionary, a computer could hack the account in about 20 seconds, on average. Users, developers, managers, and IT administrators all fall victim to shortcuts for remembering passwords, and there are those in the industry that believe that IT administrators are the single largest security vulnerability.

There's also the issue of social engineering, where users are persuaded or tricked into giving up their usernames and passwords. More sophisticated forms of social engineering have spawned "phishing" and given the proliferation of the practice, one would have to surmise that phishing is successful enough to be worth the effort. In many cases, it's just easier to ask. You'd be surprised how often people will divulge their passwords if the request appears appropriate. Have any of your IT staff call anyone in your organization and ask for their password and see how often someone is willing to divulge it.

Finally, there is the aspect of physical security. Laptops are stolen, users leave their desks unattended, and network resources are left unsecured. Physical access to a server is absolutely the best way to hack it. Sitting down at the receptionist's desk that's logged on to the network might yield useful information to an attacker. Your network assessment needs to account for the human factor in all areas of security.

Policy Issues

The quality and comprehensiveness of your security policies and practices is at the heart of your network security. Your policy should be created in conjunction with your human resources staff and your legal counsel to ensure that you're creating policies and procedures that make sense for the whole organization. Legal counsel helps ensure policies meet legal requirements, both from a human resources perspective and also from a legal risk mitigation perspective. Your policies and procedures need to be strong enough to meet standards of "reasonable care," but they also must conform to standard human resources practices.

We've discussed the importance of involving key stakeholders in your project planning process right from the start. This is one key area where outside assistance from human resources and legal can help tremendously. If security policies are mismatched to the organization, there's a very high chance that compliance will be low. The major problems users run into with security policies is that they're:

- **Too Stringent** Requiring a 35-character complex password, multiple logins, and so on. Will usually cause the user to find ways to circumvent the policy.

- **Too Old** Outdated security policies undermine the credibility of the policies that are still up-to-date. Asking users to sort through and determine which are relevant and which are not creates an inconsistent approach to security policies, which leads to security risks.

- **Unread or Unused** Security policies that are not read or enforced by the IT staff, management, and human resources are useless. It doesn't matter how many locks you put on the door if you leave the door wide open.

- **Vague or Unclear** Policies that are vague, confusing, contradictory, or that provide no clear direction on how users can comply are worse than no policies at all. If users do not understand how to comply with security requirements, they will usually resort to doing whatever they need to do in order to get their jobs done. That often means circumventing security best practices out of desperation. If users are told they cannot transmit a patient's medical data across unsecured lines or without encryption but they don't know if their lines are secure or how to encrypt a file, there's a good chance they won't comply.

Your security assessment should include reviewing, modifying, updating, and deleting all existing security policies so that the resulting set of policies is up-to-date and relevant to the current (and near future) security environment for the network. You should also make sure that your policies are clear enough that users understand and know how to comply with security policies.

Incorrect Assumptions

The difficulty about assumptions is that we don't always know we're making them, and that's the root of security issues. If we assume users behave in a particular way and we're wrong, we potentially have a security hole. If we assume a particular set of configuration settings will result in a particular outcome, we've created a potential security hole. If we assume that the technology works in one way and we're wrong, we've left the door open to attack. Testing assumptions is an important part of your security assessment process. Unfortunately, it's not always easy to see what we're assuming. There are several ways to address this including consciously asking, on a regular basis, "What assumptions are we making here?" involving those outside the IT environment to provide a fresh perspective and unbiased approach, and hiring outside experts who come in without those same assumptions in mind.

For example, suppose someone wants to get at your customer database. The attacker knows your company has a large online store with millions of transactions flowing through on a monthly basis. The attacker looks on your company Web site and eventually is able to cause the database server to generate an error that gives the attacker the information he or she was looking for. The attacker uses the result of the database error to inject code that enables him or her to hack further into the system. He or she gives themselves administrative privileges, covers their tracks, and sits in the comfort of his or her home grabbing any database information he or she wants. You may have looked hard at your Web server and made sure that it was secure and that customer transactions were secure and assumed you were all set. These are exactly the kinds of assumptions attackers hope you'll make.

Another assumption we discussed earlier in this book is the assumption that the proper steps were followed when implementing various security measures. If you simply assume the proper steps were followed and completed, you leave open the possibility that these measures were not properly completed. Using completion criteria for each task (see Chapter 6 for more detail) will help ensure that each security task is completed successfully and per your security project plan. Using completion criteria and spot checks on various security measures will help you to know, rather than assume, that your security measures have been properly implemented.

Corporate IT Security Project Parameters

After completing the risk assessment and impact analysis for your corporate IT security project, you should have a better idea of the problem(s) you're trying to solve and the desired outcomes. These should be well-aligned with your enterprise-level security strategy. If not, you'll need to circle back through the process and locate and address any disconnects. At the conclusion of this process, you should document both the problem statement and the outcome statement. This can be a relatively short few sentences just to make sure you've clearly identified the problem you're trying to solve and that you've identified the outcome you want to achieve. There will always be a balance between security and cost and between security and operational efficiency, and this is the place to begin to find that balance.

Project Objectives

Your corporate IT security solutions should include all of the security areas you need to address. Figure 9.1 shows several common security areas that are likely to be a part of your plan. These include general, infrastructure, Web, wireless, communication, and operational security, among others. You may find that you want to slice and dice your security areas differently than we have here. That's fine as long as you take a logical and comprehensive approach to the wide variety of topic areas you need to cover, and don't inadvertently omit anything.

Your potential solutions include all of the security topic areas you want to cover. We also know that in the real world of corporate finance, there's a good chance that your complete list probably falls under the label "wish list" rather than "to do list." Since you will likely be forced to make some compromises and tough choices, it's important to start with your ideal list and pare it down from there. Once you've identified your ideal solution, you need to circle back and see how it compares with your project constraints starting with the scope, time, cost, and quality.

Project Parameters

All projects have four parameters: *scope, schedule, budget,* and *quality.* As we've discussed, there is a relationship among these parameters that must be addressed at the outset of any project planning process. You can create a smaller project scope by phasing your projects and identifying ISAPs within the corporate IT security project plan. Your overall plan and your ISAPs will each have the four parameters and will move independently.

For example: Your corporate IT security project may have a schedule of 12 months and a budget of $500,000. Your communication security plan, which includes e-mail, instant messaging, Voice over IP (VoIP), and remote access, has a schedule of 30 days and a budget of $10,000. Clearly, the 30 days is part of the 12-month schedule and the $10,000 is part of the $500,000 budget. However, the priority for your corporate IT security project might be time —it must be completed in 12 months. On the other hand, your priority for your communication security plan might be budget—you don't care if it takes two months or even three months, but it can't cost more than $10,000.

This is one of the reasons it's helpful to break a project down into smaller sub-projects. You can adjust priorities for the sub-projects (in our case, the ISAPs) in a manner that drives your overall goals and objectives. This can be especially helpful if you believe that another segment of your corporate IT security project plan could take more time than allotted. In that case, you might need to allocate more funds to hire outside contractors to come in and assist in getting the job done. By having both the overall plan's project parameters and priorities identified and by working with the ISAPs, you can build in a bit more flexibility than you might have otherwise.

Scope

The scope of your corporate IT security project plan includes the scope of all the ISAPs (if you choose to break your projects out in this manner), but that's not all it should include. The corporate IT security project, in some sense, is the mortar that holds the bricks (ISAPs) together. Each individual security area is important, but without a holistic approach to security, you're bound to have gaps between these areas. The scope of the corporate IT security project should reflect this need. You can include the scope statement from each of the ISAPs and you may want to include the following items as well:

- Comprehensive review of network systems security
- Comprehensive test plan for systems vulnerability
- Vertical security assessment and hardening
- Horizontal security assessment and hardening
- Perimeter security assessment and hardening
- System-wide IT security policies and procedures
- Corporate IT security policies and procedures
- System-wide IT emergency response plan

At the risk of being repetitive, these elements should take a system-wide or corporate-wide look at the same areas that will be addressed in one or more of your individual security area plans. In some cases, there is overlap and in other cases there are gaps. The goal of the corporate IT security project plan is to ensure that any areas that overlap are appropriately resolved and any gaps that exist are addressed. Think of the corporate IT security project plan as your last line of defense.

Another useful way to look at the scope is to look at the physical elements of your network. How many locations does your company have? How many buildings does that entail? How many logical or physical subnets are there? How many servers? How many desktops? How many users? Are you planning on addressing every aspect of your IT security in this plan or are you going to take it in phases? If you remember the project management guideline that smaller projects tend to be more successful than larger projects, you can see that properly setting your scope is key to success. If you determine that your corporate IT project must address every aspect of IT security, you will definitely need to break it down into smaller ISAPs. If your network security is relatively good and you simply want to make sure things stay up-to-date with the latest threats, your scope may not need to be quite as extensive.

Finally, you might look at your network both horizontally and vertically. A vertical approach looks at a single host or single host type and looks for all vulnerabilities that might impact that host type (e.g., look at all of the desktop systems running Microsoft Windows XP Professional and look for all vulnerabilities, threats, and remediation strategies related to that operating system and those devices.) This is defined as the scope of your corporate IT security project or the scope of just Phase One. A horizontal approach is useful for spanning various platforms and might include looking for any device that could be vulnerable to a Transmission Control Protocol/Internet Protocol (TCP/IP) port scan or a Denial of Service (DOS) attack. This approach could be used to define the scope.

Ultimately, you want to review all systems top to bottom and side to side, but if you've recently completed a number of security measures or if a comprehensive corporate IT security project plan is outside of the financial means of the company, you may choose to scale it down using these various elements of scope.

Schedule

There are a number of elements regarding the schedule of a corporate IT security project and the related ISAPs. The overall schedule may be dictated by a planned, future event such as the company going public via an Initial Public Offering (IPO) or a requirement to be compliant with a particular set of regulations by a certain deadline, or maybe by a deadline determined by the executive team. These are external constraints that must be considered as you build your project plan. If schedule (time) is your top priority, you already know that something else will have to "give" if the project runs into problems (which almost all projects do at one time or another). In this case, you need to plan for the possibility that you will need to add more people to your project if work is delayed for any reason. You also need to be ready to scale your scope back a bit if you fall behind schedule. The corporate IT security plan will have to be the most flexible, because it will have to accommodate the changes to all the underlying ISAPs and it will also have to provide a thorough, integrated approach to corporate security as a whole.

In addition, you may set high-level target completion dates for various elements of your project and then set your more detailed schedule based on the ISAP schedules you develop. For example, you may choose to complete a Web security project plan first, because you know your Web systems are most vulnerable at this time. You expect that project to take two months to complete. You might choose to begin the planning stages of your infrastructure project plan, because you want to begin implementing it as soon as possible. You may also be able to utilize different members of your IT staff so that you can run these projects in parallel. These are the kinds of things you can decide on regarding your schedule when you take a holistic, system-wide look at your security initiatives.

Budget

Determining the budget for your corporate IT security project can be the most challenging aspect of developing your corporate IT security plan. How much it will cost is often a function of how much it can cost, meaning that your security budget may well be set by corporate or IT budget constraints. If your budget question is answered for you, then you'll need to reverse engineer your budget to determine just how much security you can get for some set number of dollars.

Phasing your security projects can also help when overall cost is not as much an issue as the timing of cash flow. You'll need to determine if your costs are primarily internal or external. Internal costs are those such as labor costs for staff, loss of productivity (which often isn't captured in any organization), and any other cost that essentially involves shifting money around in accounts. External expenses are the ones that often have to be timed and explicitly approved. Purchases including new security hardware, software, or external labor often require specific sponsor approval for the expenditure if it exceeds a certain threshold. Often you can negotiate a higher overall budget for your corporate IT security project by negotiating the budgets for the smaller ISAPs individually. Beware of one trap of this approach. Sometimes you'll negotiate a budget for an ISAP such as infrastructure security and, whether accidentally or intentionally, it is construed as your entire security budget. Be extremely clear in your communications that if you choose to negotiate individual project plan budgets that you're talking about a subset of your total security needs. If you are painfully clear about this, you'll avoid problems down the road, but you will likely have to answer the question, "How much will the whole thing cost?" Although you may not know (or may not want to say at that moment), you can briefly lay out your approach to managing the costs by discussing your overall corporate IT security strategy. In some companies, this piecemeal approach to budget expenditures is an effective way to reduce organizational resistance to security spending. In other companies, this approach could be viewed as manipulative or underhanded, in which case you should find a more acceptable method of presenting your budget needs.

Quality

Although even one security breach can be devastating for an organization, the cost of guaranteeing zero breaches can be astronomical. You'll have to find the balance between the quality your organization requires and the cost it can afford. In many cases, there is a direct relationship between the level of quality (or the tolerance for breaches) and the cost of the project. Therefore, if budget is your top constraint, you'll most likely need to adjust your scope or your quality. Reducing quality is not as bad as it sounds. Adobe Photoshop is a great program, but it's pricey if all you want to do is view pictures from your digital camera and add captions underneath. Less expensive programs offer lower quality, but if that's all you need, why pay more? The same holds true for your corporate IT security quality level. Deliver the highest quality you can afford, and recognize that no solution is ever perfect. Define what level of risk you can afford to operate under and let that be your guide to quality. If the level of quality your organization requires is higher than your budget allows, you will have to build a business case for increasing the budget. You may find an ally in your legal department or a legal representative who can help explain the cost of the risks (and consequences) that you're trying to mitigate.

Requirements

Every IT project should have well-developed requirements that define the boundaries of your project. Your scope statement states what is and is not included in the project, but the requirements provide the details for those scope statements. Functional requirements answer the question, "What should this project accomplish?" A good example for corporate security might be that the functional requirement specifies the implementation of a stronger authentication system, because a recently passed law or regulation requires it. The functional requirement says the project must include a "strong authentication system as defined by Regulation 123."

Technical requirements describe *how* you will accomplish the functional requirements. They are typically quite specific and binary: either it is or it isn't; either it meets specifications or it doesn't. A stronger authentication requirement might provide very detailed technical specifications for smart cards or biometric hardware in very specific language. Technical requirements are server processor speed or hard disk capacity (i.e., they are clear, tangible, and relatively easy to define.)

Project management is an iterative process—you often have to circle back to add detail as information becomes available. Requirements may be known at the outset of a project, in which case they should be included. However, it's also common for new or additional requirements to be added as you move through the definition and planning phases of your project. You may not know that strong authentication is a requirement until you've done a risk analysis or audit. You may not know that you need a biometric system for authentication until you've completed some other part of the project work or read a new section of a regulation. The key is to define what you're aware of and revise the project plan as details become known. That doesn't mean that you're shooting at a moving target—just the opposite. Pin down as many details as possible, knowing that as you gather data and do your research, you'll develop finer levels of detail. Don't get lost in the spin cycle, but do refine your data as you gather additional information.

Projects may also have some sort of organizational requirements (e.g., a particular security measure must be compatible with screen readers used by visually impaired employees, or the security measures do not violate employee privacy as defined by the organization. These typically should be translated into functional and technical specifications, but they can also be noted separately as organizational requirements to ensure they receive the attention they deserve.

Finally, IT security projects will have legal and regulatory issues that need to be defined as requirements. Again, these can be listed as legal, regulatory, or compliance requirements to give them needed visibility, but they ultimately should be translated into functional and technical requirements for the project.

Key Skills Needed

Although we touched on this in earlier chapters, this is a good time to reiterate the basics. Your corporate IT security project team should include people from all areas of your organization with both technical and non-technical skills. You can create a list of the technical skills needed for each of the ISAP projects, and roll your skills list up into your corporate IT security project plan. However, you might need to take a bit more time identifying the non-technical skills needed (e.g., you don't always need technical people to create security policies that include physical computer equipment security policies, e-mail, and Internet and training policies, and you don't always need technical people to create and deliver related user training). The following is a list of skills you may need for your corporate IT security plan:

- Technical
- Communication
- Training

- Policy development

- Technical and non-technical writing

- User requirement development

- Financial (to create the budget)

- Legal (to advise on various aspects of your project)

- Human Resources (to help develop user guidelines)

From the technical side, there are numerous skills you're likely to need. The core skills needed to assess security (which are usually the same skills needed to implement security solutions after assessment) are operating system, network, application and programming skills. These skills are often found in two different groups of people. Most of your IT staff can be divided into "network guys" and "programmers." Your network experts are the ones you turn to when you have a router outage, a server configuration issue, or a new application to install. Programmers typically look at the world in a different way; they're usually not the ones you want configuring your database server, but you do want them writing and testing the scripts. Understanding the core skills of your IT staff and where they're most appropriately applied in your IT security project plan is critical.

Most technical skill sets are either deep or broad and it's not too common to find someone whose skills are both. If someone knows routers inside and out and can list off soft switch settings for every Cisco product ever made, he or she most likely won't be able to tell you the best way to configure access control lists for the database. In fact, your department likely has a mix of generalists and specialists specific to the jobs you've needed to get done in the past. However, that doesn't necessarily help when you're looking the skills needed for your corporate IT security project. A skills assessment may be necessary before you undertake your security project and you may need to train staff or hire expertise, which should be reflected in your project budget.

Operating System Skills

You should have at least one person on staff with deep operating system expertise for each operating system deployed in your organization. If you're running Windows, Linux, and Apple, you ideally should have experts in each of those areas who are well-versed in securing each of those operating systems. Your expert(s) should have a detailed understanding of the operating system's subsystems, with special emphasis on the security subsystems. Operating system fundamentals change slowly, so this is one area where in-depth study will pay off. This is also an area where you should have good bench strength.

Create a list of all of the operating systems deployed in your organization, and make sure you have one or more experts on staff that can assist in developing, implementing, and maintaining your corporate IT security plan. Excellent training in these areas is widely available and a good investment to ensure that staff skills in this area are up-to-date.

Network Skills

As an IT Manager or IT Security Project Manager, you probably recall the Open Systems Interconnection (OSI) model in name only. However, if your job is to secure the network, the OSI model should be permanently etched in your brain. Understanding what goes on in the network at Layer 2 and 3 is critical to security, because that's where most of the routing, switching, and security controls operate. Another network skill you should have on your IT staff is Internet Protocol (IP) expertise, people who can count and add in hexadecimal format in their sleep. They should be familiar with subnetting, supernetting, IPv4, IPv6, IP telephony (VoIP), and all of the other ways the IP is implemented, used, and configured in the enterprise.

Part of your corporate IT security project plan should include a list of the network skills needed based on the type of systems you have in place and what you're planning to implement in the near future.

Application Skills

Staying up-to-date on application skills can be a challenge, because unlike operating system or networking data, applications rarely stay the same from version to version. The core application doesn't change much, but enterprise-wide applications are typically complex programs and when something changes in one area, it ripples through the application at lightening speed. This creates a security challenge, because on one hand, you don't know exactly how the latest updates impact the application and its security (i.e., did the developers do a good job testing security on this latest release?) and you also don't know exactly how the application changes might impact your business operations and security (i.e., how well-versed you are in the latest nuances of the application and how it impacts your system security).

The application skills your organization requires are database skills and Web application skills. If you don't have these skills internally, you should add them to your requirement list so that the next time you hire someone, you will hire them with these skills in mind. Database and Web-related security are two areas that hackers like to attack, so be sure you have the requisite skills in this area.

Identify the applications in your organization and check to see if you have the necessary skills. If not, seek out vendor training so that you can adequately secure your company's applications.

Security Tools Skills

Depending on the scope of your corporate IT security project plan, you may or may not need to delve into the detailed world of specific security tools. In later chapters, we take a look at various security tools. Some are simple scripting tools and others are hardware devices. Depending on your project plans, you may purchase these tools and train staff to use them, or hire external contractors who have the tools and the expertise. The decision will primarily hinge on the potential payback on the investment. If you're going to need these tools on a regular basis, it makes sense to make the investment in the tools and training. If a tool will only be used occasionally, it might make sense to hire a contractor, who can bear the time and expense of staying up-to-date. You can hire their expertise for less than it would cost you to develop that expertise in-house.

There are many training methods available including online courses, workshops, and boot camps that train staff how to use security tools. One thing to consider, though, is that not all courses teach participants to think like hackers, and using the security tools without the mindset of an attacker will likely yield less than optimal results.

Programming Skills—Compiled Languages

In order to perform security testing, you should have programmers on staff that are conversant in various compiled languages. Is it absolutely necessary? No, but it's often helpful to create automated testing procedures and to understand how to read source code and see what's going on beneath the covers. C and C++, C#, and Java are the primary languages in use, although there are others. C, C++, and C# are not the same languages. Both C++ and C# are object-oriented languages; C is not. However, all share similar syntax and semantics. C# is a relatively new variation and is used primarily in Web applications and Web services. Java is also an object-oriented language, developed by Sun Microsystems, and is used across a wide variety of platforms and devices.

Determine what security projects you're going to undertake and whether you'll need these programming language skills in-house. In some cases, you may want to hire the programming expertise you need from an employment agency, but be careful about what you provide to the contractor. You could be hiring the guy who opens the back door on your system.

Programming Skills—Scripting Languages

Scripting languages (also called interpreted languages) are often used for a variety of administrative tasks, so chances are your IT staff has a variety of scripting skills. Take a full inventory of all scripting skills in your department. This will not only help you match skills to need, but it might also prompt a few creative ideas for how to approach various security tasks.

The most commonly used scripting languages these days are Microsoft's Visual Basic Scripting Edition (VBScript), JavaScript, Python, and Perl. VBScript is typically used to automate various administrative tasks, especially in the Windows environment. It's also widely used on the client side of Web services. JavaScript is also used in client side code on Web sites. VBScript is specific to Microsoft and JavaScript works across the Microsoft, Unix, and Linux platforms. Python is also an object-oriented scripting language that is used extensively in the Google search engine. Python runs on Windows, Linux/Unix, Mac OS X, OS/2, Amiga, Palm Handhelds, and Nokia mobile phones. Python has also been ported to the Java and .NET virtual machines. Python is distributed under an OSI-approved open source license that makes it free to use, even for commercial products. Python is slowly replacing Perl, though there are still many Perl scripts running in the world.

Key Personnel Needed

Once you've identified the scope of your project and the skills needed to successfully complete your corporate IT security project plan, you can start mapping the specific people to their skills. For example:

- **Communication** - Jesse (IT), MaryAnn (HR)
- **Training** - Lisa (IT), Fernando (IT), Sonali (Training)
- **Policy development** - Bill (IT), Marcos (HR)
- **Technical and non-technical writing** - Lisa (IT), Sonali (Training), Ming (HR)
- **User requirement development** - Luisa (Business analyst), Ming (HR)
- **Financial (to create the budget)** - Deepak (Finance), Lisa (IT)
- **Legal (to advise on various aspects of your project)** - Larry (Legal)
- **Human Resources (to help develop user guidelines)** - Nels (HR), Ming (HR), Fernando (IT)

You can see from this list that there are two names that appear multiple times—Lisa from the IT department and Ming from HR. Are you sure that Lisa and Ming will be available? Can Fernando cover for Lisa in any of these areas? As you develop your list of needed personnel, also create a viable list of alternates. If these people are not available and are truly needed, your project will be delayed.

Notice we didn't list any of the technical skills or technical personnel needed. It's assumed you'll do this in each of your ISAPs and roll it up into your corporate IT security plan. However, you may need or want to include additional skills and personnel to your corporate IT security plan, if you want to provide a higher level skill set to the mix (e.g., an outside security consultant to review your overall plan or someone with a systems integration testing background who normally works in a different department or division).

Project Processes and Procedures

The overarching question is this: What processes and procedures do you need to implement to manage your corporate IT security project plan? The answer lies in your approach to your corporate IT security plan. For example, if you choose to break your corporate IT security project plan down into the underlying ISAPs, how will you manage the timing, resource allocation, reporting, and scheduling of these projects? How will you manage resource conflicts? How will you know if you're over budget or behind schedule?

The key to developing your project's processes and procedures is to look at what you've defined thus far. What does your scope look like? How are you organizing this project? Next, you'll need to find your standard project processes and procedures and review them. Are they appropriate to this project? Do they contribute to or compromise overall security? For instance, for some projects, you may want people to collaborate on particular sections of the project, but in a security project, you may want people to work independently so they can test each other's solutions. Having one person develop the solution and another devise the test of that solution can sometimes yield better results.

As part of the organizational security ISAP, we'll discuss both organizational security policies and procedures and emergency response policies and procedures, so we won't cover them here (see Chapter 13). The processes, policies, and procedures we focus on in this section are those needed to effectively plan, implement, monitor, and manage your enterprise-wide IT security plan.

In addition, you may want to implement additional procedures related to security projects including:

- Require that IT staff create special user accounts for testing so that employees who have been given permission to test security can be recognized and monitored on the system. These accounts can later be deactivated or used only in cases of security testing. This can help separate out legitimate testing from insider hacking.

- Develop specific procedures for testing security and for recovering from any unintended consequences of that testing. Sometimes pen testing (or other security testing) breaks something in ways you couldn't foresee. Having specific recovery procedures in place will help mitigate project risk.

- Develop procedures to prioritize security breaches found during testing.

- Develop procedures for notifying key staff of serious security holes found and the appropriate measures to take. The last thing you want is for one of your staff to find a significant security hole and be told, in essence, "That task isn't scheduled for another month. Remind us later." Your security procedures should include escalation and notification procedures for serious security issues uncovered during the security project.

- Create policies and procedures for emergency response teams in the event of a real security breach.

- Develop policies regarding how IT staff handles the sensitive information discovered during security assessments and audits. Remember, discovery of security holes can lead to legal liability if reasonable measures are not taken to address those shortcomings.

- Develop policies detailing how and when to perform complete backups and how to restore systems. Always perform complete backups of critical systems before performing any audit or test activities. Also ensure that backups are tested with sample restores prior to auditing activities.

There may be many other security-related policies and procedures you want to employ in order to successfully plan, implement, and run your corporate IT security project plan, but this will get you started thinking along the lines of things that are specific to security projects.

Project Work Breakdown Structure

Recall that your work breakdown structure (WBS) is created from your project objectives. Typically, you'll have three to five high-level objectives to start with. In the case of your corporate IT security plan, you'll probably end up incorporating sub-plans (ISAPs) into the master plan. To that end, you may not decide to list out each of the ISAPs for your project, but instead include those as one high-level objective. Let's look at a few examples of how you can define your corporate IT security plan. Remember that if you don't already have your core project team working with you on defining your project, there's no time like the present to get them involved. If you define your WBS without key stakeholder and subject matter expertise input, you'll have a lot of rework on your hands later on.

WBS Example 1

1. Develop enterprise security strategy
2. Perform enterprise-wide security audit

3. Implement individual security area plans based on audit results

   3.1 Develop and implement the Infrastructure Security Plan

   3.2 Develop and implement the Web and Internet Security Plan

   3.3 Develop and implement the Communication Security Plan

   3.4 Develop and implement the Wireless Security Plan

   3.5 Develop and implement the Cryptography Security Plan

   3.6 Develop and implement the Operational Security Plan

4. Perform cross-functional security review

5. Develop ongoing security maintenance procedures

In this example, developing the security strategy is the first major objective of your corporate IT security project plan. Some might argue that this step should be completed prior to developing your corporate IT security project plan, but if rolling it into your project planning process is helpful, there's no harm in doing so as long as it's completed before moving into the development of the remaining four high-level objectives (which translate into your top-level tasks in your WBS). Notice that Task 3 is a high-level placeholder for ISAPs. Several are listed underneath Task 3 for illustrative purposes only. One quick reminder is that best practices dictate that task names use a verb and a noun format so they are somewhat descriptive. Let's look at another corporate IT security WBS you might use as a starting point.

Work Breakdown Structure Example 2

1. Develop RFP to hire an outside security consultant for an enterprise-wide security audit

   1.1 Define RFP parameters

   1.2 Develop a list of companies from whom to solicit RFP responses

   1.3 Issue a RFP

1.4 Evaluate RFP responses

1.5 Hire an outside consultant

2. Perform enterprise-wide security audit

3. Implement security recommendations based on audit results

    3.1 Develop ISAPs

        3.1.1 Develop and implement Infrastructure Security Plan

        3.1.2 Develop and implement Wireless Security Plan

        3.1.3 Develop and implement Operational Security Plan

    3.2 Implement, monitor, and manage defined ISAPs

4. Develop ongoing security maintenance procedures

In this example, you've decided to hire an outside consultant to perform a security audit. From those results, you will develop your individual security plans to address the specific areas or vulnerabilities identified by the consultant. You may develop those plans with or without the consultant, and you may decide to implement and manage those projects with or without the consultant. Those are choices you can make as you move through the process based on the unique characteristics of your organization, your IT staff's capabilities, and your relationship with the consultant. However, regardless of who does the work, you are the project manager and should actively manage the process. In most cases, it is not advisable to hand off responsibility for the project to an outside consultant, unless you are explicitly hiring them to come in, assess your security needs, develop the security project plan, and implement the resulting plan. There are some instances when that might be advisable, but as a general rule, you should maintain control of the project, because you'll be held accountable for the results when it's all said and done.

As part of your WBS, you'll want to include the specific security areas you plan on addressing. You may have to circle back through your planning process to add detail once your security assessment or audit is completed. If the assessment or audit is conducted prior to planning your corporate IT security project, you most likely will have adequate detail to specify the ISAPs at the outset of your planning phase. There are numerous security areas to be considered that should be delineated as part of your assessment process. However, to give you a jump start, we've included a list developed by the International Engineering Consortium (IEC) that delineates many of the major areas to be addressed in a comprehensive security project plan. Table 9.1 provides a list to help you to start thinking about what your network includes, what your security assessment should review, and what ISAPs you may need to define.

Remember, smaller projects are more successful, so if you need or want to undertake many (or all) of the items listed in Table 9.1, you should create separate ISAPs for them and roll them up into your corporate IT security project plan. At that point, the corporate IT security project plan becomes more of a "program" than a project, because it is the roll up of a number of related initiatives. This distinction is important, because looking at the corporate IT security project as a program allows you to allocate resources (time, money, expertise) across your IT security projects in a thoughtful and predictable manner, rather than running wild through one enormous project plan that is difficult (impossible) to effectively manage.

Table 9.1 Enterprise-wide Technology List for Security Projects

Technology Category	Components
Storage and Server Technology	Backup Solutions
	Disaster Recovery/Business Continuity
	Storage Management Solutions
	Story Area Network (SAN)/Network
	Attached Storage (NAS)
	Storage Server Provider (SSP)
	PCs/Workstations/Laptops
	Server
	Server-based Operating Systems

Continued

Table 9.1 continued Enterprise-wide Technology List for Security Projects

Technology Category	Components
Mobile and Wireless Technology	Wireless/Cellular Services Personal Area Networks (PANs) Wireless Local Area Networks (LANs) Fixed-Access/Point-to-Point/MAN Wireless Wide Area Networks (WANs) Mobile Computing Platforms/Applications
Networking and Systems Management	Network/Application Monitoring/Performance Management Policy Management Traffic Management Management Service Provider (MSP) Web Monitoring Services
Security	Anti-Virus Software Virtual Private Network (VPN)/Firewalls Public Key Infrastructure (PKI) Authentication/Access Technology Intrusion Detection Systems (IDS) Encryption VPN/Security Services Certificate Authorities Security Management
Infrastructure	KVM Directory Services LAN Infrastructure WAN/MAN Infrastructure Service Provider/Carrier Class Equipment Remote Access Servers Printers UPS Caching and Load Balancing Collocation Services Internet Service Provider (ISP)

Continued

Table 9.1 continued Enterprise-wide Technology List for Security Projects

Technology Category	Components
	Carrier/Competitive Local Exchange Carrier (CLEC) Services
Digital Convergence	VoIP
	Videoconferencing
	Private Branch Exchange (PBX)
	Streaming Media Technology
	Web-enabled Call Centers
	Content Delivery Network (CDN) Services
	Unified Messaging
Business Applications	Application Servers
	Database Servers
	Web Servers
	E-Commerce
	Enterprise Resource Planning (ERP)
	CRM
	Enterprise Application Integration (EAI)
	Content Management
	Data Warehousing
	Business Intelligence Tools
	Development Tools

Once you've developed your high-level (and perhaps mid-level) WBS tasks, you can continue developing additional underlying detail as you would any WBS development process. Don't worry about defining the tasks in the correct order. The order in which tasks should be done will be determined later when you're creating your project schedule. The tasks will be undertaken based on dependencies, constraints, and available resources, so spending a lot of time ordering tasks at this point is usually unproductive. That said, there is usually a linear order in which we think about tasks; if keeping them in some semblance of order helps ensure you don't overlook any major or minor tasks, that's fine. Numbering the tasks at this point will help you keep track of them. If desired, you can renumber your tasks when you believe you have your final WBS, but don't expect numbers tasks to be performed sequentially once your project gets underway.

Project Risks

Identifying risks to the corporate IT security project plan is ideally a team effort. Everyone comes to a project with a distinct set of skills and a unique perspective. These are valuable assets in your risk identification, evaluation, and mitigation planning process. The objective of this phase of project planning is to identify all the things that could go wrong with your project and come up with specific plans for avoiding or reducing those risks.

There are three basic ways to deal with any risk. You can mitigate, avoid, or transfer. Let's look at a quick example to help illustrate these differentiations so you know how to approach project risk management.

- **Mitigation** If there is a fire danger, you buy fire sprinklers to reduce your risk of fire.

- **Avoidance** If there is a fire danger, you remove flammables from the area to avoid the risk.

- **Transference** If there is a fire danger, you buy fire insurance to make the risk someone else's.

Eight distinct steps should be taken in your risk management planning phase:

1. Identify the risk.
2. Rank the likelihood of the risk occurring.
3. Rank the severity of the impact should the risk occur.
4. Create a prioritized list of risks you will plan for and manage.
5. Develop mitigation strategies to avoid or reduce the impact of the risk.

6. Develop specific triggers for the risk mitigation (or alternative) strategy.

7. Analyze the potential impact of implementing the alternate strategy.

8. Identify any direct, indirect, and unintentional consequences of implementing the alternative strategy.

Not all risks are worth planning for, because they are either unlikely to occur or because the impact if they do occur is negligible. An asteroid hitting Earth would have a huge impact, but it's not worth planning for because the likelihood of that occurring is so small. But what about something less dramatic, such as your company's acquisition of another company? How likely is that to occur and how would it impact your corporate IT security project plan? In your case the answer might be that it is highly likely to occur and would have a major impact. What about a dramatic downturn in sales? How likely is that to occur in your business, industry or sector? If that were to occur, how would that impact your corporate IT security plan? You might decide that it's highly unlikely to occur, but it would have a major impact on your plan (because your IT budget would be slashed accordingly). What about the introduction of a new security technology? Would that impact your corporate IT security plan? It might if your security strategy involves staying on the leading edge of security and technology. How likely is that to occur? It depends largely on what technology you're talking about, but let's assume for this example that it's not very likely to occur but would have a huge impact if it did occur.

These are all high-level risks that may be appropriate because we're focusing on the corporate IT security plan, not the ISAPs. However, there may be additional risks you and your team identify that you want to address. This is where an all-out brainstorming session can be very helpful. Have everyone identify absolutely every risk you can think of, whether they're realistic, outlandish, or highly unlikely to occur. Then have the team rank each potential risk twice (independently)—once for likelihood of occurrence and once for severity of occurrence. Place the list in prioritized order and review it. Sometimes a purely mathematical ordering of a risk's likelihood and severity doesn't address contextual issues very well; a bit of human intelligence can go a long way in developing your final list. Once you've accomplished this, decide how far down the list you're willing to plan. Develop risk mitigation strategies (covered that in detail in Chapter 6) appropriate to the plan and incorporate them into your project.

Project Constraints

As you know, every project has constraints that you must deal with. It's one of the major responsibilities of the IT project manager, and is what makes the job both challenging and interesting. Your corporate IT security project plan will undoubtedly have time, budget, and resource constraints you'll have to deal with. In addition, you will likely have legal or regulatory constraints that come into play. These need to be identified at the outset of your project.

In addition, you need to look at your project's scope, budget, schedule, and quality requirements and rank them from highest to lowest priority. Put another way, you need to understand which parameters are locked in and which are flexible. It's nearly impossible to demand that scope, time, budget, and quality all be etched in stone from the outset of the project, so you're better off defining which parameters can change and which cannot.

In the case of corporate IT security, you may find that your constraints are a compilation of the underlying ISAP plans, or you may find that your high-level constraints drive your ISAP constraints. There is no one right way to approach this, but it is important that you address it early and get project sponsor agreement as to project priorities. If you're operating under the assumption that budget is the top priority and your project sponsor believes you're working to come in on schedule knowing the budget may expand a bit, you have a potentially serious disconnect. Define these at the top level for your corporate IT security project based on your stated security strategy and alignment with corporate objectives.

This should give you a bit more flexibility in defining your constraints at the corporate IT security plan level and provide guidance as to how to proceed with the ISAPs.

Project Assumptions

In order to undertake any project, you have to make a few assumptions such as that funding will be available or that resources will be released to you. The key here is to identify the assumptions you are making so that you can address them directly. If your corporate IT security project plan assumes the existence of an overarching security strategy, say so. If the strategy doesn't yet exist, then that assumption means you have some foundational work to do before you can implement your corporate IT security project plan. If you assume that your IT budget will remain a flat 5 percent of corporate revenue next year, state what dollar amount you believe that to be. When you list your assumptions, two things happen. First, you define what you're counting on as being true. Second, you're forced to look clearly at your project and think through what it is you are assuming. That's not always an easy process, because our assumptions sometimes are so fundamental that we can't see them clearly. Again, having your project team work with you on this will help avoid blind spots and make sure you clearly list the assumptions upon which this project is built.

Project Schedule and Budget

In terms of developing your corporate IT security project schedule and budget, there is one important note. If you approach it as you do any other IT project, you'll develop your schedule based on the logical order in which tasks should be performed, including the dependencies and the constraints. Your budget will be based on the calculated cost of each of the tasks and sub-tasks defined in the plan. However, there is one element to the corporate IT security planning process that is unique with regard to schedule and budget. You may choose to take a top-down or a bottom-up approach to your plan development. That is, you may choose to develop the various ISAPs and pull them altogether (with additional tasks that glue the corporate IT security project together and ensure a holistic approach) to create your project plan. This bottom-up approach means that your schedule and budget will also be built from the bottom up. Your schedule will look something like that shown in Figure 9.2, where your corporate plan is roughly the sum of the underlying ISAPs (there may be additional schedule and budget components for those "glue" tasks). In Figure 9.2, those "glue" tasks are shown as having no dependencies and 100 percent float, which is probably not how they'd be included in your project plan. They are shown in this manner to indicate there are tasks that are needed to tie these ISAPs together, such as a full systems test after all the ISAPs are complete or a complete review of all policies related to the ISAPs. The intent of the diagram is to show that the ISAPs roll up and essentially define the corporate IT security project schedule and budget.

Notice that in Figure 9.2, there is overlap of some of the ISAPs. This might occur if you have enough IT staff time, resources, and expertise to undertake projects in parallel (e.g., you might use completely different staff to implement your Web and Internet security plan versus your wireless security plan). Based on other projects and workload, you determine if you can run these projects almost in parallel and that the first of those two can start when the communication security project is about 50 percent complete. Therefore, your total duration for your project is not the sum of the duration for each ISAP, but rather the total duration for all ISAPs to be completed.

Figure 9.2 Bottom-up Schedule and Budget Development

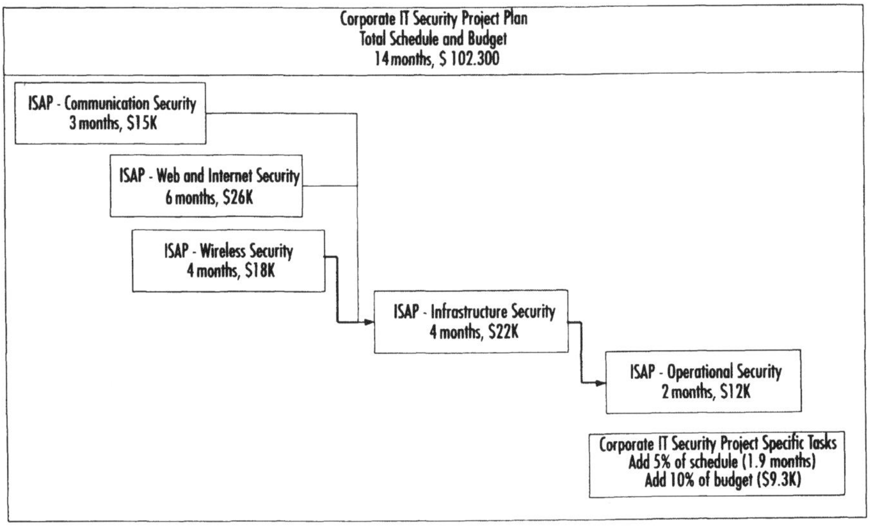

Alternately, you can define your schedule and your budget from the top-down, as shown in Figure 9.3. In this case, your total budget and schedule are defined and each ISAP underneath (as well as any "glue" tasks) are parsed out of the total. In this example, the total schedule allotted for your corporate IT security project plan is 18 months and your budget is $250,000. All of the ISAPs underneath are allocated a percentage or portion of the total. This may mean you have to scale time and budgets for the ISAPs down in order to meet your schedule and budget requirements, but you'd have to do that with either the approach anyway, since we're assuming you don't have unlimited time and unlimited funds to accomplish your goals.

Figure 9.3 Top-down Schedule and Budget Development

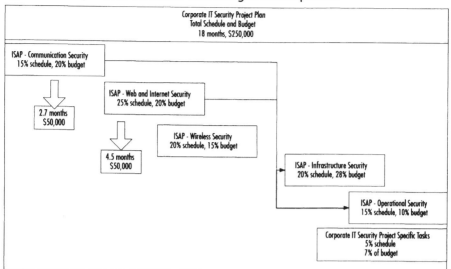

As with the bottom-up approach, some of your ISAPs may run in parallel or may begin before another project is complete. In the example shown in Figure 9.3, the wireless security plan begins when the Web and Internet project is about 50 percent complete, but that project can't commence until the communication plan is complete.

These examples are two ways you can incorporate your ISAPs into your corporate IT project plan and come up with a fairly accurate initial estimate for schedule and budget. It will have to be revised a number of times based on additional detail that is developed through the project planning stages, but deciding on your high-level approach to developing your corporate IT security project plan schedule and budget will help get you started for your initial estimates. This also gives you the opportunity to look at and address known parameters, constraints, and assumptions.

Business Intelligence…

Project Estimating: Part Science, Part Art

Project estimating—whether for scope, budget or schedule—is part science and part art. The science involves taking a consistent and methodical approach toward defining your tasks. The more detailed your WBS, the easier it becomes to define a unit of work (task) that can be clearly defined in terms of duration, effort, and cost. At the outset of project planning, you don't have that level of detail, but are often required to drawn a line in the sand and commit to the maximum cost and time the project will take. Dangerous waters, to be sure, but something we have to do almost daily. The process of defining the project schedule and cost can be termed *progressive elaboration* where you progressively gather more detail as you move through your project planning phases. The art form comes from understanding how to generate that initial estimate, how to manage expectations, and how to estimate various unknowns. As you become more experienced in project management and estimating, you should find that your estimates are closer to reality than fiction. That's the fine art of estimating.

Managing the Project

We're assuming that your corporate IT security project is a series of ISAPs and that you will manage them accordingly. You will have the additional burden of balancing conflicting demands for resources and addressing the impact of one ISAP on another. There is no cookie cutter approach that will work in all circumstances. Program management is outside the scope of this book, but suffice it to say that it will test your skills as a project manager.

Closing Out the Project

Any project close out includes standard steps (see Chapter 8), but closing out the corporate IT security project plan also includes a number of elements unique to this type of project. It's entirely possible that you want to perform another security test or audit once all work is completed before officially closing out the project. This is one last check before you close the books on this project, and hand off the management of security for day-to-day management by your IT staff. Along the way, you should have developed processes and procedures for maintaining security on an ongoing basis; developed user training and guidelines, and developed an updated set of documentation for your IT staff to review, modify, and update on an ongoing basis.

There may be particular tasks or duties that need to transition out of the project mode and into the maintenance mode. Ongoing operations should support, sustain, or even improve the security set through the project activities. Documents, processes, and procedures should be reviewed and finalized for the operational team.

As with other important projects, your high-level corporate IT security project plan may also require a large presentation to executives or other key staff. Don't miss this chance to tout your team's efforts and project results. Highlight the positive, calmly explain the negative, and if necessary, explain what you've learned and how it will benefit the company in the future.

Summary

We've covered a tremendous amount of territory in this chapter, with the intent of helping you define your corporate IT security project plan based on the specific needs of your organization. Your corporate IT security plan should start with a well-defined enterprise-wide security strategy. This is the glue that binds all of your security activities together and provides the rationale for all IT security activities. Ideally, this is developed prior to trying to plan your corporate IT security plan, but in some cases, it might make sense to list it as the first major objective in your plan.

We took a look at various legal standards related to your corporate IT security plan, because in this day and age, security has become a legal issue. While this chapter won't make you an attorney, it should have provided enough of an overview to help you understand the larger legal environment. Of course, you should consult your firm's legal counsel for additional information on the potential legal implications of security in your particular company.

The bulk of this chapter walked you through the standard project management steps with an eye toward corporate IT security project planning. While the generally accepted project management methods apply in this case, there are areas specific to corporate IT security planning that we called out along the way. These are typically high-level issues that should be addressed in a top-level project plan. We also noted areas where the corporate IT project plan provides the mortar or glue for the ISAPs. Each individual plan should be complete unto itself, but there are necessary connections between and among the ISAPs required to implement a comprehensive, holistic IT security solution for your company.

At the end of all of this, you should have a fairly clear view into how to approach your unique corporate IT security project plan. Every company and every IT security solution has standard components as well as very distinct organizational requirements. Your challenge is to apply standardize methodologies while addressing the aspects unique to your company and your IT environment. This chapter provided the foundation upon which to build your corporate IT security project plan.

Solutions Fast Track

Defining Your Security Strategy

☑ Your IT security strategy should be aligned with the business objectives of your organization.

☑ IT security strategies developed without aligning with business objectives are far less likely to benefit from executive support or to receive needed funding.

☑ The five key success factors for an IT security strategy are: 1) The skills, capabilities, and efforts of the entire organization must be utilized and mobilized, 2) Key functions and processes in the organization must collaborate on shared security goals and strategy, 3) The organization's security objectives or an articulation of its "desired state" must be developed and understood, 4) Critical assets that are essential to achieving the organization's mission must be identified and protected, and 5) IT operations and support must enable security goals.

☑ Your corporate IT security plans also have to align with the reality of your organization. You must live within the company's constraints, which may include budget, schedule, staffing, or other overarching organizational limitations.

Legal Standards Relevant to Corporate IT Security

☑ There are numerous federal laws that impact corporate IT security. Some of the more well-known ones include: GLBA, HIPAA, SOX, FISMA, FERPA, TEACH, ECPA, and CFAA.

☑ There are numerous state laws that pertain to corporate IT security that you should be familiar with, especially with regard to all states in which your company has a physical presence.

☑ There are three key fallacies that can trap corporate and IT staff when planning for IT security: The "Single Law" fallacy, the "Private Entity" fallacy, and the "Penetration Test Only" fallacy.

☑ There are a number of things you can do to reduce your company's legal liability including: Understand your legal environment, perform comprehensive and ongoing security assessments, evaluations, and implementations, use contracts to define rights and protect information, and use qualified third-party professionals.

☑ Nothing in this chapter or book should be construed as legal information or advice. You should consult with a qualified legal professional to assess your firm's specific legal liabilities and to develop optimal legal risk mitigation strategies.

Corporate IT Security Project Plan Overview

☑ Your corporate IT security project should be based on your overall security strategy for the organization.

☑ As with any project, you should define the problem you're trying to solve so your project solves the right problem.

☑ An integral part of the problem definition in IT security is the security assessment or audit.

☑ You may choose to perform the assessment as a separate project or as the first major task in your corporate IT security project plan.

☑ The remaining steps mirror standard project management steps: Define the desired (required) outcome(s), identify potential solutions, define project constraints, define project requirements, select optimal solution, define project team, define project procedures, define project WBS, tasks, owners, resources, budget and schedule, monitor and manage project, and hand off and close out project.

Corporate Security Auditing

☑ Security assessments and auditing are a natural first step for any IT security project. Your corporate IT security project may have such an assessment as the first major objective or you may develop your plan based on the outcome of a separate security assessment project.

☑ Security fails for a variety of reasons, the primary reasons being: Improper configuration, failure to update, faulty requirements, human factors, policy issues, and incorrect assumptions.

Corporate Security Project Parameters

☑ Your corporate IT security plan should start with defining the key objectives.

☑ Every project includes four parameters that must be balanced: scope, cost (budget), time (schedule), and quality.

☑ There are numerous skills needed for each IT security project. These generally can be organized into these categories: Operating system skills, network skills, application skills, security tools skills, programming skills, compiled languages and programming skills, and scripting languages.

☑ As part of the initial project definition, you will also need to identify the key personnel needed.

☑ Defining project processes and procedures is an important part of any IT project, but in the corporate IT security project plan, you need to define enterprise-wide processes to address the unique characteristics of this type of plan.

Project WBS

☑ Creating a WBS for your corporate IT security project may involve developing high-level tasks that include development of ISAPs as single task, or you may develop a WBS that pulls of the ISAPs in as separate project plans.

☑ There are numerous areas that must be addressed in the corporate IT security project plan including people, process, and technology.

☑ The WBS should include all subtasks and should be an iterative process to produce ever expanding levels of detail.

Project Risks

☑ Defining project risks and mitigation strategies is a fairly standard process, but at the corporate IT security project level, there are organizational issues that must be addressed.

☑ One risk unique to the corporate IT security strategy that you might not find in other types of IT projects is the legal risk.

Project Constraints

☑ If your corporate IT security project plan is well-aligned to your current business strategies, you should be able to identify your project constraints in a manner consistent with organizational goals.

☑ Understanding at a corporate level how scope, budget, schedule, and quality all come into play and what the priorities should be for both the corporate IT security project plan and the ISAPs, will help you manage the program (collection of related projects).

Project Assumptions

☑ Many of your project assumptions will be related to the underlying ISAPs, but they can also be captured in the corporate IT security project plan.

☑ Your high-level assumptions about your business environment are assumptions that should be captured in your plan. These may include assumptions about your overall level of funding in the coming year, planned acquisitions or divestitures, and so on.

Project Schedule and Budget

☑ When creating your corporate IT security project plan, your initial schedule and budget estimates can be developed using a bottom-up or top-down approach.

☑ A bottom-up approach allows you to create your best estimates for the underlying ISAPs, add some factor for the corporate IT security project-specific activities, and develop a top-level project schedule and budget.

☑ A top-down approach allows you to determine the total time and budget for all corporate IT security projects, and allocate time and dollars as percentages of the whole. This might be desirable if you have very specific deadlines and budgetary targets you're trying to meet.

☑ Running the corporate IT security project is like managing a program because you'll have to deal with potentially conflicting needs of the various ISAPs as well as corporate constraints.

☑ Closing out the project should include transitioning needed ongoing security activities to the daily operational staff. Documentation should be reviewed, revised, and finalized to provide the procedures, policies, and documentation needed to support, sustain, and improve security in the future.

Chapter 10

General IT Security Plan

Solutions in this chapter:

- IT Security Assessment and Audit
- Authentication
- Access Control
- Auditing
- Attacks
- Assessment and Audit Report
- General IT Security Project Parameters
- General IT Security Project Plan

☑ Summary
☑ Solutions Fast Track

Introduction

In this chapter, we provide the framework for creating a general Information Technology (IT) security project as part of your overall corporate IT security project plan strategy. As with all of the individual security area projects (ISAPs) discussed in this book, this is intended to be a template to use as a starting point. You might be wondering what a "general" IT security project plan consists of. In this chapter, we'll discuss the security assessment and auditing function in great detail. Most corporate IT security plans start with a thorough assessment so that the problem statement can be developed. As discussed in Chapter 9, you might perform your assessment as one of the major objectives of your corporate project, or you might implement the assessment as a separate project whose results feed into your corporate IT security project plan. Either way, your planning begins with an assessment, which is covered in detail here. We also look at access control, authentication, and attacks, and how to build a project plan that addresses these core areas.

IT Security Assessment and Auditing

For the purposes of this chapter, let's define assessment as the act of testing network security to determine the strength of current security measures. Furthermore, let's define auditing as the act of examining, recording, and evaluating security configurations. Clearly these two activities should work in tandem. If all you do is run some tests against your network, you've performed an assessment that might yield important information. However, if your test misses some critical area, you're still vulnerable. If you perform an audit, you might see that your server configuration is air-tight. Again, you might miss a vulnerability caused by the interaction of security in one network system (e.g., servers) and another network system (e.g., firewalls or routers). These two activities are, in a sense, two sides of the same coin and together they provide as complete a picture of your network security as possible. Let's begin by talking about assessments.

People are always the weakest link in security. Take the recent cases of hackers getting into corporate credit card databases. In many of these recent stories, someone on the inside of the organization made a poor decision (whether malicious or not) about how to handle the data, resulting in a vulnerability that was exploited by an outsider. Social engineering, lack of awareness of security best practices, and malicious intent are ranked very high on the list of vulnerabilities from the people perspective. Assessing your vulnerabilities from a people perspective should include these methods.

Processes are the security processes maintained by the company from top to bottom. Vulnerabilities occur because IT security processes, such as analyzing key network traffic, are poorly defined or poorly executed. Corporate policies with regard to security processes often fall behind known threats and fail to address new threats. A good example is having a policy about reporting new or unexpected equipment found on or near one's desk. Since rogue wireless networks are easy to install, if employees are not vigilant about investigating new or unusual equipment (they often assume someone from IT put it there), there is a risk. In addition, if IT policy doesn't specifically define a procedure for installing new equipment, you are losing an opportunity to maintain security. It's a two-sided process. IT should define clear procedures for how things will work, so that users can be educated as to standard operating procedures. Both groups can therefore keep an eye out for rogue or unusual activity that falls outside standard policies and procedures. In addition, processes such as how employees are removed from access control lists when they leave the organization, should be part of the assessment to ensure standard procedures maintain strong security.

Technology vulnerabilities are the most tangible of the three vulnerabilities and are the ones that most people in IT start out looking for. While these are found in abundance in technical trade magazines and Web sites, don't make the mistake of thinking that the most important vulnerabilities are those with the actual technology. While important, they are part of this triad of people, process and technology that, when addressed holistically, gives your network the highest possible security. In many ways, assessments, access control, authentication, and auditing address all three aspects of security. There are technology assessments and risk assessments, both of which are discussed in this section.

Business Intelligence...

Lingo

For what it's worth, the National Security Agency (NSA) and the National Institute of Standards and Technology (NIST) use slightly different lingo. They use management (people), operations (process), and technology. In *How to Cheat at IT Project Management* and throughout this companion book, we use the terms people, process, and technology, which are slightly different but the intent is the same.

We can also look at security through a layered approach. In fact, the more ways you parse out your environment, the more likely you are to find vulnerabilities. In Figure 10.1, you can see that your first line of defense consists of your policies, procedures, and user awareness. These form the foundation of all network security, because people and process are two of the three major components of security. The physical environment includes physical access to equipment and the general security of the facility. If a hacker gains legitimate (though unauthorized) access to someone's desk and is able to root around amongst all the sticky notes to find a username and password, you essentially have wasted all those thousands (or millions) of dollars on protecting the network from outside attack. Finally, there are both physical and virtual security elements related to the perimeter, the internal network, servers and hosts, applications and databases, and the data itself. The virtual elements include all the ways someone could access this information from outside the organization, while the physical elements include the ways someone could physically access these components.

Figure 10.1 Layered Approach to Network Security

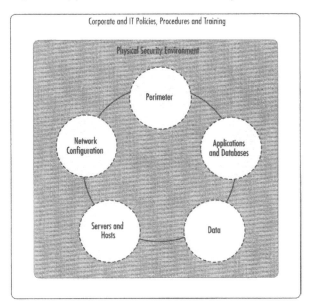

Perimeter or Boundaries

First, you should define your perimeter and determine where your border areas are. (Some people use the term "perimeter," and others prefer the term "boundaries.") Be clear that the perimeters or boundaries are either physical or logical. The port of a router is a physical boundary. A network segment is a physical boundary. The Internet Protocol (IP) subnet is a logical boundary. The responsibility for securing data from Point A to Point B is a logical boundary. Next, you should define the components that protect your perimeter, which typically include firewalls, routers, proxy servers, and Demilitarized Zones (DMZ's), to mention a few. After user awareness and adherence to policies and procedures, your perimeter defense is often your first line of defense against external attacks. Remember, many attacks or security breaches are internal, so an obsessive fixation with just the perimeter is not going to keep your network safe.

Internal Network

How your network is configured and segmented is of great interest to hackers, because once they learn this, they can navigate easily through your entire internal network. Information regarding the segmentation and addressing of network segments as well as the presence and configuration of any network intrusion detection systems (IDS), would also be a real bonus for a hacker, and would provide a great jump start to many types of intrusive attacks.

Servers and Hosts

Information about the types, locations, and numbers of servers and hosts (for our purposes, any non-server network device with an IP address,) is great information for a hacker. This is an area where a fair amount of effort is expended to harden the devices against attack. System hardening includes tasks such as disabling unused protocols and ports, removing unused applications, implementing access control and authentication requirements, maintaining up-to-date anti-virus, anti-spyware applications, maintaining up-to-date operating systems and applications, and performing ongoing and meaningful intrusion detection and auditing functions.

Applications and Databases

Applications and databases are also common targets for attackers. If a hacker can gain access to an application, he or she might be able to modify data, insert data, or steal data. The same holds true for a database application except that with databases, there is often a wealth of information a hacker would really like to get their hands on. In addition, sometimes the objective is to simply corrupt the database to cause financial or political problems for the company. Think of a database used for an online application in which a hacker changes the product pricing or inserts bad language into the product description. Think of a database that becomes corrupted, and mailings regarding the results of Human Immunodeficiency Virus (HIV) testing are mailed to people's work addresses instead of home addresses. The list of possibilities is endless, and part of your assessment should be how the data could be corrupted and what the potential implications of such a result would be.

Data

Ultimately, hackers want data of all kinds. Sometimes the hacker doesn't know exactly what data he or she wants, but they'll take whatever they can get their hands on. Sometimes there's a ripple effect to data acquisition. A hacker might start with just the name of a technical contact listed in the WHOIS database for a Uniform Resource Locator (URL). He then uses that information to call the company and, through social engineering, convince the technical contact to give him the username and password for the account on the hosting company's Web site. He or she then logs on and installs some tracking software. Now, every time a customer logs into his or her account on your Web site, the bad guy gets instant access. Clearly, this is just one type of data a hacker can use, but you can see how it can ripple down into your organization.

Unfortunately, there is a lot of public information out there on both publicly and privately owned companies. There is no way to avoid that. However, a good rule of thumb is to only disclose required information, and to verify the entity you are disclosing the information to. Let's look at some of the kinds of data a hacker might put to use.

Contact Information

As mentioned, various kinds of contact information can be extremely useful to attackers. They can use it to represent themselves as an employee or agent of the company, or they can use it to talk to the internal contact directly, pretending to be a legitimate external representative of a service provider. Employee names, mailing addresses, e-mail addresses, and phone numbers are excellent resources for social engineering.

Business Information

Who are your company's business partners? Who are your vendors, suppliers, and contractors? This information is also extremely helpful for an attacker, because it can be used to impersonate people with legitimate ties to your company. In addition, if your company is acquiring or divesting another company or division, it creates security holes that can be exploited by an attacker who is aware of this activity.

Extranet and Remote Access

While extranets and remote access channels are great tools for employees and vendors for a variety of purposes, unfortunately they are also magnets for hackers. Especially vulnerable are accounts used by external business partners, which typically use weak or default passwords. Unused or forgotten modems are another great source of unauthorized remote access.

Valid User Accounts

To a hacker, valid user accounts with passwords are the mother lode, but even just a valid user account is a great starting point. It provides the attacker with information about the format of your user accounts and allows them to quickly figure out other valid user names based on the contact information provided. Some companies use a different username format than their e-mail addresses to protect the user login format information (e.g., your e-mail address format might be *first initial_lastname@ yourcompany.com* whereas your user login information might be *first name_middle initial_first four letters of your last name*. While it's a bit more difficult for users to remember, they'll quickly get the hang of it. It won't necessarily prevent a hacker from figuring out your username format, but it might slow them down a bit. It might also help you to see any attempts at brute-force attacks, if they follow the format for your e-mail addresses and not your standard username format.

   If an attacker has a valid user account and can figure out the format, he or she can then start a brute-force attack to crack the password. Thus, protecting user account formats is one half of the equation; the other half is requiring strong passwords.

System Configuration

System configuration information is also extremely valuable to an
attacker, because he or she can determine what types of attacks to launch.
If someone knows you're running Microsoft Windows Server 2003, he or
she can specifically attack vulnerabilities of those systems, including
exploiting systems that have not been kept up-to-date with critical security patches. An example of this can be found at www.netcraft.com.

Business Intelligence...

Deterrence Tactics

An alarm on your car doesn't prevent it from being stolen, it simply
deters the would-be thief. They have to think twice about whether or
not they can boost your car before someone pays attention to the alarm.
Similarly, protecting your corporate data from attacker reconnaissance
missions is not going to increase your security, it will simply help deter
would-be hackers. Putting up barriers wherever you can without
impeding your own business processes (or without unduly impeding
users) reduces the chances that an attacker will select your network as a
target. In the end, your layered security systems are what will protect
you, but why not make it as difficult as possible for a would-be attacker
to get any helpful information?

Types of Security Assessments

There are various types of assessments you can perform on your overall
network security. We're not going to go into complete detail here,
because these topics are large and ever-changing. However, there are two
major categories worth addressing: vulnerability scanning and pen testing.

Vulnerability Scanning

Vulnerability scanning slices both ways. You're doing it to keep the bad guys out and the bad guys are doing it to find a way in. From the IT administrator's perspective, the goal of vulnerability scanning is to identify devices on the network that are open to known vulnerabilities. Despite your best efforts, there will always be new vulnerabilities discovered, and your activities in this area will likely be almost non-stop. However, you have to begin from a known starting point, and performing vulnerability scanning begins with addressing the obvious first. Also, keep in mind that vulnerabilities encompass people, processes, and technology, so be sure to look at all three areas when addressing vulnerabilities. It doesn't matter how locked down your systems are if you have a power user lose a laptop or hand out a password to someone posing as an IT staffer. Also, keep in mind that penetration (pen) testing is not useful for scanning for vulnerabilities if the system hasn't been secured. Other methods are more productive on the front end; pen testing can be more helpful on the back end after security measures have been implemented.

Enumeration

The most common type of vulnerability scanning is done using software tools that attempt to enumerate, or list, all of the network components. Enumeration includes scanning to identify network segments, IP ranges, IP addresses, network configuration, names, addresses, and version numbers for network devices, protocols, ports, versions, users, groups, directories, patches, updates and any other information about the network. Enumeration is possible because system vulnerabilities lead to unauthorized exposure of important system information and because system capabilities are actually designed to help administrators manage networked systems, which also helps attackers. When vulnerabilities exist, they allow for exposure of information that can be exploited by an attacker.

Security Mistakes

Most organizations have a lot of data stored in various locations, directories, and servers across the enterprise. Are you absolutely sure each of those areas is properly secured? Systems are often configured to replicate settings from the top of the hierarchy down through the lower layers of the directory or file hierarchy. Did those settings replicate properly? Were the original settings correct, or were mistakes replicated throughout the organization as well? These kinds of security mistakes can create huge security holes; therefore, vulnerability scanning should look for weak passwords, incorrect user, file, or folder permissions, default configurations, and unused features that should be disabled. In addition to errors, you also need to ascertain whether any settings have been altered or modified by a user within your organization. If a user's permissions were accidentally misconfigured, he or she may have had the ability (even if for a short time) to increase their permission levels or even create a new user account for themselves.

Known Vulnerabilities

Known vulnerabilities are the first things exploited by attackers, but they're also addressed by software makers through patches and updates. While a vulnerability might become known before a patch is available, often the patch is available before the attacker finds your network and your vulnerability. Such was the case in 2003, when the Blaster virus hit many corporate networks. The patch had been available for about three weeks before the attack occurred, but many organizations' computers were not patched; best estimates place the infection rate at about 500,000 computers. Patching and updating are important in addressing known vulnerabilities, and since 2003, most organizations have developed better systems for patch and update management. Microsoft has new tools available, including the automatic update feature on desktop systems and the Microsoft Security Baseline Analyzer tool that allows you to scan for known vulnerabilities from a Microsoft systems perspective. Some scanning tools look for registry settings to determine whether or not the system is up-to-date, and more extensive programs attack the system via the known vulnerabilities to see how it responds. A wide variety of tools are readily available and are usually a good investment for companies of all sizes. However, remember, these tools are also available to the bad guys.

Common Attacks

Vulnerability scanning has to look at both sides of the equation. Are known vulnerabilities addressed? Are known attacks addressed? There are many known attacks and attack methods that should be addressed in your security assessment. It's not enough to cover known vulnerabilities; it's possible that if you simulate attacks on your network you may uncover previously unknown vulnerabilities. Not all vulnerabilities can be patched or updated. Some vulnerabilities are the result of the interaction of two or more network components or systems. Therefore, it's important that you include common attack scenario testing in your security assessment.

Pen Testing

Pen testing by itself proves nothing. So what if you can penetrate an insecure network? It's akin to walking in the open front door of a house; it doesn't tell you if the locks work. Second, pen testing is by no means comprehensive. In fact, it is like a laser; it goes directly at a particular target in a very focused manner. It will give you a result based on a specific circumstance, but it won't give you a broad overview of your network security. If you're going to use pen testing as a tool, start with the "low hanging fruit"; in other words, make sure the front door is locked, and then work your way up from there. Performing pen testing after a security project is far more useful than doing it beforehand, so be sure you understand when and why you'd use pen testing in IT security projects. Be clear about what the results of a pen test will tell you, not what you assume they'll tell you. As an assessment tool, pen testing should be limited in scope (e.g., if you believe some specific part of your network is locked down you might perform a pen test on that area to verify your assumption).

Pen testing can be a tricky area, because you essentially have to hack your own network. So, before you head off to do a pen test, make sure you have the appropriate sign-off from corporate executives. The last thing you need is for you or one of your staff to be falsely accused of attacking the network when, in fact, you were legitimately testing the security of the network. Having a security testing plan in hand and getting sign off from your project sponsor is the best way to ensure there are no negative repercussions. Also keep in mind that an inexperienced pen tester could cause unintended problems ranging from minor to severe. Think carefully about how and when these tests should be carried out and by whom. If you retain an outside firm to perform this type of testing, be sure they come well-recommended and with the appropriate credentials and a spotless reputation. Also, make sure that they sign the appropriate paperwork to shield you and them from liability. Finally, keep in mind that many companies think that hiring an outside firm to "just do the pen testing" is sufficient. What they fail to realize is that performing pen testing absent other security planning and implementation activities, can actually lay the company wide open for legal liability. If you are aware of the problem but do not take "reasonable care" in addressing it, you could be worse off than not knowing about the vulnerability in the first place.

Keep in mind that the ultimate goal of pen testing is to obtain administrator-level privileges. Therefore, your testing should start from the same place as an outsider—without a username or password. Pen testing usually tries to exploit known vulnerabilities first, so this is a logical place to start. Not all vulnerabilities can be addressed, however. Remember, there is a limit to what you can protect and what you should protect. In keeping the balance between security and cost and security and reasonable business operations, you will probably find yourself making conscious trade-offs between security and other business objectives. Therefore, you may have to be creative and find alternate ways to address vulnerabilities besides simply closing and locking the door on them.

There are various methodologies you can use to perform a pen test. Here's one to get you started:

1. Think like the attacker. Determine how the attacker would most likely try to attack your network. This normally begins by locating all publicly available information on the target and using that information as a starting point.

2. Locate vulnerabilities and areas of weakness. Use the elements in Figure 10.1 to ensure you're looking across the entire enterprise.

3. Determine all the ways (currently known) a hacker could exploit the vulnerabilities and weaknesses found in Step 2.

4. Determine which assets might be attacked to access, alter, or destroy data based on the likely attack scenarios defined in Step 1 and the vulnerabilities identified in Step 2.

5. Determine whether an attack can be detected. If you are performing a pen test, determine if you were able to detect the attack, either in real-time or in retrospect.

6. Determine the attack footprint. The attack footprint is the size of the target. If you're shooting an arrow, it's harder to hit the stem of a plant than the side of a barn. The same holds true for your network. Determine how big a target you're providing.

7. Analyze results, formulate remediation strategy, and implement.

Risk Assessment

We know there is a trade-off between total security and total risk. There are financial and operational trade-offs that every organization must make. In the risk assessment phase of your audit, you need to look at your risks in four specific categories: *asset protection, threat prevention, legal liabilities*, and *costs*. This is a good time to sit down with key stakeholders, including your executive sponsor or team, your financial, legal, human resources, and operational experts to determine what your company's specific risks are. As mentioned in Chapter 5, your IT security project plan team membership will likely change as you move through the phases of your project. Risk assessment is a part of the initial definition stage, and should include all of the key stakeholders you can think of. At this point, it might be better to invite too many people to attend this meeting rather than too few. Anyone who finds their participation is not needed can opt-out, but you want to avoid forgetting a key player who can help you and your IT team perform a thorough risk assessment.

The risk assessment itself should be thorough; skimp here and you will likely end up with a less-than-optimal security solution. Even if your company can't afford to implement all the recommended security solutions, at least you'll have a thorough assessment of what's needed. This may be important later on, because if a security breach does occur, you can point to documentation showing that your assessment indicated the breached area was a risk (which might save your job down the line). However, rather than be right later on, use the results of the assessment to pro-actively push for a bigger budget and implement those changes now. If there's documentation showing that you were aware of the potential security risk and did not implement a solution, your firm might have a huge legal and financial liability on its hands. So, the thorough assessment cuts both ways. It gives you the data you need to make your case for appropriate funding, but it can also be used by attorneys to prove your company was aware of the risk and chose not to act.

Risk Assessment: Asset Protection

As we have continually stressed throughout this book, you have to find the right balance between protecting corporate assets and the cost of doing so. In any network assessment scenario, you should begin by understanding what you're trying to protect and why. You may have adequately addressed this issue during your overall IT corporate security planning process. If so, you should review the data, assumptions, and outcomes at this stage to ensure your conclusions are still relevant and correct. Things change so quickly in most corporate environments, that a quick review of previous assessment data is almost always a good use of your time. You should review what data is on your corporate network and what needs to be protected. This is also a good time to find out what is on your corporate network that perhaps should not be. If you recall the case studies from Chapter 1, it's not uncommon for corporate networks to store confidential data on the corporate network, such as credit card numbers or social security numbers.

In addition to discovering what is on your network (and what's there but shouldn't be), you also need to assess the relative value of that data. While it can be argued that all corporate data is valuable, some data is clearly more valuable than other types of data. Remember that you need to think like a hacker to make these assessments. A list of nuts, bolts, and cable lengths are not worth as much in value as personal data such as credit card numbers, social security numbers, and bank access codes. Correlate the data on your network with the perceived value of the data to an outsider, to understand the relative risk to your network. This will help you determine how much security is appropriate for your specific situation.

A good example of this is a home wireless network. Most people using home wireless networks for things such as logging onto their online brokerage account or doing some online shopping with a credit card, do not secure them. This data is transmitted in an unsecured manner from their laptop or wireless device to their wireless access point, and then to the router or cable modem and out to the Internet. How likely is it that a hacker is going to grab that data? If you live in a dense urban setting where a hacker can sit in a nearby coffee shop and peruse wireless data like yours, then the likelihood is high. If you live in a more suburban or rural setting where it would be difficult for someone to get close enough to receive your wireless signal, the risk drops significantly. If you're in an urban setting and you run an unsecured wireless network, your risk is probably four times higher than someone in a more rural setting. That said, your overall risk is still about 50 times lower than that of any corporate network, because a hacker would have to sift through a fair amount of mundane wireless traffic at someone's home before being able to grab usernames, passwords, and so forth; the upside potential for that hacker is minimal. Why go after a single person's data if you can access thousands or millions of people's data? Looking at the risk/reward proposition from a hacker's perspective will help you assess the relative value of your assets and what level of protection is warranted. Keep in mind there is always the hacker of convenience, who hacks because he or she can, whether there is a big payoff or not.

Sensitive Data

Sensitive data is defined differently from one company to the next. What's sensitive at one company may not be sensitive at another. However, in most companies, there are clearly segments of data that are sensitive and, therefore, your security audit should identify those areas. As part of your corporate security project plan definition stage, you must clearly understand how sensitive your corporate data is. It goes beyond the legal implications and into the business aspects. Lists of customers, vendors, suppliers, or employees can be sensitive, especially if you're in a medical setting. Trade secrets, formulas, and research and development (R&D) data can be extremely sensitive, especially in industries that work in leading edge or groundbreaking areas. This is a great place to get feedback and input from the various departments in your company. Ask them what data they work with that they would not wanted posted on a Web site or printed in a newspaper. That usually gets people's attention and helps them to begin looking at the data they work with on a daily basis from a slightly different perspective. Here's a quick list of data typically considered sensitive:

- Customer databases
- Employee lists
- Identity information (e.g., customer, employee, vendor)
- Credit card or other financial data
- Health information
- Intellectual property
- Trade secrets
- R&D

Remember, too, that there are two ways sensitive data is at risk. First, it can be stolen and used inappropriately by your competition, your

www.syngress.com

employees, or by those who can gain financially from the data. Second, it can be compromised. Imagine the damage that could be done if a publicly held corporation's financial statements were changed without the company's knowledge, just before being released to the Securities and Exchange Commission (SEC) or just before a major announcement. Sensitive data must be protected from theft and from modification. Keep that in mind when you're looking at your corporate IT security auditing plans.

Network Services and Business Operations

Sometimes an attacker is less interested in stealing or compromising data than they are in disrupting business operations (e.g., shutting down a Web site through a Denial of Service (DOS) attack, or corrupting a customer database or modifying financial statements). Whether it's the external link (Web site) or the internal network, some hackers are simply looking to undermine the availability of the network. There are numerous areas to look for vulnerabilities in business and network operations. The following is a list to start with; your organization may have additional operations that need to be included on this list.

- Internet connectivity
- Web site connectivity
- Web-based applications
- Database services
- Directory services
- File services
- E-mail services
- Virus and intrusion prevention and detection services
- Custom application services
- Voice over IP (VoIP) services

Take an inventory of the various ways your company uses the network and electronic communications to understand the vulnerabilities that your corporate IT security project plan should address. More than likely, you'll want to create ISAPs to address the various categories, because smaller projects are more manageable.

Risk Assessment: Threat Prevention

Threat prevention starts with the IT security project problem statement. What problems are we trying to solve with this project? In other words, what threats do we perceive that we need to address? What is the company trying to protect through these security measures? What kinds of threats are likely or possible? Are you most concerned about an attack, a theft, or a breach and which is most likely to occur? Answering these questions will help you define your problem and your outcome statements, and will also help form a solid foundation for your corporate IT security project plan.

Because past security measures may be in place, there is not always a direct relationship between the importance of data and the threat to that data. If you process credit card transactions through a third-party company, you do not store the credit card data any longer than it takes to transmit it to that third-party company. Also, if all of your transactions are conducted using a secure Internet protocol (Hyper Text Transfer Protocol Secure sockets [HTTPS] and so forth), the risk of credit card data being stolen from your company is fairly low. When looking at your threats and vulnerabilities, you should rank both the importance (the relative financial value) of the data and the relative threat or risk to that data. You want to make sure your most important data is properly secured while also ensuring that your biggest vulnerabilities are addressed. By identifying vulnerabilities and their likelihood of occurrence, you can create a prioritized list that will help you make smart decisions should you be forced to choose to implement only a portion of your total corporate IT security strategy. If you need to stage your corporate IT security project implementation to meet the financial needs of the company (e.g., breaking it down into phases that can be funded each fiscal quarter), this prioritized list can also help you decide which projects should be addressed during each phase of funding.

Denial of Service

A DOS attack is usually launched at a company's Web site with the clear intention of making it unavailable to legitimate users. However, a DOS attack can also be launched in a variety of ways to deny service to Web sites, Internet access, network access, or wireless network access. When looking at your vulnerability to a DOS attack, don't just look at the risk to your Web site; look at the risk to any network component that provides vital business service that could be attacked.

Unauthorized Access

The threat of unauthorized access to network resources comes in various forms, all of which must be considered. It's important to assess any points of entry (e.g., the Web site, any dial-in communications that are still enabled (remember, you may not use dial-in access any more, but you may still have modems with live phone lines connected to your servers that have never been removed); network login and wireless access points are the most common. In addition, unauthorized access can be gained through various protocols being left open including Simple Network Management Protocol (SNMP), telnet, serial ports, and a variety of Transmission Control Protocol (TCP)/IP ports. Using default settings on routers and wireless access points also leaves you vulnerable to unauthorized access, as does providing more lenient access to users and user accounts than needed. Finally, there is the issue of social engineering that is often successfully used on sophisticated IT staff and unsuspecting users alike, in order to gain access to legitimate network credentials and to unauthorized.

Identity Theft

Identity theft is on the rise and while most people assume it happens as a result of online fraud, there are numerous ways identity theft can occur. However, we confine our discussion of identity theft to the kinds most likely to occur within the business environment. As we've repeatedly discussed, any company that collects, stores, or transfers credit card data can be a source of identity theft. In addition, companies that collect, store, or transfer other personal information including names with addresses, social security numbers, and various account numbers (mortgage, brokerage account, bank account, insurance, and so on) can also be a source for information used to steal someone's identity. It's also important to secure employee's personal data including the above-mentioned information, because even a company with 50 employees is a decent coup for someone attempting identity theft.

Individual consumers must take steps to secure and protect their personal information when interacting with businesses; however, even then there are limits to what a consumer can do. Take the well-publicized cases discussed in Chapter 1. Those are clear indicators that businesses are the more likely target for identity theft, since hackers would clearly like to get their hands on 100,000 names and not just one or two. It's critical that you take an inventory of the data your company collects, stores, and transfers, and identify any data that could be used to perpetrate identity theft on your consumers, your employees, or any other individuals your company deals with.

Personal Information Exposure

Personal information exposure can be the source of identity theft, but it's not exactly the same thing. Exposure of personal information could be private or personal data that would not necessarily facilitate identity theft but some other type of harm. For example, suppose a medical supply company's list of people and their associated medical problems was stolen and that the information was made public. That information couldn't be used to steal someone's identity, but it could reveal other personal information that customers don't want to share. If your company has any sort of sensitive information including age, marital status, vacation schedules, alarm codes, and so forth, your firm could be liable if that information is stolen and used in any malicious way. A recent episode of a new television program featured a group of robbers that broke into an architectural firm and stole blueprints to a bank. While such a robbery would be outside your control, if a hacker broke into your network and stole the electronic blueprints to someone's home, another company, or a financial institution, your company could be held liable for a related robbery.

At the risk of redundancy, review all of the data your company stores, even data that appears to be useless to outsiders, and think about how that data could be used if it fell into the wrong hands.

Credit Card Fraud

We've talked extensively about personal information and we've referred repeatedly to credit card information as some of the most sensitive information companies work with. For most hackers, the bigger the potential gain, the more desirable the target. Therefore, any company that runs an online store is clearly a more interesting target than a home computer. Online stores use secure Web protocols to ensure personal information, including credit card data, is secure when the user data is transmitted via the Internet to the company's Web site. Many smaller e-commerce sites use a third-party credit card processing company to handle the entire credit card transaction so that the data never sits on the company's server for more than the time it takes to authorize the transaction. Still, there is a vulnerability there. Hackers can compromise the Web site, redirect Web traffic, spoof the URL, send bogus e-mail that appears to be from your company and your Web site, redirect users to an alternate URL; the list goes on and on. Also, keep in mind that the threat is increased if you have an unsecured wireless network connected to your wired network. Any hacker than can gain access through the wireless network can work his or her way onto the wired network and into your credit card data.

Corporate Trade Secrets or Competitive Data

We can become so focused on personal user data such as social security numbers or credit card numbers, we might easily overlook corporate trade secrets or competitive data. There's a long list of information that can be considered trade secrets or competitive data. The list for your company will be very specific to the business you're in. We've included a generic list to help prompt your own investigation of data that could be considered confidential to your company. These include:

- Customer or employee databases (used to steal customers or employees)

- E-mails among employees discussing confidential matters

- E-mails among executives discussing company secrets, financial status, or future plans

- Competitive information

- Formulas for products and descriptions of soon-to-be released products

- Design specifications, engineering specifications, and technical diagrams or drawings for current or new products

- Confidential reports, audits, or memoranda

- Personnel files, performance reviews, pay rates

- Financial reports

- Source code for software projects

- Marketing or technical project plans

Unfortunately, due to the variety of data listed here, it's often difficult to definitively point to one or two network locations where this type of sensitive information exists. Usually, it's spread across the enterprise in department-level folders, on e-mail servers, and on individual desktops and laptops. As part of your corporate IT security planning process, you may decide to designate specific locations for this type of sensitive data, to be sure it's properly backed up on a regular basis, and so that you can control, monitor, and audit access to these files. In addition, pay special attention to executives and others who might have access to sensitive information and who travel with laptops. There have been several well-known cases of laptops with confidential or sensitive data being stolen from hotel rooms, locked cars, and airports. In some cases, the thief is just after the laptop. In worst case scenarios, these thefts constitute industrial espionage and are intended to garner trade secrets from a competitor or to steal plans, information, or other sensitive data.

Malicious Data Insertion

Malicious data insertion is a huge problem that is on the rise. Part of the reason is the increase in Internet usage and in the collaboration of malicious software (malware) writers. Hackers are getting along well these days, working together to create bigger corporate security headaches. Malicious data insertion is a risk to every computer on the planet, save those that (for some reason) are completely isolated from the Internet. The risk to individual user computers is clear: malware can steal user names and passwords, track where you go on the Internet, capture your instant messaging, and copy your e-mail. Pretty scary stuff. In the corporate environment, that problem is multiplied by the number of hours the average user is on the network, the type of data carried on the corporate network, and the number of potential "back doors" available to hackers.

Rootkits are one of the most malicious and growing forms of malicious data insertion (see the following sidebar), but they're not the only problems. Viruses, worms, corrupted or modified data, illegal, illicit, or unethical data can all be inserted into your network. We often think of security as preventing unwanted intrusion, which it is, but we sometimes forget that when the bad guys get in, they often want to leave something on your computer so they can continue to siphon data.

In addition, this malicious code can cause computers to become unstable which can result in thousands of lost hours and dollars trying to recover from these incidents. Some viruses or malware are intended to do nothing more than cause the computer to run slowly, generate errors, become unstable, or simply not boot.

Malicious data can also involve inserting bad, erroneous, or illegal data into the company's network. Think about the last time you shopped online: almost every online store uses some sort of database to present product information, including product name, description, specifications, and price. What if a hacker inserted data into that database so that the pricing was wrong, or a competitor's products were displayed, or the company's President's social security number was displayed instead of the product number? In some cases, hackers are pulling a prank; in others, they want to create serious problems and may specifically target a company they want to disrupt.

Business Intelligence…

Malware Threat Rises

An article written by Matt Hines in an April 2006 issue of eWeek.com is titled *Rootkits, Smarter Hackers Pose Growing Security Threats*. The article points to a study released by anti-virus maker, McAfee, on the growing sophistication of hackers and malware writers. According to the article, "Factoring into the issue, and the continued maturation of malicious attacks on enterprise systems, is the growing tendency toward collaboration among hackers." McAfee said its research indicates that the use of so-called 'stealth technologies' has jumped by over 600 percent during the last three years."

    If you're not already aware, a rootkit is a set of software tools typically used by an attacker to hide unauthorized activity on the computer, and to evade anti-virus program detection. The tools are intended to conceal processes, files, or data running on the computer in order to evade detection. The issue made headlines in 2005, when Sony BMG music CDs placed a rootkit on Microsoft computers in order to prevent CD copying.

    A recent report by Microsoft, the biggest target for hackers, announced it was practically impossible in some cases to get rid of a rootkit. In a separate eWeek.com article, Ryan Naraine reported that Mike Danseglio, program manager in the Security Solutions group at Microsoft, stated at a presentation at the InfoSec World conference that, "When you are dealing with rootkits and some advanced spyware programs, the only solution is to rebuild from scratch. In some cases, there really is no way to recover without nuking the systems from orbit." In fact, when a branch of the U.S. government discovered over 2,000 user computers infected with a rootkit, it had no viable way to quickly scrub those systems and reinstall the operating system.

Continued

www.syngress.com

As malware threats rise, it's even more important to train users, lock down systems, and have a solid plan in place for wiping out systems and starting from scratch if malware can't be removed in any other way. Be sure your audit looks for these problems as part of your project plan, and as part of your ongoing security operations. (See http://www.eweek.com/article2/0,1895,1949650,00.asp, http://www.eweek.com/article2/0,1895,1945782,00.asp.)

Equipment Theft or Damage

The threat of equipment theft or damage should be carefully assessed and is typically addressed through physical security planning; how buildings, offices, servers, and other network resources are physically secured. Obviously, some items are easier to steal or break than others. It's pretty hard to sneak out of a building with a desktop computer under your coat, but a blade server, router, or laptop is much easier. Your threat assessment should include taking a look at your physical premises to determine how easy (or hard) it would be for someone (insider or outsider) to steal or damage equipment. Network, communication, Web, database, and application servers would be at the top of the list and should be physically secured. Beyond servers, there are plenty of network resources that, if stolen or damaged, could hinder or halt business operations. Items such as routers, gateways, hardware firewalls, and network storage devices are critical to daily operations, and should be included in your physical security assessment.

Risk Assessment: Legal Liabilities

You may need executive or legal input to understand the company's legal liabilities, so make sure you have the right people involved in this assessment. For example: A specialty food distribution company sells to other businesses and directly to consumers through an online Web store. The company carries an inventory of about 5,000 products and its product catalog is available online. It keeps track of various data (e.g., business customers' purchase orders, order history, returns, and so forth.; consumer names, addresses, phone numbers, and order history; and vendor order history, stocking levels, pricing, transportation costs, and discounts. It processes credit cards through a third-party credit card processing company, and does not store credit card numbers, expiration dates, or related data. What are the company's legal liabilities? On the vendor side, they're pretty low because the data is probably not very interesting to most hackers (excluding industrial espionage). On the customer side, the business customer's order numbers, order history, and purchase order numbers are also not particularly useful to a hacker, unless someone wants a list of customers. Again, not particularly useful or lucrative data to go after. Finally, the consumer data (e.g., credit card information, expiration dates, names, addresses, phone numbers, and so forth. What's the liability here? If the company has a secure connection to the credit card processing company, and if they never store that data, then the liability is more limited than if they inappropriately store credit card data in order to do a bit of "data mining." However, the security of the transmission between the credit card processing Web site and the company Web site should be assessed, as should the overall security of the Web site itself.

As you can see, by looking at your business processes from the hacker's perspective, you can better determine where your legal liabilities lie and how best to address them. It's important to understand what a hacker might go after and what the legal liabilities are in each of those scenarios. Make sure you also understand what, if any, legal protection your firm has in the event of a breach, and what impact a breach might have on your organization such as blacklisting your domain name due to unauthorized spamming stemming from a breach. Make sure to include your firm's legal representative in this discussion, to make sure you haven't overlooked any legal elements. For a more detailed look at legal liabilities, pick up another Syngress title, *Network Security Evaluation: Using the NSA IEM* (see Chapter 5).

Third-party Attacks

Third party attacks are most common in the wireless arena, where an attacker (usually a spammer) sends unsolicited e-mail via your network connection. It's simple enough once an attacker gains access through an unsecured wireless network connection. In those cases, it is your net-work's IP address that will be tagged as the source of this spam, even though no one from your company actually sent the e-mail. Many states are instituting legal and financial penalties for spamming, and your com-pany could be found liable for spam it never sent. Beyond the possible legal and financial penalties, your networks' IP address could be black-listed or shutdown due to this type of activity, unless you have some way of proving you were the victim of a third-party attack. Even then, restoring order and connectivity can be extremely difficult. Another growing and disconcerting kind of attack are zombie nets, which are Distributed Denial of Service (DDOS) attacks.

Illegal Data Insertion

We talked about malicious data insertion, but we didn't specifically discuss the legal liabilities that can come from it (as opposed to malware, rootkits, and so on). There are two ways illegal data ends up on your network. First, stolen content could be placed on your network from an attacker who gains unauthorized access to the network. They may place stolen data there in order to blackmail the company, to embarrass the company, or to get the company in legal hot water. Suppose a hacker (or disgrun-tled employee) places unlicensed, stolen software on your network and then reports your company to the authorities? Suppose a competitor's blueprints or technical drawings end up on your network and it is somehow discovered? These kinds of activities may not steal your data, but they can certainly disrupt business operations, cost a lot of money, and create significant legal liabilities.

Risk Assessment: Costs

At some point in every project planning process, you should ask the question, "What if we do nothing?" The reason for this is to avoid solving a problem that doesn't need to be solved. In the case of corporate IT security, you shouldn't just "do nothing," but if you start from there and work your way up, you can begin to understand what is required and what might be optional, since you're likely to have to make trade offs at some point.

Once you've decided to implement corporate IT security, you'll need to include the initial and ongoing costs of securing the network to your cost estimates. If you already have an IT security solution installed, you'll have to address the cost of both the ongoing (in place) IT security, and the new security initiatives. Your costs include securing the network data, securing the network connection, securing network communications, and securing end-user devices (laptops, Personal Digital Assistants [PDA's]). You will continually have to balance operational security with operational efficiency and security costs with remediation costs.

In addition to these implementation costs, you need to assess the cost of a network security breach to the organization. If the network is compromised, how much will it cost you to repair the damage? What are the costs of remediation, legal defense, and possibly marketing and public relations to address a potential breach? Finally, you need to look at the cost/benefit analysis to determine how all the potential costs of a breach compare to the cost of securing the network in the first place. Though the answer almost always comes out in favor of pro-active security solutions, you need to be comfortable with your analysis so that you can defend it to your executive team or project sponsor.

People

When performing a risk assessment and looking at costs, you need to start with the people needed to design, implement and maintain security. Without the right people in place, your costs (or schedule) can mushroom and you can still end up with a network full of security holes. Critically assess your team's skill set and be brutally honest with yourself about the skills your team has and the skills it lacks. Hiding your head in the sand won't change the cost of the project but it will change the outcome if you don't have the needed skills. As mentioned earlier, hiring an outside security consultant can be costly but the quality of the result can end up saving you time and money on the other end of the project. If an outside consultant isn't warranted or affordable, you'll need to find alternative ways of gaining the expertise you need at a reduced cost. That might involve training current staff (which still leaves them at the early stage of the learning curve), hire a well-qualified temporary employee (which comes with the danger that he or she will open a back door into your network), or hire a full-time employee with the requisite skills. It's going to cost you no matter which way you approach it, so you might as well find your best alternatives early in the process. It's usually an investment that's well worth it.

Training

As part of your security assessment, you'll need to look at the training needs of the entire organization related to security. As we've stated, security is not a one-time activity; it takes the awareness, attention, and compliance of all network users to help ensure a secure network. As such, there are a variety of training activities that will probably be needed and which should be assessed early in the planning process.

- **Installation and Configuration** Equipment that is improperly installed and configured creates a huge security hole. Think of all the wireless routers out there using the default administrator username and password. IT staff may require vendor-specific training on equipment, especially servers, routers, and firewalls, among others. Remember that training provides the necessary knowledge to IT staff, but there's no substitute for hands-on experience.

- **Network Operations Training** The ongoing operations of the network is where security is monitored, maintained, and managed once the security plans have been implemented. Therefore, as part of the assessment, it's important to begin identifying what ongoing operations are required to maintain security once it's established. It's important for those responsible for managing the day-to-day network operations to be well-versed in secure operations, and to be well-trained in operational issues. Whenever possible, send your employees to vendor-sponsored training on the equipment you use. It's a great way to ensure your employees are well-trained on network equipment, and a great way for your employees to learn about the latest tips, trick, and threats from the instructor or other class participants.

- **End-user Training** End-user training is often overlooked in the security planning process, yet we all know that users can be the first line of defense. When users understand the threats that exist, they can actively participate in keeping the network secure. For instance, if employees understand that downloading files from unknown sources (and some known sources) can result in malware being installed, they tend to be a bit more cautious about downloads. If they understand that an unusually slow computer or altered files can be a sign of virus, worm, or malware infection, they can quickly report it rather than disregard it. Also keep in mind that each company should have policies in place regarding safe and approved computer behavior. Each employee should be trained in these policies and ideally should have to acknowledge, in writing, that they will comply with these policies. While training can be a significant expense, the upside is that properly trained users are less likely to put the network or the company's data at risk. We know the cost of remediation is very high both in real dollar costs and in lost productivity. The cost of training is almost always offset by the real reduction in security risks.

Equipment

When performing a risk assessment and looking at costs, it's important to include equipment—both equipment that needs to be protected and equipment that protects the network. Equipment that needs to be protected are all network servers, routers, switches, hubs, firewalls, desktops and mobile devices (your list might be longer). These devices need to be physically protected from theft, damage or unauthorized use. In addition, these devices need to be protected from remote attack such as data inser-

www.syngress.com

tion, data manipulation, or data theft. On the other side of the spectrum is the equipment you use to protect your network, including firewalls, isolated network segments (and the equipment used to create those subnets), routers, and more.

Sometimes it's helpful to look at what network level (data link, network, application, and so forth) your equipment is operating and how it needs to be protected. In other cases, it might be more helpful to look at your network map and determine where security is needed.

Regardless of the security solution you're working on (corporate IT security or one of the individual security area plans), you're probably going to have to buy software or hardware to complement your security efforts. You can harden your servers, disable unused TCP/IP ports, set up auditing, and tighten access controls but you still need firewalls, anti-virus, anti-spyware, and other security systems to complement those efforts. Again, be sure you do a thorough inventory and assessment before sitting through any company's sales presentations. Define your goals, your needs, and your parameters first, then sit through the presentations. Companies will almost always try to up-sell you. Sometimes that's a good thing because they add value to the process; however, other times it's just about making more money. If you are clear about the equipment and the solutions you need before you sit down and talk with anyone, you're more likely to purchase just the solutions you need, not the ones the company wants to sell you.

Time

When IT staff members are on salary, there's a tendency to forget that time is money. IT security can take up tremendous amounts of time in many different areas, and the risk assessment and the associated costs should include the cost of people's time. When planning the time for the risk assessment and the security plan implementation, include tasks such as:

- Equipment specification development
- Equipment purchase (direct purchase or through a bid process such as Request for Quote [RFQ])

- Equipment set up, staging, testing, configuration, and installation
- Integrating security solutions into existing infrastructure (planning, staging, testing, implementing)
- Maintenance, operations, and recovery procedures
- Baseline testing and documentation
- Security policies and procedures
- Vendor contract negotiation and contract management

Time is a cost that should be captured within your assessment and in your project plan. When you delineate your project's tasks, you'll capture the estimated duration (how long you'll allow for the task to be completed) so you can create a project schedule. Depending on how your company works, you may also be required to capture labor costs. In these cases, you'll need to estimate the time (effort) it will take to complete a task, and calculate the labor cost based on the wages of those who will be completing the task. Add tasks like those in the above bulleted list, so that you don't inadvertently underestimate your labor costs in both the assessment and project implementation phases.

Impact Analysis

How much would it cost your business to be down for one hour? One day? One week? As part of your risk assessment, you need to identify your critical business systems and processes that most impact your business revenues, your assets, and your clients or customers. These should be ranked in order of direct and indirect costs. It's not enough to merely determine that you'd lose $54,000 per hour of revenue. What is the cost in terms of lost productivity, IT staff time spent on remediation, employees unable to access critical data, and the press getting wind of your security breach? Identify your business systems, evaluate the impact of an outage, and prioritize them so you can focus your attention on addressing the most critical aspects first. You can use a model like the one shown earlier (in Figure 10.1) as an aid in defining your impact analysis.

Since you're likely to implement your security plan as a corporate IT security plan with smaller individual plans incorporated, you can choose to implement the most critical ISAPs first. This reduces your security risks quickly while providing a comprehensive approach to corporate security. As we've discussed throughout this chapter, the potential impact goes far beyond the financial impact and can include:

- Immediate financial loss
- Long-term financial loss
- Loss of customer confidence
- Industry or market loss of confidence
- Bad press or intensive press scrutiny/investigation
- Regulatory, statutory, or legal investigation
- Shareholder scrutiny or lawsuits

There are companies that perform impact analysis as part of their consulting services, but in many cases, you can perform this assessment yourself or with help from key members of your company. The analysis should include identifying the most critical business processes across your entire company (not just the headquarters or location you're most familiar with). After identifying these critical business processes, you should identify the maximum outage your company can afford to sustain before it severely impacts the well-being of the company. According to the Gartner Group, 50 percent of all businesses that suffer a data loss due to attack or system failure went out of business within three years of the attack if they failed to restore the lost data within 24 hours. Your impact analysis should include the impact of both a full and partial outage. Your recovery and remediation plans should also be well-documented, so that you are able to recover quickly. Your impact analysis should address the financial, productivity, and personnel impact of an outage, and you will also need to account for the potential legal liability (and the related financial impact of legal defense and litigation) of a security breach that exposes confidential or personal information.

   The impact analysis should also take into account the priority of recovery. Clearly, when a security breach is discovered, the first priority it to close the gap and secure the network. Once that is accomplished, however, additional work must be done to assess the scope, nature, and impact of the breach. Recovery and remediation plans should be prioritized based on business impact, so that the most important systems are brought back online as quickly as possible. Sometimes in the heat of the moment, people tend to go after the "low hanging fruit" and focus on the tasks that are easiest or fastest to accomplish. Having an impact analysis and prioritized list at your disposal during these crises can help you focus on getting the most important work done first without having to try to evaluate priorities during an "emergency."

Public Access Networks

One of the most neglected areas is that of public access security and the impact to business via a breach in this arena. Here's the most common scenario: A busy VP of Marketing is traveling to an important client meeting. She's waiting in an airport for her flight and is waiting for one of her staff to make a key revision in the presentation she's making at the client site. She fires up her laptop and checks her e-mail. While online, she opens another document, makes a few changes, and saves it. She logs off, saves the updated presentation to her laptop, turns off the computer, and boards her plane. It all sounds innocent enough until she checks into her hotel room and fires up the laptop. Now she finds that she can't logon to her e-mail account. She gets a message saying username or password is invalid. She contacts the IT help desk but it's after hours and she gets a recording and the option to page someone. She's very tired, it's been a long day so she lets it go until morning. What she doesn't know is that sitting in the airport was someone just waiting for someone else (the VP of Marketing in this case) to log onto an unsecured wireless network that appeared to be the airport network. The bad guy now has her corporate username and password, which happens to be the same for her e-mail. The bad guy now has access to everything on her corporate network, and he's been reading her e-mail while she is in meetings.

Because she's a fairly high level corporate employee, chances are good her user account has permission to access highly confidential material. Certainly she (and now the bad guy) have access to marketing plans and projections, financials, and more.

Most IT staff will focus intently on the impact to business operations if the corporate network is attacked directly, but the scenario described is becoming more commonplace. When looking at the potential impact, look at all of the ways your company's employees connect to corporate data and look at the potential impact of these means of access.

Legal Implications

We discussed the legal implications at great length, so we won't repeat that here other than to say that it should be abundantly clear to you by now that there are significant legal aspects to IT security that must be assessed and addressed in a clear, thoughtful, and intelligent way. The future of your company literally depends on how well you do your job in this area. No pressure.

After performing a thorough risk assessment, audit, and/or impact analysis, you should have a very clear idea of what needs to be secured and what the priorities are. When you looked at the impact of systems outages to your business, you should have developed a prioritized list that would help you in two ways: you know what you need to secure first, and you know where you need to focus your IT resources, including your staff, your budget, and your project planning efforts. You can prioritize your ISAPs based on this analysis and build them into your corporate IT security plan in a phased manner. This helps by reducing the project scope, schedule, and budget and allows you to focus completely on one particular security area at a time. Granted, not everyone can implement security solutions in a sequential manner, in some cases you'll have to run security projects in parallel. We also recognize you don't have the luxury of just running a security project. IT staff have multiple ongoing responsibilities on a daily, weekly, and monthly basis. The security project will be "just another task" on the long to-do list for many. Breaking your corporate IT security project plan down into smaller s can help staff focus on the tasks at hand without overwhelming them with a massive corporate security plan.

Thus far in this chapter, we've talked about your risk assessment and impact analysis. We've gone into great detail, but you can dig even deeper. This should provide you with an excellent framework for understanding your corporate IT security needs. As we mentioned, you will have to circle back through this more than once, because the corporate IT security plan depends on a full assessment. Regardless of your approach, you will want to revisit your data at least once and refine it as you go, to make sure your corporate IT security plan is as comprehensive as possible. Remember, there is no perfect security solution and you can far outspend your need for security; thus, striking a balance should be your goal. Next, we discuss the parameters for your corporate IT security plan.

Business Intelligence...

Scan the Headlines to Avoid Common Mistakes

We all have those "duh" moments when we realize we've made an incredibly dumb mistake by overlooking the obvious. One way to avoid common security mistakes is to scan the headlines for what's happening in the rest of the world. Many IT professionals subscribe to a variety of online newsletters including security-related newsletters, which is one way to stay on top of changes in the world. In addition, scan newspaper and magazine headlines on a regular basis. If possible, include a "what's new in the world of security" segment in your IT staff meetings, and assign one or more people each week to come prepared with a five minute presentation (sans PowerPoint) on a security-related topic. Look at the problem, how it was detected, and how it was corrected. This information can be extremely useful in detecting and avoiding security problems internally. It keeps you and your staff up-to-date, sharpens your skills, and can also make for very interesting staff meetings. And, chances are if they were exploited elsewhere, they'll be exploited in your organization before long.

Authentication

Authentication is the process of verifying the identity of any entity requesting access to network resources. Authentication encompasses server and host authentication, router or wireless access point authentication (where applicable), process authentication, and user authentication.

Authentication and authorization are not exactly the same thing, though in some cases such as legal or technical requirements, they are often paired or confused with each other. However, authentication is the process of making sure you are who you say you are, and authorization allows access based on that identity.

Your project plan should dig into your authentication security to determine how effectively you've implemented authentication systems, where your vulnerabilities lie, where and how an attacker might strike, and what you need to do to improve security. While ever-changing, the list presented here shouldn't change too dramatically in the near-term, unless some major event or discovery obliterates previous authentication solutions.

- **Basic Authentication** Users signing into a guest account have to know the guest account name and password.

- **Two-factor Authentication** The username and password are two factors required to log onto a network. This is similar to entering a credit card number and the expiration date for an online transaction.

- **Multi-factor Authentication** The username, password, and pin number are all part of multi-factor authentication. Many banks use multi-factor authentication to prevent theft based on URL spoofing. Multi-factor authentication includes entering a user name and then being presented with a unique key such as a picture or key word, and then entering your password only after the correct key is presented to you. This prevents specific types of attacks, such as man-in-the-middle (MITM) attacks.

- **Public Key Infrastructure (PKI)** PKI is a form of cryptography that is implemented as part of a security project. PKI allows users to communicate securely through the use of a pair of cryptographic keys. One of the keys is the "public" key and one is the "private" key, and they are related to one another mathematically.

- **Geo-location** Geo-location is a method of determining where in the world a particular computer resides. It's used for a number of legitimate purposes, but it can also be used for illegitimate purposes. Many companies sell IP address geo-location databases that can locate the city and the street Justas well as the country of an IP address. Anonymous traffic can help deter geo-location efforts, but many Internet companies will not accept or forward anonymous traffic.

- **Kerberos** An Internet security protocol that prevents eavesdropping and replay attacks, and ensures the integrity of the data. It is implemented between clients and servers and provides mutual authentication.

- **Secure Shell (SSH)** SSH is one implementation of public key cryptography that provides for mutual authentication of user to a remote server. It also provides data confidentiality and integrity.

- **Secure Remote Password (SRP) Protocol** The Secure Remote Password Protocol is a password-authentication system that allows users to authenticate with a server. This method is resistant to dictionary attacks and does not require a trusted third party.

- **Closed-loop Authentication** Closed loop authentication is a means by which one party verifies him or herself to another party by requiring the use of a token transmitted from a trusted point of contact.

- **Remote Authentication Dial-In User Service (RADIUS)**
  RADIUS is a protocol that provides authentication, authorization, and accounting (AAA) for network access and mobility. It works in both local and roaming situations.

- **DIAMETER** DIAMETER is an AAA protocol that is purported to be the "upgrade" to RADIUS, although it is not backward compatible.

- **Hashed Message Authentication Code (HMAC)** HMAC is a type of message authentication code that uses a cryptographic hash function in combination with a secret key.

- **Extensible Authentication Protocol (EAP)** EAP is a fairly universal authentication mechanism that is often used to secure wireless networks and point-to-point connections. There are variations of the EAP protocol that are incorporated into recent Wireless Protected Access (WPA) and Wi-Fi Protected Access 2 (WPA2) standards for wireless networking security.

- **Biometrics** Biometrics are used in computer security through fingerprint, retinal, and facial recognition, among others. Recent studies have shown that some of these methods are easily spoofed.

- **Completely Automated Public Turning Test to Tell Computers and Humans Apart (CAPTCHA)** You may have run into this type of authentication without knowing its name. It's used to tell humans apart from machines by preventing automated responses. It falls into the category of challenge-response authentication. Typically, a word or set of numbers and letters are presented that are obscured or modified in some manner to prevent computers from responding to a prompt. Figure 10.2 shows an example of a CAPTCHA.

Figure 10.2 Sample of CAPTCHA Used to Prevent Automated Responses

Authentication can be accomplished in a number of ways. This section is not meant to teach you about authentication as much as it is meant to get you thinking about the kinds of authentication you may have or may want to research as you begin developing your IT security project plan. We discuss cryptography in a later chapter, with an eye toward developing individual security area project plans.

Business Intelligence...

CAPTCHA

You may not need to know about CAPTCHA to develop your authentication and authorization assessments, audits, and recommendations, but it's a very interesting concept that's worth knowing about. This is one of those areas that you'll learn about sooner or later if you have your staff actively looking for innovations in the security world. Developed by the brilliant folks at the School of Computer Science at Carnegie Mellon University, the CAPTCHA can be used in a variety of applications, among them thwarting automated responses. There are several iterations of this method. The most basic is called "Gimpy," which distorts text so that

Continued

human eyes can still recognize and read the text, but computers cannot use automated programs to discern the letters in the text image. "Bongo" is a system where the user is shown visual images and asked to determine where a third image should be placed. "Pix" relies on a large database of labeled images. The database then pulls four (or some number) of related images together and asks the user to identify the unifying element (e.g., it might show a picture of a lake, an ocean, a sailboat, and a glass of water). The unifying element can be selected from a long list that includes the word "water." CAPTCHA uses a sound file to say or spell a word, and then the listener must type in the word he or she heard.

CAPTCHA's are good for a lot of things, but keep in mind that they're not friendly to those who have sight or hearing problems (e.g., visually impaired people often use screen readers to determine what's on their computer screen. Clearly, visually based CAPTCHA's can be problematic, because aurally based CAPTCHA's would exclude people who are hearing impaired. While this may be a small portion of your population, it is something to consider before implementing this type of system. For more information on CAPTCHA, go to www.captcha.net.

Access Control

Access control can be thought of as authorization and encompasses three areas: physical access to equipment, local access to the network, and remote access to network resources through Virtual Private Network (VPN), the Internet, or wireless connections. As shown earlier in Figure 10.1, the layered approach might help you visualize your network and look at access control from that perspective (e.g., how do you physically control, monitor, and detect a breaches access to the elements defined? How do you virtually control, monitor, and detect breaches to access?

Physical Access to Equipment

As part of your ISAP, you need to assess and audit the physical access to your equipment, and devise strategies for improving that aspect of security based on the results of your assessment, testing, and auditing. Restricting and monitoring access to key network components such as servers and routers, is an important part of securing the network that should be addressed in your security project plan. Obviously, there are limits to how secure you should make equipment. Users need access to some of the network resources, including desktops, laptops, PDAs, and other wireless devices. These assets should be protected to the greatest extent possible to prevent an unauthorized person from using or stealing the equipment (e.g., What happens when the receptionist steps away from his or her desk? Is the front door locked? Is there a security person or camera? Does your company's security policy dictate that he or she lock his workstation first?). Also, compliance issues such as the Health Insurance Portability and Accountability Act of 1996 (HIPAA) can come into play. What if the receptionist who leaves the desk unattended works in a doctor's office or a hospital emergency room? In that case, you have two issues—the security risk and the HIPAA risk.

Local Access to Network

Local access is typically controlled through username login requirements, although as mentioned in the previous section, it is also tied to actual physical access to the system. Look for ways that unauthorized persons might gain access to the local network. This is clearly the largest area, because we have to include usernames, passwords, access control lists, security and user groups, permissions, and how they replicate throughout the organization. These areas should be reviewed and addressed as part of your assessment and included as discrete tasks in your security project plan. Local access can also include someone slipping a wireless access point onto a network node that is hidden or in an obscured location.

Remote Access to Network

Remote access includes access to the corporate network by employees physically located outside your network, as well as other connecting points into the network such as extranets and Web sites—anyplace that the inside and outside come together. An attacker would prefer to sit in the comfort of home to wander undetected through your network, so all external-facing access points must be assessed and addressed in your project plan.

Auditing

Different people view auditing in different ways, but the net result is that auditing should examine and expose any shortcomings of IT and company security policies in a systematic manner. The challenge for many IT departments is twofold. First, policies almost always come from outside the IT department, so you have to actively advocate for policy change and work collaboratively on a cross-functional team to accomplish this goal. For many in IT, that's not an appealing proposition. Second, developing policies and procedures based on the outcome of your auditing, is a task that requires less technical ability and more organizational agility, which are two primary reasons why IT audit results sometimes don't make their way back into organizational policies and procedures.

Many IT security experts agree there are five major components of a security audit: policy review, process and procedure review, operational review, legal requirements, and reporting requirements. Let's look at each of these areas in more detail so you can include tasks in your IT security project plan to address these components.

Policy Review

There are all kinds of corporate policies that directly and indirectly impact network security. This is an area that you should have representatives from different areas of your company provide input. At minimum, you should have one or more representatives from Human Resources to provide guidance on current policies, how suggested changes to policies might be implemented, and whether there are any legal or Human Resources considerations for such policy changes.

There are three basic kinds of policies, as shown in Figure 10.3. The physical policies truly govern who can physically access equipment, including servers and other mission critical components. Technical policies govern who can do what with a network resource. Technical policies are often governed by or created from administrative policies, the third piece of this puzzle, which outline how corporate resources are used.

Figure 10.3 Three Layers of Security-related Policies

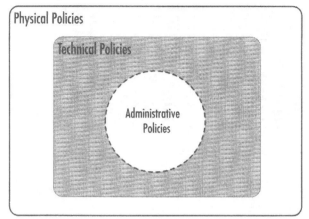

Physical

Physical policies prevent unauthorized access to network resources, which basically prevents theft and tampering on a physical level. Physical policies are often dictated by administrative policies (e.g., you might have an administrative policy that says that only senior IT staff have access to server rooms. You might enforce that policy through physical policies such as installing a card key system that only senior IT staff identification (ID) cards can open, or using a keypad with unique Personal Identification Number (PIN) numbers for each senior IT staff member. While these are clearly physical barriers to entry, they also reflect or enforce administrative policies through technical policies (which card keys or PINs are authorized). Notice that these three areas are always intertwined.

Technical

Technical policies are enforced by the operating system or other related technology, not by physical means. A technical policy addresses various technical requirements such as the requirement to use strong passwords or a policy regarding how confidential data is encrypted. These technical policies are, in a sense, the second line of defense after physical policies. However, since attackers often don't require physical access to the network, physical policies are inadequate by themselves.

In addition, technical policies that should be audited include the full scope of how users access the network and what methods are in place to monitor network activities (e.g., how user groups are created and maintained, how it is determined which user gets membership to which groups, how group permissions are assigned and replicated through the enterprise, the administrative procedures for maintaining appropriate group permissions, and related activities).

When we talk about auditing, we're talking about looking at the security environment, but there is also the discrete activity of auditing that involves tracking various network events through the use of log files and alerts. What you audit is strictly dependent on your unique network environment. If you audit too many events that don't directly help you manage security (or other critical network aspects), you risk becoming bogged down in mundane log files and non-critical event evaluation. If you audit too few events, you may miss seeing a pattern of repeated attack or inquiry (perhaps an attacker is gathering information and has not yet performed an intrusive attack). In this case, auditing is part science and part art. You have to carefully determine which events are worth auditing, understand what the audited event will actually tell you about your network activity, and create a process for routinely reviewing log files. A log file containing all the clues to an imminent network attack is useless if no one ever looks through it and analyzes the logged events.

Providing a full list of auditable activities is outside the scope of this chapter, but there are great resources available to help you develop a meaningful network auditing process so that you can be sure you're looking at log files and audit files that help you maintain security across the enterprise. To get you started thinking about log files and auditable events, we've created this high level list for you:

- IDS logs and session logging

- Firewall reporting

- Systems and network reporting

- Report management (what needs to be reported to whom and how files are managed)

- Managing log files with a log parser

Business Intelligence...

Buried by Log Files

You've undoubtedly had a lot of experience with log files. You know that you can set auditing requirements in just about any way you want, and at the end of the day, those audit activities create alerts and log files. While there are automated ways of reviewing log files, they're not without flaws. Being overrun with data is not helpful if you can't discern the potentially important events from normal daily network activities. As Jacob Babbin puts it, it's really about "identifying the patterns in the chaos." (*Security Log Management*, Jacob Babbin, Syngress Publishing, Inc., 2006). Jacob (and others) put together a great resource to help you figure out what you need to log, what you need to do with those logs, and ultimately, how you can see "the forest through the trees" when you're managing security logs in the enterprise. You can also find articles specific to managing log files in the Windows environment on the Microsoft Web site at www.microsoft.com/technet. When all is said and done, it's your job to determine which events to audit and to manage log files in a manner that enhances and maintains security. A log file that isn't read and acted on is just a waste of 1s and 0s on your network storage device.

Administrative

A variety of administrative policies are required to describe in detail how security is maintained. These run the gamut from policies regarding which level of access a manager is granted, which employees should be granted remote access capabilities, and how passwords should be created, secured, and maintained. Policies regarding the use of the Internet, the ability to download from the Internet, or the ability to install new programs fall under both administrative and technical policies. The administrative policy describes what is and is not allowed and technical policies are created to enforce those administrative policies. This can include blocking certain Internet sites and disabling the feature that allows users to install new programs and other technical safeguards. Administrative policies are typically included in employee handbooks, reviewed during employee orientation or awareness campaigns, and maintained through active management.

Administrative policies also help define the culture and attitudes toward security within an organization. While some companies go a little crazy with policies and procedures, others are far too lax. You'll need to work with key stakeholders in your organization to find the right balance between securing the network and over-burdening management with policies that are unenforceable or unmanageable.

Process and Procedure Review

Here is another area in which you should have strong Human Resources input, because many of the security processes and procedures are directly related to personnel management (e.g., what happens when an employee is hired or fired?). In some organizations, it can be days before a fired employee's account is disabled. A policy that states that the account of any terminated employee should be disabled within ten minutes of termination should then be coupled with a process for doing so. This might involve having the firing manager or Human Resources notify IT through a defined process so that the account is quickly disabled. What about when a new employee is hired? Are there any policies regarding background checks for employees working in Human Resources, IT, or finance? If so, you also need to have a process for making sure the background check is performed.

Operational Review

Your operational review should accomplish the following:

- How consistently are the policies and procedures related to security applied and enforced?

- How do day-to-day operations enhance or degrade IT security?

- What operational plans are in place to address security in the various areas? Ideally, each area should be assessed individually and as part of a holistic system.

Your operational audit should look at four discrete elements that help build a secure framework. First, you should provide the least privilege necessary for any user to perform the functions of their job. Second, you should reduce the attack footprint by disabling, removing, and uninstalling anything on the system that is unused, including equipment, modems, ports, software packages, protocols, and the like. You should also look at the various security layers, sometimes called *depth-of-defense*, to ensure your policies, procedures, and operations support your security objectives. Finally, you should work diligently to identify the inherent assumptions you're making about your network, your users, and potential attackers (people, process, and technology assumptions).

Legal and Reporting Requirements

Although listed last, it might actually be the first task, chronologically, that you perform in your audit function because it often helps to know what your legal requirements are for your audit. If you must conform to various government or legislative regulations, you should state these at the outset of your audit process. As part of your project plan, you should have defined your various requirements and all legal requirements should be listed. This will help you devise an audit plan that ensures you meet these requirements. In addition, you may have legal or corporate reporting requirements. Again, these should be defined at the outset so that your audit is conducted in a manner that facilitates the required reporting. For example, you may need to collect a particular type of data that can only be collected at the time the activity occurs. Therefore, your audit requirements should list this and these requirements should be built into your task's completion criteria.

Attacks

Attacks come in all shapes and sizes, and the list of common attacks provided here will no doubt change before the ink on the page has dried. Still, old habits die hard and some of the most common attacks have been around for a long time. In this section, we provide a list of attacks to look for, to prompt you to think along these lines. However, be sure to sit down with your team and research the latest attack methods as well as the best practices for addressing these attacks.

Attacks can generally be categorized as *intrusive* and *non-intrusive*. Intrusive attacks include password attacks, DOS attacks, network sniffing, spoofing, session hijacking, and application and database attacks. Non-intrusive attacks include network and host discovery (using a variety of techniques), port scanning, war driving (and related activities), and information reconnaissance. Intrusive attacks usually cause damage; non-intrusive attacks are typically the precursor to intrusive attacks, because they involve gathering information about their target prior to the actual attack. Therefore, let's start by talking about various non-intrusive attacks that provide vital information to an attacker in preparation for the actual assault.

Non-intrusive Attacks

Non-intrusive attacks are intended to gather information typically needed to perform an intrusive attack. There are various kinds of non-intrusive attacks; the following list is just a sampling. You need to look at all the different ways your network can be evaluated or sized up by the bad guys, so you can determine how a non-intrusive attack would generate needed data for a later, more invasive attack. Let's look at a few of the more commonly used non-intrusive attacks and how they should be incorporated into your own assessment, testing, and audit plans.

Information Gathering

We previously discussed various kinds of data that hackers try to access, including user account information, contact names, e-mail addresses, and phone numbers, as well as system configuration data and external connection data (extranets, phone lines, and so forth) This type of non-intrusive attack is called information gathering (also known as *information reconnaissance*), because the attacker is simply gathering data from public or easily available sources. While you can't prevent this information from being gathered, you can think of ways to reduce the value of this data, such as using generic e-mail addresses for public use. Your audit activities should include an examination of all of the public data you can find on your company (e.g., phone book, Web site, search engine, public records, domain name registration, and so forth), and ensure it is as minimal and generic as possible.

Server and Host Discovery

Finding the addresses of key servers is one of the goals of most hackers. There are two distinct ways to accomplish this task. One is to access the network and start "taking inventory." The other is to find a source that will tell you everything you need to know. One of those sources is the Domain Name Server (DNS) directory, that will give you all kinds of information about the structure of the network. The variety of record types used in the DNS can yield a wealth of hacker-friendly information. A thorough discussion of DNS is far outside the scope of this book, but it is an area your IT security project plan should incorporate. Active Directory (in the Microsoft world) and other directory services are also potential gold mines for attackers.

Aside from DNS and other directory services, there are many other kinds of information about your server and hosts that a hacker would love to get their hands on. This includes all network configurations, system components (routers, switches, hubs, and so forth), wireless networks, telephony equipment and configuration data, power and control systems for your network, and other data that generally cannot be enumerated via a directory scan.

Your audit should perform the same kinds of enumeration and discovery techniques that a hacker would use to try to determine the configuration and layout of your network. There are numerous techniques and tools you can use for this set of tasks.

War Dialing and War Driving

War driving (also known as *war dialing*) is when an attacker drives around looking for open wireless networks. Many organizations have dial-in connections to their networks that are no longer used but still active, or that are active but not secured. It's easy to dial phone numbers during off-hours to try to find a modem that automatically throws handshakes at you. Your audit should identify all existing modems and the current state of the security on those lines.

Port Scans

Another non-intrusive attack is a *port scan*. When an attacker is looking for a way in to your network, he or she may perform an initial port scan to see what ports are sitting open for them to enter through. The TCP and the User Datagram Protocol (UDP) both use ports to identify session and services information, and to transmit this data back and forth among machines using these protocols. Ports should be scanned on your end, and your security project plan should include ports that are listening, filtered, and closed.

Intrusive Attacks

Intrusive attacks intrude into your network for a definite purpose. Once an attacker has gathered data using non-intrusive techniques, he or she now have the needed data to actually get into the network and do some damage. Two major objectives for hackers are to get in and out quickly, and to do so in an undetected manner. Therefore, your job is to make it hard to get in and out, and even harder to do so without detection. It's a never-ending high stakes game of "cat and mouse." Let's look at some of the intrusive attack techniques you should include in your network security assessment and audit.

Password Attacks

Password attacks are the easiest and most commonly used intrusive attacks. They can be done through social engineering (e.g., "Hey, Jake, I forgot the password for the database, can you e-mail it to me? I'm working from home today. Thanks!"), brute-force attacks, dictionary attacks, and password capture.

DoS

Traditional DoS attacks flood Web servers with so many packets, that it is forced to deny service to legitimate users. This was a very popular attack style about ten years ago but is still used in a variety of less-well known ways. A DoS can happen at a Web or Internet connection point or at a server, where the CPU is overloaded with bogus requests it must respond to, thus forcing out any legitimate CPU requests. A new variation, DDoS, gained favor among hackers in the recent past.

Network Sniffing

Network sniffing is the process of capturing and examining network packets to gather information to be used in an attack. Your assessment and testing should include network sniffing, but keep in mind that sniffing must be done on the local network. That means that you can't do it remotely. Your policies, procedures, and technology should help ensure that sniffers are not used on your network; however, there is no danger of remote sniffers. Also keep in mind that switches, which are "smarter" than hubs, are designed to send traffic to one specific host instead of broadcasting to everyone on the segment. As a result, switches are vulnerable to network sniffing attacks and should be tested in your organization.

Spoofing

The three most common kinds of spoofing are DNS, e-mail, and IP. Each type of spoofing attempts to impersonate legitimate network or electronic traffic in order to gain access to valuable data. Your assessment and testing plans should include tests to see how easily (or not) spoofing can be used on your network.

Session Hijacking

As you know, a session is a specific connection between two computers. Sessions are created in order to exchange information between hosts on a network. If a session can be hijacked, a hacker can insert his or her computer into the exchange and gather information. Sessions can be hijacked at the application level, the host level, or the network level. Your assessment and testing should include a determination as to whether your network uses transport protocols that are unencrypted (which could lead to session hijacking vulnerabilities), if you have ports that could be easily hijacked, or if you have applications that have been written with security in mind (terminating idle sessions, testing user input, use digital signatures, and so on).

Application Attack

Commonly used application attacks that have received a fair amount of publicity include buffer overruns (stack and heap) and integer overflows. Assessment and testing plans should address these issues.

Database Attack

Database management and the attendant requirements for security can fill volumes on their own. Databases are becoming more complex and securing them is becoming more difficult. Ironically, even today, many databases are the weakest link in the security chain. Database servers should be tested for proper configuration, all updates and patches should be applied, and access should be strictly controlled. Scripts should be tested to ensure that errors that can be forced (or are accidentally generated) do not compromise the security of the database server or the database itself.

Assessment and Audit Report

Once you've completed your assessments, testing, and audits, you need to generate a report that helps you, the team, and management understand the findings of these activities. If you're performing the assessment and audit as a separate project in preparation for the development of your corporate IT security plan, these findings will form the basis of that project plan's requirements and assumptions. If you're performing these tasks as the first major objective within your corporate IT security project plan, you'll need to take these findings and circle back into some of your earlier planning tasks to revise your plan based on the results of this first phase. In either case, it's not enough to simply record the results of various assessments, including vulnerability assessment and auditing. This data needs to be turned into actionable information that is incorporated into later stages of your project. Information without action is as bad as no information. You and your team should spend time thinking about the types of data that will result from these activities and how that information can be used to increase security across the enterprise.

The results of your assessments and audits might become legal documents if your network is later breached, so you should be cognizant of the potential implications of these reports. That is not to say you should omit or minimize negative information. To the contrary, you should document the issues found with the clear understanding that you will take action—within a reasonable time and in a reasonable manner—to mitigate or resolve these issues.

It is easy to forget that this document essentially lays out every vulnerability and weakness discovered. What a great resource for a hacker! Be sure that the document is not widely distributed and that you maintain strict control of it. You may choose to create several versions of this document, most of which do not specifically delineate the vulnerabilities and weaknesses in a way that could be exploited (e.g., your executive team does not need to know the all the details, and you don't need to worry about where the document ends up. There might also be some legal liability issues with regard to executives being made aware of specific problems.

You may want to sit down with your project sponsor to discuss the reporting requirements for this project. Since there are potential legal issues related to this type of reporting, you may also want to consult with your firm's legal counsel before you begin your security project plan, to determine the most appropriate way to proceed. Again, the intent is to ensure that your firm stays within the realm of legal and ethical behavior; your job is to help your company navigate that sometimes circuitous path.

Elements of a Findings Report

The elements that should be included in your report should be, at a minimum:

- The steps taken to assess vulnerabilities and weaknesses

- A list of vulnerabilities and weaknesses found

- An assessment of the risk (criticality and likelihood of occurrence) of each vulnerability or weakness

- The specific steps to mitigate each vulnerability or weakness

- The specific owners, timelines, and deliverables for each mitigation strategy

Let's look at these elements in more detail.

Defining the Steps Taken

Through the Work Breakdown Structure (WBS), your project plan should describe all of the steps taken to assess, test, and audit security across the enterprise, so that you can easily recap these activities in the beginning of your report. Rather than put copious amounts of detail in this section, you may choose to put a reference or link to the project plan itself.

Defining the Vulnerability or Weakness

After the assessment, you should have an excellent idea of what vulnerabilities were found. You should describe in detail the source and nature of each vulnerability. If possible, organize them using some logical system, whether by system (external, network configuration, servers and hosts, and so forth), or by source (network protocol, operating system, scripts, and so forth). Beware of standard security definitions that come "out of the box" with various security applications. They are intended to be one-size-fits-all definitions, but they often don't fit. Use the expertise of a security professional (whether internal or external) to define the importance of the vulnerabilities.

Defining the Criticality of Findings

Each vulnerability or weakness should be assessed for criticality (i.e., how important is this vulnerability?). As you know, there are some vulnerabilities that would be devastating if exploited, but the likelihood of such an exploitation is statistically insignificant. Remember that your findings report may serve two purposes: internal and external. The internal purpose might be to document findings in preparation for an IT security project, or it might be used as a tool to negotiate for a higher IT security budget based on vulnerabilities discovered. On the external side, this may become a legal document if something goes wrong down the road. Be aware of the potential uses of this document. Create a document with the right amount and level of detail regarding your assessment of the criticality and potential impact of vulnerabilities.

You can use whatever ranking system works for you. Some people use a numbering system where 10 is the highest criticality and 1 is the lowest. Others use words such as critical, high, medium, and low. Whatever ranking system you use should be defined so that everyone understands the meaning. What does "critical" or "10" mean? You could say that "critical" is defined as any activity that can cause bodily harm or death, significantly compromise the company's financial future, significantly compromise the company's ability to remain an ongoing concern, significantly damage the company's brand or reputation, or result in significant legal liability or lawsuits.

Defining Mitigation Plans

Your mitigation plans might be part of this project plan or they may feed into your larger corporate IT security project plan, because a solid assessment should be the starting point for most (if not all) IT security projects. Therefore, how you address your mitigation plans will depend on how you're approaching the project as a whole.

Mitigation plans should be clear, specific, and measurable. They should include which specific vulnerability they are addressing, how the vulnerability will be mitigated, and what the result should be. It might also include how you'll test the results of the mitigating action as well as how these results should be rolled into ongoing security processes and procedures. Finally, it should include recommendations for changes to physical, technical, and administrative policies, as appropriate.

Defining Owners, Timelines, and Deliverables

In the project management world, a task with no owner most likely will not get done, or the task will default to the project manager. To avoid either of these scenarios, you should include owners, timelines, and deliverables in your finding report. If these tasks are going to be rolled into a higher level corporate IT security project plan, you should still define these elements and then make sure they are incorporated into the details of the corporate plan. Deliverables might include functional, technical, legal, financial, or regulatory requirements. They might also include specific acceptance criteria and should include success criteria. If you recall, acceptance criteria are those standards by which a project result is accepted (typically by a client, but in this case it might be acceptance by a regulatory or compliance authority). Success criteria are those standards by which the task owner knows the task was successfully completed. They are closely related, but are not the same in every case.

Format of a Findings Report

You don't necessarily need to hire a graphic designer to format your findings report for you, but you should create a professional presentation. If you're going to present it to senior management, it should be well-prepared so that it provides information in a clear, concise, and professional manner. It should be technically accurate and as objective as possible. While it's tempting to become a bit defensive if the results are not stellar, it's more important to stick to the facts. Executives typically hate spin and obfuscation, therefore, your best bet is to calmly and rationally state the facts. That also means that you should avoid presenting the information in an overly pessimistic way as well. Executives also don't like to hear "the sky is falling," even if it is. Try to be fair and balanced. One way to do this is to include measurable statements. This helps prevent an "all or nothing" presentation.

The actual presentation for your findings will vary based on your corporate culture. If creating a PowerPoint presentation is how you disseminate information, go for it. Otherwise, write the report in a format that's aligned with the relative formality of your organizational reporting norms. For starters, here's an outline you can use to begin the process:

1. **Cover Sheet** Cover sheet with title, author name, contact information, and date.

2. **Table of Contents** If the document is long, a TOC is helpful.

3. **Executive Summary** Write this after you've completed writing the report. Think of what you'd say if you ran into an executive in the elevator and had one minute to summarize your findings.

4. **Summary of Findings** Discuss the project background briefly as well as the scope, key findings, and methodologies used.

5. **Detailed Findings** Include relevant detail that you want to capture and report. You may choose to leave some detail out and reference an external document that contains all the detail, depending on how much detail is available. A 9,000 page detail document might not be helpful for anyone but the IT staff.

6. **Remediation** If you haven't included remediation recommendations or actions in your findings, include them here.

7. **Timelines and Deliverables** Any follow up action required should have assigned owners of specific tasks. These tasks should define clear timelines and deliverables.

We'll discuss more about various security reporting processes and tools when we discuss operational security later in this book. For now, we're focusing on reporting needs during the assessment and auditing phase.

Project Plan

We've covered a number of related topics in this ISAP, including managing assessments, audits, access control, authentication, attacks, and reporting. Now you should have the data needed to put together your security project plan. As with all projects, let's start with the problem statement and the major objectives. Once those are defined, you and your team will be in a better position to select the optimal solution for your organization.

Project Problem Statement

Your problem statement for this security project plan should focus on the need to ascertain how secure your network currently is, what processes, procedures and systems are in place to maintain security, and how that security can be supported, maintained, or enhanced. The problem statement you generate will be specific to your organization. However, three statements are provided here as generic starting points.

> We do not have a benchmark for our current level of security, and we are not confident that our network is as secure as it can be given our size, resources, and vulnerability profile.

> As our company has grown, our public profile has also grown, and we are concerned that our network may now be

a valuable and sought-out target for attacks. We are particularly concerned about maintaining confidentiality of certain data.

Our company is now subject to several governmental regulations regarding the confidentiality, integrity, and availability of our data. We are not confident that we currently meet those standards; we need to ensure that we meet or exceed them within the next six months.

Problem Mission Statement

As with the problem statement, your mission statement will be highly unique to your company and this project. However, here's a starter for you:

To assess how well IT security systems protect the confidentiality, integrity, and availability of critical network resources, and to generate specific actionable data that can be used to increase security across the enterprise.

Project Objectives

Once you've defined your problem and mission statements, you are ready to create a short list of high-level objectives. In this project, we're focusing on assessing and auditing your network for vulnerabilities. You can lay out your objectives in one of several ways, depending on your preferred approach to IT project management. Some people like to combine their major objective and follow-up action into one objective (i.e., if you test for vulnerabilities, you also want to create a process for addressing those vulnerabilities, which can all be put into one high-level objective. On the other hand, you could make vulnerability scanning one high-level objective and remediation another. Thus, the objectives for this individual security area project look something like the list shown in Figure 10.4.

Figure 10.4 Sample Objectives for Security Assessment and Audit Project

```
IT Security Assessment and Audit

1. Define Network Environment

2. Perform Vulnerability Scans

3. Perform Penetration Testing

4. Perform Security Audit
        4.1 Access Control
        4.2 Authentication
        4.3 Attack

5. Develop Security Assessment Report

6. Develop and Implement Security Action Plan
```

We've talked about each of these elements throughout this chapter. The objectives here are clear and will form the foundation of the project's WBS. Your security project plan's objectives may vary from those shown in Figure 10.4, but the overall result should be the same—a list of high-level objectives you want to accomplish in this project.

Potential Solutions

Your potential solutions are varied, but let's start with the fact that you can perform these assessments and audits internally using IT staff, or you can outsource this function. There are pro's and con's to both approaches and you may have a third or fourth viable option you want to consider. When you look at your potential solutions for this particular ISAP, you need to consider the following factors:

- Do we have the internal expertise we need to ensure we're effectively looking at all systems?

- Do we have the time to perform as extensive an assessment, audit, and test as is needed?

- Do we have the budget or time to train internal staff to perform these tasks? If so, is that desirable?

- Do we have the budget or time to locate and retain an external firm to perform these tasks? If so, is that desirable?

- Do we have the tools and resources we need internally to perform these project tasks? If not, is the cost of acquiring and learning them a wise investment?

- Is there any benefit to not acquiring the needed tools internally?

- Are we confident we have trustworthy individuals internally that will perform these tasks as needed?

- Are we confident we can hire an external firm that we trust to perform these tasks as needed?

- Are there organizational or political considerations that will impact this decision?

- Are we subject to specific legal or regulatory requirements that would impact this decision? If so, what are they and how will they impact this decision?

- Are there other organizational resources we can call upon to assist with some of the non-technical elements of this project?

- What are the environmental constraints (technology changes, industry changes, pending litigation, pending acquisition, and so forth) that might impact this project?

How you approach your list of potential solutions is up to you, but if you ask and answer these questions, you'll at least start out with a clear idea of some of the factors impacting your decision. These questions (and any others you want to add to the list) should be addressed by the core IT project team with key stakeholders, if possible. Remember, user input early in the process will help avoid disconnects that often lead to security problems later. While users may not understand some of the more technical elements of the project (e.g., vulnerability testing or assessing the risk of various types of attacks), they can be very helpful in letting you know how current security is working and how they work with the current security processes. In fact, they may very well have great ideas on how security could easily be improved that you might never think of.

Selected Solution

Once you've looked at your potential solutions and thought through all of your organizational constraints and considerations, you should be able to identify the optimal solution for this project. Remember, at this point you want to focus on the optimal solution, knowing that you'll more than likely have to scale it back in one way or another once you start addressing project constraints. In some ways, organizational constraints are project constraints, but it's often helpful to separate them into two distinct categories.

Organizational constraints that impact your solution selection might include the fact that the president of your company sits on the board of a company that uses solution X, and has therefore mandated that you consider using solution X. It might be that you know your company is in the process of acquiring another company and that your IT budget will be strained with acquisition-related activities. These are organizational constraints you'll have to deal with. Once you begin defining your project, there will be additional constraints (e.g., a specific project budget, allocation of resources, and project timing that will impact the project even more directly). You'll have to bounce your ideas about your optimal solution against these organizational constraints to see what is most optimal at this juncture. The key is to start from the best possible solution and shave it back from there. If you start placing too many constraints on your project at the solution selection point, you may miss an opportunity to create an optimized plan. It's like digging around in your pocket to see how much cash you have and then deciding what to have for lunch. You may have failed to take into account that you also have your debit and credit cards with you, which would open up more possibilities. Don't limit yourself too early in the process.

When you have identified your optimal solution, take time to clearly describe and record it. The last thing you want is to sit through long meetings to reach consensus only to have to re-visit the decision in 30 days when a new vice president comes on board. While you might still have to re-visit the decision, if you have adequately documented the process of coming to the solution, the rationale behind it, and the factors considered, you may be able to short-circuit these kinds of endless loops that can drive even the most sane IT person over the edge.

General IT Security Project Parameters

We've defined our project's problem, mission, and objectives very clearly. Next, we need to define the project's environment. Again, the specifics of these sections will vary from company to company and from project to project, so don't just cut and paste these into your plan. That said, you can use these if they apply directly to your unique set of circumstances. You'll need to look at the requirements for this particular project as well as define the scope, schedule, budget, and quality of the project. Once you understand what's involved (at least in a preliminary way), you also need to describe the skills you'll need to successfully carry out the project. After the required skills are documented, you'll need to assign key personnel to the project and form your project team. The final stage of the definition stage is to develop and document project processes and procedures. Ideally, you're already working with a core project team, but if not, this is a good time to pull in additional resources to help in the initial project definition stages.

Requirements

What are the requirements for a project whose objectives include performing security assessments and audits as well as developing recommendations for remediating or removing any vulnerabilities discovered? As discussed in earlier chapters, there are a wide range of requirements that often impact IT projects. We're not going to run through all of them again, but we will provide a quick list of the major categories of requirements you should consider including. Then, we provide a few specific requirements for this type of security project plan and let you take it from there.

Types of Requirements

The following are the types of requirements you should consider including in this project. Also, check with your team, your human resources group, your legal representative and your project sponsor before finalizing your requirements list.

- User requirements

- Functional requirements

- Technical requirements

- Legal or financial requirements

Project Specific Requirements

The types of requirements needed for an assessment and auditing project plan include the technical requirements for the various assessments and tests to be performed. When looking for security vulnerabilities, you should specify the specific target of the assessment, the specific tests or actions that will be taken, how results will be monitored, recorded, and reported, and how recommendations will be made. These might fall under functional, technical, legal, or financial requirements. Technical specifications should encompass methods, tools, and techniques that will be used to test and assess security. The audit function should include very clear specifications regarding functional and technical requirements.

While you might not specifically think of user requirements in this type of project, a user requirement in this context might include that tests be run at night or on the weekend when the fewest users will be impacted; that users be selected at random (or via some specified system) to review current security practices; or that users will be needed to perform certain testing or auditing functions due to specific subject matter expertise that you want to bring onto your IT project team.

You may choose to develop your requirements using the elements shown in Figure 10.5 as your guide. Look at your perimeter, network configuration, servers and hosts, applications and databases, and data needs as you develop this project's functional and technical requirements.

Figure 10.5 Element of IT Security Requirements

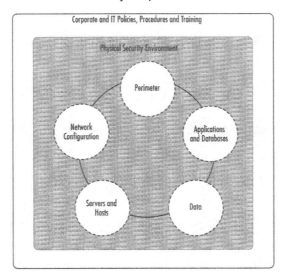

Scope

The scope of this project is up to you and your team. If you choose, you can parse out these different topic areas (as shown in Figure 10.5) into separate sub-project plans that roll up into your general IT security project plan. If so, each of the sub-project's scope would be limited to the topic area. If we assume these elements are part of one project, the scope is all the work to be done to assess, test, and audit security in each of these areas as well as the security at the intersection of these areas.

The scope statement should be as specific as possible about what the project includes and what it doesn't include. Here are a few examples of statements that help you define the scope of your project:

1. The company has 47 servers, including infrastructure, systems, and applications servers, which are all included in this project. The organization may acquire the business operations of CompanyZ during this project and CompanyZ servers are specifically excluded from the scope of this project. CompanyZ servers will

be included in a separate project plan should the acquisition go through.

2. The company has 3,243 host computers, including 2,844 desktop computers and 399 laptops and other mobile devices. These are all included in the scope of this project. All CompanyZ host computers are excluded from this project.

3. The company has four separate geographic locations. Each location is a separate domain within the corporate forest. Each of these four domains is included in this project plan. Domains external to these four domains are specifically excluded. The four domains are: *east.company*, *west.company*, *north.company*, and *south.company*.

Each of the above statements is a clear, specific statement. We could continue to delineate which operating systems the servers and hosts are using, and we could specifically exclude all operating systems that are not listed as currently under use. Or, we could have delineated all the operating systems and specifically included or excluded Linux and Apple operating systems in this project.

The key is to be very clear about what you're going to include in this project. Later, as you develop your WBS, you can keep an eye on your scope statements to make sure you don't define a larger project than your scope statements describe. On the other end of your WBS development, you can circle back and determine if your WBS describes a bigger project than your scope statements. A good checks-and-balances approach to developing and defining your project helps mitigate scope creep.

Scope—Best Practices

Scope creep happens in even the best-planned and managed projects. The key is how well you can manage that creep so it doesn't get completely out of hand. While it's true that there are some projects in which scope does not creep, it seems to be one of the most common areas to shift and change as a project moves forward. One way to contain or even prevent scope creep is to define not only what the project includes, but also what it specifically excludes. The project management gurus in Stanford University's Advanced Project Management program suggest defining what a project is and is not. Sometimes by forcing yourself to specifically say what is not included, you can better define the boundaries of scope and prevent it from oozing out in all directions. It may not cure all scope creep problems, but it will help you draw a line in the sand.

Schedule

You're most likely familiar with the concept of the WBS, which is your detailed list of project tasks broken down into manageable work units. Until you develop your WBS, you can't create a detailed or meaningful schedule. However, at this juncture, you should have a sense of how much work this assessment, testing, and auditing project is going to require. Therefore, you should at least begin to develop your first pass schedule. Will this take 6 weeks or 6 months or 60 months? Based on the high-level objectives and your scope statement, you should begin narrowing this down to a ballpark duration for the project, with high-level milestones you might want to include. For example, you might look at your objectives and scope and determine that this is about a 4-month project. You might also know that your company is being investigated by the SEC for potential violations related to the disclosure of confidential data and that your project will come under intense scrutiny. Therefore, you may choose to shorten this proposed schedule, knowing it will cost more to get it done quicker, so that you can complete your assessment within 60 days in order to comply with one of the SEC's recommendations (or requirements). Remember, too, that if you shorten your estimated project time, you'll have to modify the scope, budget, or quality to compensate.

Budget

As with your schedule, you're not completely ready to sign on the bottom line for the project cost estimate, but you should have a sense of what this project will likely cost. If your company has a set budget for this project, you have to find ways to work within that pre-determined budget by adjusting the scope, schedule, or quality. On the other hand, if there is no set budget for this project at this time, you can develop a high-level guess based on your experience and expertise. If possible, avoid tossing around schedule or budget estimates at this point, as they often "stick" and you end up with a ballpark estimate becoming your actual schedule or budget.

Once you develop your detailed WBS, you can better estimate the time and cost of each task and activity and roll it up into a project budget. Remember to involve subject matter experts who can best estimate both time and cost for specific tasks within the project plan.

Quality

Defining quality in the assessment, testing, and auditing area is tricky. If you determine that zero intrusions is your requirement, then your quality metrics are very high. You will always have to balance security against cost and against usability. Where you draw these lines is how you are, by default, defining quality. If you tolerate some security vulnerabilities or weaknesses due to user requirements or cost constraints, you have essentially lowered the quality. This is not necessarily a bad thing as long as it's done consciously and intentionally, and as long as you can justify the reduction in quality. As stated, you don't need the same security as the U.S. Treasury if you're selling granite to landscape companies. Keep this in mind as you define what level of quality is acceptable.

By the same token, be cognizant of the costs of reduced quality in terms of potential legal liability. This may be an area in which you choose to consult with your legal representative to determine what "reasonable care" in your company and industry would consist of. While there may be no definitive answer, getting expert guidance can reduce your overall risks, especially when it comes to making decisions about the trade-offs between security and cost or security and usability. Although quality is a difficult area to tackle, quality goals and metrics help define the maturity of the processes that are in place. The ultimate goal is continuous improvement, but you have to start on a very solid foundation to build quality into all of your security and IT processes.

Key Skills Needed

In a project of this nature, you need a variety of skill sets. First, you need extremely savvy technical people who can think and test like hackers. This is a slippery slope, indeed, because it's always a bit unnerving to have people on your IT staff who think like hackers. On the other hand, is it any safer or more reassuring to hire an external firm that thinks like hackers and hand them the keys to your system? As the old expression states, "better the devil you know than the devil you don't." There is no single right answer, but you should be aware of the risks. You'll also need people who are less technical, who would be excellent at reviewing policies and procedures as they relate to security practices in the company. These people are sometimes found in the IT department, but might also be found elsewhere in the company. This list is not exhaustive but should give you an excellent running start.

Technical Skills

1. Physical layer protocols, processes, and services
2. Network layer protocols, processes, and services
3. Operating systems
4. Applications

5. Databases

6. Internet

7. Wireless

8. Intrusion Prevention System (IPS) and IDS

9. Attack methodologies

10. Attack testing tools

11. Vulnerability and intrusion testing tools

12. Reporting tools

13. Remediation tools, techniques, and recommendations

Non-Technical Skills

1. Public information reconnaissance (what information can be found about your company)

2. Review of security policies

3. Review of procedures and policies (might also require technical review or assistance)

4. Recommendations for implementation (from a non-technical and user perspective)

5. Documentation

6. Training

7. Project communication

Key Personnel Needed

Once you've defined your technical and non-technical skill sets, you need to locate and acquire the right people for the project. In any project, this can be a challenge for a number of reasons. However in the case of a security assessment, you need to be sure you have the right players on your team. If you don't have the depth and breadth of skills needed, you will have to devise a strategy for acquiring those skills. Depending on a number of variables, you will have to decide whether to train, hire, or contract out for those skills. Whatever route you take, be sure you have people who are well-versed and experienced in the technologies related to security vulnerability and testing, as well as assessments and audits. This is one area where you could have some serious gaps in skills; it's better to address them now than face a potentially devastating security breach later. Since you can't personally perform and monitor every single task in this project, you need to have a high level of confidence that the team you do have has the requisite skills, because at the end of this security project plan, you will be held accountable for results.

Form the Project Team

Forming the project team is listed here to remind you that if you haven't yet put together a preliminary team, you've missed a few opportunities to actually gain expert input and assistance. However, if you've been working with your core team up until this point, now is a good time to begin defining the ongoing project team, which might mean creating several sub-teams to address various sub-sections of the project based on expertise, availability, or other pertinent factors. At this point, you should have a clear idea of how readily available your needed resources are and what strategies you'll need to use to acquire the right talent at the right time in your project lifecycle.

Project Processes and Procedures

With your project team, you should define the processes and procedures for this project. You should have many standard templates for things like task status reporting (to you), project status reporting (to management), project status reporting (to the user community), issue tracking, escalation procedures, and more.

In addition, you need to define very specific procedures and processes for implementing your assessment, testing, and auditing (e.g., if you hire outside contractors to perform these tasks, you should have very clear legal documents drawn up that might include non-disclosure agreements, specific agreements about what to test and when to test it, and specific guidelines on what should be done with the resulting information.

www.syngress.com

Even if you're working internally, pen testing is a tricky situation, because you don't want employees getting in trouble for performing a pen test and exposing a serious vulnerability. Be sure you get the proper authorization and document the specific people, responsibilities, tasks, and timelines. These should be part of your project processes and procedures in this type of project, due to the sensitive nature of this kind of work. Remember that pen testing on the front side is most useful to test areas that you believe you've previously secured, not to just go after the network prior to implementing your security plans.

You'll also need to define what should occur in the event a vulnerability scan or pen test reveals a very serious problem. If you've defined "very serious" as "critical" or as a "10," what should the tester do? These should be thought of in advance to protect everyone involved. Deciding on these actions ahead of time helps set expectations and helps keep everyone calm when something significant occurs.

General IT Security Project Plan

We've defined the environment for the project, now it's time to get into the details of the project plan. The next step is to take the high-level project objectives and create the WBS. Whatever method you use for creating the WBS is fine, but remember to follow a few best practices:

- Use the verb/noun format to describe tasks so they are clear and unambiguous.

- Don't spent time placing tasks in order until later; just make sure they all get captured.

- Gather subject matter experts to assist in developing a detailed WBS.

- Use a numbering scheme that helps you understand the relationship between and among tasks.

Project WBS

Your WBS will vary depending on the specific objectives you've developed for this project plan. However, to give you a running start, we've included a sample in Figure 10.6. If you're familiar with developing a WBS (which we're assuming you are), you can follow whatever methodology you're most comfortable with. If this is all new to you, you can use the structure shown in Figure 10.6 as a solid starting point. Be sure to include reporting and close out activities in your project plan, as you would with any type of IT project.

Figure 10.6 Sample WBS for General IT Security Project Plan

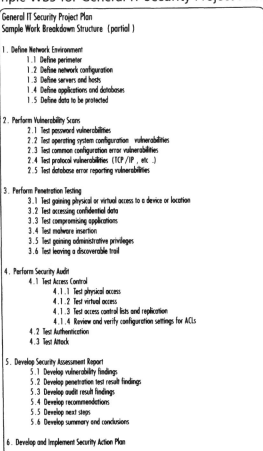

```
General IT Security Project Plan
Sample Work Breakdown Structure (partial)

1. Define Network Environment
      1.1 Define perimeter
      1.2 Define network configuration
      1.3 Define servers and hosts
      1.4 Define applications and databases
      1.5 Define data to be protected

2. Perform Vulnerability Scans
      2.1 Test password vulnerabilities
      2.2 Test operating system configuration vulnerabilities
      2.3 Test common configuration error vulnerabilities
      2.4 Test protocol vulnerabilities (TCP/IP, etc.)
      2.5 Test database error reporting vulnerabilities

3. Perform Penetration Testing
      3.1 Test gaining physical or virtual access to a device or location
      3.2 Test accessing confidential data
      3.3 Test compromising applications
      3.4 Test malware insertion
      3.5 Test gaining administrative privileges
      3.6 Test leaving a discoverable trail

4. Perform Security Audit
      4.1 Test Access Control
            4.1.1 Test physical access
            4.1.2 Test virtual access
            4.1.3 Test access control lists and replication
            4.1.4 Review and verify configuration settings for ACLs
      4.2 Test Authentication
      4.3 Test Attack

5. Develop Security Assessment Report
      5.1 Develop vulnerability findings
      5.2 Develop penetration test result findings
      5.3 Develop audit result findings
      5.4 Develop recommendations
      5.5 Develop next steps
      5.6 Develop summary and conclusions

6. Develop and Implement Security Action Plan
```

Project Risks

There are always risks to any project and this one in particular is fraught with possibilities. You and your team should spend time discussing your project's risks as well as your plans for mitigating those risks. Included should be your triggers (how will you know the risk has occurred) as well as your assessment of the potential risks involved in your mitigation plan.

Risks to this type of project include (but are not limited to):

- Missing a significant vulnerability or weakness

- Failing to fully implement recommended solutions

- Changes to corporate objectives, structure or funding

You can define as many risks as you choose. As with other risk assessments, you should determine the likelihood of the risk occurring and the impact should it occur. Then create mitigation plans for those risks that weigh in on the top of your list. The biggest single risk is that your project will fail to find a significant vulnerability or weakness. The bigger risk is that you will fail to find it and someone will exploit it. How do you mitigate this type of risk? In part, through sound project planning and consistent methodologies. Don't let egos drive this process. If you believe your team members have the requisite skills, fine. Otherwise, find outside resources to assist you.

Project Constraints

Constraints on any project often include time and money, but more specific to this project plan, one of the typical constraints, is the ability to perform these assessments. Non-intrusive attacks are generally safe and can often be performed at just about any time. On the other hand, intrusive attacks are more dangerous and could potentially disable a server, network segment, or the entire network. Therefore, the timing of these various tests is often constrained by user schedules and higher level corporate events. It would be pretty dismal if your testing brought down the network on the same day your boss was holding a press conference in the conference room using network-based resources.

Another common constraint in this type of project is the availability of highly qualified personnel. This project requires a very specific set of skills for many aspects of the assessment and testing functions. Having the wrong people performing this work can result in wasted time or increased vulnerabilities. However, you may have difficulty finding, training, hiring, or contracting out for these services, especially if your budget is locked in. This is the place in your project plan where you review and work through these various constraints to determine what impact they will have on your project. If they are significant, it will require you to sit down with your project sponsor to work through these problems before proceeding. If you believe the constraints on this project are serious, don't agree to a project plan that is faulty from the start. Negotiate with your project sponsor to address these problems.

Project Assumptions

Project assumptions in this type of project might include a list of the known vulnerabilities you'll be testing for, and the assumptions about the skills or availability of key technical resources. If you have two people on your team who are able to perform the bulk of the vulnerability scanning and testing, you should list this as an assumption about your project.

While some project management methodologies list "success factors" as discrete elements of the security project plan, they can also be incorporated into assumptions. If you assume that the things you need to be successful are included, you can list them in this section (e.g., if continued executive support is one of the factors you deem essential to the success of the project, or if you believe that a 25 percent increase in your IT budget will come through and is fundamental to the success of the project, list these as assumptions.

Project Schedule and Budget

Now that you've developed your WBS, you have a list of the tasks needed to successfully complete this project. Therefore, you should be able to look at your tasks and develop a more detailed schedule and budget. The schedule must take into consideration the various constraints as well as resource scheduling, corporate event coordination (e.g., avoiding an outage during a press conference or VIP tour of the facilities) and task dependencies.

Projects with more milestones tend to be more successful than those with fewer milestones. Add milestones as checkpoints throughout your project, so that you can keep the team focused on the next steps and you can measure progress more effectively.

Once you've concluded these tasks, you're ready to launch, manage, and close out the project.

Summary

In this chapter, we looked in detail at how to develop a security project plan for a security assessment and audit project. It should form the foundation of any IT security planning process, whether you undertake the project as a standalone project or as part of a larger corporate IT security project plan. We looked at different ways to view the security assessment as a whole, including looking at the perimeter systems, internal network, server and host systems, applications and databases, and data. It's important to understand the elements that comprise an assessment, which typically fall into the vulnerability scanning, pen testing, and risk assessment with the caveat that any pen testing should be limited in scope prior to implementing a security project. The audit function includes auditing physical, technological, and administrative policies and procedures. We also looked briefly at access control, authentication, and auditing as part of our overall security assessment, and will re-visit some of these topics briefly in our operational security project plan. Finally, we developed a security project plan that includes a problem statement and a mission statement, potential solutions, the selected solution, and the high-level objectives. We also developed other project details including the skills required, the WBS, the project risks, and the assumptions.

At this point, you should have a solid start on your general IT security project plan focused on assessment, testing, and auditing. While this initial project plan will not be your end-point, it should give you a reasonable start on defining and planning a security project plan customized to your company's unique situation.

Solutions Fast Track

IT Security Assessment and Audit

☑ A security assessment and audit is a typical starting place for any IT security project.

- ☑ People, processes, and technology must all interact effectively to maintain and enhance security.

- ☑ It's often helpful to categorize the components that should be included in your assessment. One way to parse these out is: policies, procedures and training; physical security; perimeter; network configuration; servers and hosts; applications and database; and data.

- ☑ The types of assessments usually include vulnerability scanning, pen testing, and risk assessment.

- ☑ Pen testing prior to implementing a security plan should be limited and very focused. Gaining access through an open door doesn't prove the locks don't work.

- ☑ Types of auditing include authentication, access control, and auditing (at a systems level).

- ☑ An impact analysis helps define what would happen if these vulnerabilities or weaknesses occurred. This can help you prioritize activities and expenditures.

Authentication

- ☑ Authentication proves the identity of an entity trying to gain access to network resources.

- ☑ There are many different kinds of authentication schemes available today. They span many different network types, operating systems, and devices.

- ☑ Authentication is managed through a variety of methods and each should be assessed and tested during this project.

Access Control

- ☑ Access control limits access to devices, resources, and data in the organization, based on pre-existing rules and policies.

☑ Access control can be developed on several levels, including physical, local, and remote.

☑ Testing access control spans all systems and networks, and requires a thorough audit of processes, procedures, and configuration data.

Auditing

☑ Auditing is used in two ways with regard to this project. There is the task of auditing current security settings and there is the ongoing activity of auditing key network activities.

☑ Auditing current security settings includes reviewing physical, technical, and administrative policies.

☑ Auditing should also include a thorough review of processes and procedures, operational issues, and any legal and reporting issues.

Attacks

☑ Your vulnerability scan and pen testing should include various known attack types.

☑ Your plans should also include an assessment of your firm's attack footprint and plans for reducing that footprint.

☑ Attacks can be non-intrusive or intrusive. Non-intrusive attacks typically involve gathering information in preparation for an intrusive attack.

☑ Intrusive attacks typically include stealing, modifying, or destroying critical data or systems.

☑ A list of attacks as well as the likelihood of or vulnerability to various attacks should be included in the security project plan, to ensure a comprehensive plan and to document what should be included.

Assessment and Audit Report

☑ Once you've completed your assessment, testing, and auditing activities, you will need to generate a findings report.

☑ Remember that the data contained in this report enumerates your company's vulnerabilities, and may become a legal document. Handle this document with extreme care and maintain close control over it.

☑ Include the following items in your report:

- Define what steps were taken
- Report the results of the steps taken (vulnerabilities and weaknesses found)
- Define the criticality of findings
- Describe mitigation plans
- Define owners, timelines, and deliverables.

General IT Security Project Parameters

☑ As with any project, your planning process should begin with clearly defining the problem statement, mission statement, and high-level objectives

☑ After defining the basic elements, you and your team should look at all potential solutions and then select the optimal solution. If you don't look at all potential solutions, you might inadvertently overlook an excellent but somewhat unconventional solution.

☑ An assessment and auditing project has a very specific set of requirements. Carefully define functional and technical requirements to ensure you create a thorough assessment plan.

☑ The scope of your assessment and audit plan may be part of a larger corporate IT project plan, or it may be a standalone project. Clearly define the scope by describing what is and is not included.

☑ You won't have enough detail at this juncture to commit to scope, schedule, budget, or quality, but you should begin defining these so they can be refined as you gather additional information.

☑ Don't let egos drive your decisions about needed skills and personnel. Your company's future may rest on the skills and expertise of the people you select, therefore, be diplomatic but honest in your assessment.

General IT Security Project Plan

☑ Your WBS should be developed from your high-level objectives specific to assessment, testing, and auditing activities.

☑ Include reporting and close out activities in your WBS.

☑ Risks in security assessment and auditing type projects require that specific attention is paid to the risks of not finding vulnerabilities and weaknesses, and the risks of finding those weaknesses and not addressing them adequately.

☑ Assumptions should be examined and well-documented, because the success of the project ultimately rests on the assumptions you make about the project and its environment.

☑ Assumptions can also include critical success factors. If a budget of $100,000 has been discussed and you believe it is critical to the success of the project, state that as an assumption.

☑ Once you've developed a detailed WBS, you can hone your schedule and budget.

☑ Be sure to include reporting and close out activities, and roll these into your corporate IT security project plan, if appropriate.

Chapter 11

IT Infrastructure Security Plan

Solutions in this chapter:

- Infrastructure Security Assessment

- Project Parameters

- Project Team

- Project Organization

- Project Work Breakdown Structure

- Project Risks and Mitigation Strategies

- Project Constraints and Assumptions

- Project Schedule and Budget

- Infrastructure Security Project Outline

☑ Summary

☑ Solutions Fast Track

Introduction

Infrastructure security is at the root of your entire corporate security plan. Other individual security area plans (ISAPs) may overlap with your infrastructure security plan to some extent. For example, a wireless network is part of your infrastructure, but it's also a large enough area to be addressed in a separate project plan. You'll need to ensure that your corporate IT security project and your ISAPs cover all the bases, but be aware that there are overlapping areas that should be clearly delineated if you're working on several projects in parallel. You don't want project teams wrestling over ownership of one part of your network or another. In this chapter, we'll look at the basic infrastructure components and how to secure them; then we'll create a project plan utilizing this information.

Infrastructure Security Assessment

There are two distinct processes: audit and assessment. An *assessment* is intended to look for issues and vulnerabilities that can be mitigated, remediated, or eliminated prior to a security breach. An *audit* is normally conducted after an assessment with the goal of measuring compliance with policies and procedures. Typically, someone is held accountable for audit results. Some people don't like the term *auditing;* perhaps it's too reminiscent of ol' Uncle Sam scouring through your tax return from three years ago when you claimed that one vacation as a business trip because you talked to your boss on your cell phone while waiting at the shuttle to your beachfront hotel. Though the terms *assessment* and *audit* are often used interchangeably, in this chapter we focus on assessments.

As we've discussed throughout this book, there are three primary components of IT security: *people, process,* and *technology.* A balanced approach addresses all three areas, because focusing on one area to the exclusion of others creates security holes. People, including senior management, must buy into the importance of security, and they must understand and participate in their role in maintaining security. Process includes all the practices and procedures that occur and reoccur to keep the network secure. Technology obviously includes all hardware and software that comprises the network infrastructure. Part of the technology assessment required to assess and harden infrastructure security includes deploying the right technological solutions for your firm and not the "one size fits all" or the "it was all we could afford" solution. In IT, we often focus a disproportionate amount of time and energy on securing the technology and overlook the importance of both people and process to the overall security environment.

To secure your infrastructure, you need to understand its building blocks. These include:

- Network perimeter protection
- Internal network protection
- Intrusion monitoring and prevention
- Host and server configuration
- Protection against malicious code
- Incident response capabilities
- Security policies and procedures
- Employee awareness and training
- Physical security and monitoring

We'll discuss policies, procedures, and training in the chapter on operational security later in this book, so we won't discuss that material here.

We can look at the infrastructure security assessment in three segments, as shown in Figure 11.1.

Figure 11.1 Infrastructure Assessment Overview

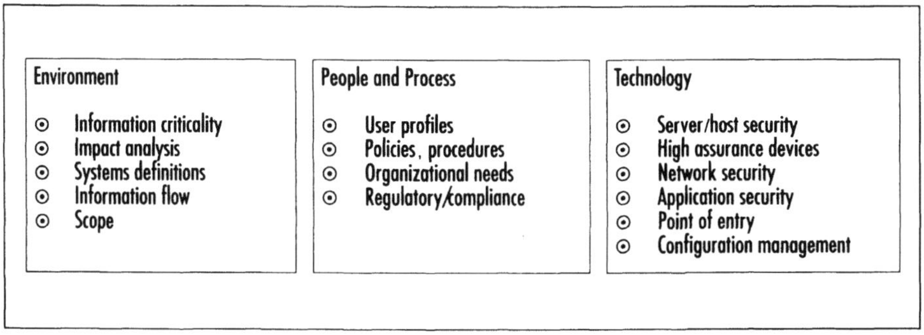

Environment	People and Process	Technology
⊙ Information criticality	⊙ User profiles	⊙ Server/host security
⊙ Impact analysis	⊙ Policies, procedures	⊙ High assurance devices
⊙ Systems definitions	⊙ Organizational needs	⊙ Network security
⊙ Information flow	⊙ Regulatory/compliance	⊙ Application security
⊙ Scope		⊙ Point of entry
		⊙ Configuration management

Internal Environment

Security assessments should begin by looking at the overall environment in which security must be implemented, since security does not exist in a vacuum. Looking at the relative importance of your company's information is a good starting point, because you need to find the right balance between security and information criticality. As part of that analysis, you also need to look at the impact of a network infrastructure intrusion and what that would cost to defend and repair. You need to define the various systems you have in place and look at how information flows through your organization to understand the infrastructure you're trying to protect. Finally, you need to create an initial assessment of scope to define what *is* and *is not* included in your project. We'll look at scope later in the chapter, when we begin developing our project plan.

Information Criticality

It's important to begin by looking at information criticality. We've discussed this topic throughout this book, and it will continue to be a common theme because there's really no point in securing something that no one wants. It's why a new Lexus RX-330 comes with a lo-jack system, but a 1993 Dodge Dart with serious body damage is not likely to need any protection (in fact, there might be an economic benefit to having such a vehicle stolen—no offense intended to any 1993 Dodge Dart owners). Information criticality is an assessment of what your network holds and how important that is in the overall scheme of things. Not all data is created equal, and if your company manufactures steel troughs for horse feed, there's a good chance your network data is not nearly as interesting to a potential attacker as the data in an online stock brokerage firm or a bank or credit card processing house network. Therefore, you need to look at the criticality of your information and decide how much you're willing to spend to secure that information. No one ever wants a security breach, but it would not make good business sense to spend $15 million to secure a network for a company that pulls in $5 million annually and doesn't store sensitive personal data such as credit card numbers or medical records. That said, just because your company makes $5 million annually doesn't mean that you *shouldn't* look seriously at the criticality of your data, to be sure you don't have excessive exposure. If you are storing credit card numbers or medical records, you'd better be sure your security solutions are up to standards, because your legal liability could significantly outstrip that $5 million annually in a big hurry.

Impact Analysis

You'll notice as you read the chapters for the individual security area plans that some of this information overlaps. It's hard to perform an impact analysis on an infrastructure breach without also seeing how it would impact your wireless network components, your Web site, or your policies and procedures. However, in looking at the impact to your infrastructure, you'll need to understand how a breach could impact the very foundation of your organization. The impact analysis should include:

- **Cost of network infrastructure—failure (downtime)** Server down, database server down, routers down, etc.

- **Cost of network infrastructure—unavailable (slow or unresponsive)** Denial-of-service attacks, packet flooding, etc.

- **Cost of network infrastructure breach—data confidentiality, integrity, availability** Man-in-the-middle, spoofing, phishing, etc.

- **Cost to company reputation** Lost sales, lost customers, loss of long-term business relationships.

- **Cost to company** Cost of remediation, cost of litigation.

You should combine information criticality with the findings of your impact analysis to form a clear picture of what you're trying to protect and why. When you understand the impact, you can see where the important areas are in your organization, and you can use this information, in part, to prioritize your approach to securing the network.

System Definitions

Infrastructure systems clearly include the "backbone" services, including DHCP servers, DNS servers, Directory Services servers, e-mail servers, database servers, firewalls, DMZs, routers/switches, operating systems, Web servers, and security applications (antivirus, antispyware, IDS/IPS, etc.). If it's helpful, you can also look at your systems from the OSI model perspective—from the physical layer all the way up through the application layer, whatever makes the most sense to you and your team.

Creating (or updating) network diagrams can also be included in the system definitions overview, since the way everything fits together is part of understanding the whole.

Information Flow

One area that is sometimes overlooked in the assessment phase is the flow of information through the infrastructure. This area can be used in conjunction with your systems definitions to help map your network and to discover the key areas that need to be protected and how an attacker would get to those assets.

It sometimes helps to look at information flow from different perspectives. For example, how does information from a user computer flow? How does DNS or DHCP traffic flow through the network? How is external traffic coming into the network managed, and where and how does it enter? How is traffic leaving the network for the public network (Internet) managed? Creating a map of your network infrastructure and information flow will help you visualize your network and identify potential weak spots.

Scope

You might want to limit the scope of your infrastructure security project for a variety of reasons. While you're looking at your internal environment, you might choose to limit the scope. "Scoping" is often done at this point when you're engaging an external security consultant. However, if you're doing this work internally, you may limit your scope here, or you may choose to do a full assessment and then limit the scope after you see what's what.

People and Process

Clearly, people and processes impact network security in a big way. Most security breaches occur from the inside, not the outside, despite the media's sensationalized focus on external security breaches. The people in your organization can be your defenders or your downfall, depending on how they approach security. Savvy, well-informed users can augment the technical security measures by avoiding becoming victims of social engineering, by reporting suspicious activity, by avoiding responding to phishing e-mail, or by not leaving their computer logged in and unattended. All the security in the world can't prevent problems if users are not pulling their weight. There are many ways to inform and involve users, and unfortunately, many IT departments don't leverage these opportunities very successfully, because they often fall victim to a "user as pain in the hind quarters" mentality. Let's look at how users and organizational processes should be reviewed during an infrastructure assessment.

User Profiles

What kinds of users do you have? Where and how do they work? If you begin by looking at your user population, you will see segments that have higher and lower risk profiles. The clerk in the mailroom might only have access to e-mail and the mailroom application, but does he or she also have Internet access and the ability to download and install programs? What about the marketing staff who travel worldwide? What kinds of information do they keep on their laptops (usernames, passwords, domain names, sensitive documents, contacts, and the like), and how does this impact your network security?

Users can be categorized in whatever ways work for you in your organization, but here's a list of potential risks by employee type, to get you thinking:

- **Executive** High-profile targets, often not extremely "tech savvy," potentially easy to get information about (from press releases, public filings, legal filings, and so on).

- **Director** High-profile targets, may travel extensively with sensitive information, may need to connect to the network in a variety of insecure locations.

- **Finance, marketing, HR, legal** Access to extremely sensitive data, may be high-profile targets due to their access to sensitive data, may travel extensively and be desirable targets of social engineering.

- **IT staff** Access to network resources, ability to grant/deny access, potentially desirable targets of social engineering (especially via help desk), highly desirable targets (IT usernames and passwords with administrative privileges are the Holy Grail for hackers).

- **Users** Access to sensitive company information, often targets of social engineering.

In addition to these categories, you may have user groups defined in your network security management system (which manages access control) that you want to use. Microsoft defines users as administrators, power users, and the like, and that might also work for you. Again, the point is to use a categorization method that's meaningful to the way your company and your existing network infrastructure are organized, so you can understand the risks users bring into the organization and the strategies for keeping the network secure in light of the way various users work.

Policies and Procedures

We won't spend a lot of time discussing policies and procedures in this chapter; we'll focus on them in an upcoming chapter on operational security. As we've discussed, no single security topic exists in a vacuum or silo, and as you move through your project planning, you'll notice areas of intersection and overlap. There are few hard-and-fast rules about where these overlapping elements should be placed; the important factor is to be sure they *are* included *someplace*.

Infrastructure policies and procedures touch on the day-to-day operations of the IT staff, including the way security is monitored (auditing functions, log files, alerts) and how it is maintained (backups, updates, upgrades). Policies regarding user behavior are also crucial to ensuring that the network infrastructure remains safe. Finally, corporate policies regarding the use of data, computer and electronic equipment, and building access, to name just three, are areas that should be reviewed and revised to support and enhance security across the enterprise. For more specific information on polices and procedures, see Chapter 13, "Operational Security."

Organizational Needs

The internal environment is shaped by the organization's business profile, including the type of business, the nature of sales and marketing functions, the types of customers, the kinds of employees, and the flow of work through the company. What does your company require from the network services you provide, and how can these needs be secured? If you believe your organization's network, data, and computer needs are being met, delineate what they are and check with a few users to see if you're on the mark or if you're really off-center by a wide margin. Make sure that you understand how the network fits into the organization, not the other way around, and then design your security solution around it.

Regulatory/Compliance

Any infrastructure assessment and security plan must incorporate regulatory and compliance requirements. These vary greatly from state to state and country to country, and as you're probably well aware, keeping up with them can be more than a full-time job. Many companies are hiring compliance officers whose primary job is to manage corporate compliance. If your company has a compliance officer, you should certainly make sure he or she is a member of your IT project team, at least during the definition phase, when you're developing your functional and technical requirements, since these are often the method by which compliance occurs. We've included a short list here with a few Web site links, but it's not exhaustive; you should seek legal advice regarding regulatory and compliance requirements for your firm if you don't have a knowledgeable and experienced compliance officer in place.

Business Intelligence...

Common Compliance Standards

There are numerous compliance issues facing organizations today. Below are just a few of the compliance standards you should be aware of and should evaluate whether your firm is subject to these regulations or not.

British Standard 7799 (BS7799), eventually evolved into ISO17799.

Child Online Protection Act (COPA), www.copacommission.org.

Continued

Health Insurance Portability and Accountability Act (HIPAA), www.cms.hhs.gov/hipaa/hipaa1/content/more.asp.

Family Educational Rights and Privacy Act (FERPA), www.ed.gov/policy/gen/guid/fpco/ferpa/index.html.

Federal Information Security Mgmt Act (FISMA), csrc.nist.gov/seccert/.

Gramm-Leach Bliley Act (GLBA), www.ftc.gov/privacy/glbact/.

Homeland Security Presidential Directive 7 (HSPD-7), www.whitehouse.gov/news/release/2003/12/20031217-5.html.

ISO 17799, www.iso.org (International Organization for Standardization's INFOSEC recommendations).

National Strategy to Secure Cyberspace, www.whitehouse.gov/pcipb/.

Sarbanes-Oxley Act (SOX), www.aicpa.org/sarbanes/index.asp.

Technology

The technology assessment involves the three elements: people, process, and technology. However, the technology portion of the assessment will probably take up 80% of your time due to the vast number of technological components involved in securing the infrastructure. Servers and hosts must be updated, patched, and secured. Applications must be updated, patched, and secured. The perimeter of your network must be secured, tested, and monitored. Remote access and wireless access must be secured, tested, and monitored. Data traveling across the network needs to be secured against a variety of attack types, which is done through various protocols at different network layers, depending on where the data originates, where it's headed, and what it contains. We'll spend the remainder of the chapter looking at the technology components of infrastructure security, holding off discussing the policies and procedures (which impact user behavior and the *people* aspect) until a later chapter.

Establishing Baselines

The point of performing these assessments is not to prove that your network is secure or insecure but to find out exactly what level of security you actually have and to establish baselines. When you know the starting point, you can improve security incrementally and document it as you go. Baselines are created by establishing a known starting point, in this case your current settings.

It might be tempting to correct problems as you perform this assessment, but it's not the best way to proceed. As you know, making a configuration change at Point A can cause a ripple effect through your network and show up at Point C in a strange and unexpected way. As you develop your project plan, be clear with your project team that they need to document existing configurations, settings, versions, and so on, without making changes. If a team member finds a serious security hole, it should be brought to your attention immediately for action. The point is that if a serious problem is found, it should be quickly addressed but not in an ad hoc manner. It should be assessed and addressed in a calm, rational, thoughtful manner, and possibly incorporated into your project plan. Does that mean that you wait until your project planning is complete to address a serious security hole? Absolutely not. You should, however, use a well thought out strategy for addressing it outside the project planning cycle, then document the changes and incorporate them into your project plan. What you want to avoid is having every person looking at the network making small tweaks here and there to "tighten up security" as they go, because you'll end up with a mess at the end of your evaluation period. Serious problems should be brought to your immediate, and minor issues should be well documented.

Addressing Risks to the Corporate Network

Once you have created a prioritized list of risks to your network as well as their associated costs, your next step will be to determine a course of action in handling each risk. When deciding how to address risks to your network, you typically have one of four options:

- **Avoidance** You can avoid a risk by changing the scope of the project so that the risk in question no longer applies, or change the features of the software to do the same. In most cases, this is not a viable option, since eliminating a network service such as e-mail to avoid risks from viruses would usually not be seen as an appropriate measure. (Network services exist for a reason; your job as a security professional is to make those services as secure as possible.) One example of how avoidance would be a useful risk management tactic is a case where a company has a single server that acts as both a Web server and a database server housing confidential personnel records, when there is no interaction whatsoever between the Web site and personnel information. In this scenario, purchasing a second server to house the employee database, removing the personnel database from the Web server entirely, and placing the employee database server on a private network segment with no contact to the Internet would be a way of avoiding Web-based attacks on personnel records, since this plan of action "removes" a feature of the Web server (the personnel files) entirely.

- **Transference** You can transfer a risk by moving the responsibility to a third party. The most well-known example of this solution is purchasing some type of insurance—let's say flood insurance—for the contents of your server room. Although the purchase of this insurance does not diminish the likelihood that a flood will occur in your server room, it does ensure that the monetary cost of the damage will be borne by the insurance company in return for your policy premiums. It's important to note that transference is not a 100-percent solution—in the flood example, your company will likely still incur some financial loss or decreased productivity in the time it takes you to restore your server room to working order. As with most risk management tactics, bringing the risk exposure down to zero is usually an unattainable goal.

- **Mitigation** This is what most IT professionals think of when implementing a risk management solution. Mitigation involves taking some positive action to reduce the likelihood that an attack will occur or to reduce the potential damage that would be caused by an attack, without removing the resource entirely, as is the case with avoidance. Patching servers, disabling unneeded services, and installing a firewall are some solutions that fall under the heading of risk mitigation.

- **Acceptance** After you have delineated all the risks to your infrastructure that can be avoided, transferred, or mitigated, you are still left with a certain amount of risk that you won't be able to reduce any further without seriously impacting your business (taking an e-mail server offline as a means to combat viruses, for example). Your final option is one of acceptance, where you decide that the residual risks to your network have reached an acceptable level, and you choose to monitor the network for any signs of new or increased risks that might require more action later.

There is no one right way to address all risks to your infrastructure; you'll most likely take a blended approach to security. There are some risks you absolutely need to avoid, other risks you can reasonably transfer or mitigate, and still others that you simply accept because the cost of avoiding them is just not worth it.

Business Intelligence...

Depth in Defense

Depth in defense is a key concept to understand before heading into an infrastructure security project. The concept is a fairly straightforward one: Security comes not from one source but from many layers of protection. Almost any attacker can find a way in through a single-defense

Continued

system, but it's much more difficult (but not impossible) to find a way in through a maze of security measures. When security measures are used in combination, it's like having a deadbolt, a padlock, a keypad, a card reader, and a biometric scanner attached to the network. An attacker can get through one or two, maybe even three, but it's the fourth and fifth layers that finally stop the would-be intruder and cause him or her to look for another, easier target. In the world of IT security, nothing is 100-percent secure unless it's powered off and locked in an isolated box, at which point it becomes completely useless. Understanding the depth-in-defense approach will help you as you try to evaluate the measures you should take to secure your network infrastructure. You may choose to implement something less iron-clad (at a drastically lower cost) in one area, knowing that the "layering" effect will likely give you a strong enough level of defense against most known threats.

External Environment

The external environment includes the changes in technology that might impact your business, the changes in the regulatory and legal environments that could impact your business, and the changing landscape of threats to your network. It's not a static picture; you'll need to implement policies and procedures that allow you and your IT staff to remain up to date with these changes so that you can continually monitor, assess, and address these changes in a proactive and positive manner.

We've talked about the legal implications of compliance and the importance of understanding those compliance issues when you're planning your IT security project. Because these issues are numerous, industry specific, and ever changing, we're not going to get into specific compliance data in this book. We recap some of the more common ones in this section, just in case you missed them earlier. We've also provided some Web links for you to learn more about these standards. There may be serious legal issues involved with compliance and noncompliance, so be sure to check with your firm's legal counsel to determine the regulations that apply to your firm. You might want to complete the internal assessment prior to contacting your attorney, so that you have a clear understanding of the kinds of information your network stores and the criticality of that information. For example, if your company recently started storing segments of people's medical records as part of a new business partnership with another firm, you will most likely have to comply with HIPAA standards (and possibly others). Recent changes to your company's business may have pulled you into areas in which regulation and compliance are mandatory, so be sure to do a full assessment here.

Threats

Predicting network threats and analyzing the risks they present to your infrastructure are among the cornerstones of the network security design process. Understanding the types of threats that your network will face helps you in designing appropriate countermeasures and in obtaining the necessary money and resources to create a secure network framework. Members of an organization's management structure will likely be resistant to spending money on a threat that they don't understand; this process will also help them understand the very real consequences of network threats so they can make informed decisions about the types of measures to implement. In this section, we discuss some common network attacks that you will likely face when you're designing a secure network and how each of these attacks can adversely affect your network.

When classifying network threats, many developers and security analysts have taken to using a model called STRIDE, which is an acronym for the following terms:

- **Spoofing identity** These include attacks that involve illegally accessing and using account information that isn't yours, such as shoulder-surfing someone's password while he types it on his keyboard. This type of attack affects the confidentiality of data.

- **Tampering with data** These attacks involve a malicious modification of data, interfering with the integrity of an organization's data. The most common of these is a man-in-the-middle (MITM) attack, where a third party intercepts communications between two legitimate hosts and tampers with the information as it is sent back and forth. This is akin to sending an e-mail to Mary that says, "The meeting is at 3:00 P.M.", but a malicious attacker intercepts and changes the message to, "The meeting has been cancelled."

- **Repudiation** These threats occur when a user can perform a malicious action against a network resource and then deny that she did so, and the owners or administrators of the data have no way of proving otherwise. A repudiation threat can attack any portion of the confidentiality, integrity, and availability (CIA) triad.

- **Information disclosure** This occurs when information is made available to individuals who should not have access to it. Information disclosure can occur through improperly applied network permissions that allow a user to read a confidential file or give an intruder the ability to read data being transmitted between two networked computers. Information disclosure affects the confidentiality of your company's data and resources.

- **Denial of service** So-called DoS attacks do not attempt to alter a company's data; rather, they attack a network by denying access to valid users, by flooding a Web server with phony requests so that legitimate users cannot access it, for example. DoS attacks affect the availability of your organization's data and resources. A new variation is a distributed DoS (DDoS), also called a *zombie net* or *zombie attack*.

- **Elevation of privilege** This type of attack takes place when an unprivileged, nonadministrative user gains administrative or "root level" access to an entire system, usually through a flaw in the system software. When this occurs, an attacker has the ability to alter or even destroy any data that he finds, since he is acting with administrative privileges.

This type of threat affects all portions of the CIA triad, since the attacker can access, change, and remove any data that he or she sees fit. When you are analyzing a potential network threat, try to remember the

STRIDE acronym as a means of classifying and reacting to the threat. You can use the STRIDE model throughout the life of your corporate network when you're designing and maintaining security policies and procedures.

Recognizing External Threats

Now that we've discussed a model for classifying network threats, we can look at some of the common attacks in more detail. Entire books can be (and have been) written that solely discuss the kinds of threats that we look at in this section, so we'll be giving you a "birds-eye" view of the kinds of attacks that your network security design will need to guard against.

Denial-of-Service Attacks

As we've already mentioned, the DoS attack (and its first cousin, the DDoS attack) works to disrupt services on a network so that legitimate users cannot access resources they need. Some examples include attempts to disrupt the connection between two specific machines, or more commonly, attempts to flood an entire network with traffic, thereby overloading the network and preventing legitimate traffic from being transmitted. There can also be instances in which an illegitimate use of resources can result in denial of service. For example, if an intruder uses a vulnerability in your FTP server to upload and store illegal software, this can consume all available disk space on the FTP server and prevent legitimate users from storing their files. A DoS attack can effectively disable a single computer or an entire network.

A common venue of attack for DoS is against an organization's network bandwidth and connectivity; the attacker's goal is to prevent other machines from communicating due to the traffic flood. An example of this type of attack is the *SYN flood attack*. In a SYN flood, the attacker begins to establish a connection to the victim machine but in such a way that the connection is never completed. Since even the most powerful server has only a certain amount of memory and number processor cycles to devote to its workload, legitimate connection attempts can be denied while the victim machine is trying to complete these fake "half-open" connections.

Another common DoS is the so-called *Ping of Death,* where an attacker sends so many *PING* requests to a target machine that it is overloaded and unable to process legitimate network requests. An intruder might also attempt to consume network resources in other ways, including generating a massive number of e-mail messages, intentionally generating system errors that need to be included in Event Viewer logs, or misusing FTP directories or network shares to overload available disk space. Basically, anything that allows data, whether on a network cable or hard drive, to be written at will (without any type of control mechanism) can create a DoS when the attack has exhausted a system's finite resources.

Distributed Denial-of-Service Attacks

Distributed denial-of-service (DDoS) attacks are a relatively new development, made possible (and attractive to attackers) by the ever-expanding number of machines that are attached to the Internet. The first major wave of DDoS attacks on the Internet appeared in early 2000 and targeted such major e-commerce and news sites as Yahoo!, eBay, Amazon, Datek, and CNN. In each case, the Web sites belonging to these companies were unreachable for several hours at a time, causing a severe disruption to their online presence and effectiveness. Many more DDoS attacks have occurred since then, affecting networks and Web sites large and small.

WARNING

Most publicity surrounding DDoS attacks has focused on Web servers as a target, but remember that any computer attached to the Internet can fall victim to the effects of a DDoS attack. This can include everything from file servers or e-mail servers to your users' desktop workstations.

The DDoS attack begins with a human attacker using a small number of computers, called *masters*. The master computers use network scanners to find as many weakly secured computers as it can, and they use system vulnerabilities (usually well-known ones) to install a small script or a service (referred to in the UNIX world as a *daemon*) onto the insecure computer. This machine becomes a *zombie* and can now be triggered by the master computer to attack any computer or network attached to the Internet. Once the organizer of the DDoS attack has a sufficient number of zombie machines under control, he or she will use the "zombi-fied" machines to send a stream of packets to a designated target computer or network, called the *victim*. For most of these attacks, these packets are directed at the victim machine. The distributed nature of the DDoS attack makes it extremely difficult to track down the person or persons who began it; the actual attacks are coming from zombie machines, and the owners of these machines are often not even aware that their machines have been compromised. Making matters even more difficult, most network packets used in DDoS attacks use forged source addresses, which means that they are essentially lying about where the attack is coming from.

Viruses, Worms, and Trojan Horses

Viruses, Trojans, and worms are quite possibly the most disruptive of all security threats that we discuss in this section. These three types of threats, working alone or in combination, can alter or delete data files and executable programs on your network shares, flood e-mail servers and network connections with malicious traffic, and even create a "back door" into your systems that can allow a remote attacker to entirely take over control of a computer. You'll often hear these three terms used interchangeably, but each type of threat is slightly different. A *virus* is a piece of code that will alter an existing file and then use that alteration to recreate itself many times over. A *worm* simply makes copies of itself over and over again for the purpose of exhausting available system resources. A worm can target both hard drive space and processor cycles.

Business Intelligence...

Even Symantec Is Vulnerable

On May 24, 2006, a research company, eEye Digital Security, announced it had discovered a *high severity* security vulnerability in the Symantec antivirus program used by 200 million computers worldwide. The vulnerability was characterized as severe because it didn't require any user interaction to be exploited, making it highly susceptible to worm attacks. The irony is, of course, that this vulnerability was discovered not a week after the CEO of Symantec slammed Microsoft's "security monoculture" as a source of vulnerability. Since no one single product or defense will provide adequate security in today's threat environment, this finding underscores the need for depth in defense. And, as Symantec's CEO discovered, it also underscores the danger of tossing rocks at security "glass houses."

Software Vulnerabilities

Some network attacks target vulnerabilities in the way that a software application or entire operating system has been programmed. For example, a buffer overflow attack occurs when a malicious user sends more data to a program than it knows how to handle. For example, we've all seen Web forms that ask you to fill in personal information: first name, last name, telephone number, and so forth. A careless developer might program the "First Name" field to only be able to handle 10 characters; that is, a name that is 10 letters long. If the Web application does not check for buffer overflows, an attacker can input a long string of gibberish into the First Name field in an attempt to cause a buffer overflow error. At this point, the attacker could even embed the name of an executable file into that long string of text and actually pass commands to the system as if he or she were sitting at the server console itself. A similar software vulnerability is a format string vulnerability that would allow an attacker to insert random data into a file or database, including malicious code that can be executed against the server as though the attacker were sitting right in front of the keyboard.

Another attack that is specifically common to Web and FTP servers is a *directory traversal vulnerability*. This type of vulnerability allows a user to gain access to a directory on a server that he hasn't been specifically given permissions to, by virtue of having permissions to a parent or child directory. Say that someone goes to the URL www.airplanes.com/biplanes/cessna/model1.html. He decides to manually change this URL (in other words, not following an <HREF> link on the site itself) to www.airplanes.com/biplanes/piper, to see if the directory structure holds any information there. If the Web site hasn't been properly patched and configured with the correct security settings, the user might find that he now has access to every single file in the piper/ directory. Even worse, he can once again execute a command from the Web browser by changing the URL to something like www.airplanes.com/biplanes/piper/del%20*.*. (*%20* is used in HTML to represent a space, so that command would read *del *.** on a regular command line.)

Another common attack also occurred in NetMeeting and Windows Media Player some time ago, where an attacker could insert special characters during a file transfer that would allow him to browse an unsuspecting user's hard drive directory structure.

Unfortunately, the breadth and depth of software vulnerabilities grows almost daily due to the wonderfully wide variety of applications available on the market. This variety provides new and useful functionality to users, but it obviously can create headaches for IT staff just trying to keep up.

Nontechnical Attacks

A final category of attack that we'll discuss here are those that use less technical means to circumvent network security. *Social engineering attacks* rely on an unsuspecting user's lack of security consciousness. In some cases, the attacker will rely on someone's goodwill, using a tactic like, "I've really got to get this done and I don't have access to these files. Can you help me?" (This works because most of us, at heart, really want to be helpful to those around us.) Other social engineering attacks use a more threat-based approach, insisting that the attacker is the secretary for Mr. Big-Shot VP who needs his password reset right away and heaven help you if you keep him waiting. This method relies on the assumption that a show of authority will cause someone without adequate training to bypass security procedures, to keep the "big-shot important user/client" happy. Since social engineering attacks are nontechnical in nature, the measures required to defend against them are more administrative than anything else. It's critical to have well-understood security policies in place that apply to everyone, regardless of their position in your company. This will assist in preventing an attacker from circumventing security procedures because a help desk or other staff member is unaware of them. We discuss user education and awareness campaigns later in this book.

Top 20 Threats

The SANS organization publishes and maintains a top-20 list of network threats. You might want to refer to this list as you're developing your infrastructure security plan; it will give you excellent insight into the latest threats and how to address them. For the most up-to-date list, visit www.sans.org/top20/#threatindex. The current Top Vulnerabilities in Windows Systems list contains the following categories:

- W1. Windows Services
- W2. Internet Explorer
- W3. Windows Libraries
- W4. Microsoft Office and Outlook Express
- W5. Windows Configuration Weaknesses

The Top Vulnerabilities in Cross-Platform Applications list:

- C1. Backup Software
- C2. Antivirus Software
- C3. PHP-based Applications

- C4. Database Software

- C5. File Sharing Applications

- C6. DNS Software

- C7. Media Players

- C8. Instant Messaging Applications

- C9. Mozilla and Firefox Browsers

- C10. Other Cross-platform Applications

The Top Vulnerabilities in UNIX Systems list:

- U1. UNIX Configuration Weaknesses

- U2. Mac OS X

The Top Vulnerabilities in Networking Products list:

- N1. Cisco IOS and non-IOS Products

- N2. Juniper, CheckPoint and Symantec Products

- N3. Cisco Devices Configuration Weaknesses

Later in this chapter, we'll look at the major threats and vulnerabilities so you can build these into your project plan, as appropriate, based on your own unique network configuration.

Business Intelligence...

Hackers Turn to Security Software

An article in the *Washington Post* in late 2005 highlighted a new and growing trend among hackers: the new focus on security software used by millions of end users. In the "old days," hackers focused on attacking operating systems and exploiting known vulnerabilities. Although that still occurs, the new threat front is in the very software you rely on to secure your computer from the bad guys. As hackers look for and exploit

Continued

these vulnerabilities, they expose users to a whole new realm of risk. Operating systems such as Windows and Linux are now regularly updated and patched, but security software programs typically were only updating virus signature files, not the program itself. Now security software program makers are finding their products under attack and are having to respond as operating system companies once did.

For more information and to read the whole article, head to this URL: www.washingtonpost.com/wp-dyn/content/article/2005/11/21/AR2005112101424.html.

Network Security Checklist

This section is a lengthy one and is intended to provide you with a thorough review of the types of things you should review, assess, and think about when you prepare your infrastructure security project plan. Even though we've created a detailed list, there's always a chance there are additional elements your plan will need. Certainly, there's also a strong likelihood that there are things in these checklists that you don't have and don't need. That's okay. The point is to try to help you think through all the details you possibly can about your network infrastructure, to ensure that you are thorough and don't leave any stone unturned. At the end of this process, you may decide not to address some aspects of infrastructure security, or you might choose to work on some of these items in a Phase 2 or Phase 3 project plan. This should give you a great start in thinking all this through.

We've divided the infrastructure project into four main areas, though you may choose to parse it out differently. We'll look at devices and media and ways to secure network devices (excluding servers and user computers) and the network media. Media could mean secure network area storage devices (NAS), backup media, or other storage devices. The "Topologies" section includes how you segment the network for security, including creating DMZs and implementing firewalls, and how you secure network traffic. Intrusion detection and prevention systems are pretty popular these days (for good reason), so we'll look at best practices for implementing IDS/IPS that you can utilize in your project plan.

Finally, we'll look at system hardening, including hardening infrastructure servers (DNS, DHCP, and so on), application and database servers, and other computers on the network. Keep in mind that this is not a "how to" as much as it is a list of things to consider and include in your project plan. There are volumes filled with information on these topics; it would be far outside the scope of this book to talk about how you do these things. Our intent is to provide a framework and a solid starting point for your infrastructure security project-planning process. If you're not sure what some of these things are or if you're uncertain as to how to address these issues, you'll need to do further research on these topics.

Devices and Media

Network devices typically include routers, switches, firewalls, and other communication devices. We cover these items extensively at the end of this section (we placed it there because it's a long, wide-ranging list). The short story is that routers, switches, and other communication devices should be:

1. **Physically secured** Place devices in a locked cabinet, locked room, and locked building, where possible. Where that's not possible, devices should be closely monitored or access should be controlled or limited.

2. **Physically inspected** Remove extra cables, disable external ports, and disconnect unused connections.

3. **Hardened** Remove unused software, disable unused ports, stop or uninstall unused protocols and services, disable unused functionality, remove unused user accounts, change default settings, use strong passwords, and remove or limit all but one administrative account.

4. **Monitored** Audit, log, and monitor all access to devices, both physical and logical; monitor all successful logons; monitor all failed logons; review log files frequently; and store configuration data in a safe, secure location.

5. **Encrypted** Encrypt sensitive data files; encrypt and secure all removable media; create a secure system for handling removable media, including backup files; create a log file to track media handling; secure removable media in locked, access-controlled location; and store archives in a secure, off-site location.

Topologies

Network infrastructure security:

1. Create secure boundaries using firewalls, DMZs, and proxy servers.

2. Create secure remote access.

3. Create secure wireless access.

4. Implement a segmented network.

5. Implement network traffic security protocols for sensitive network traffic.

6. Deploy network security technologies.

   - Use Encrypting File System (EFS) or similar file encryption.

   - Require and use strong user authentication, passwords and account policies.

   - Employ the concept of "least privileges" when assigning user rights.

Security infrastructure components include routers, proxy servers, firewalls, and DMZs. Firewalls are pretty straightforward and can be implemented as hardware or software solutions. Let's take a side street and take a quick look at DMZs.

Demilitarized zones, or *DMZs,* are isolated network segments that typically sit between the Internet and your network, whether in front of or behind your firewall (or between two firewalls). There are many different ways to set up a DMZ; again, it's outside the scope of this book to discuss the design, implementation, and configuration of a DMZ. However, it might be helpful to discuss a few highlights of DMZ design that might help as you look at implementing or tightening a DMZ for your network.

Designing DMZs

DMZ design, like security design, is always a work in progress. As in security planning and analysis, we find DMZ design carries great flexibility and change potential to keep the protection levels we put in place in an effective state. The ongoing work is required so that the system's security is always as high as we can make it within the constraints of time and budget, while still allowing appropriate users and visitors to access the information and services we provide. You will find that the time and funds spent in the design process and preparation for the implementation are very good investments if the process is focused and effective; this will lead to a high level of success and a good level of protection for your network.

In this section of the chapter, we explore the fundamentals of the design process. We incorporate the information we discussed in relation to security and traffic flow to make decisions about how our initial design should look. Additionally, we'll build on that information and review some other areas of concern that could affect the way you design your DMZ structure.

Design of the DMZ is critically important to the overall protection of your internal network—and the success of your firewall and DMZ deployment. The DMZ design can incorporate sections that isolate incoming VPN traffic, Web traffic, partner connections, employee connections, and public access to information provided by your organization. Design of the DMZ structure throughout the organization can protect internal resources from internal attack. As we discussed in the security section, it has been well documented that much of the risk of data loss, corruption, and breach actually exists inside the network perimeter. Our tendency is to protect assets from external harm but to disregard the dangers that come from our own internal equipment, policies, and employees.

These attacks or disruptions do not arise solely from disgruntled employees. Many of the most damaging conditions occur because of inadvertent mistakes made by well-intentioned employees. Each of these entry points is a potential source of loss for your organization and ultimately can provide an attack point to defeat your other defenses. Additionally, the design of your DMZ will allow you to implement a multilayered approach to securing your resources that does not leave a single point of failure in your plan. This minimizes the problems and loss of protection that can occur because of misconfiguration of rule sets or ACL lists, as well as reducing the problems that can occur due to hardware configuration errors.

Remote Access

Remote access is granted in a number of different ways, so the way it should be secured varies widely. The basics are that the remote access servers should be physically secured (as should all infrastructure servers) in an access-controlled location. The number of accounts that are authorized to log onto the server for administrative purposes should be limited and audited. The communication link between the RAS and the remote users should be secured, as should the data on that link, if needed. The network traffic security methods include signing, encryption, and tunneling. The level of these methods is determined by the system with the least capabilities. Older operating systems cannot utilize the latest encryption technologies, for example, so you might include policies that require that remotely connecting users use the latest version of Windows XP Professional, to enable the entire end-to-end communication link to use the strongest available encryption. You can also require strong authentication across remote links. Different operating systems implement this differently; in Windows Server 2003, for example, it's implemented through policies set in Administrative Tools | Routing and Remote Access.

Wireless Access

We've devoted a whole chapter to wireless security, so we will only discuss the top-level items here:

- Change access point default settings.

- Disable SSID broadcasting; create a closed system (does not respond to clients with "Any" SSID assigned).

- Transmission power control (limiting the amount of power used for transmission to control the signal range).

- Enable MAC address filtering.

- Enable WEP or WPA.

- Filter protocols.

- Define IP allocations for the WLAN.

- Use VPNs.

- Secure users'computers.

All these choices have pros and cons, distinct advantages and disadvantages; you'll need to decide the right approach for your organization. As with all things in IT security, it's important that you understand the result of the solutions you're using, understand the configuration and maintenance of these elements, and be sure you test them well in a lab or isolated setting before implementing them across the enterprise.

Intrusion Detection Systems/ Intrusion Prevention Systems (IDS/IPS)

First, let's define IDS and IPS, because they're not one and the same. *Intrusion detection systems* (IDS) are passive in nature; they let you know an intrusion is taking place or has occurred. They do nothing to stop an intrusion. On the other hand, an *intrusion prevention system* (IPS) is an active system that works to stop an intrusion or to prevent one when "it thinks" one is occurring. How does "it" think? It does so based on how you configure it, so we end up back at that persistent *people* problem we've mentioned once or twice. An IPS has one major drawback, and that is the high likelihood of false positives. Depending on how you configure the IPS, the results of a response to a false positive might be far more devastating than an actual intrusion, so you're walking a fine line with IPS. That said, some excellent hardware and software solutions are available on the market today, many of which are a great improvement over IDS/IPS systems of the past. It is far outside the scope of this book to discuss the pros and cons, the highlights and lowlights of these systems, so we're not going there. However, we will mention a few different ways you can implement and secure your IDS/IPS systems and leave it up to you to develop a specific plan for implementing these systems, since they are so varied.

A word of caution: IDS/IPS is not a standalone defense. You should implement it with the understanding that it contributes to your depth of defense, but alone it will not keep your network safe. It's a great tool to have in your security toolkit, but it's not the magic bullet everyone wishes they had.

IPSs introduce fundamental performance and stability issues within the network or system they are designed to protect. The act of implementing automatic controls in response to detecting attacks does not come without a price. For example, an inline network IPS will not forward packets before inspecting Application-layer data. This inspection takes time and can result in a slowdown in the responsiveness and throughput of the local network. A host IPS that has been charged with the inspection and validation of an application's system calls can impact a kernel's ability to quickly service system calls, which may only be 1 to 15 percent but is probably noticeable.

Network Active Response System

A *network active response system* has the ability to interact with network traffic indirectly through the modification of firewall policies and router Access Control Lists (ACLs). They also have the ability to take down switch ports (for locally generated attacks) and to spoof error code packets such as Transmission Control Protocol (TCP), RST (Reset), or Internet Control Message Protocol (ICMP) unreachable packets. Such an active response system is commonly implemented directly within a network IDS, where it can easily take advantage of its detection capabilities.

This is useful for tearing down individual sessions or for trying to convince an attacking host that the target is unreachable due to ICMP errors. However, there is not usually much time between these measures and the goal of the attack. It's unclear whether the countermeasure will be successful.

There are four classes of countermeasure that a network IPS can utilize to thwart a network-based attack. Each class applies to one layer of the protocol stack, beginning at the Data Link layer:

- **Data Link layer countermeasures** Administratively shut down a switch port interface associated with a system from which attacks are being launched. This approach is feasible only for attacks that are generated from a local system. Having the ability to timeout the downed switch port is important, since the port probably should not be shut down indefinitely.

- **Network layer countermeasures** Interact with the external firewall or router to add a general rule to block all communication from individual IP addresses or entire networks. An inline IPS can accomplish the same thing without having to appeal to an external device, since packets from specific IP addresses can simply be blocked after an attack has been detected. Similarly to Data Link layer responses, timeouts are important at the Network layer, since the firewall rule set or router ACL modifications should be removed after a configurable amount of time.

- **Transport layer countermeasures** Generate TCP RST packets to tear down malicious TCP sessions, or issues any of several available ICMP error-code packets in response to malicious UDP traffic. (Note that ICMP is strictly a Network layer protocol and is the standard method of communicating various errors to clients that utilize UDP). Timeouts are not applicable here, because countermeasures are leveraged against an attacker on a per-session or per-packet basis.

- **Application layer countermeasures** Alter malicious Application layer data so as to render it harmless before it reaches the target system. This countermeasure requires that the IPS be in line in the communication path. Any previously calculated Transport layer checksum must be recalculated. Similarly to the Network layer, timeouts are not applicable here, since the effects of replacing Application layer data are transitory and do not linger once an altered packet is forwarded through the IPS.

Later in this chapter, we'll walk through a number of "generic" countermeasures and hardening tasks related to these layers when we look at various ways routers, switches, and other network devices can be hardened in conjunction with whatever IDS/IPS system you implement.

Host Active Response System

A *host active response system* is usually implemented in software and is deployed directly on a host system. Once a suspicious event has been detected on a host (through any number of means, such as log file analysis, detection of specific files or registry keys associated with known exploits, or a suspicious server running on a high port), a host active response system is charged with taking an action. As with network active response, the expectation for a host active response system is that countermeasures will not necessarily prevent an attack from initially being successful. The emphasis is on trying to mitigate the effects and damage caused by an attack after detection. After an attack is detected, automated responses can include alteration of file system permissions, changes in access that a system grants to users, automated removal of worms or viruses (anti-virus), and additions of new rules to a local firewall subsystem.

Before we move into system hardening, let's take a look at how IDS/IPS systems are implemented in the network infrastructure. Figure 11.2 shows the IDS system as part of the infrastructure. The IDS server, in this case, would be connected to a span port so that it would monitor all traffic on the local network. The IDS system is capable of spoofing a TCP RST or ICMP error code packet to thwart the attack but would not be effective against single-packet attacks.

Figure 11.2 IDS System Placement in Infrastructure

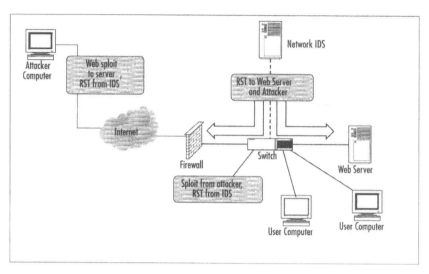

An inline system performs a bit differently, as shown in Figure 11.3. In this case, the inline system captures the sploit (short for *exploit*) and modifies it to protect the local network. A typical deployment of the IPS occurs just inside the firewall. In this position, it captures all incoming traffic before it goes to the local network, providing ubiquitous protection, even for single-packet attacks. Because all traffic flows through an inline IPS, downsides such as false positives and slower response times must be factored in.

Next Generation Security Devices

As you look at your current implementation of IDS or IPS (or if you're considering an implementation), you should also keep an eye on recent developments in the world of security devices. *Network processors* can be deployed in various architectures including parallel, where each processor handles $1/N$ of the total load or pipeline, where, as a packet moves through the pipeline, each processor typically handles a single specific repetitive task. The network processor was originally targeted to the routing market, but it is easy to see how it can be applied to the increased demands of packet inspection in network security. For example, one processor could handle the pattern matching for known worm signatures, another could analyze for protocol standards compliance, and yet another could look for protocol or usage anomalies. The network processor would have direct access to fast memory that stores policies and signatures, whereas slower, larger memory would store state information and heuristics information. New attacks could be mitigated by adding new code to the network processor. A separate processor can handle management functions such as logging and policy management. Network processors also offer the ability to scale, much like CPUs on computer systems.

Figure 11.3 IPS System Inline Placement in Infrastructure

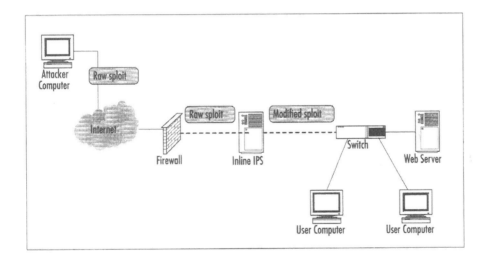

System Hardening

Server security:

1. Always control physical and network access to critical servers,
   especially domain controllers, DNS servers, DHCP servers, and
   other infrastructure servers. Keep infrastructure servers in an
   access-controlled location.

2. Always perform tasks on the servers with the least possible privileges. Do not perform tasks with Administrator privileges, if possible. Use the *Run As* command (or equivalent) when needed.

3. Restrict user and machine access to groups that have loose security settings. Provide users and computers with the least possible

permissions while still meeting their needs to access and use network resources.

4. Secure the data on the computers using strong ACLs and, if needed, the *syskey* utility. The *syskey* utility provides protection against password-cracking software that targets the Security Access Management (SAM) database or directory services. It uses strong encryption that is much more difficult (if not close to impossible) and time consuming to crack.

5. Require the use of strong passwords via password policy settings.

6. Restrict the downloading and installation of programs that do not come from known, trusted sources.

7. Maintain up-to-date virus protection on all systems.

8. Keep all software patches up to date. Patches often address newly discovered security holes. Applying patches in a timely manner on all affected machines can prevent problems that are easily avoided.

9. Deploy server, application and client-side security technologies:

   ■ Secure server traffic traveling on the network.

   ■ Secure application and user data traveling on the network.

   ■ Secure network access points and network access.

   ■ Secure client devices including desktops, laptops, and PDAs.

   ■ Implement automatically updating virus and spyware protection systems.

Other Infrastructure Issues

1. Deploy network monitoring and auditing.

2. Develop a disaster recovery plan that includes creating backups, documenting recovery options and using repair and recovery tools. (See Chapter 13 for more on disaster planning and recovery.)

www.syngress.com

3. Develop standard operating procedures that include strong monitoring, auditing, and documentation.

Business Intelligence...

Rootkits

There's been a lot of news in the recent past about the problems presented by rootkit attacks. As you're well aware, those little pieces of malware reside so deep in the system that you can't possibly remove them without completely starting from scratch. After a system is compromised, all the affected software must be reinstalled from known "clean" sources. Since it can be difficult to determine precisely which pieces of software have been affected, the best way to guarantee security is to reinstall the entire operating system (OS) and all applications. OS kernels can also be compromised (see www.rootkit.com), and when they are, nothing on the system (even the most basic file system, memory, and network status information) can be trusted. An after-the-fact forensic analysis of the file system may turn up useful information if the disk is mounted underneath an uncompromised OS, but this is a time-consuming operation.

Other Network Components: Routers, Switches, RAS, NMS, IDS

There are numerous components that should be checked during an infrastructure security project. The list in this section was compiled, in part, from a network checklist developed by the Defense Information Systems Agency (DISA) for the Department of Defense (DoD). Although not all items listed will apply to your network and it's possible that not all items that apply to your network appear on this list, this is an extensive list that you can use as the starting point for your own checklist. Some of the items in this list contain brief explanations included to help you understand their importance. Our assumption is that you're familiar with the ins and outs of network security, but there are a few places where a quick clarification will help, and we've included them as well. These are written in language that reflects problems you would find that should be remedied (for instance, highlighting the problem you're looking for, not necessarily the solution you should implement). The list is organized by device type, beginning with routers and other network devices and moving on to firewalls, VLANs, RAS servers, and so on.

Network

- **Network infrastructure is not properly documented** You should begin with a clear understanding of how your network infrastructure is currently configured. This should be well documented and kept up to date.

- **Network connections exist without approval** All network connections should exist only with explicit approval or knowledge of the IT department. This is typically a problem with modems, wireless access points, and USB-type network devices.

- **Unmanaged backdoor connections, backdoor network connections bypass perimeter** Every network in the world has a variety of backdoor connections that network administrators use (or that software developers build in). When unmanaged, these connections create security problems for your network infrastructure. These are especially problematic when these backdoors bypass perimeter security systems. If you can use them, so can the bad guys.

- **Circuit location is not secure** The location of network circuitry, including the backbone and other highly critical components, should be secured physically.

- **Network devices are not stored in secure communications room** This is part of physical security; to the extent possible, network devices should be stored in a secure communications room. This should certainly be true for mission-critical devices. Physical security of the company's premises, coupled with physical security of key network devices, is part of a depth-in-defense strategy.

- **Minimum operating system release level** All network devices—from desktop computers to servers to firewalls to routers—should have the latest updates and patches for the operating system they are running. As seen from the top-20 threat list, many are threats to portions of the operating system, so all device operating systems should be kept up to date. Where possible, you may also choose to upgrade the operating system itself to a newer, more secure version, where appropriate. This OS release-level maintenance should also apply to routers and other devices that have operating systems, firmware, or other embedded software functionality.

- **DNS servers must be defined for client resolver** If a router or similar network device is specified as a client resolver (resolves DNS to IP address), the router should have a DNS server defined. If the DNS server is specified, it makes it more difficult for an attacker to substitute his or her IP address for that of the destination host. If this type of man-in-the-middle attack is successful, the unsuspecting host user could transmit sensitive information, including logon, authentication, and password data, to the attacker.

External Communications (also see "Remote Access")

- **Modems are not disconnected** In Chapter 12 ("Wireless Security"), we discuss the problem with unsecured modems. Briefly, these can be attacked by wardialers who simply look for modems connected to corporate networks. These can create significant security holes and are often overlooked in our quest to lock down the wired network.

- **An ISP connection exists without written approval** In most companies, this might be a difficult trick to achieve, but it certainly warrants examination to ensure that the ISP connection(s) is managed by the IT department and not some errant user who managed to get the local ISP provider to run a cable into the office on a Saturday morning.

- **Communications devices are not password protected** This seems like a giant "Duh!" but you'd probably be surprised how often communication devices such as modems, routers, switches, and other "smart" devices are left unprotected by even a simple password or that use the default password that came with the device out of the box.

- **No warning banner** Failure to display the required login banner prior to logon attempts will limit the site's ability to prosecute unauthorized access. It also presents the potential for criminal and civil liability for systems administrators and information systems managers. Not displaying the proper banner will also hamper the site's ability to monitor device usage. Displaying a banner warning users of the consequences of unauthorized access helps warn off the bad guys and draws a line in the legal sand that you might need later.

TCP/IP (Some TCP/IP Information Also Found in the "Routers" Section)

- **LAN addresses are not protected from the public** In later versions of the Windows operating system, even home users were able to easily implement Network Address Translation (NAT) to protect internal IP addresses from Internet users. Most businesses these days have implemented some method of protecting internal IP addresses so that hackers can't use this information to decipher the network structure and plan an attack.

- **The DHCP server is not configured to log hostnames** To identify and combat IP address spoofing, it is highly recommended that the DHCP server log MAC addresses or hostnames on the DHCP server.

- **TCP and UDP small server services are not disabled** TCP and UDP services are often available on network devices, including routers and servers. Disabling these services if they're not used helps reduce the attack footprint. TCP and UDP protocols include services that routers can support; however, they are not required for operation. Attackers have used these services to cause network DoS attacks.

- **TCP keepalives for Telnet session must be enabled** Enabling TCP keepalives on incoming connections can help guard against both malicious attacks and orphaned sessions caused by remote system crashes. Enabling the TCP keepalives causes the router to generate periodic keepalive messages, letting it detect and drop broken Telnet connections.

- **Identification support is enabled** Identification support allows you to query a TCP port for identification. This feature enables an unsecured protocol to report the identity of a client initiating a TCP connection and a host responding to the connection. With identification support, you can connect a TCP port on a host, issue a simple text string to request information, and receive a simple text-string reply. This is another mechanism to learn the router vendor, model number, and software version being run. Identification support should be disabled on routers and other network devices that provide this functionality.

Whitelisting

Whitelisting is the ability to easily specify IP addresses or networks that should never be the subject of an automated response in an IDS/IPS system. For example, IP addresses associated with systems that are critical to a network (for example, the Domain Name Server, or DNS, or upstream router) should not be automatically blocked by an active response system, nor should sessions be altered by an inline IPS. Some active response systems include the ability to whitelist IP addresses and networks and to specify which protocols should be ignored. For example, if a DNS server sends an attack across the network to a Web server, it may be permissible for an active response system to capture the individual TCP session on port 80 but ignore everything else.

- **IP-directed broadcasts are not disabled** An *IP-directed broadcast* is a datagram sent to the broadcast address of a subnet that is not directly attached to the sending machine. The directed broadcast is routed through the network as a Unicast packet until it arrives at the target subnet, where it is converted into a link layer broadcast. Due to the nature of the IP addressing architecture, only the last router in the chain, which is connected directly to the target subnet, can conclusively identify a directed broadcast. IP-directed broadcasts are used in the extremely common and popular *smurf*, or DoS, attacks. In a smurf attack, the attacker sends ICMP echo requests from a falsified source address to a directed broadcast address, causing all the hosts on the target subnet to send replies to the falsified source. By sending a continuous stream of such requests, the attacker can create a much larger stream of replies, which can completely inundate the host whose address is being falsified. This service should be disabled on all interfaces when it's not needed to prevent smurf and DoS attacks.

- **Ingress filtering inbound spoofing addresses** Inbound spoofing occurs when someone outside the network uses an internal IP address to gain access to systems or devices on the internal network. If the intruder is successful, they can intercept data, passwords, and the like and use that information to perform destructive acts on network devices or network data.

- **Egress outbound spoofing filter** You should restrict the router from accepting any outbound IP packet that contains an illegitimate address in the source address field via egress ACLs or by enabling Unicast Reverse Path Forwarding. ACLs are the first line of defense in a layered security approach. They permit authorized packets and deny unauthorized packets based on port or service type. They enhance the network's posture by not allowing packets to even reach a potential target within the security domain. Auditing packets attempting to penetrate the network but that are stopped by an ACL will allow network administrators to broaden their protective ring and more tightly define the scope of operation.

Administration

- **Devices exist that have standard default passwords** This is another major "Duh!" item; again, it's surprising how easy it is to get into a large number of devices just by using the default password that the device shipped with. Want to know the default password? Go up on the manufacturer's Web site, look for the user guide for the specific device, and the default password is almost guaranteed to be listed in the first five pages of the manual.

- **Group accounts or user accounts without passwords** Without passwords on user accounts for network devices, one level of complexity is removed from gaining access to the routers. If a default user ID has not been changed or is guessed by an attacker, the network could be easily compromised, since the only remaining step would be to crack the password. Sharing group accounts on any network device should also be prohibited. If these group accounts are not changed when someone leaves the group, that person could possibly gain control of the device. Having group accounts does not allow for proper auditing of who is accessing or changing the network. Only allow individual user account access and require each user to have a unique user ID and a strong password.

- **Assign lowest privilege level to user accounts** Across the enterprise, you should always assign the least privilege possible for all users. This prevents users from getting into places they shouldn't, and it also prevents hackers from upgrading their privileges if they manage to get in on a user account that has too many privileges. Even IT staff should have user accounts with least privileges for most day-to-day network tasks, and they should only log on with administrative privileges when needed. Network outages and security holes can be created by users with too many permissions or even by a well-meaning but inexperienced net admin.

- **Strong password policies are not enforced** Strong passwords is an inadequate defense on its own, but it slows down a would-be intruder and can also alert a net admin to a potential problem if failed password attempts are monitored and accounts are locked down after too many failed attempts. Requiring users to use strong passwords, to change them periodically, and to prevent them from repeating old passwords too frequently are all parts of strong password policy. In addition, you can audit failed attempts, notify a net admin of too many failed attempts, and lock out an account with too many failed accounts as part of your strong password policy implementation.

- **Passwords are not recorded and stored properly** User passwords should not be recorded and stored, but certain administrative ones absolutely should be. You can probably think of several scenarios where someone who doesn't normally require administrative access requires it. For example, suppose as part of your disaster recovery plan, you have an executive VP who is responsible for coordinating recovery efforts. He or she should have access to these passwords only for these emergency situations, because on a day-to-day basis, you operate on the principle of "least access" and the EVP really has nothing more than the equivalent rights of a power user. Having these passwords on a network server in plain sight or in a paper file someplace obvious is not a good idea. Making sure these emergency passwords are recorded and stored properly ensures security for the network on a day-to-day basis but provides an important fail-safe option in emergencies as well.

- **Passwords are viewable when displaying the router or other device** Many attacks on computer systems are launched from within the network by unsatisfied or disgruntled employees. It's vital that all router passwords be encrypted so they cannot be intercepted by viewing the console. If the router network is compromised, large parts of the network could be incapacitated with just a few simple commands.

- **Passwords are transmitted in clear text** There are many types of situations in which passwords are transmitted in clear text. This creates an opportunity for an attacker to seize passwords. Review how and where passwords are transmitted and secure the communication lines if the passwords themselves are transmitted in clear text.

- **Emergency accounts should be limited to one** Emergency accounts on devices such as routers or switches should be limited to one. Authentication for administrative access to the router should obviously be required at all times. A single account can be created on the router's local database for use in an emergency, such as when the authentication server is down or connectivity between the router and the authentication server is not operable. Verify that there is one and only one emergency account to prevent unnecessary opportunities for attack.

- **Unnecessary or unauthorized router or device accounts exist** This point is related to the previous item. You should eliminate any unused, unnecessary, or unauthorized device accounts except for one authorized emergency account.

- **Disable unused ports and services** On every server, every firewall, and every device, disable unused ports and services. Microsoft took a giant leap forward in the more recent versions of the Windows operating system when the company changed the default configuration from "open" to "closed." This meant that the net admin had to consciously enable and open services and ports after installation. Earlier versions came open and unlocked out of the box, and the net admin had to sift through the system to lock it down. For all devices, disable unused ports and services, uninstall unused applications, and remove unused hardware.

- **Auditing and logging files are not set to record *denied* events, not set to record system activity** Auditing and logging are key components of any security architecture. It is essential that security personnel know what is being done, being attempted, and by whom in order to compile an accurate risk assessment. Auditing the actions, particularly *denied* events, on routers provides a means to identify potential attacks or threats. Maintaining an audit trail of system activity logs (*syslog*) can help you identify configuration errors, understand past intrusions, troubleshoot service disruptions, and react to probes and scans of the network.

- **Configurations are stored in unsecured locations** To ensure network and data availability, the configuration data of key network infrastructure components should be maintained in a secure, offsite location. This is part of good disaster recovery planning practices and adds to security if these configurations are stored in secured locations offsite rather than in an unlocked file cabinet in the mailroom. Access to these configuration files should be restricted and logged to prevent unauthorized access.

Network Management

- **Out-of-band network management not implemented or required** It's outside the scope of this chapter (and book) to get into a deep discussion of in-band and out-of-band network management, but we will toss out a couple of quick explanations before discussing the infrastructure security implications of both. In-band network management uses the same network infrastructure as the devices and data being managed. Most networking equipment basically sends out IP traffic for network management on the same medium as the traffic it's managing (routers, switches, and so forth). Out-of-band network management uses a separate connection, often a serial RS-232 port, instead of the network port used for in-band management. There are security pros and cons to both, so the key is to secure whichever method(s) you implement.

  Without secure out-of-band management implemented with authenticated access controls, strong two-factor authentication, encryption of the management session, and audit logs, unauthorized users may gain access to network managed devices such as routers or communications servers (CS). If the router network is compromised, large parts of the network could be incapacitated with only a few commands. If a CS is compromised, unauthorized users could gain access to the network and its attached systems. The CS could be disabled, therefore disallowing authorized subscribers from supporting mission critical functions.

From an architectural point of view, providing out-of-band management of network systems is the best first step in any management strategy. No network production traffic resides on an out-of-band network.

- **Use of in-band management is not limited, restricted, or encrypted** It is imperative that communications used for administrative access to network components are limited to emergency situations or where out-of-band management would hinder daily operational requirements. In-band management introduces the risk of an attacker gaining access to the network internally or even externally. In-band management should be restricted to a limited number of authorized IP addresses to improve security. The in-band access should also be encrypted for added security. Without encrypted in-band management connections, unauthorized users may gain access to network managed devices such as routers, firewalls, or remote access servers. If any of these devices are compromised, the entire network could also be compromised. Administrative access requires the use of encryption on all communication channels between the remote user and the system being accessed. It is imperative to protect communications used for administrative access because an attacker who manages to hijack the link would gain immediate access to the network.

- **Log all in-band management access attempts** Since in-band traffic travels on the same pathways as normal network traffic, be sure that all in-bound management access attempts are logged. This will give you an indication as to whether an intruder is attempting to gain control of key network devices. These attempts should not go unnoticed and should be verified against legitimate management activity of that device. For example, if the access attempts happen after business hours, it's possible (or likely) that the attempts are unauthorized.

- **Two-factor authentication is not used for in-band or out-of-band network management** Without strong two-factor authorization, unauthorized users may gain access to network managed devices such as routers, firewalls, and remote access servers. If any of these devices are compromised, the entire network could also be compromised.

- **Filter ICMP on external interface** The Internet Control Message Protocol (ICMP) supports IP traffic by relaying information about paths, routes, and network conditions. ICMP unreachable notifications, mask replies, and redirects should be disabled on all externally-interfaced routers to prevent hackers using these messages to perform network mapping and infrastructure discovery.

- **SNMP access is not restricted by IP address** Detailed information about the network is sent across the network via SNMP. If this information is discovered by attackers, it could be used to trace the network, show the network topology, and possibly gain access to network devices. Access to SNMP should be for specific IP addresses only.

- **SNMP is blocked at all external interfaces** Clearly, using SNMP to map a network and discover the network infrastructure is a great hacker tool that should be secured to the greatest extent possible. This includes blocking SNMP on all external interfaces.

- **SNMP write access to the router is enabled** This allows an intruder to set various configuration settings to allow him or her greater access to the router and hence to the network. SNMP write access should be disabled.

- **Block identified inbound ICMP messages** Using inbound ICMP Echo, Information, Net Mask, and Timestamp requests, an attacker can create a map of the subnets and hosts behind the router. An attacker can perform a DoS attack by flooding the router or internal hosts with Echo packets. With inbound ICMP Redirect packets, the attacker can change a host's routing tables.

- **Block identified outbound ICMP traffic** An attacker from the internal network (behind the router) may be able to launch DoS attacks with outbound ICMP packets. It is important to block all unnecessary ICMP traffic message types.

- **Block all inbound *traceroutes*** If you're ever had to troubleshoot a network or Internet connection, you're familiar with the *traceroute* command. This is a helpful tool in troubleshooting, but it also provides great information to a would-be attacker to create a map of the subnets and hosts behind the router. These should not be allowed into the network through the router or other externally facing devices.

- **Secure NMS traffic using IPSec** To securely protect the network, Network Management Systems (NMS) and access to them must be controlled to guard against outside or unauthorized intrusion, which could result in system or network compromise. Allowing any device to send traps or information may create a false positive and having site personnel perform unneeded or potentially hazardous actions on the network in response to these false traps. These sessions must be controlled and secured by IPSec.

- **An insecure version of SNMP is being used** SNMP Versions 1 and 2 are not considered secure and are not recommended. Instead, use SNMP Version 3, which provides the User-based Security Model (USM), which gives strong authentication and privacy. Without Version 3, it's possible an attacker could gain unauthorized access to detailed network management information that can be used to map and subsequently attack the network.

- **SNMP standard operating procedures are not documented** Standard operating procedures will ensure consistency and will help prevent errors or omissions that could create a security hole.

- **NMS security alarms not defined by violation type or severity** Ensure that security alarms are set up within the managed network's framework. At a minimum, these will include the following:

  - **Integrity violation** Indicates that network contents or objects have been illegally modified, deleted, or added.

  - **Operational violation** Indicates that a desired object or service could not be used.

  - **Physical violation** Indicates that a physical part of the network (such as a cable) has been damaged or modified without authorization.

  - **Security mechanism violation** Indicates that the network's security system has been compromised or breached.

  - **Time domain violation** Indicates that an event has happened outside its allowed or typical time slot.

  Also ensure that alarms are categorized by severity using the following guidelines:

  - Critical and major alarms are given when a condition that affects service has arisen. For a critical alarm, steps must be taken immediately to restore the service that has been lost completely.

  - A major alarm indicates that steps must be taken as soon as possible because the affected service has degraded drastically and is in danger of being lost completely.

  - A minor alarm indicates a problem that does not yet affect service but may do so if the problem is not corrected.

- A warning alarm is used to signal a potential problem that may affect service.

- An indeterminate alarm is one that requires human intervention to decide its severity.

Without the proper categories of security alarm being defined on the NMS, responding to critical outages or attacks on the network may not be coordinated correctly with the right personnel, hardware, software, or vendor maintenance. Delays will inevitably occur that will cause network outages to last longer than necessary or expose the network to larger, more extensive attacks or outages.

- **The NMS is not located in a secure environment** Any network management server (or any other highly critical network component) should be kept in a physically secure location with restricted access. Since many attacks come from inside an organization, by people who are authorized to be on the premises, it's important to physically secure all critical network components to the greatest degree possible. Using keypad or card-swipe access control can also help identify specific administrative access, to allow you to further control and monitor access.

  Access to NMS and other network critical components should be restricted via access controls as well, and all activity, including all successful and failed attempts to log on, should be logged. The log file, as with all log files, should be reviewed regularly, stored for 30 days, and archived for a year, unless regulatory or compliance requirements differ.

- **NMS accounts are not properly maintained** Only those accounts necessary for the operation of the system and for access logging should be maintained. This is true for all servers and network devices. Good "housekeeping" is an essential element to network security, and removing or disabling unused accounts as well as removing and investigating unauthorized accounts is critical.

www.syngress.com

Routers and Routing

- **No documented procedures and maintenance for MD5 keys** Routing protocols should use MD5 to authenticate neighbors prior to exchanging route table updates, to ensure that route tables are not corrupted or compromised.

- **MD5 Key Lifetime expiration is set to never expire** MD5 is a public key encryption algorithm that uses the exchange of encryption keys across a network link. If these keys are not managed properly, they could be intercepted by unauthorized users and used to break the encryption algorithm. This check is in place to ensure that keys do not expire, creating a DoS due to adjacencies being dropped and routes being aged out. The recommendation is to use two rotating six-month keys, with a third key set as infinite lifetime. The lifetime key should be changed seven days after the rotating keys have expired.

- **Console port is not configured to time out** Console ports on routers or other network devices should be set to time out after some specified period of inactivity. In most cases, a 5- or 10-minute timeout is appropriate. A router is a highly desirable asset to an intruder, so setting a low threshold on timeout will help increase security.

- **Modems are connected to the console or aux port** There may be valid reasons to have a modem connected to the console or auxiliary port of a router or other network device, but you should first ensure that this connection is absolutely necessary. If not, remove it. If it is needed, be sure to secure it by requiring a username and password (and other security measures) and avoid default configurations.

- **The router or network device's auxiliary port is not disabled** If the router or other network device has an auxiliary port, be sure it is disabled it if it's not in use. These are the kinds of welcome backdoors hackers look for.

- **Login is not limited to three attempts** Login attempts for any network device that exceed three tries are likely the work of a hacker. Limiting login attempts to three is a reasonable limit, and most net admins will stop after three attempts if they cannot recall the appropriate login. This won't stop a hacker who is willing to try three times, wait some specified interval, and try again, but it will prevent automated attacks from going through quickly (or at all).

- **Secure Shell timeout is not 60 seconds or less** Many routes and network management devices use the Secure Shell (SSH) protocol to secure communications to the device. Reducing the broken Telnet session expiration time to 60 seconds or less strengthens the router or network device from being attacked using an expired session.

- **Key services are not disabled on all routers** The DHCP, finger service, HTTP, FTP, and BSD *r*-commands and *bootp* services should be disabled on routers and network devices for added security. All unused protocols and services should be disabled to prevent unauthorized use of these services.

- **Configuration autoloading must be disabled** The routers can find their startup configuration in their own NVRAM or load it over the network via TFTP or Remote Copy (*rcp*). Obviously, loading in across the network is a security risk. If an attacker intercepted the startup configuration, it could be used to gain access to the router and take control of network traffic.

- **IP source routing is not disabled on all routers** IP source routing is a process whereby individual packets can specify routing. This is a method that attackers can exploit, so this ability should be disabled on routers and network devices with this capability.

- **Proxy ARP is not disabled** When proxy ARP is enabled on some routers, it allows that router to extend the network (at Layer 2) across multiple interfaces (LAN segments). Because proxy ARP allows hosts from different LAN segments to look like they are on the same segment, proxy ARP is safe only when it's used between trusted LAN segments. Attackers can leverage the trusting nature of proxy ARP by spoofing a trusted host and then intercepting packets. You should always disable proxy ARP on router interfaces that do not require it, unless the router is being used as a LAN bridge.

- **Gratuitous ARP is not disabled** A gratuitous ARP is an ARP broadcast in which the source and destination MAC addresses are the same. It is used to inform the network about a host's IP address. A spoofed gratuitous ARP message can cause network mapping information to be stored incorrectly, causing network malfunction and resulting in various types of service denials, leading to an *availability* issue.

- **Routers are not set to intercept TCP *SYN* attacks** The TCP *SYN* attack involves transmitting a volume of connections that cannot be completed at the destination. This attack causes the connection queues to fill up, thereby denying service to legitimate TCP users. Routers and similar network devices should be configured to intercept TCP *SYN* attacks to prevent DoS attacks from an outside network.

- **Router is not configured to block known DDoS ports** Several high-profile DDoS attacks have been launched across the Internet. Although routers cannot prevent DDoS attacks in general, it is usually sound security practice to discourage the activities of specific DDoS agents (a.k.a. *zombies*) by adding access list rules that block their particular ports.

- **TFTP used without specific need or approval, access is not restricted** Trivial File Transfer Protocol (TFTP) is a simple form of FTP that uses the User Datagram Protocol (UDP) and provides no security features at all (not even a password). It is often used by routers, X-terminals, and servers to boot diskless workstations, but by its very nature it is an insecure protocol. It should not be implemented without a very specific need to do so, and access to the TFTP server should be restricted and monitored.

- **The FTP username and password are not configured** The FTP server should require the use of usernames and passwords to prevent anonymous use of the FTP functionality on the network.

Firewall

- **Firewall not implemented and configured properly** You should ensure that one or more firewalls are installed and properly configured. The default configuration should be the most restrictive configuration, *deny-by-default,* so that only specifically allowed traffic is allowed into the network.

- **A screened subnet (DMZ) is not implemented** Without the dual-homed screened subnet (a DMZ), architecture traffic that would be normally destined for the DMZ would have to be redirected to the site's internal network. Computers on the inside of the firewall should send outbound requests through the firewall and into the DMZ. The DMZ, in turn, routes or redirects these outbound requests. Typically, a firewall will not accept inbound requests from the DMZ computers, which adds another layer of protection to the network clients.

- **Using an application-level firewall** All networks should use an application-level gateway or firewall to proxy all traffic to external networks. Devices such as SSL gateways, e-mail gateways that will proxy services to protect the network, are also acceptable. A Layer 4 or stateful inspection firewall, in collaboration with application-level proxy devices, can be used to secure all connections.

- **Firewall does not require authentication, does not lock out after three attempts** Firewalls are the enforcement mechanisms of the security on the network, and they are ideal targets for attackers. Firewall placement in the network and the level of access granted to the users accessing the device also increase the risk profile associated with remote management. Therefore, all personnel who access the firewall both locally and remotely should be granted the minimum privilege level needed to perform their duties. The standard three-attempt lockout should be enforced, with the exception that when a firewall administrator is locked out, the senior net admin (or network security officer, if one exists) should be responsible for unlocking the account.

- **Firewall remote access is not restricted** Only the firewall administrator should be able to access the firewall remotely. Remove unused accounts and remove access for all staff other than the administrator.

- **Firewall is not configured to protect the network** Ensure that the firewall is actually configured to protect the network. Configuration of the firewall will vary from site to site, but in general, it should at least be configured to prevent TCP *SYN* flooding and the Ping of Death attacks.

- **Firewall has unnecessary services enabled** As with all network devices, disable, uninstall, and deconfigure any unused or unnecessary services. The fewer services that are enabled, the smaller the attack footprint.

- **Firewall version is not a supported or current** As with all network devices, it's critical to keep the firewall software (and hardware, if appropriate) up to date with current versions, patches, and updates. It's extremely common for attackers to exploit known security issues days, weeks, or even months after a patch is available. This type of hacking is pretty lazy stuff and is a bit of an embarrassment if it occurs, because it's 100-percent preventable. Keep your firewall up to date.

- **The firewall logs are not being reviewed daily** There's really no point in creating log files if you're not going to review them. Reviewing and analyzing log files is part art, part science, but the only way you'll ever know what's going on is to actually review those files on a regular basis. If you don't know that a hacker was chopping away at your network security last night, you'll probably be surprised when he or she manages to hack in tomorrow night.

- **Firewall log retention does not meet policy** The firewall logs can be used for forensic analysis in support of incidents (after the fact) as well as to aid in normal traffic analysis. It can take numerous days to recover from a firewall outage when a proper backup scheme is not used. Firewall logs should be stored in secure locations; they should be stored for 30 days and archived for one year.

- **The firewall configuration is not backed up weekly** It's quite a chore to properly configure a corporate firewall, as you probably well know. Therefore, it's wise to back up the configuration data for the firewall on a weekly basis or whenever the firewall configuration changes. This provides excellent forensic support and helps in disaster recovery efforts.

- **The firewall is not configured to alarm the admin** If someone is knocking at the door but no one's home, an intruder may well decide to just barge right in. That's the net result of having a firewall that is not configured to alarm the administrator to unusual traffic.

- **The firewall is not configured properly** The firewall should be configured to protect the network. The following are suggested settings:

  - Log unsuccessful authentication attempts.

  - Stamp audit trail data with the date and time it was recorded.

  - Record the source IP, destination IP, protocol used, and the action taken.

  - Log administrator logons, changes to the administrator group, and account lockouts.

  - Protect audit logs from deletion and modification.

Intrusion Detection/Intrusion Prevention

- **The company does not have an incident response policy** An IDS is pretty worthless if you don't also have an incident response policy in place. Develop an incident response policy so there are clear lines of responsibility and reporting. Also clearly delineate how, where, and to whom to report suspicious activity.

- **Unauthorized traffic is not logged** Audit logs are necessary to provide a trail of evidence in case the network is compromised. With this information, the network administrator can devise ways to block the attack and possibly identify and prosecute the attacker. Information supplied by an IDS can be used for forensic analysis in support of an incident as well as to aid in normal traffic analysis.

- **No established weekly backup procedures** IDS data needs to be backed up to ensure that it is preserved in the event of a hardware failure of the IDS or in the event the IDS is breached.

- **IDS antivirus updates procedures not in the standard operating procedure** IDS systems require antivirus updates. Be sure that these updates are in the standard operating procedures for IT staff. Sometimes it's the little things we overlook that bite us the hardest; this one's a no-brainer but easy to overlook.

- **Switches and cross-connects are not secure** Since the intrusion detection and prevention system includes all hardware required to connect horizontal wiring to the backbone wiring, it's important that all switches and associated cross-connect hardware are kept in a secured location, a locked room or an enclosed cabinet that is locked. This will also prevent an attacker from gaining privilege mode access to the switch. Several switch products require only a reboot of the switch to reset or recover the password.

Remote Access

- **The management VLAN is not secured** In a VLAN-based network, switches use VLAN1 as the default VLAN for in-band management and to communicate with other networking devices using Spanning-Tree Protocol (STP), Cisco Discovery Protocol (CDP), Dynamic Trunking Protocol (DTP), VLAN Trunking Protocol (VTP), and Port Aggregation Protocol (PAgP)—all untagged traffic. As a consequence, VLAN1 may unwisely span the entire network if it's not appropriately pruned. If its scope is large enough, the risk of compromise can increase significantly.

- **Remote Access Servers do not require encryption for end-user access** You should ensure that only users who require remote access are granted it and that all remote access traffic is encrypted to the fullest extent possible.

- **RAS does not use two-factor authentication** Without strong two-factor authorization, unauthorized users may gain access to network services, devices, and data. Clearly, if an intruder gains control of network infrastructure devices, he or she could inflict damage to either the data or the network, causing loss of confidentiality, integrity, or availability.

- **Remote Access Server connectivity isn't logged** Logging is your friend; keeping a log file of RAS connectivity is critical to keep track of who is attempting to log in, who did log in and when, and how long they were logged in. Reviewing log files daily will help you notice patterns and problems earlier in the cycle than reviewing log files infrequently (or never).

- **RAS session exceeds 30-minute inactivity** An RAS session that is inactive should be terminated to prevent session hijacking. Terminate idle connections after no more than 30 minutes of inactivity.

- **RAS log retentions do not meet requirements** Depending on organizational, legal, or regulatory requirements, you should keep log files for 30 days and archive them for one year.

- **The logs are not viewed on a weekly basis** Reviewing log files daily will help you notice patterns and problems earlier in the cycle than reviewing log files infrequently (or never).

- **Modems are not physically protected** Limiting the access to infrastructure modems and keeping accurate records of the deployed modems will limit the chance that unauthorized modems will be placed into the infrastructure. If an unauthorized person has physical access to a site's modems, the switch or software settings can be changed to affect the security of a system.

- **An accurate list of all modems isn't maintained** Keeping accurate records of the deployed modems will limit the chance that unauthorized modems will be placed into the infrastructure. It will also help you keep track of modems that are no longer used so they can be physically removed or disabled.

- **Modems are not restricted to single-line operation** Modems should be connected to phone lines that have very basic capabilities. If a phone line has advanced features such as call forwarding, it's possible an intruder could take control of a modem, computer, or network. Keep it simple for better security.

- **Proper call logs are not being maintained** Logs of all inbound and out-bound calls for modems and phone lines should be logged and reviewed on a regular basis. Hijacked modems could conceivably allow an attacker to steal phone time and incur long-distance charges on your company's dime. Make sure you know what's going on with modems and phone lines to avoid big phone bills or network intrusion.

- **Callback procedures are not configured correctly** One way to increase security is to implement a callback feature on the modem so that a caller's call disconnects and the modem calls back a preprogrammed number. Ensure that if callback procedures are used, on establishment of the callback connection the communications device requires the user to authenticate to the system.

- **RAS/NAS server is not located in a screened subnet** Allowing a remote connection to the private network unchecked by the firewall enables a mobile user to violate the security policy and put the network infrastructure in a vulnerable position. The risk would be magnified if a remote access session were hijacked.

- **The RAS/NAS is not configured to use PPP** To securely protect the network, Network Access Servers (NAS) and access to them must be controlled to guard against outside or unauthorized intrusion, which could result in system or network compromise. If the NAS is accessed remotely, the risk of compromising a password or user ID increases. The authentication of the remote nodes must be controlled by encryption such as CHAP with MD5 or MS-CHAP with MD4.

- **VPN gateway is located behind the firewall** Allowing a remote connection to the private network unchecked by the firewall enables a mobile user to violate the security policy and put the network infrastructure in a vulnerable position. The risk would be magnified if the VPN connection were hijacked.

■ **The VPN connection is not using IPSec's ESP tunnel**
Ensure that remote access via VPN uses IPSec ESP in tunnel
mode. For legacy support, L2TP may be used if IPSec provides
encryption or another technology that provides security such as
AES, 3DES, SSH, or SSL.

■ **VPN is not configured as a tunnel type VPN** Be sure that
VPNs are established as tunnel type VPNs, which terminate outside the firewall (in other words, between the router and the firewall, or connected to an outside interface of the router). If VPNs
terminate inside the firewall, you basically have taken the firewall
out of the security mix and reduced your line of defense by one.
Improperly deployed VPNs take away a firewall's ability to audit
useful information.

We've walked through a lot of very specific security information in
this section, some of which might be relevant to your organization, some
of which might not be. What is highly likely, though, is that if you even
scanned this section, you thought of a few things you might otherwise
have overlooked, or it sparked you to make a note to check one thing or
another. The key is to be thorough, and to that end, this list should have
helped you make sure you covered some of the nitty-gritty details of network infrastructure security.

Project Parameters

It's time now to plan your infrastructure security project. We've covered a
lot of detail, and now we'll try to focus it down into a project plan that
you can use to secure your infrastructure. Let's start with our problem and
mission (outcome) statements. Remember, this is a good time to gather
your core IT project team together to help you begin defining the basic
project parameters. You probably could do some (or all) of this preliminary work on your own, but there's a lot to be said for getting the core
team fired up and engaged with the project from the very start. You're less
likely to have gaps in the project plan if you start relying on the "two

heads are better" theory right from the start. Here are two sample problem statements you can use to begin developing your own:

> Our network infrastructure is vulnerable to attack because our security technologies have not kept pace with changes in the external environment. We currently do not have a meaningful approach to security, and all measures in place have been ad hoc or reactive. We are not confident of our level of security across the enterprise.

> We recently experienced a security breach that caused a network outage for three days. We were fortunate that no sensitive data appears to have been stolen or compromised. We took remedial measures, but we are not confident that our data or our network is secure.

Next, let's look at the mission or outcome statement for these problem statements. What's the desired outcome in both of these cases? The short answer is a secure network. We can probably use a single outcome statement for both problems, and it might look something like this:

> We want to create and implement a comprehensive infrastructure security plan so that we are confident we have developed and can maintain as secure a network environment as is reasonably possible.

Your possible solutions run the gamut, but we're going to assume that you've made the decision to secure your network infrastructure by developing a security plan focused on network infrastructure. That being the case, let's look at the requirements for this project.

Requirements

If you haven't done so, gather your core project team to work with you on the requirements. Requirements are those areas the project must address; in some respects, this is the real foundation of your project. Whatever is defined in the requirements should be implemented in the project, and whatever's in the project should be defined by the requirements. Success factors, those things required to make the project successful, can be defined within your requirements here or as part of your assumptions (discussed later in this chapter).

Functional Requirements

The functional requirements for your infrastructure security project will vary from the list we're providing, but your list should have the same overall elements. Where we would expect to see more divergence is in the technical requirements, which we'll discuss in a moment. Functional requirements might include:

- Physically secure premises

- Secure network infrastructure servers

- Secure network components (firewalls, routers, switches)

- Secure local communication (authentication, access control, encryption)

- Secure remote communication (authentication, access control, encryption)

- Secure user devices (operating system, antivirus, antispyware, application, file system)

- Create secure operating procedures

- Create documentation

Technical Requirements

Clearly, the technical requirements for your infrastructure security project will vary greatly from whatever list we provide, because the technical requirements are based on the specific network topology, server types, server operating systems, communication methods, authentication methods, and more. The lengthy list of items presented earlier in this chapter should provide you with plenty of ideas and material for creating your technical requirements for the project. Instead of going into detail here, we present the categories that you should include; the details under those categories are up to you, based on your unique requirements.

Remember, technical requirements should describe the "how" of your functional requirements. So, as you work through this section, keep in mind that you should be describing, very specifically, how you will implement the functional requirements via technology. Your technical requirements should be detailed in describing how these things will be accomplished, but be careful to stick to describing the *requirement*. Let's take "Physically secure the premises" as an example. You don't need to describe how the premises will actually be secured ("Phil will get a screwdriver and install a deadbolt …"); you need to describe the *technical details* of how it will be secured. So, let's say you're the only tenant in a building. You might describe your technical requirement in this manner:

- Upgrade all external entry doors to card-swipe system. Card-swipe system should be compatible with the existing employee card system, XYZ. (You might include the technical specs of this system here as well.)

- Install security monitoring system (with cameras) focused on parking lot and all external doorways (3). System should be able to record continuously for 24 hours, cameras should be able to record in slow motion and high resolution, the system should be able to "respond" to potential incidents, and the system should record events and have at least three methods of administrator alert.

These are just some of the ways you can capture technical requirements. Clearly, if you're talking about a server, you would include processor speed, memory specifications, disk drive specifications, operating system, and so on. However, other kinds of less technical elements, such as how to secure the premises, might look like the example provided. If your card-swipe system, for example, must conform to certain standards, those standards should be included as well.

Legal/Compliance Requirements

Create a list of the functional, technical, and administrative requirements for your infrastructure security project based on the legal, regulatory, and compliance requirements. Taking time to translate these requirements into project requirements at this juncture will help ensure that you build compliance requirements into your project. In standard project management, it's always easier to build something in at the front end than to add it at the back end (it reduces errors, omissions, time, and cost), so now's the time to add these requirements to the greatest extent possible. Also, be sure to add milestones and documentation requirements to your project plan based on compliance needs.

Policy Requirements

Policy requirements may fall under functional requirements, but there's no rule that you can't include policy requirements as a distinct category of requirements if doing so helps you cover all the bases. We'll look at policies in more detail in a later chapter, but for now, let's walk through a few ideas for policies related to securing the infrastructure:

- User policies
- Network access policies
- Remote access policies
- Wireless policies
- Network administration/network management policies
- Server policies
- Firewall, IDS/IPS, DMZ policies
- Regulatory/compliance policies
- Corporate policies
- Legal policies

Scope

At this point, you should have an idea of the scope of your project. You could choose to address your complete infrastructure security needs during this project, or you might choose to parse it out into smaller sub-projects and time them in stages or phases to meet organizational needs. Making changes to the infrastructure comes with risk, and you'll need to be careful to take this fact into consideration as you plan your project. This starts with determining the proper scope for your project. For example, you might have recently implemented an IDS that you're satisfied with, so you could choose to include IDS in your project only to the extent that it ties in with other infrastructure security measures. However, you might feel that your biggest exposure is on network servers such as DHCP, DNS, and directory servers, so your primary focus will be to harden these servers and related network traffic. Your assessment should tell you where you need to focus and what must be included in the plan and perhaps what can safely be omitted from your plan. Then clearly define what is and what is not part of your project so that you leave nothing open to interpretation.

Schedule

Since we haven't created a detailed work breakdown structure (WBS) yet, we can't develop a detailed schedule, but we can begin to develop a higher-level schedule. First, you should take a look at your organization and see if there are any events or timelines that might come into play. You certainly don't want to be in the middle of a network outage (due to an upgrade) when an important client is visiting, when your marketing department has a big presentation coming up, or when your manufacturing group is working overtime to get a large order out. Taking organizational needs into consideration is critical to project success and helps grease the political gears as well.

In addition to organizational needs, you might know about other timelines or constraints that should be considered in the schedule. Are other security initiatives being planned or under way? If so, is there a logical order to the plans themselves? It might make sense to complete early phases of an infrastructure security project before implementing a new wireless network security plan, for example. Also, look at other IT projects to determine how they might impact the infrastructure security plan or how the infrastructure security activities might disrupt or alter other projects that are in the planning or implementation stages.

Finally, look at your talented IT staff and determine if there are any scheduling issues that would impact your project, such as your best wireless or IP person heading out for vacation or your encryption specialist planning to be out for a month on paternity leave. Whatever the case, if you already know about these scheduling issues, you might as well begin addressing them here.

You might have a rough idea of how long this project will take, given what you've looked at thus far, and you may be able to see where it will fit in your overall IT schedule. You'll have to balance the demands for your IT resources with the need to secure the infrastructure, so this is a good point to try to get a handle on some of those schedule constraints.

Budget

Your budget will be large or small depending on how well secured your infrastructure currently is and how large your company is. For example, if you already know that you're going to have to upgrade some of those old servers still running Windows NT (gasp), then your budget is going to have to include a whole host of things like the server box itself, the operating system, license upgrades, and updated applications. As with scheduling, you won't have an exact amount in mind yet, but you might have some large segments defined or at least identified. Begin making a list of the components you believe you've identified in terms of purchases so you can verify (or modify) this list after you've created your WBS. Also keep in mind that with an infrastructure security project, a large percentage of your budget might be expended on labor costs (if you track internal labor costs in your project) because much of the work entails checking configurations and modifying settings.

Quality

You could define quality as the level of protection you're willing to accept, though it might be difficult to quantify. As we've stated, quality is a mindset, and you should instill this mindset in your IT project team. As you define your project plan, you'll have the opportunity to create specific quality metrics related to your infrastructure and incorporate them into your task details. Remember that security comes from depth of defense, so you want each layer you build to be as strong as it can be, within the defined constraints (time, cost, criticality, and so on) and understanding that no system is 100-percent secure.

Once you've defined the project parameters, it's essential that you develop your priorities. If you haven't checked in with your project sponsor, this would be a good time to discuss the priorities. What's the least flexible element here? Are you expected to meet a particular deadline, or were you handed a set budget? Understanding which of these parameters must be met will tell you how to make decisions during the project work phase. If you have a deadline, you'll focus your efforts on making sure that the schedule stays on track, which might mean spending a bit more on overtime than was in the original budget. As you know, in projects something always changes and something *has* to give. Understanding where that flexibility should come from will help you meet organizational requirements. Understand which parameter is least flexible and which is most flexible. Discuss this with your project sponsor, and make sure you're clear and in agreement. That way, when project work is under way, you won't have to keep going back to your sponsor to make basic decisions, and you'll know you're making decisions that support these priorities.

Key Skills Needed

For your network infrastructure security project, you're going to need a very wide variety of skills. Here we list some of the obvious ones; you can add to (or modify) this list as you define your project:

- **Network services** Securing the infrastructure requires a solid look at security settings on infrastructure servers such as DHCP, DNS, and directory services servers. These key servers require a deep understanding of the services they provide as well as an understanding of best practices in each of these areas.

- **Network perimeter services** Securing the perimeter involves installing, configuring, and managing components such as firewalls, routers, proxy servers, and DMZs. These typically require a strong background and ability to work with various protocols, including SNMP, ICMP, TCP, IP, FTP, HTTPS, SSH, SSL and more.

- **Intrusion detection/intrusion prevention** Installing and configuring IDS/IPS systems require a strong skill set in networking, understanding how information and IP traffic flows through the network infrastructure, and understanding the kinds of threats that are commonly launched (TCP, ICMP, etc.).

- **Remote access** Securing remote access requires an understanding of communication devices and protocols as well as of various authentication and encryption standards and methods. RAS, VLAN, VPN, and tunneling are just a few of the concepts needed in this area.

- **Wireless access** Securing a wireless LAN is discussed in a later chapter, but the skills here are the ability to understand and use various wireless network tools (the same ones the hackers use) and an understanding of how wireless networks are vulnerable and can be protected using a variety of tools.

- **Servers and hosts** These entail understanding operating systems, patches, upgrades, and vulnerabilities as well as how to secure files, folders, data, and user accounts.

- **Network administration** A strong understanding of network administration tools and techniques, including the ability to audit, review, and manage user and group accounts, access control lists, services and protocols, and other administrative tasks, is critical.

- **Documentation** You need people who are excellent at documenting the systems, the proposed changes, the implemented changes, and the final infrastructure configuration data. Documentation may be required for legal or compliance requirements as well.

- **Communication** You should have one or more people on your team who are good at communicating and creating connections within the organization. Since infrastructure changes can have a big impact on business operations, you will need to effectively and proactively communicate with various stakeholders and users during the course of the project.

- **Training** You might need to train users or IT staff on new methods, technologies, or other changes that occur as a result of implementing the infrastructure project plan.

Key Personnel Needed

Now that you've developed your list of needed skills, you can develop your wish list for project team members. You might want to create your "A" list and a backup list, but for political purposes, you might want to call it your Primary and Secondary teams, to avoid ruffling any feathers. Be sure to highlight the skills needed for which there are no internal matches. This will indicate places you need to seek staff training or external expertise. Also look at your personnel needed and get a sense for how much you're relying on a two or three people. It's often the case that we want the three people who are best to work on everything, but that will slow your project down tremendously. Develop your personnel list, then determine where your gaps are and how you'll address those gaps.

Project Processes and Procedures

As with any project, you should identify the processes and procedures you'll use during the duration of the project. We are assuming you have a whole stash of those at your disposal, so we won't run through the basics here. However, there are five areas to keep in mind when you're working on an infrastructure security project; you might want to check that these are in your processes and procedures. If not, add them as needed:

- **Testing procedures** Define how, when, and where you'll test security solutions before implementing them on the live network. Clearly, some things can be done on live systems; others should be tested before going live. Define what should be tested offline and how those testing scenarios should proceed.

- **Rollback procedures** For any major changes you're making, be sure you've identified and tested reliable rollback plans so you can roll back to a known good state in case things go wrong.

- **Escalation procedures** These are standard in any project, but when you're dealing with the infrastructure, you might need to beef this area up a bit to make sure you have the right people on standby or on call when critical portions of the project are being implemented.

- **Critical issue reporting** As with other security projects, you might want to review your critical issue-reporting procedures to see whether you need to create a "team red response" that will enable you and your project team to quickly address any vulnerabilities or issues that are deemed critical, severe, or extreme. Develop the process for defining these kinds of issues, and develop an agreed-on scale or measurement system so your team can quickly deal with imminent or urgent issues that may arise.

- **Documentation** Depending on the nature of your project as well as your regulatory or compliance requirements, you might need to revisit your typical project documentation processes and procedures so that you can create the kinds of documentation your project requires, without sorting back through the project to develop the documentation after the fact.

Project Team

We always recommend gathering at least your core team together to help define the project, but at this point, you have defined the skills and personnel you need, so you should be ready to create your project team. As with almost all IT projects, you should involve subject matter experts from outside the IT department so that you get a well-rounded view of life within the organization, not just within the IT department. Also keep in mind that with infrastructure issues, many areas are technically beyond the grasp of many employees within the organization (well, most everyone outside the IT department). Be patient, be prepared to explain things in nontechnical ways, and don't discuss technical details when it isn't absolutely necessary. You want to involve users and stakeholders in appropriate ways, but there will be a more limited role for them in this type of project than in most of the other kinds of IT security projects you might undertake.

An infrastructure security project spans the entire enterprise and is as deep as it is wide. To be successfully completed, the project requires an extensive set of first-rate skills. Be sure that your project team has all the skills delineated in your skills assessment. If it does not, your project is at risk because gaps in skills or skills that are not up to standards will create problems in quality or scheduling down the line. Be sure you have all the requisite skills; if you don't, be sure to create a plan to address those gaps. Whether you need additional external staff or just some training for internal staff, be sure to add this to your budget and possibly your schedule.

Develop your team, create a team roster, and get the team ready to create the detailed project plan, especially the work breakdown structure.

Project Organization

You might want to organize your project by the topic areas we've defined so that you have subteams dedicated to: devices and media, topologies, IDS/IPS, and system hardening. You could choose to parse it out differently, or you might have the whole team, if it is small, work through each stage of the project plan together. It's up to you, and it's certainly somewhat dependent on the size of your company, the size of the project, and the size of your IT staff. Be sure that everyone is clear about what their roles are within the team and within the project. Organizing your team will provide the necessary structure for the team to be productive. Since we're assuming you've managed a lot of projects (or have read up on your project management skills recently), we won't delve into the details of organizing this project except to make one note: The work in the various segments of this project overlaps a lot, and if your project and team are not well organized, you're going to have people working at cross-purposes and creating a big mess. Keep the project and your team organized to avoid this scenario.

Project Work Breakdown Structure

Your approach to creating your work breakdown structure (WBS) might be different from the method we provide; that's fine as long as you cover the basics. Our recommended approach is to start with your mission statement and your selected solution and create three to five high-level objectives. From there, you can parse each of those objectives down into smaller components until you have tasks that actually make sense and are understandable. Tasks should be broken down until they represent an understandable and manageable unit of work. The 80/8 rule is a good one to keep in mind; it states that no task should exceed 80 hours or be less than 8 hours. If a task is longer than 80 hours, it needs to be broken down into smaller components. If you define tasks of less than 8 hours, you'll end up with a scheduling nightmare on your hands.

We'll start with the four major areas we discussed at the opening of this chapter:

1. Devices and media

2. Topologies

3. Intrusion detection/intrusion prevention

4. System hardening

If you recall from prior chapters, these are not properly written as tasks or even as objectives; they're topic labels. So, let's fix that and create the top-level objectives based on these four areas of concern:

1. Audit and secure devices and media

2. Audit and secure network topology

3. Implement or harden intrusion prevention/detection systems

4. Harden systems

Now we have a better starting point for our WBS. From here, we can break these down into smaller tasks. We're not going to dig down as deep as you'll need to, because once you get beyond a certain level of detail, the plan is very much dependent on the nature and structure of your organization and how you and your team decide to approach the project. So, don't fight with the structure presented here; use it as a guide to create one that works for you. Also note that where servers or other devices may be called out, the numbers or types of devices may not track with standard networking practices. They are presented as examples of a WBS tree, not necessarily examples of best practices in networking. In reality, you will have more or fewer DNS servers, but we only mention one. You will have a long list of tasks under Task 3.4, "Assess and harden routers, switches, and other network communication devices." We didn't dig down at all levels of the WBS but provided samples of how or where you might develop additional tasks and subtasks. And, while this list is long, it's not as long as your infrastructure security project plan's WBS will end up being. However, this should give you a running start:

1. Audit and secure devices and media.

2. Audit and secure network topology.

    2.1 Create secure boundaries using firewalls, DMZs, and proxy servers.

    2.2 Create secure remote access.

    2.2.1 Secure all Remote Access Servers.

    2.2.1.1 Physically secure Remote Access Servers.

    2.2.1.2 Secure Remote Access Servers.

    2.2.1.2.1 Remove excess administrative accounts.

    2.2.1.2.2 Disable all unused services, ports, and protocols.

    2.2.1.2.3 Remove all unused applications.

    2.2.1.2.4 Disable all unused modems.

    2.2.2 Secure remote communications.

    2.2.2.1 Evaluate the feasibility and desirability of implementing VLAN.

    2.2.2.1 Evaluate the feasibility and desirability of implementing VPN.

    2.3 Create secure wireless access.

    2.3.1 Change all wireless access points' default settings.

    2.3.2 Disable SSID broadcasting, create a closed system.

    2.3.3 Enable MAC address filtering.

    2.3.4 Evaluate and implement encryption (WEP or WPA).

    2.3.5 Filter wireless protocols.

    2.3.5 Define IP allocations for the WLAN.

    2.3.6 Evaluate VPNs for possible implementation.

    2.3.7 Secure users' wireless devices.

2.3.8 Develop wireless policies for users.

2.3.9 Develop wireless policies for IT operations.

2.4 Implement a segmented network.

2.5 Implement network traffic security protocols for sensitive network traffic.

2.6 Deploy network security technologies.

2.6.1 Use Encrypting File System (EFS) or similar file encryption.

2.6.2 Require and use strong user authentication, passwords, and account policies.

2.6.3 Employ the concept of "least privileges" when assigning user rights.

3. Implement or harden intrusion prevention/detection systems.

3.1 Assess security of current IDS/IPS system or evaluate need for implementing IDS/IPS system.

3.1.1 Evaluate intrusion detection system feasibility and desirability.

3.1.2 Inline intrusion prevention system feasibility and desirability.

3.1.3 Network active response system feasibility and desirability.

3.1.4 Host active response system feasibility and desirability.

3.1.5 Network processors feasibility and desirability.

3.2 Assess and harden DMZ or evaluate need for implementing DMZ.

3.3 Assess and harden firewall or evaluate need for implementing additional firewalls.

3.4 Assess and harden routers, switches, and other network communication devices.

4. Harden systems.

4.1 Evaluate physical security and access control to critical servers.

4.1.1 Evaluate and secure access to domain controllers.

4.1.1.1 Evaluate and secure domain controller 1.

4.1.1.2 Evaluate and secure domain controller 2.

4.1.1.3 Evaluate and secure domain controller 3.

4.1.2 Evaluate and secure access to DHCP server.

4.1.3 Evaluate and secure access to DNS server.

4.2 Review and revise administrative accounts on infrastructure servers.

4.2.1 Remove unused or superfluous administrative accounts.

4.2.2 Remove unused or unnecessary non-administrative accounts.

4.2.3 Remove unused rights and privileges.

4.3 Implement strong authentication and password policies on all infrastructure devices.

4.4 Review, record and update (as needed) operating system and application version levels.

4.4.1 Review and record operating system versions on all infrastructure servers.

4.4.1.1 Review and record operating system version on domain controller 1.

4.4.1.2 Review and record operating system version on domain controller 2.

4.4.1.3 Review and record operating system version on domain controller 3.

4.4.1.4 Review and record operating system version on DHCP server.

4.4.1.5 Review and record operating system version on DNS server.

4.4.2 Update operating systems on all infrastructure servers.

4.4.2.1 Update operating system on domain controller 1.

4.4.2.2 Update operating system on domain controller 2.

4.4.2.3 Update operating system on domain controller 3.

4.4.2.4 Update operating system on DHCP server.

4.4.2.5 Update operating system on DNS server.

4.5 Review current status of virus protection software installed on servers.

4.6 Assess and implement server, application, and client-side security technologies.

4.6.1 Secure server traffic traveling on the network.

4.6.2 Secure application and user data traveling on the network.

4.6.3 Secure network access points and network access.

4.6.4 Secure client devices including desktops, laptops, and PDAs.

4.6.4.1 Upgrade all insecure "legacy" operating systems.

4.6.4.2 Update all operating systems with latest revisions, patches, and updates.

4.6.4.3 Update all applications with latest revisions, patches, and updates.

4.6.4.4 Update all virus protection programs.

4.6.4.4.1 Ensure latest virus definition file is loaded.

4.6.4.4.2 Ensure virus program is configured to automatically download the latest definition file from secure server or Internet site (WSUS in Windows or vendor Web site).

4.6.4.5 Enable file encryption for mobile devices.

4.6.4.6 Implement strong passwords.

4.6.4.7 Update user policies to prevent downloading or installing of unsigned programs.

5. Document all infrastructure changes.

5.1 Document changes to all infrastructure configuration settings.

5.2 Document changes to network topology, layout, or structure.

5.3 Document changes to standard operating procedures.

5.4 Document changes to user policies and procedures.

6. Perform compliance audit.

Once you've completed the WBS, you need to go through with your subject matter experts and develop the task details. Details can include task owners, resources, known constraints, or requirements for the task, task duration, task cost or budget, tools or equipment needed for the task, completion criteria, deadline or due date, and any other data relevant to the task and its successful completion. Remember that the functional, technical, and legal requirements should be fully incorporated into the project task detail or they will get lost. This is a great opportunity to review your requirements and go through your task details to ensure that everything is included, before project work starts.

This is also a point at which you should do a scope check and make sure that the WBS describes your intended scope. It's fairly common for the scope described by the WBS to be larger than the stated scope. In fact, this is often the first source of "scope creep." Look at your scope statement and at your WBS and reconcile any discrepancies. For example, you might have stated in your scope statement that something was not part of the project scope but that element shows up in the WBS. Decide if that element should be in or out, then adjust either your scope statement or your WBS accordingly. If there are substantive changes to your scope, check in with your project sponsor to gain agreement as to the modified or updated scope and WBS.

Project Risks and Mitigation Strategies

This section of your project plan defines the risks to your project and the strategies you'll use to avoid or mitigate your risk. There are always risks with every project, and it's important to take time to identify those risks while you're calm, cool, and collected. There are some projects for which the risks outweigh the benefits and you decide, as a team or an organization, to not go down that path. Securing the infrastructure is not likely to fall into that category, but it's always important to keep this in mind—that sometimes doing nothing is a better choice.

However, you've decided to strengthen security on your network infrastructure and there are attendant risks. Let's look at one risk you might have, and you can then use this structure to develop additional risk and mitigation strategies. We'll use the following ranking system: 1 = Extremely high, 5 = Extremely low.

Risk: Improper configuration could completely disable network.

1. Criticality: 1

2. Likelihood of occurrence: 3

3. Relative risk ranking: 2

4. Mitigation strategy 1: Test all configurations in lab prior to rollout.

5. Risk of mitigation 1: Not all lab tests will completely mirror actual conditions.

6. Mitigation strategy 2: Develop fail-safe rollback plans for all critical configuration changes.

7. Risk of mitigation 2: Rollback will take time and set back project completion timelines.

8. Trigger 1: One week prior to scheduled configuration change.

9. Trigger 2: Forty-five minutes after network outage occurs.

10. Notes: All configuration changes will be tested in the lab first, but the there is still a chance that the configuration change could cause the network to crash. If this occurs, rollback plans will be implemented after 45 minutes of network downtime have elapsed.

As you can see from this single example, you can develop sound contingency plans for risks you decide are worth planning for. Some risks are too small to bother planning for; other risks are significant but unlikely to occur, and planning for them would also not be a good use of time.

Once you've listed every risk you can think of, you can develop a ranked list based on both criticality and likelihood of occurrence. From there, you can develop mitigation strategies for just the most critical and most likely-to-occur risks. You may choose to develop more than one mitigation strategy. In our example, our first choice was to test in the lab, but we also conceded that testing in the lab may not mirror real-world results and the risk of our mitigation strategy had to be addressed as well. In this case, we developed a secondary or backup mitigation strategy as a fail-safe option. Both mitigation strategies require a defined trigger—how will you know when to implement your risk mitigation plan? In this case, you might choose to build lab testing into your project plan for all configuration change tasks and avoid this first mitigation strategy. However, you would still need the second mitigation strategy and trigger in the event that you ran into a configuration problem that you couldn't immediately find. In this case, after a 45-minute outage you'd go to Plan B, your predetermined rollback plan. It's nice to have Plan B ready to go when you're running around like you hair is on fire because you have 47 different people asking you when the network will be back up, what the problem is, and why they can't log onto the network.

Project Constraints and Assumptions

Constraints for an infrastructure security project might come in all shapes and sizes. You may well face budgetary constraints that limit the scope of your project. You might face scope problems because the infrastructure needs a lot of upgrading but your company isn't willing to implement all the changes needed, for a variety of financial, political, and organizational reasons. You might face resistance within the organization because some changes impact users' computing behaviors, and this can cause problems. In addition, you may face specific constraints or limits within portions of your project. For a variety of reasons, you might not be able to make changes to application servers or database servers due to other projects under way or other organizational issues. The infrastructure security is core to your network's security, so constraints to the project should be clearly identified and discussed. If the constraints are too great or impede your project too much, you should have a talk with your project sponsor. Although every project has to deal with a variety of constraints, you must decide whether the constraints are reasonable or if they place an undue burden on your project. You are responsible for project success and, ulti-mately, for the security of the infrastructure, so it's up to you to clear away these obstacles or get your project sponsor involved with removing them so the project can be successful.

Equally important is delineating the assumptions you're working under as you move into the project. For example, if you assume certain resources will be available or if you assume that other projects will be completed first, you should state that clearly. Your assumptions should be clearly delineated so that you and your team can *challenge*, *clarify*, or *confirm* those assumptions before proceeding with the project. The most dangerous assumptions are the ones we don't know we're making.

For example, if you've been in the midst of deploying a particular encryption method, your project would work on the assumption that the encryption scheme was already in place or was being deployed. This fact is critical to note in your project because, if something outside your control changes the encryption scheme on which your infrastructure project is based, you'll have to rework your project plan. This could (and probably would) impact both your schedule and your budget. It's hard enough to bring a project in on time and on budget without having the project environment shift around on you. Listing the assumptions you're making going into the project will help you as you develop your plan as well because others on the team or in the organization can challenge your assumptions, if they know what they are. To go back to the encryption example, if you list this as an assumption and someone on your project team lets you know that the encryption project was put on hold for one reason or another, it's good to know that ahead of time rather than planning based on that incorrect assumption.

Some project managers like to list project success factors in their list of assumptions because they are assuming these factors will be in place or will occur. You can also discuss and define success factors at the front of your project-planning process, if that's a more logical flow for you. Some teams don't know what it will take to be successful until they've neared the end of their definition and planning work; others like to define these elements right up front. Whatever works for you is fine. Just be sure to define these so you'll know what it will take for your project to succeed.

You and your project team will have to look at the project environment and list the constraints and the assumptions you're making in order for your project to get off to a good start and to have a better-than-average chance for success. These elements are unique to each project and each company, so we can't give you a list of things to place in this section, but now that we've discussed them in general terms, you and your team should be able to dig in and find the constraints and assumptions for your own, unique infrastructure security project.

Project Schedule and Budget

You can see from the lengthy project plan we've created that your schedule and budget are going to be challenging to develop. Once you've created your WBS, you can look through your task details and begin developing your schedule. The schedule is best developed in a project management software program since you will have a lot of moving parts to handle. If you have subteams working in parallel on different aspects of the project plan, be sure you address this in your schedule. First, you'll have to be sure you're not double-booking someone and throwing your schedule off. Second, you want to keep an eye on how different segments of the project will impact other segments so you don't end up working at cross-purposes, or worse, damaging something another team just implemented. If one team is upgrading the firewalls and another team is working on IPS, it's entirely possible one team's work will greatly impact the other team's work and cause confusion, problems, errors, or omissions.

Be sure to check your critical path tasks after you've loaded your schedule into the software program, since these tasks will determine the longest, least-flexible path through your project. Although we haven't discussed the more technical aspects of scheduling (we assume you know them), recall that you can indicate lead and lag times as well as float to create a more realistic schedule. If everything in your project plan ends up on the critical path, or if none of your tasks end up on the critical path, there's a good chance you have a fundamental problem with how your schedule is set up.

As for budget, you should have a pretty clear idea of what this project will cost at this point, with one notable exception. If you are using your infrastructure security project plan to evaluate the need for an IDS, IPS, DMZ, or other network equipment, you might not yet have sufficient data with which to get bids for these systems. In that case, you need some sort of placeholder to indicate that a system will be purchased but the system has yet to be clearly defined and therefore cannot be spec'd out or priced. If you know the order of magnitude, it might be good to add a dollar-amount placeholder. For example, suppose you know that one type of system you're looking for costs about $18,000, plus or minus $2,000. You might want to put $20,000 into your budget as a placeholder so that when your project budget is approved, you have that cost built in. It's usually difficult to get your budget increased after it's been approved, unless you specifically get your budget approved with the understanding that it does *not* include the cost of new hardware or software solutions that may be recommended as a result of the project assessment.

If you've made it this far, you've made it to the end of the chapter and the end of your planning cycle for your infrastructure security project plan. It's a lot to cover because the infrastructure is wide and deep, but if you take time to step through your planning in a measured, thoughtful manner, you'll end up with better results than if you just rush headlong into the project work. That's a guarantee. Your project might not be perfect, it could come in late or over budget, but whatever result you turn in will be far better than if you used no consistent approach or framework at all.

IT Infrastructure Security Project Outline

- Audit and secure devices and media.
- Audit and secure network topology.
  - Create secure boundaries using firewalls, DMZs and proxy servers.
  - Create secure remote access.
  - Create secure wireless access.
  - Implement a segmented network.
  - Implement network traffic security protocols for sensitive network traffic.
  - Deploy network security technologies.

- Implement or harden intrusion prevention/detection systems.
    - Assess security of current IDS/IPS system *or* evaluate need for implementing IDS/IPS system.
    - Assess and harden DMZ *or* evaluate need for implementing DMZ.
    - Assess and harden firewall *or* evaluate need for implementing additional firewalls.
    - Assess and harden routers, switches, and other network communication devices.
- Harden systems.
    - Evaluate physical security and access control to critical servers.
    - Review and revise administrative accounts on infrastructure servers.
    - Implement strong authentication and password policies on all infrastructure devices.
    - Review, record, and update (as needed) operating system and application version levels.
    - Review current status of virus protection software installed on servers.
    - Assess and implement server, application, and client-side security technologies.
- Document all infrastructure changes.
    - Document changes to all infrastructure configuration settings.
    - Document changes to network topology, layout or structure.
    - Document changes to standard operating procedures.
    - Document changes to user policies and procedures.
- Perform compliance audit.

Summary

We've covered a lot of ground in this chapter because your network infrastructure is literally and figuratively the backbone of your network. Infrastructure security touches every aspect of your network, and a thorough assessment will take time and careful effort to complete so that your network is as secure as it can reasonably be, given the organizational constraints and considerations you'll have to deal with. It's often helpful to break the network infrastructure down into it systems or areas to help ensure that you cover all the areas, including devices and media, topology, intrusion detection and prevention, system hardening, and all the network components such as routers, switches, and modems. Once you've identified all the areas, you need to take a top-to-bottom look at how security is currently implemented and what threats exist. By looking at issues such as information criticality and performing an impact analysis, you can decide what should be included in your project and what can reasonably be left out or delayed for a later phase if needed. Understanding the threat environment and your network's vulnerabilities is also important during your planning phase.

Requirements need to be thoroughly developed because they form the foundation of your project's scope. Functional requirements should be developed first, followed by technical, legal, and policy requirements. Be sure to build these into your task details when you create your WBS so that all required elements will be present and accounted for in your project plan.

In an infrastructure security project, you'll need a wide variety of skills that span the depth and breadth of networking knowledge. Be sure you define the skills you'll need so that you can assess your team and your organization to identify skills gaps. These will have to be addressed before your project can proceed, and this often requires hiring outside contractors or providing training for internal staff members. Either way, this can impact both your budget and your schedule, so be sure you do a gap analysis between needed and available skills prior to proceeding with your project.

The WBS defines the scope of your project, so once you've identified all the work through delineating the tasks, be sure to do a scope check. If the defined scope is smaller than the scope outlined in your WBS, you need to reconcile the differences. Also be sure to discuss any scope changes with your project sponsor so that you start off with the same expectations about project results.

Scheduling an infrastructure security project can be challenging due to all the moving parts involved. You'll run into scheduling conflicts, resource usage conflicts, timing issues, and more. These should be resolved to the greatest degree possible before starting the project, because things will only get more complicated and difficult to resolve once project work is under way. One important scheduling note is that with all areas of your network being poked and prodded, you'll need to make sure subproject teams are not working at cross-purposes and undoing work just done or inadvertently injecting false indicators into the process through their own task work.

When it's all said and done, you should be able to define, implement, manage, and close a very successful infrastructure security project, if you follow a consistent methodology and make teamwork and quality topmost priorities. This is the foundation of all other security projects; it touches on everything in your organization, so success here will create the framework for a very secure network that will help you sleep at night, knowing you've done everything possible to keep your organization's assets secure.

Solutions Fast Track

Infrastructure Security Auditing

☑ Auditing or assessing the infrastructure security is a large task that encompasses every aspect of your network.

☑ Infrastructure projects cross several boundaries, and you should be sure that any overlap is addressed so you are not working at cross-purposes.

☑ The infrastructure project can be parsed out in numerous ways. One way is to look at it in terms of these systems: network perimeter, internal network, intrusion monitoring and prevention, host and server configuration, malicious code protection, incident response capabilities, security policies and procedures, employee awareness and training, and physical security and monitoring.

☑ The internal and external environments should be assessed thoroughly prior to planning your project.

☑ Internal factors include understanding information criticality, the potential impact of a breach, the information flow, policies and procedures, user needs, and regulatory/compliance issues.

☑ Externally, you need to consider the types of threats your network is vulnerable to, including spoofing, repudiation, data tampering, denial of service, and elevation of privileges.

☑ The SAN Institute publishes a list of the top 20 vulnerabilities that can serve as a great starting point for assessing your network's vulnerabilities.

☑ The assessment should look at devices and media, topologies, intrusion detection/intrusion prevention systems, and system hardening.

☑ Devices and media include all the network infrastructure devices that must be secured, including routers, switches, and modems.

Project Parameters

☑ Defining the functional and technical specifications for your infrastructure project will define the scope of work you need to accomplish.

☑ There could be specific legal or regulatory compliance issues to be addressed within the scope of your infrastructure security plan; you should include these issues in the early stages of project planning.

☑ Defining scope, initial budget, initial schedule, and quality guidelines based on the functional, technical, legal, and policy requirements gives you a solid starting point.

☑ Developing the relative priority of your parameters and gaining project sponsor agreement is important in helping you know how to make decisions for your project, moving forward. The least flexible parameter will be your constraint; the most flexible parameter will be what "gives" when things change in the course of project work.

☑ Technical skills needed for the project include network services, network perimeter, intrusion detection/prevention, remote access, wireless access, server and host administration, familiarity with protocols, ports, and services as well as skills in documentation, communication, and training.

Project Team

☑ Your core project team should help in defining the project.

☑ Your infrastructure project team should include people with the needed skills, which, in an infrastructure security project, are extensive.

☑ Your project is at risk if you don't have the skills you need on your team. Be sure to address skills gaps before you start project work and add any associated costs into your project budget.

Project Organization

☑ The project should be organized around areas of the network and areas of expertise.

☑ Typical organizational methods should form the foundation of your project organization.

☑ Infrastructure projects require extra coordination to ensure that subteams are not working at cross-purposes.

Project Work Breakdown Structure

☑ The work breakdown structure, or WBS, for an infrastructure project should begin with the high-level objectives for your project, which might include securing devices and media, securing the perimeter, securing infrastructure components, or whatever way you choose to segment the work in this project.

☑ Task details should reflect the functional, technical, and regulatory requirements for your project. Check task details against requirements to be sure everything is included at the outset.

☑ The scope statement and the scope described by the WBS might not be in sync. Compare them and make any modifications needed to either your scope statement or your WBS before proceeding.

☑ If there are significant changes to your scope statement, check in with your project sponsor before proceeding to ensure that you're both on the same page with regard to scope.

Project Risks and Mitigation Strategies

☑ The risks inherent in an infrastructure project are many because this type of project touches every aspect of your network.

☑ Identify all potential risks and rank them according to criticality and likelihood of occurrence, then look over the list and make any reasonable adjustments.

☑ Determine how far down your risk list you will plan, then develop mitigation strategies and triggers for each defined risk.

☑ If you determine that there are one or more significant risks, you should sit down and talk them over with your project sponsor. In some cases, the risks outweigh any potential benefit and the project should be canceled, redefined, or postponed until those risks can be more clearly evaluated and addressed.

Project Constraints and Assumptions

☑ Constraints are present in every project, but in an infrastructure security project, you could have constraints on several fronts.

☑ If the constraints are too great, they can hinder or prevent project success. Discuss major constraints with your project sponsor to determine the best course of action. Otherwise, develop ways to address these constraints or plan around them.

☑ Clearly delineating assumptions is an important part of your infrastructure security plan because you have to work from a known good point.

☑ If your assumptions are stated, they can be challenged, clarified, or confirmed.

☑ Assumptions may also include success factors, since you might be assuming certain factors must be in place for the project to succeed. Success factors are also sometimes developed in the requirements phase of the project-planning process, depending on how you go about identifying them.

Project Schedule and Budget

☑ After you've developed your project's WBS, you should have sufficient data to create a fairly realistic and feasible project schedule and budget.

☑ Keep in mind that the project schedule has a lot of moving parts, and you're likely to run into issues around conflicting resource demands or subteams working at cross-purposes.

☑ Be sure your budget provides for adequate training or hiring of needed resources.

☑ Large purchases such as IDS/IPS or other major components might not be decided at the outset of the project. Create ballpark estimates or insert placeholders in your budget so it is clear whether or not large-ticket items are included or specifically excluded from your project budget.

Infrastructure Security Project Outline

☑ Audit and secure network topology.

☑ Audit and secure network topology.

☑ Implement or harden intrusion prevention/detection systems.

☑ Harden systems.

☑ Document all infrastructure changes.

☑ Perform compliance audit.

Chapter 12

Wireless Security Project Plan

Solutions in this chapter:

- Wireless Security Auditing
- Project Parameters
- Project Team
- Project Organization
- Project Work Breakdown Structure
- Project Risks and Mitigation Strategies
- Project Constraints and Assumptions
- Project Schedule and Budget
- Wireless Security Project Outline

- ☑ Summary
- ☑ Solutions Fast Track

Introduction

In this chapter, we'll provide the framework for creating a wireless security project as part of your overall corporate IT security strategy. As with all the individual security area projects (ISAPs) discussed in this book, it is intended to be a template to use as a starting point. There is no one-size-fits-all project plan for any security topic, and wireless security is no exception. You will need to modify this project plan to fit your organizational needs in many different ways but you will find the basic building blocks here.

Wireless technology continues to evolve and so, too, do the tools hackers use to gain unauthorized access to wireless networks. Even as recently as two years ago, a majority of corporate wireless networks were unsecured, allowing anyone with a wireless card to access the network. In the past couple of years, more companies have begun securing their wireless networks in a variety of ways (though a surprising number are still unsecured). Some companies have created a separate wireless network for customers or guests that does not connect in any way to the corporate network (such as those often found in hotels, coffee shops, and airports). Other companies have applied basic security such as Wired Equivalent Privacy (WEP), which was once thought to be secure but has since been shown to be hackable; or Wi-Fi Protected Access (WPA), a stronger but more difficult-to-administer security solution for wireless. We won't get into the pros and cons of various wireless security solutions in this chapter, though we will discuss various technical elements and let you decide what will work best for your organization.

Even if your company does not have a wireless network, you still need to perform an audit because an intruder or employee can easily install a rogue wireless access point at just about any place on the wired network to provide unauthorized wireless access. So, don't think that because your IT department hasn't implemented a wireless network that others (inside and out) haven't already done so without your knowledge. The bottom line is this: wireless networks must be secured to meet the specific needs of *your* organization and you must also be aware of all wireless access to the network. In this chapter, we'll get you started down that path.

In addition, a laptop with a wireless connection at an airport or hotel lobby accessing the corporate network via the Internet exposes your firm to the same wireless hazards as a corporate wireless network does, so you do need to have a wireless security plan for your organization.

Wireless Security Auditing

Before you can embark on just about any IT security project, you need to understand the current environment. In project management, as we've stated several times, you should start with a problem statement. The problem statement for wireless security can be as general as, "We don't have adequate security for our wireless network and corporate resources are at risk." However, the more specific you get, the better your solution will be. If you say, "We currently have 25 wireless access points (WAP) that are operating without security and we have no idea how many rogue WAPs we have," you are getting closer to defining the real problem and closer to identifying the real need. One way to develop a solid problem statement can be through auditing.

Auditing means different things to different people but we'll use a definition commonly used in the IT security world: a thorough and methodical review of systems and technologies focusing on finding vulnerabilities. Some companies hire outside security consultants to assist with their security auditing. If you choose to perform your own wireless security audit, you're going to need several tools to do so and you're also going to need to put on your "hacker's hat" so you can discover vulnerabilities hackers would likely exploit.

Hackers, like robbers or car thieves, will attack the easiest targets first. In the case of wireless networks, they'll certainly take an unsecured wireless network over a protected one any day. Although both WEP and WPA can be hacked, both require more time, effort, data, and sophistication to do so. Just like the car thief, the easiest car to steal is a car that is (in this order):

1. Running with the key in the ignition.

2. Unlocked.

3. Locked.

4. Locked and using a security device (e.g., a steering wheel lock).

5. Locked, with an alarm system.

6. Locked, with an alarm system and an engine-disabling device.

For a hacker, the easiest networks to hack are those that are unsecured. However, corporations can be pretty rich targets for hackers—either because of the presence of personal data on the network (credit cards, personal identification, etc.) or because they can access corporate trade secrets, R&D, and other confidential corporate data. Hackers will try to find a way in if they believe it's fun, interesting, or lucrative to do so. Finally, there is simply the hacker-of-convenience who hacks into a network just to see if he or she can. Therefore, your goal in wireless network auditing is to find the vulnerabilities from easiest to hardest (just like our car thief). If you plug the obvious holes, you're better off than doing nothing, but you're not secure.

Also keep in mind that there are a growing number of wireless devices, all of which you need to manage. Users with laptops, PDAs, smart phones, and other devices are accessing all kinds of information on the Internet, both from your corporate network and elsewhere. They're like little kids out playing at school—you have no idea what they may have gotten into and what kinds of viruses they may bring into the organization, all through relatively innocent activities. It doesn't really matter how secure your network is if traveling employees access confidential data across an unsecured link. These are the kinds of things you need to be aware of when you assess your wireless environment from end to end.

Types of Wireless Network Components and Devices

There is a long list of actual devices that can be used in a variety of wireless environments. For now, let's look at the top-level categories. These include:

- Wireless Local Area Network (WLAN), including wireless access points (WAP), bridges, wireless keyboards, WLAN clients, or Wireless Personal Area Network (WPAN) Bluetooth clients

- Cellular phones with Internet capabilities or camera capabilities

- Radio Frequency Identification (RFID)

- Broadband wireless networks or cellular data interface cards (3G) in PDAs

- Two-way pagers and Short Messaging Service (SMS) devices

- Blackberry devices and Blackberry Enterprise Server

Wireless devices and technology are changing all the time and the wireless capabilities continue to expand, so be sure to take a look at the technological landscape at the time you plan your wireless security project to determine if the list provided should be expanded for your project. Table 12.1 also categorizes wireless devices by network connection, operating system, and how it participates in a wireless network. This may be helpful to you in looking across your organization at all wireless devices.

Table 12.1 Wireless Devices to Secure

Wireless Technology	Environment
Wireless network	Wireless Local Area Network (WLAN), Wireless Personal Area Network (WPAN), Wireless Wide Area Network (WWAN)
Radio Frequency Identification (RFID)	
Wireless camera	Wireless client, network device, embedded OS
Wireless access point (WAP)	Infrastructure, operating system, network access
WLAN Security gateway, router, bridge, or switch (functionality often imbedded with WAP)	Infrastructure, operating system, network access

Continued

Table 12.1 continued Wireless Devices to Secure

Wireless Technology	Environment
WLAN or WWAN (Broadband) Network Client (including laptops and other clients)	Wireless client, network device, operating system, applications, anti-virus, IP address
Personal Digital Assistant (PDA) with Network Interface Card (NIC)	Wireless client, network device, embedded OS, applications, IP address
PDA without NIC	Network device (via docking or sync station), embedded OS, applications, no IP address
Blackberry Enterprise Server	Wireless server, network (member) server, operating system, server application, anti-virus
Blackberry client devices	Wireless client, network device, embedded OS, applications
Wireless phone	Wireless client, network device, embedded OS
Wireless Voice over IP (VoIP) system and telephone devices	Embedded OS, wireless telecom
Wireless keyboards and mice	None

Adapted from "Wireless Security Checklist, Version 3, Release 1.3, 20 April 2006." Developed by Defense Information Systems Agency (DISA) for the Department of Defense (DOD).

If you're interested in reviewing the entire spectrum of security checklists available from DISA, visit the National Institute of Standards and Technology (NIST) Web site at http://csrc.nist.gov/pcig/cig.html. The checklists are written in a very specific format that may not be useful to you, but the information contained within the templates may be useful. They can be used as a starting point for creating a detailed security assessment or audit for a variety of topics including access control, Microsoft's Active Directory, biometrics, Cisco's IOS Router, and many more.

Wireless Technologies

Although it's important to be aware of the various kinds of wireless technologies, the primary focus is on the standard wireless networking components we're all pretty used to by now. Let's take a brief detour to understand the wireless standards.

The wireless standard issued by the Institute of Electrical and Electronic Engineers (IEEE) is known as IEEE 802.11. Here's a quick summary:

- **802.11** Has data speeds of up to 2 megabits per second (Mbps) and uses either Frequency Hopping Spread Spectrum (FHSS) or Direct-Sequence Spread Spectrum (DSSS) transmission techniques. Even though both are based in the ISM (Industrial, Scientific, and Medical) radio band, FHSS and DSSS devices cannot network with each other.

- **802.11a** Has data speeds of up to 54 Mbps and uses the Orthogonal Frequency Division Multiplexing (OFDM) technique in the U-NII (Unlicensed National Information Infrastructure) radio band.

- **802.11b** Has data speeds of up to 11 Mbps and uses only the DSSS technique in the ISM radio band. It's backward-compatible with 802.11 DSSS devices.

- **802.11g** Has data speeds of up to 54Mbps and uses both OFDM and DSSS techniques in the ISM radio band. Use of the DSSS allows it to be backward-compatible with 802.11b and 802.11 DSSS devices.

- **802.11n** This is the latest Wi-Fi standard but results aren't in yet. There are reports that there are interoperability problems so most consumers and businesses are taking a wait-and-see approach.

Although 802.11 debuted in the mid-1990s, wireless networking didn't become a big consumer item until the introduction of inexpensive 802.11b equipment in 2001. Even though the 802.11a standard was ratified just prior to 802.11b, most manufacturers made "b" equipment first. 802.11a has a very short range in comparison to any of the other standards, due to the U-NII band, and has never gained much popularity. The subsequent standard, 802.11g, was ratified in 2003, and is backward-compatible with 802.11b and 802.11 DSSS equipment. For these reasons, 802.11b enjoys the most popular use, though 802.11g has caught up quickly. Next up, 802.11n. If you want to learn more about the standards, www.hpl.hp.com/personal/Jean_Tourrilhes/Linux/Linux.Wireless.std.ht ml has some detailed information on how they came about. You can also read through the IEEE standards; they're located at http://standards.ieee.org/wireless. Another good resource is http://www.netstumbler.com.

Types of Threats

There are three primary categories of threats we'll discuss in this chapter: War dialing, war driving, and Bluetooth attacks. In a moment, we'll look at each one in detail. The majority of this chapter will be devoted to "traditional" wireless security—meaning the wireless networks created by wireless network interface cards and wireless access points connected to a wired network. This is where the bulk of the risk comes from in any company and therefore it should be the place where most attention is placed (from a wireless security perspective). However, there are several other types of attacks that fall within the "wireless" realm that should be understood and assessed in your network. Most of these "alternate" connection types can be quickly and easily located and secured, but the point is that you must be thorough in your wireless assessment so you don't overlook these easily secured openings. We'll begin by looking at attack methods from oldest to newest. *War dialing* started back in the days when remote computers communicated with one another only via modems over the public telephone systems. *Wardriving* is the updated version of that and uses wireless technologies rather than phone lines. Bluetooth, a short-wave radio signal communication method, also has its perils.

War Dialing, Demon Dialing, Carrier Signal Scanning

Although war dialing (a.k.a. demon dialing or carrier signal scanning) is not technically a wireless technology, it belongs in this arena due to the nature of the attack. *War dialing*, for those of you not familiar with this attack type, is when hackers dial phone numbers looking for misconfigured or unsecured modems. Remember modems? Many desktop computers and even many servers have modems sitting in them, even if they are unused and getting dusty in a virtual sense. War dialing can yield unexpectedly large rewards for hackers since modems are often forgotten elements and are therefore overlooked as part of a risk assessment or security monitoring project.

In a standard network configuration, all incoming traffic is routed through an external firewall and/or a perimeter network along with an internal firewall. However, with a modem in the mix, a hacker can essentially bypass all those layers of protection and go directly into the computer or server with the modem installed. The modem in and of itself is not a problem but because it may not be secured, it may create a security hole that you're not even looking for. You should take an inventory of all computers in your network to determine if they have modems and if they have phone lines connected to them. A modem by itself can't be utilized unless it's connected to a phone line, and some companies' phone systems don't connect well with standard RJ-11 jack types, so this may not be an issue for you. However, it never hurts to look. For example, if your company used to use modems, are you sure you're no longer paying for those modem lines from the phone company? Many corporate phone bills go directly to finance, not to the IT department, so it's entirely possible you have active phone lines that users might still be connected to (or that they could connect to). For example, if a corporate computer is configured with Symantec's pcAnywhere without username and password required, it's a wide open door for anyone looking to circumvent network firewalls and security measures, as shown in Figure 12.1. A hacker can easily bypass all the well-designed security systems and get right in an open backdoor without any security measures at all. It doesn't take any very sophisticated tools or techniques to do this.

Keep in mind that if your company is still running legacy systems or components, many require the use of modems for maintenance and support activities. If these systems are connected to the network, they are part of your security environment. One of the best ways to secure these types of systems is to enable the dial-back feature so that an incoming call is disconnected and the call is returned to a specified phone number.

Figure 12.1 Network Exposed Via Modem

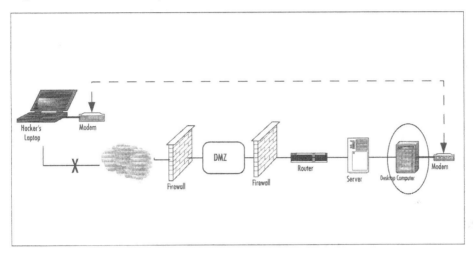

Business Intelligence...

The Art of War Dialing

Peter Shipley and Simpson Garfinkel wrote a document called "An Analysis of Dial-Up Modems and Vulnerabilities" in 2001 (http://www.dis.org/filez/Wardial_ShipleyGarfinkel.pdf). They used an automated process to dial over 5.7 million phone numbers looking for

Continued

unsecured modems in the San Francisco area. Although the method they used was dialing blocks of numbers within area codes, an easier way is to dial blocks of numbers associated with a business's main phone number. If your company's phone number is 555-1000, a war dialer would dial every number between 555-1000 and 555-9999 looking for a modem. Of the 5.7 million numbers Shipley and Garfinkel called, 49,192 modems respond. What they found was that many of these modems were connected not just to open dial-up lines, but directly to application servers. Even though that was five years ago, the emphasis on high-speed Internet connections via cable modems, broadband, and T1 lines has left little attention focused on these "legacy" devices. A well-publicized event cited by these authors was a teenager who stumbled upon a dial-up line and was never asked for a username or password. With open access, he was presented with various commands he could use, so he began experimenting. According to the article, the result was that the teen managed to shut down power to a regional airport and 600 nearby houses. Even though the teen was really just monkeying around, his rather innocent exploration had a major impact. The lesson—don't overlook modems as part of your security patrol. For the full story, check out the full article by Peter Shipley and Simpson Garfinkel at the link provided; it's a fascinating read and will open your eyes to a lot of security issues, not just war dialing techniques.

Wardriving, NetStumbling, or Stumbling

Wardriving is a term many IT people are familiar with—the term is a take off on the original term *war dialing* (based on a 1980s movie starring Mathew Broderick called *War Games*) and involves actually driving around in a car with a good antenna looking for unsecured wireless networks. Before we jump to any rash conclusions, however, let's hear what security experts have to say about *war driving*. This is an excerpt from *WarDriving: Drive, Detect, Defend: A Guide To Wireless Security* (Chris Hurley, Frank Thornton, Michael Puchol, and Russ Rogers, Syngress Publishing, Inc. 2004).

> These days, you might hear people confuse the terminology *WarDriver* and *hacker*. As you probably know, the term hacker was originally used to describe a person that was

able to modify a computer (often in a way unintended by its manufacturer) to suit his or her own purposes. However, over time, owing to the confusion of the masses and consistent media abuse, the term *hacker* is now commonly used to describe a criminal; someone that accesses a computer or network without the authorization of the owner. (If you choose to hack or modify your own computer, you're not engaging in a criminal activity.) The same situation can be applied to the term WarDriver. WarDriver has been misused to describe someone that accesses wireless networks without authorization from the owner. An individual that accesses a computer system, wired or wireless, without authorization is a criminal. Criminality has nothing to do with either hacking or WarDriving.

The news media, in an effort to generate ratings and increase viewership, has sensationalized WarDriving. Almost every local television news outlet has done a story on "wireless hackers armed with laptops" or "drive-by hackers" that are reading your e-mail or using your wireless network to surf the Web. These stories are geared to propagate Fear, Uncertainty, and Doubt (FUD). FUD stories usually take a small risk, and attempt to elevate the seriousness of the situation in the minds of their audience. Stories that prey on fear are good for ratings, but don't always depict an activity accurately.

An unfortunate side effect of these stories has been that the reporters invariably ask the "WarDriver" to gather information that is being transmitted across a wireless network so that the "victim" can be shown their personal information that was collected. Again, this has nothing to do with WarDriving and while a case can be made that this activity (known as *sniffing*) in and of itself is not illegal, it is at a minimum unethical and is not a practice that WarDrivers engage in.

These stories also tend to focus on gimmicky aspects of WarDriving such as the directional antenna that can be made using a Pringles can. While a functional antenna can be made from Pringles cans, coffee cans, soup cans, or pretty much anything cylindrical and hollow, the reality is that very few (if any) WarDrivers actually use these for WarDriving. Many of them have made these antennas in an attempt to both verify the original concept and improve upon it in some instances.

The reality of WarDriving is simple. Computer security professionals, hobbyists, and others are generally interested in providing information to the public about security vulnerabilities that are present with "out of the box" configurations of wireless access points. Wireless access points that can be purchased at a local electronics or computer store are not geared toward security. They are designed so that a person with little or no understanding of networking can purchase a wireless access point, and with little or no outside help, set it up and begin using it. Computers have become a staple of everyday life. Technology that makes using computers easier and more fun needs to be available to everyone. Companies such as Linksys and D-Link have been very successful at making these new technologies easy for end users to set up and begin using. To do otherwise would alienate a large part of their target market.

The Legality of WarDriving

According to the FBI, it is not illegal to scan access points, but once a theft of service, denial of service, or theft of information occurs, then it becomes a federal violation through 18USC 1030 (www.usdoj.gov/criminal/cyber-crime/1030_new.html). While this is good, general information, any questions about the legality of a specific act in the United States should be posed directly to either the local FBI field office, a cyber crime attorney, or the U.S. Attorney's office. This information only applies to the United States.

> WarDrivers are encouraged to investigate the local laws
> where they live to ensure that they aren't inadvertently vio-
> lating the law. Understanding the distinction between
> "scanning" or identifying wireless access points and actually
> using the access point is the difference between WarDriving,
> a legal activity, and theft, an obviously illegal activity.

One of the more commonly used tools for wireless network detection
is *NetStumbler*, which was created by Marius Milner and released in May
of 2001. There is a PocketPC version of this program called *MiniStumbler*.
As a result of the ease-of-use of this program and the proliferation of its
use, many now refer to the activity of wireless network detection not as
wardriving but as *netstumbling*, or simply *stumbling*. Since it is often an
activity done with no malice whatsoever, stumbling certainly is more representative of what most people do with these programs.

Clearly, the downside to the proliferation of easy-to-use wireless components is that they come with no security configured right out of the
box. More recent releases of the Microsoft operating system come locked
down, by default, but earlier versions had been set to "open" by default
and the system administrator had to lock down anything he or she didn't
want open, on, installed, or available. Now, the operating system takes just
the opposite approach—things are locked down, disabled, and not installed
by default, and the system administrator has to make a conscious effort to
open things up. This approach is much better for network and server security but certainly doesn't encourage first-time users to give it a whirl. The
balance between encouraging users and providing security is a delicate
one, and most user-grade component companies like Linksys and D-Link
are focused on the home user. As such, their equipment comes ready to
install and use out of the box. Does that mean your home wireless network is at risk? Absolutely. Does it mean someone is going to come and
steal your personal data? Who knows? If you live in a rural area, the likelihood of someone getting close enough for long enough to steal data is
unlikely but certainly possible. If you live in an urban area, the risk obviously climbs because your neighbor in the downstairs apartment might be
sitting there watching all your unsecured network traffic go by. However,

to go back to the comments made by the WarDriving experts, the real issue is that WarDriving itself is not an illegal activity and someone who uses your open wireless network may be unethically using your network, but if he or she does nothing harmful, it's a bit like running an extension cord to your neighbor's house to run your television set—it *is* stealing but it does not damage your television in any way. We're not here to support stealing unsecured wireless access, but to help you understand that not everyone who engages in wardriving has ill intentions.

If you perform a Web search for images using the search phrase "war driving maps," you'll find thousands of access point maps out on the Internet. Some sites keep up-to-date maps in a database, other sites are abandoned or outdated, but the overall impression you should get is that there are thousands of people looking for unsecured access points everyday for all kinds of reasons, and if you think your corporate wireless network or your wireless users are safe, think again. Figure 12.2 shows a sample map of the Los Angeles area.

Figure 12.2 Wardriving Map of Los Angeles, California

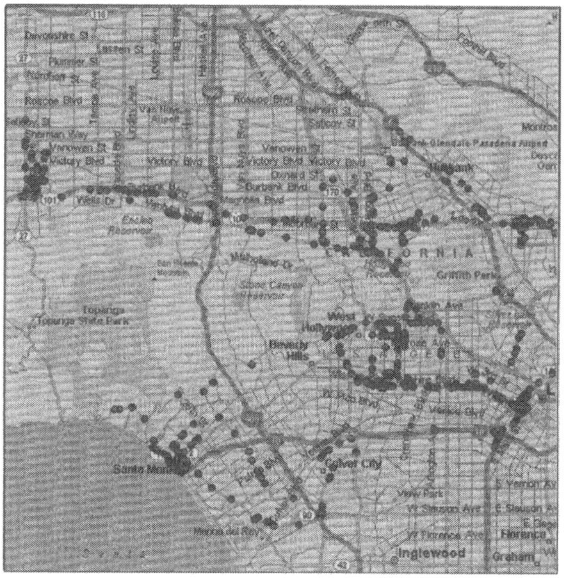

Source: http://www.cybergeography.org/atlas/wireless.html, Frank Keeney.

You can see that wireless networks are clustered, and anyone looking for wireless access could take a nice slow drive down Wilshire Blvd. or find a comfy coffee shop and take a look at tons of unsecured network traffic. The point is not to feed into the fear factor but to help you understand the reality of wardriving and the need to secure your corporate network and wireless users' wireless devices so that your network assets remain secure against the bad guys and the good guys who might accidentally stumble in.

Business Intelligence...

Wardriving for Fun and Profit

If you pay attention to what's happening in the outside world, you'll notice there's been a proliferation of information about wardriving in the past few years. At first, it was a subversive, secret underground world (or so it seemed), but these days there are many people who view wardriving as cheap entertainment—well not so cheap with the price of gas these days, but still very affordable. The tools and techniques are readily available for anyone seeking them. A laptop with a wireless card, a small fairly inexpensive antenna, and a tank of gas will get you started. If you're really strapped, you could do this on foot (some do in urban areas) with a well-equipped PDA (see Figure 12.3). Wardriving itself is not illegal when it's done simply to find and map secured and unsecured wireless access points (fun). Wardriving that leads to using someone else's unprotected network or network intrusion (profit) is illegal. Stumbling = ok, intrusion = not ok. It's a simple rule to follow for most.

There are thousands of Web sites that discuss wardriving and wardriving adventures. One that comes up in a search engine search is http://www.unwiredadventures.com, though there are many out there. On this particular site, the wardriver talks about his adventures in wardriving while vacationing with his family. This is a leisure activity he engages in to map wireless access points in various locations. Think of it as local geography with a twist. This excerpt from his Web site indicates his intention (from 2001): "Our trip was fun for all of us. Lots of good food and fun with our relatives. The kids were well behaved in the car

Continued

and my wife was understanding about the extra equipment in the car. 802.11b wireless equipment is very easy to install and has become very inexpensive. It's everywhere now, in homes and businesses. Wireless network technology has made the use of computer systems so very easy and convenient. Let's be sure to understand the equipment that we plug into our networks. Read the manuals, or hire an experienced security consultant to make sure that you are secure in your use of this technology." He mentioned that he has TCP/IP disabled on the computer he uses for wardriving so that he cannot inadvertently gain unauthorized access to corporate networks, though he admits that "Otherwise, it would have been easy to get free Internet access behind many corporate firewalls. Nearly all of the 802.11b wireless equipment that I have evaluated is factory configured with the lowest possible security settings. No access control and no encryption. It's up to the user to secure the equipment that is plugged into their network."

http://www.unwiredadventures.com/unwire/2005/12/vacation_war _dr.html.

A word to the wise: If you decide to give wardriving a try to hone your own skills, be sure to disable the TCP/IP stack on your wardriving device before you head out. This will prevent accidental intrusion to an unsecured network and keep you on the right side of the law.

Figure 12.3 Well-Equipped PDA for WarDriving

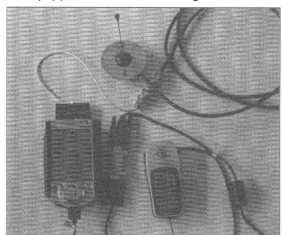

Some critics get upset by the proliferation of information available on how to set up equipment for wardriving. This is true for just about every computer activity that can be used for good or evil. E-mail communication is not a bad thing, phishing is. They both use the same tool (e-mail) for different purposes. The same is true of wardriving. The activity can be done innocently for fun or to hone technical skills, or it can be done to gather information in advance of an attack. Many in the security world are frustrated by the easy access people have to sniff, attack, and hack, but most also grudgingly agree that the more information that's out there, the more tools one has to understand and prevent unauthorized access. It's a never-ending cycle and you and your IT project team need to be on top of the latest tools, techniques, and tips that hackers have available so that you can secure your network—wired and wireless—from unauthorized access and harmful activities. We'll discuss the tools of the trade later in this chapter when we look at risk assessment for your wireless security project.

Bluetooth Attacks

As you probably know, Bluetooth uses a short-range radio signal to provide wireless communications, typically between various personal communication devices such as cell phones and headsets or PDAs. Bluetooth allows you to create a wireless personal area network (WPAN) that can communicate with other Bluetooth devices within a small physical radius (about 10 meters). Bluetooth relies on the use of radio waves and overcomes earlier infrared (IR) technologies that were used for personal communication devices. IR required line-of-sight for communicating with another device and it was a one-to-one connection. Bluetooth overcomes these limitations because it does not require line-of-sight and it allows many devices to communicate simultaneously. Bluetooth limits interference with other radio signals and other Bluetooth devices by limiting its broadcast range to 10 meters and by using a random frequency hopping algorithm. If interference does occur, it would be extremely short-lived since frequency hopping involves changing frequency several times per second.

Let's take a short side-trip to understand how Bluetooth devices communicate with one another so you can better understand the threat. Bluetooth devices "pair up" by exchanging a passkey (depending on the type and level of authentication selected). Once this occurs, the devices have essentially created a personal area network (PAN) in which one of the devices assumes the lead role ("master"). A single device can participate in multiple PANs, creating a *scatternet*, as shown in Figure 12.4. PAN1 and PAN2 form the scatternet and by design, the hand-held computer could be communicating, via the cell phone with the laptop computer. Since radio signals move through walls, the scatternet can be formed much like a standard wireless network. Some Bluetooth users mistakenly believe that their devices are safe but if you have Bluetooth enabled and you're not actively using it, it's possible your device is part of a scatternet without even knowing it.

Figure 12.4 Bluetooth Devices Forming a Scatternet

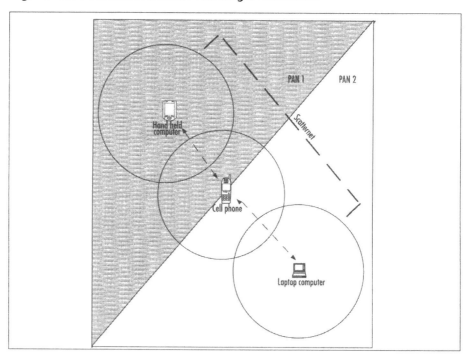

Business Intelligence...

The Art of Bluejacking and Bluesnarfing

Bluejacking first showed up in popular use in 2003 or so when Bluetooth devices gained popularity. Bluejacking is more of a prank than an attack, and an annoying one at that. The term apparently was coined in late 2002 by a fellow going by the moniker *ajack*. Although there are some rather amusing stories about bluejacking, to date there are no stories of unmitigated corporate network attacks having their genesis in a blue-jacking. A story in 2003 by the Associated Press is a great example of how bluejacking typically works.

"The group of lanky tourists strolling through Stockholm's old town never knew what hit them. As they admired Swedish handicrafts in a storefront window, one of their cell phones chirped with an anonymous note: "Try the blue sweaters. They keep you warm in the winter." The tourist was **"bluejacked"** — surreptitiously surprised with a text message sent using a short-range wireless technology called Bluetooth. As more people get Bluetooth-enabled cell phones — both sender and recipient need them for this to work — there is bound to be more mischievous messaging of the unsuspecting. It's a growing fad, this fun with wireless. Already, Web sites are offering tips on **bluejacking**, and collections of startled reactions are popping up on the Internet." —Matt Moore, "Cell phone messaging takes a mischievous turn," *The Associated Press*, November 13, 2003 (from http://www.wordspy.com/words/bluejacking.asp).

Bluesnarfing, on the other hand, is an illegal activity that involves stealing data from a Bluetooth-enabled device. Typically, this involves stealing contacts or calendar entries. The calendar entries might be embarrassing ("Cosmetic surgery, 4 pm") but rarely damaging unless the calendar entry also has confidential information in it ("Meet Doug M. at 2 am in southwest corner of parking lot to hand off illegally gotten trade secrets"). More importantly, most of us don't want our contacts just handed over to a complete stranger. If you're like most people, you have a mixture of personal contacts (Mom, Dentist, Local Pizza Place) and business contacts (Boss: Home, Boss: Work, Boss: Cell, Boss: Husband, Boss: VacationHome, CEO of Company A, CIO of Company B). It would

Continued

be pretty creepy (and potentially dangerous) to have your mother get phone calls at 2 am from someone telling her that he knows her home phone number, address, zip code, and alarm code.

Stealing calendar and contact information via bluesnarfing requires both Bluetooth devices be on and available. The quickest and easiest way to avoid bluesnarfing (which requires about two to three minutes of continuous connection time) is to disable Bluetooth when not specifically in use. If you're using a cell phone with a Bluetooth headset, you can disable *Discovery* mode (sometimes called *Visible* mode), which makes it difficult for someone to find your Bluetooth-enabled device.

There's an excellent article you can read from 2004 that contains in-depth information about various Bluetooth attacks and the devices that were (at that time) vulnerable to such attacks. Head to this URL for more information: http://www.thebunker.net/security/bluetooth.htm.

One might argue that the threats to Bluetooth devices are greatly exaggerated by the media. At the same time, if you're sitting in a crowded airport awaiting your flight, there's always a chance someone could grab your contacts and have a field day with them. Suppose you were fortunate enough to get the home phone number (or the private line at the remote cabin) for the CIO of your company, a Fortune 500, publicly traded company. Do you really want someone getting that number, calling the CIO in the middle of the night saying that the Director of IT Security (you) gave the caller his number? Talk about a CTM (*Career Terminating Move*). The point is that confidential information is routinely stored on Bluetooth devices from PDAs to cell phones and data is at risk, regardless of how great or small you perceive that risk to be. This is an excellent example of a case where evaluating risk and remediation is pretty simple. You'll most likely create a user policy guideline (see the chapter on security policy later in this book) that requires users to set their Bluetooth devices so they are not in *Discovery* or *Visible* mode except when purposely participating in a Bluetooth network in a relatively safe location (at a business meeting, for example). Most (if not all) newer Bluetooth devices are updated to protect against attack but attackers are often smart, persistent folks and they'll no doubt find the next open door to go through. Staying up to date on attack types is a never-ending task, so make sure there are people on your IT staff that are specifically tasked with doing so and keeping the rest of the team informed. Dividing this work into topic areas is a good way to keep everyone on the prowl for the latest data, and can be a great way to improve the skills of everyone on your team.

Risk Assessment

We know there is a trade-off between total security and total risk. There are financial and operational trade-offs that every organization must make. In the risk assessment phase of your audit, you need to look at your risks in terms of CIA: *confidentiality*, *integrity*, and *availability*. Data that is accessed wirelessly is most at risk of loss of confidentiality because it's relatively easy for a hacker to jump into the middle of an unsecured wireless stream and grab any data desired. However, he or she could also modify data (integrity) or simply make that data, network, or service unavailable, if desired.

Other key components of the wireless risk assessment are the *people*, *process*, and *technology* components. We'll talk about creating security policies for the organization in Chapter 13, which are used to help dictate and guide people's behaviors. *People* are almost always the weakest link in the security chain and your risk assessment should look at the risks people's behaviors (intentional and unintentional) have on security in the wireless realm. *Processes* must be assessed for risk as well. How do wireless users connect on-site? How do wireless users connect off-site? How should guest accounts be handled for wireless connections? There are a variety of process issues that should be assessed from end-to-end. Finally, the *technology* assessment should include an assessment of various wireless technologies in use along with the strengths and weaknesses of each. You also need to understand the technology available to the hackers and determine how to secure your wireless connections in light of hacker capabilities. Let's look at an example. It is possible to crack WEP encryption if a hacker has enough time, a powerful enough computer, and enough data to do so. Therefore, WEP is usually sufficient for home wireless networks because a hacker rarely will be able to gather enough data in a short enough time frame to crack WEP on a home network and because there usually isn't a big enough pot of gold at the other end to entice a hacker to work that hard to break WEP on a home network (except in cases where there is targeted malicious intent or utter boredom). Contrast that to a corporate network where financial data including customer credit cards or bank account numbers or whatever are stored. Now there's a big enough payoff to make the time and effort worthwhile. So, you have to choose your battles and understand the relative attack footprint of your organization to understand where and how to secure your assets. That said, wireless is just a ridiculously easy target and you should take stronger precautions here than you might have otherwise considered necessary.

Remember, too, that there is no magic bullet. Wireless networking cannot be secured with 100 percent confidence. Security is often a matter of applying layers of protection to create a maze of problems most attackers will walk away from. A smart determined attacker with the right tools and enough time can probably crack anything, including the once-sacred WPA security. However, if you use MAC address filtering, you suppress SSID broadcasting, you use WEP or WPA and you educate your users, you've done all you can do. The rest is a matter of intelligently installing, configuring, maintaining, and monitoring an intrusion detection system and performing regular scans to make sure no ad hoc networks pop up.

Although we talked about risk assessment in Chapter 10, it's worth walking through a few of the risks inherent in a wireless network environment. There is some overlap but we will keep an eye focused specifically on wireless risks.

Asset Protection

As we have continually stressed, you have to find the right balance between protecting corporate assets and the cost of doing so. In any network assessment scenario, you should begin by understanding what you're trying to protect and why. You may have addressed this issue adequately during your overall IT corporate security planning process. If so, you should review the data, assumptions, and outcomes at this stage to ensure your conclusions are still relevant and correct. Things change so quickly in most corporate environments that a quick review of previous assessment data is almost always a good use of your time. You should review what data is on your corporate network and what needs to be protected. This is also a good time to find out what is on your corporate network that perhaps should not be. If you recall the case studies from Chapter 1, it's not uncommon for corporate networks to have data on it that should not be there, such as credit card numbers or social security numbers that were stored inappropriately and in violation of corporate policy or vendor policy (as was the case with the credit card processing company, which violated its own policies and that of the credit card companies for whom they processed data).

In addition to discovering what is on your network (and what's there but shouldn't be), you also need to assess the relative value of that data. Though it can be argued that all corporate data is valuable, some data is clearly more valuable than other types of data. Remember that you need to think like a hacker to make these assessments. If all you have are lists of nuts, bolts, and cable lengths, there's not as much value to that data as there is with personal data such as credit card numbers, social security numbers, or bank access codes. Correlate the data on your network with the perceived value of the data to an outsider to understand the relative risk to your network. This will help you determine just how much security is appropriate for your specific situation.

A good example of this is a home wireless network. Most people using home wireless networks do not secure them even though they may log onto their online brokerage account or do some online shopping using a credit card. This data is transmitted in an unsecured manner from their laptop or wireless device to their wireless access point, then to the router or cable modem and then out to the Internet. Even if the Web site they are using is secured using SSL or HTTPS (for example), the link between the user's wireless device and the wireless access point may not be secured. This is the weak link in this transaction. The same holds true of a corporate user at a coffee shop, hotel, or airport waiting area.

The question is this: how likely is it that a hacker is going to grab that data? Well, if you are in a dense setting where a hacker can sit in a nearby location and peruse wireless data like yours, then the *potential* is extremely high but the *likelihood* is somewhere in the mid-range on the risk scale. If you live in a more suburban or rural setting or are in a remote location of any kind where it would be difficult for someone to get close enough to receive your wireless signal, the risk drops significantly. The *potential* drops to low and the *likelihood* drops to near zero. Looking at the risk/reward proposition from a hacker's perspective will help you assess the relative value of your assets and what level of protection is warranted.

Sensitive Data

Sensitive data is defined differently from one company to the next. What's sensitive at one company may not be particularly sensitive at another. However, in most companies, there are clearly segments of data that are sensitive and your security audit should identify those areas. As part of your wireless security project definition stage, you need to clearly understand what data can be accessed via the wireless network (typically the connection in a corporate setting is to the wired network) and how sensitive that data is. It goes beyond the legal implications and into the business aspects. Lists of customers, vendors, suppliers, or employees can be sensitive, especially if you're in a medical setting, for example. Trade secrets, formulas, and research and development (R&D) data can be extremely sensitive, especially in industries that are working in leading edge or ground-breaking areas. This is a great place to get feedback and input from various departments in your company. Ask them what data they work with that they would not want posted on a Web site or printed in a newspaper. That usually gets people's attention and helps them begin to look at the data they work with on a daily basis from a slightly different perspective.

Sensitive data can be stored in a variety of locations, most notably (and insecurely) on laptops that leave the building. Employees could intentionally boost sensitive data and if they are legitimate users of that information, it would be hard to know if they're doing something wrong. However, you also need to look at the possibility that users will transmit sensitive data via wireless laptop connections or that these laptops themselves might be stolen. In the chapter on operational security, we'll talk about physical laptop security, but for now, let's focus on laptops containing sensitive data that users transmit across unsecured wireless connections. Here's a quick list of data typically considered sensitive:

- Customer databases
- Employee lists
- Identity information (can include customer, employee, vendor)
- Credit card or other financial data
- Health information
- Intellectual property
- Trade secrets
- Research and development

Network Assets

In addition to data assets that hackers might target, there is another type of data that is often sought out by hackers and that is network data. If a hacker can get into the network using an unsecured wireless access point (or by any unsecured means, really), he or she will try to enumerate the network assets to find out where servers, databases, and sensitive information are located. Therefore, understanding the network configuration is often not the end-game but the intermediate step toward the final target. If you can prevent a hacker from gaining access to this network configuration data, you may prevent an intrusion. Network data that is helpful to a hacker includes (but certainly is not limited to):

- Usernames and passwords
- Directory listings

- Network firewalls, routers, switches, and hubs

- Network segmentation, including DMZs

- IP addresses for servers

- Ports and protocols in use

Business Intelligence...

The Cost of Identity Theft

The growing focus on IT security in all realms is because there is a growing problem with data theft—both corporate and personal. Companies must secure personal information but consumers must also do their part. There are 10 million identity theft victims in the United States each year. The average ID theft victim spends over 175 hours trying to fix the damage done and at a cost of over $1500 per incident. The total annual cost in the United States attributed to identity theft tops $15 billion. There are four basic types of identity theft:

- **Financial ID Theft**—This type of case typically focuses on your name and Social Security number (SSN). This person may apply for telephone service, credit cards or loans, buy merchandise, lease cars or apartments.

- **Criminal ID Theft**—The imposter in this crime provides the victim's information instead of his or her own when stopped by law enforcement. Eventually when the warrant for arrest is issued it is in the name of the person issued the citation—yours.

- **Identity Cloning**—In this crime, the imposter uses the victim's information to establish a new life. They work and live as you. Examples: Illegal aliens, criminals avoiding warrants, people hiding from abusive situations, or becoming a "new person" to leave behind a poor work and financial history.

- **Business or Commercial Identity Theft**—Businesses are also victims of identity theft. Typically the perpetrator gets credit

Continued

cards or checking accounts in the name of the business. The business finds out when unhappy suppliers send collection notices or their business rating score is affected.

Tips for businesses from the ID Theft Center include:

- **Information acquisition**—Do you need the information? Are you acquiring it in a safe manner?

- **Storage**—What computer security measures have you placed around the systems storing personal data? It should be considered highly classified and not common access.

- **Access**—Who has access? Is it on a need to know basis and access audited? Is there password control over systems? Is there a cafeteria worker asking your child for his/her SSN prior to receiving lunch? Did you do a background check on those who have access to personal information of employees and customers? Do temps have access to secure info?

- **Disposal**—Are electronic and paper documents containing personal information rendered unreadable prior to disposal? What is in your dumpster? Is it a treasure chest for thieves and for consumer action attorneys ready to sue you for placing their clients in jeopardy?

- **Distribution**—How do you handle information? Is your employee requiring a member of the public to repeat a SSN out loud where it can be overheard? The public display, use, and exchange of SSN (including on membership cards carried in wallets) needs to be reconsidered. You place people at much higher risk when you do so.

Understanding identity theft is an important aspect of securing your network and it certainly can help you secure your own personal identity as well.
(Source: http://www.idtheftcenter.org)

Threat Prevention

Threat prevention starts, in many respects, with the IT security project problem statement. What problem are we trying to solve with this project? In other words, what threats do we perceive that we need to address? What is the company trying to protect through these security measures? What kinds of threats are likely or possible? Are you most concerned about an attack, a theft, or a breach, and which is most likely to occur? Answering these questions will help you define your problem and your outcome statements and help form a solid foundation for your wireless security project plan. In this section, we're going to outline the current threats to wireless networks. Some of this might overlap with other kinds of threats, but it's included here so that you have a fairly comprehensive list in front of you. Clearly, you'll need to do additional research when you sit down to define your wireless security plan because threats change and morph on a regular basis.

In order to understand how to protect your network, you need to understand what you're protecting against. This segment provides detailed information on threats to wireless networks. It should be used in the planning of your wireless security plan, though be clear that this same information can be used to attack your wireless network. It can be used for a friendly penetration test to find weak spots but it can also be used for an unfriendly penetration event to cause harm to your network or company. Most network tools can be used for both good and evil, so don't shoot the messenger.

War Dialing Prevention

War dialing typically occurs during off-hours to prevent phones ringing all over the office, though computers with modems may be turned off after hours, causing you to miss some devices. You may choose, as part of threat prevention, to notify users that if they hear phones ringing, especially after hours, and they are answered with screeching modem tones, that they should report it to the IT security officer. Also, your threat prevention in this case first should be to identify all live modems and phone lines. A scan of your company's phone bill may show existing dial-up lines that everyone had forgotten about (which the phone company just loves). Second, you can war dial your own company (during off-hours to avoid disruption) to see if you find any open modems. If you do so after hours, you risk the chance that users have turned computers off and that existing modems will not answer. If you suspect rogue modems may be a problem, you'll need to do your war dialing during working hours. Clearly, an e-mail blast letting people know that you're scanning for modems would be counterproductive since the point of the exercise is to *find* modems. If a user with a rogue modem is given a heads up, there's a strong chance you'll never find the modem without going desk by desk and inspecting computers. You can do an inventory of your corporate ownership of Symantec's pcAnywhere and look for existing versions. You can also check system inventory lists and look at all computers that have modems installed. If the modem is not in use and can be removed (as opposed to those that are embedded in the computer's mother board), it should be removed. If it is embedded in the mother board, it should be disabled, if possible.

Once you've gone through and discovered any modems not in use, you next need to check those that are still in use. First find out if they can be disabled. If they are still needed, ensure they require the use of usernames and strong passwords (you'd be shocked how many dial up connections require no username or password) and use the callback feature, if available. Next, look at what software is being used on those dial-up systems and ensure that the latest patches and updates are applied. If the application is deemed to be inherently insecure, look for a newer, better application that could be used instead or a way to divert this dial-up traffic to another connection method. Finally, look at the system and application configuration to ensure it is configured to be as secure as possible. Eliminate unused accounts, disable default or guest accounts, require strong passwords, and so on.

Direct Access

According to statistics from the third World Wide WarDrive, approximately one of every four access points currently deployed is in a default configuration. The default configuration means that there is no encryption enabled and the Service Set Identifier (SSID) has not been changed from the factory settings. The "direct
approach" can be used to gain access to wireless networks in the default configuration. The direct approach, in a nutshell, refers to "requesting" a

connection to the access point. This is an extremely simple process in both Windows and Linux. In order to access a wireless network with a default configuration from a

Windows machine, all that you need is a wireless client manager. The wireless client manager is the configuration software that either ships with the wireless card, or is built into the operating system (as is the case with Windows XP). It scans for wireless networks, finds one, and, depending on configuration settings on the client, connects automatically.

Defeating MAC Address Filtering

One security measure that many wireless network administrators put in place is filtering by MAC address. Enabling MAC address filtering allows only network cards with certain MAC addresses to connect to your network. However, as with any security measure, a determined, knowledgeable attacker usually can find a way around such an obstacle.

Most commercial- and consumer-grade wireless networking equipment sends the MAC address clear text even if Wired Equivalency Protection (WEP) is enabled. This means that if you passively sniff the traffic on a wireless network using a freeware tool such as Ethereal (www.ethereal.com), you can determine one or more MAC addresses that are allowed to connect to the network. If MAC address filtering is the only security measure in place, you just need to change your MAC address to one that is allowed access. This is a relatively easy thing to do in both the Windows and Linux environments. In Windows, it's a matter of editing a registry key manually or using an automated tool. In Linux, it's a matter of changing the MAC address in the interface. This also can be done manually using the *ifconfig* command or using an automated tool.

Finding Cloaked Access Points

Many wireless network administrators "cloak" their access points by putting them in "stealth" mode. This is accomplished by disabling the SSID broadcast. Active scanners, like NetStumbler, do not detect cloaked access points. These access points can be found using passive scanners like Kismet or AirSnort. Keep in mind that while you may have cloaked your access points, an intruder could have installed an access point on your network and cloaked it. Therefore, you need to use these same tools to find cloaked access points that may be attached to your network. One of the biggest benefits that passive scanners like Kismet have to offer is the ability to detect access points that are not broadcasting their SSID. Discovering cloaked access points with Kismet is accomplished by placing your wireless card in monitor mode. Older versions of Kismet required that Kismet be placed in monitor mode manually using the *kismet_monitor* command. When Kismet discovers a cloaked access point, it will initially list it as having no SSID. As Kismet collects more packets, it will be able to determine the SSID.

AirSnort is a passive wireless scanner developed by the Shmoo Group (http://airsnort.shmoo.com). Like Kismet, AirSnort will automatically activate your card in monitor mode when it is started. Any cloaked access points that AirSnort initially finds will project a blank SSID, but after enough packets are collected, AirSnort is able to determine the SSID of the cloaked network. Unlike Kismet, AirSnort has additional functionality that is also extremely valuable to an attacker. We'll discuss AirSnort in more detail later when we look at how one attacks WEP.

Man-in-the-Middle Attacks

Placing a *rogue AP* (an unauthorized access point placed on a network by an individual) within range of wireless stations is a wireless-specific varia- tion of a *man-in-the-middle attack*. If the attacker knows the SSID the net- work uses (which, as we have seen, is easily discoverable) and the rogue AP has enough strength, wireless users have no way of knowing that they are connecting to an unauthorized AP.

Using a rogue AP, an attacker can gain valuable information about the wireless network, such as authentication requests, the secret key that is in use, and so on. Often, the attacker will set up a laptop with two wireless adapters, in which the rogue AP uses one card and the other is used to forward requests through a wireless bridge to the legitimate AP. With a sufficiently strong antenna, the rogue AP does not have to be located in close proximity to the legitimate AP. For example, the attacker can run the rogue AP from a car or van parked some distance away from the building containing the network. However, it is also common to set up hidden rogue APs (under desks, in closets, and so on) close to, and within, the same physical area as the legitimate AP. Due to their virtually unde-tectable nature, the only defense against rogue APs is vigilance through frequent site surveys (using tools such as AirMagnet, NetStumbler, and AiroPeek) and physical security.

Frequent site surveys also have the advantage of uncovering the unau-thorized APs that company staff members might have set up in their own work areas, thereby compromising the entire network and completely undoing the hard work that went into securing the network in the first place. These unauthorized APs usually are set up with no malicious intent but rather were created for the convenience of the user, who might want to be able to connect to the network via his or her laptop in meeting rooms, break rooms, or other areas that do not have wired outlets. Even if your company does not use, or plan to use, a wireless network, you should consider doing regular wireless site surveys to see if someone has violated your company security policy by placing an unauthorized AP on the network, regardless of that person's intent.

Hijacking and Modifying a Wireless Network

Numerous techniques are available for an attacker to *hijack* a wireless net-work or session. Unlike some attacks, network and security administrators may be unable to distinguish between the hijacker and a legitimate pas-senger. Many tools are available to the network hijacker. These tools are based on basic implementation issues within almost every network device available today.

As TCP/IP packets go through switches, routers, and APs, each device looks at the destination IP address and compares it with the IP addresses it knows to be local. If the address is not in the table, the device hands the packet off to its default gateway. This table is used to coordinate the IP address with the MAC addresses that are known to be local to the device. In many situations, this list is a dynamic one that is built up from traffic passing through the device and through Address Resolution Protocol (ARP) notifications from new devices joining the network.

There is no authentication or verification that the request the device received is valid. Thus, a malicious user is able to send messages to routing devices and APs stating that his MAC address is associated with a known IP address. From then on, all traffic that goes through that router destined for the hijacked IP address will be handed off to the hacker's machine. If the attacker spoofs as the default gateway or a specific host on the network, all machines trying to get to the network or the spoofed machine will connect to the attacker's machine instead of their intended target. If the attacker is clever, he will use this information only to identify passwords and other necessary information and route the rest of the traffic to the intended recipients. If he does this, the end users will have no idea that this *man in the middle* has intercepted their communications and compromised their passwords and information.

Another clever attack can be accomplished through the use of rogue APs. If the attacker is able to put together an AP with enough strength, the end users might not be able to tell which AP is the authorized one that they should be using. In fact, most will not even know that another AP is available. Using this technique, the attacker is able to receive authentication requests and information from the end workstation regarding the secret key and where users are attempting to connect.

These rogue APs can also be used to attempt to break into more tightly configured wireless APs. Utilizing tools such as AirSnort and WEPCrack requires a large amount of data to be able to decrypt the secret key. An intruder sitting in a car in front of your house or office is noticeable and thus will generally not have time to finish acquiring enough information to break the key. However, if the attacker installs a tiny, easily hidden machine in an inconspicuous location, this machine could sit there long enough to break the key and possibly act as an external AP into the wireless network it has hacked. Once an attacker has identified a network for attack and spoofed his MAC address to become a valid member of the network, the attacker can gain further information that is not available through simple sniffing. If the network being attacked is using SSH to access the hosts, just stealing a password might be easier than attempting to break into the host using an available exploit.

By simply ARP-spoofing the connection with the AP, the attacker can appear to be the host from which the attacker wants to steal passwords. The attacker can then cause all wireless users who are attempting to SSH into the host to connect to the rogue machine instead. When these users attempt to sign on with their passwords, the attacker is then able to, first, receive their passwords, and, second, pass on the connection to the real end destination. If the attacker does not perform the second step, it increases the likelihood that the attack will be noticed because users will begin to complain that they are unable to connect to the host.

Attacking Encrypted Networks

One of the most common ways that administrators attempt to protect their wireless networks is with encryption. Unfortunately, the two primary means of protection, Wired Equivalent Protection (WEP) and Wi-Fi Protected Access (WPA), have flaws that allow them to be exploited. This section discusses how to attack networks that are protected by WEP and WPA.

The most commonly used form of encryption protecting wireless networks is WEP. WEP is a flawed implementation of the Rivest Cipher 4 (RC4) encryption standard. Scott Fluhrer of Cisco Systems, Itsik Mantin, and Adi Shamir of the Weizmann Institute detailed the flaws in WEP in their joint paper *Weaknesses of the Key Scheduling Algorithm of RC4* (www.drizzle.com/~aboba/IEEE/rc4_ksaproc.pdf). In short, WEP utilizes a fixed secret key. Weak initialization vectors sometimes are generated to encrypt WEP packets. When enough weak initialization vectors are captured, the secret key can be cracked. There are a two popular tools available on the Internet that can be used to crack WEP encryption.

1. Windows WEPCrack (Windows)

    WEPCrack (http://wepcrack.sourceforge.net) is a set of Open Source PERL scripts intended to break 802.11 WEP secret keys. It was the first publicly available implementation of the attack described by Fluhrer, Mantin, and Shamir in their paper. Since a PERL interpreter is not installed by default with Windows Server 2003 (or any version of Windows, for that matter), you will need to install one to run the scripts. One or both of the following freely available solutions will give you what you need: Cygwin (www.cygwin.com) or ActiveState ActivePerl (www.activestate. com/Products/ActivePerl). The more robust option is to install Cygwin. Cygwin is a Linux-like environment for Windows that consists of a DLL (cygwin1.dll) to provide Linux emulation functionality and a seemingly exhaustive collection of tools, which provide the Linux look and feel. The full suite of PERL development tools and libraries are available; however, the PERL interpreter is all that is required to run the WEPCrack scripts. The other option, using a Windows-based PERL interpreter, may be desirable if you have no need for Linux emulation functionality on your workstation or server. ActiveState ActivePerl, available by free download from the ActiveState Web site (www.activestate. com), provides a robust PERL development environment that is native to Windows. WEPCrack was written so that it could be ported to any platform that has a PERL interpreter without needing to modify the code.

2. AirSnort (Linux)

When enough weak initialization vectors are identified, AirSnort begins attempting to crack the WEP key. There are about 16 million possible initialization vectors generated by wireless networks using WEP. Approximately 9 thousand of these are weak. AirSnort considers these 9 thousand weak initialization vectors as "interesting." According to The Shmoo Group, most WEP keys can be guessed after collecting approximately 2 thousand weak initialization vectors.

After some weak initialization vectors have been collected, AirSnort will attempt to crack the WEP key. A vast majority (approximately 95 percent) of weak initialization vectors provide no usable information about the WEP key. One way you can try to decrease the amount of time it takes to crack the key is by increasing the crack breadth in AirSnort. According to the Shmoo group's Frequently Asked Questions site for AirSnort (http://airsnort.shmoo.com/faq.html), this will increase the number of key possibilities examined when AirSnort attempts to crack the WEP key.

The most difficult part of attacking wireless networks deployed with WEP encryption enabled is the amount of time it takes. It usually requires a minimum of 1200 weak initialization vectors to crack the WEP key. It can take days or even weeks to capture this many weak initialization vectors.

Once you have the cracked key, it's a simple matter of adding a preferred network in the wireless networking properties (Windows), entering the SSID and the cracked WEP key. In Linux, edit the *wireless.opts* file to include the cracked key and then restart PCMCIA services.

Wi-Fi Protected Access (WPA) networks were discovered to be less secure than originally thought when Robert Moskowitz of ICSA Labs discovered that WPA is vulnerable to an offline dictionary attack, a brute force attack that tries passwords and/or keys from a precompiled list of values (http://wifinetnews.com/archives/002452.html). WPA utilizes a 256-bit preshared key or a passphrase that can vary in length from eight to 63 bytes. Short passphrase-based keys (less than 20 bytes) are vulnerable to the offline dictionary attack. The preshared key that is used to set up the WPA encryption can be captured during the initial communication between the access point and the client card. Once you have captured the preshared key, you can use that to essentially "guess" the WPA key using the same concepts that are used in any password dictionary attack. In theory, this type of dictionary attack takes less time and effort than attacking WEP. Although there are currently no tools available to automate cracking WPA, it is only a matter of time before they are available. If you're using WPA, you should use a long, complex string that is less vulnerable to a dictionary attack than a short, simple one would be.

Legal Liabilities

We discussed legal liabilities in detail in Chapter 9, and if you skipped that chapter for any reason, be sure to read up on the legal issues surrounding IT security these days. The bottom line is that the laws are changing. Requirements are sometimes unclear or conflicting and lack of attention to detail, and lack of "reasonable care" can be cause for litigation in the event of a serious security breach. Companies that are attacked that fail to recover quickly have a 50 percent chance of failing within three years of the attack. Beyond that, your company and its executive team could face stiff penalties if reasonable care is not taken.

With wireless networking on the rise and the price of wireless components falling, it's easy to see how a company could experience a wireless breach perhaps more easily than an attack via the Internet or some other opening. Therefore, you should be sure that your wireless security plan is thorough *and* an assessment should be conducted even if your company does not officially have a wireless network. You never know if your users (or the bad guys) have installed access points until you scan for them. Saying that your company did not install or sanction a wireless network will be no defense if your network is breached and you find yourself being sued by customers whose personal data was stolen.

Business Intelligence...

Lawmakers Crack Down on Wi-Fi Crime

According to an April 26, 2006 article on internetnews.com, by Tim Scannell, if you're a business owner in New York and you use a wireless LAN to handle sensitive customer data, you had better make sure it's secure. Lawmakers in White Plains, New York (Westchester County, north of Manhattan) passed a law making it illegal for a business not to take necessary precautions to protect its wireless networks from accidental or deliberate abuse. The new law is less restrictive of public Wi-Fi hotspots like those found in coffee shops and hotels. While many members of the

Continued

business community support this legislation, not everyone is a big fan of this approach. It's an issue that needs to be addressed, and according to Andrew Neuman, senior assistant to the county executive, "At the end of the day, not one person has said it's a bad idea.

"IBM's corporate headquarters is located in White Plains, and therefore must also comply with the new law, which goes into effect in October. Executives there have not yet responded to the legislation," Neuman said.

Experts from the technical community have a mixed reaction to the legislation.

"Strong authentication and encryption combined with Wi-Fi security technologies will ultimately be the best remedy for keeping the bad guys off the network while protecting users from connecting to unauthorized devices." Some experts are not convinced that forcing businesses to secure their wireless networks is the best approach. "As much as the local government thinks they're doing the right thing by enforcing some sort of wireless security, is it really within their rights to do so?" said Doug DiNunzio, senior product manager for Bluesocket in Burlington, Mass.

To read the full article, head to http://www.internetnews.com/wireless/article.php/3601886.

Costs

Remember that in every project planning process, at some point you should ask the question, "What if we do nothing?" The reason for asking this question is to avoid solving a problem that doesn't actually need to be solved. In the case of wireless security, you can't just "do nothing" if you have a wireless network, but suppose you don't have a wireless network yet, and you're planning security for your proposed wireless network? Now the question makes a bit more sense—in essence "What if we don't have a wireless network?" Don't start with the assumption you *should* have a wireless network just because everyone else does or because it's the latest, greatest thing. If you haven't developed a strong business case for why you should have a wireless network, you've skipped an important step. Most companies these days can make the case for having a wireless network, if only from the perspective of providing flexibility and avoiding the need to run more cabling. Make sure you start with a clean baseline and add from there. However, even if your firm decides against deploying a wireless network, you can't assume your employees (or vendors, visitors, or intruders) haven't installed wireless access points that create rogue wireless networks on their own. In this case, you would need to look for wireless networks attached to the corporate network on a regular basis as part of your operational security.

Once you've decided to implement a wireless network, you'll need to include the initial and ongoing costs of securing the wireless network to your cost estimates. If you already have a wireless network installed, you'll have to address the cost of the wireless network security component separately, as we're doing here. Your costs include the cost of securing the network to which wireless access points connect, securing the communication between wireless devices (WEP, WPA) and securing the wireless devices themselves (laptops, PDAs). You should also ask yourself whether the cost of securing all of this is worth either having a wireless network or securing the wireless network. Using the hotel guest wireless network example, there's no reason to implement security because it would be an extremely high-maintenance activity to provide secure access to guests who may stay for only a night or two. However, since the WAP has to connect to the Internet, you will need to plan how to provide this access without risking your own network's security.

In addition to these implementation costs, you need to assess the cost to the organization of a wireless security breach. If the network is compromised, how much will it cost you to repair the damage? What are the costs of remediation, legal defense, and possibly marketing/PR to address a potential breach? Finally, you need to look at the cost/benefit analysis to determine how all the potential costs of a breach compare to the cost of securing the network in the first place. Though the answer often comes out in favor of security solutions, you want to be comfortable with your analysis so you can defend it to your executive team or project sponsor.

Time

Perhaps the biggest cost (other than potential legal bills) is the time lost due to investigating and repairing a security breach that occurs, especially a wireless attack that can be a bit more obscure in some ways. As you're probably painfully aware, a security breach takes time away from other IT projects and IT work but it also causes lost productivity for everyone in the organization. Although you may not be able to specifically quantify the cost of a potential security breach in terms of the time it would take to address such a breach, you can certainly look at it from a macro level. If your company is highly dependent on computers and electronic communications, your time costs will be higher than if your company uses computers but doesn't rely significantly on them. Take a look at the cost of downtime and give it an overall assessment if you can't specifically quantify it.

People

The people risk is the risk that is incurred from people's actions. In a wireless networking situation, your people risk is twofold. First, has anyone inside the organization installed a wireless access point? Whether their intentions are good or bad, the result will be the same—a huge security hole that circumvents all the best network security measures you've put in place. Therefore, while you need to assess the risk in this regard, you also need to implement policies regarding the unauthorized implementation of *any* technology, including wireless devices, and you need to implement a procedure for sweeping your network on a regular basis looking for rogue access points.

Another people risk is the risk of users with wireless devices connecting to the network via unsecured channels. If they are working with sensitive data on a laptop and they connect via an unsecured connection from a hotel or airport lounge, there is some danger their wireless communication could be hijacked. Implementing policies and procedures for secure wireless communication for mobile users is key to assessing your risk in this area.

The outside people risk is that a vendor, supplier, or visitor could install a rogue access point anywhere in your building. Assessing the risk includes reviewing the physical environment of your building and finding places an access point could be installed in an unobtrusive manner. Your risk assessment might include a physical risk review to find spots where a WAP could be installed and creating tasks in your project plan to make those spots more secure and/or more visible.

Finally, you'll need to look at the external risk of people who may come in close enough contact with your physical premises to interfere with wireless network operations. This might include RF jamming, intrusion, spoofing, and more.

Impact Analysis

The impact analysis is an essential element in a security project because, as we've stated numerous times, you have to balance the time and cost of implementing security against the potential impact of a security breach. If your company makes nuts and bolts, stores no real confidential information, and doesn't store personal information such as credit card numbers or medical records on your network, the impact of a security breach is far lower than for a high-profile hospital or major university. No doubt a security breach could potentially cause embarrassment and lost productivity if intruders impacted the confidentiality, integrity, or availability of network resources, but the chance you'd end up in a law suit for failing to protect certain data would probably be low. Therefore, it's important that you perform an impact analysis to understand how an intrusion of your wireless network could impact your company. Your analysis should include (but should not necessarily be limited to):

1. Data loss—confidentiality, integrity and/or availability

2. Productivity loss—direct and indirect (what was *not* getting done when the situation was being repaired)

3. Financial loss—direct and indirect

4. Loss of reputation—customers, vendors, employees, public markets

5. Loss of trust and confidence—customers, vendors, employees, public markets

6. Legal or regulatory implications—what are the legal, financial, and regulatory implications

Business Intelligence...

The Proliferation of Wireless Technologies

A recent article on MIT's Technology Review Web site highlights the new ways Wi-Fi technology is being used. Researchers at Brigham & Women's Hospital in Boston are collaborating with Harvard Medical School and MIT to test what they're calling "Scalable Medical Alert and Response Technology" (SMART) for use in ER waiting rooms. Researchers hope this wireless medical technology using sensors will make waiting in the emergency room a bit less life-threatening. The author of the article says: "Here's a scenario: You find yourself sitting in a local emergency room, or standing in the admitting line of an emergency clinic. But instead of just cooling your heels (and having a cardboard tag tied around your neck, as Gulf Coast clinics did after Katrina), you've been given a fanny pack containing a pocket-sized computer and ultrasound transponder. And wires come out of it, leading to a sensor on your finger and some more on your chest. Now, if something happens—say, you quietly go into a cardiac arrest—the doctors will know and can come running." Let's hope hackers don't find a way into this one.

Head to this URL to read the whole story by Lamont Wood dated May 5, 2006:

http://www.technologyreview.com/read_article.aspx?id=16776&ch=infotech

Wireless Security Project Parameters

We've looked at many aspects of wireless networking, the risks and threats, the tools both you and the hackers can use. Now, let's start planning the wireless security project. We'll begin where all projects should begin, with the problem statement and mission statement.

Your problem statement should reflect the current situation in your company, whether you have a wireless network or not. We've included a couple of sample problem statement to get you started; you'll need to tweak it to reflect your company's situation.

> We currently have a wireless network that is unsecured. We also have business users who travel frequently and utilize wireless connections to check e-mail and log into the network. We do not know our level of exposure and we have no security measures in place.

> We currently do not have a wireless network but we do not know if there are ad hoc wireless networks in existence putting our network assets at risk. We have users with wireless devices including laptops and PDAs and want to ensure they are secure when connecting to our network, whether internally (unauthorized wireless networks) or externally.

Your mission or outcome statement should focus on the other side of the problem statement—where do you want to be when your project is complete? We've included two mission or outcome statements to give you a running start.

> We will have a reasonably secure wireless network that will keep out most intruders. We will implement security measures on all wireless mobile devices and create new operating procedures and user policies to support this higher level of desired security.

> We will continue to operate without an official corporate wireless network but will implement IT operational plans that include scanning for rogue wireless networks on our

corporate network. We will also educate users and provide policy guidelines and best practices to keep our corporate mobile users safe when connecting to our network from external locations.

Requirements

As you recall from standard project management, we need to define the various requirements for this project. They include functional (often user-driven), technical, and legal or compliance requirements. It's usually best to start with functional requirements and develop technical requirements from there. We'll discuss functional and technical requirements but as with everything in these project plans, you'll need to tailor it to your specific organizational needs. Remember that, in general, the functional requirements describe "what" and the technical requirements describe "how."

Since wireless network security does not exist in a vacuum, it's important to remember that the solutions you develop for your wireless security project will very likely impact some other project. For example, if you decide you want to implement authentication or encryption protocols, these may impact all remote connections, all wireless connections, all users, and so on. Therefore, be sure to check with other IT security project teams or with your IT security program manager (if one exists) to coordinate the implementation of these across the enterprise. These may end up rolling up into the corporate IT project plan so that all the individual security area project (ISAP) plans coordinate their use of authentication or security protocols. You don't need four different groups identifying and implementing security protocols and work at cross-purposes in the organization.

Some people also like to include "success factors" in project requirements because they want to define what is required to be successful. That is certainly one way it can be documented and if that is the method you use, that's fine. In this methodology, we use "assumptions" (defined later in this chapter) to capture the things we're assuming will be in place so the project will be successful. There are probably 9 million opinions on how to approach this and the important point is that you do address it either as requirements for success or assumptions about what will be in place to help the project be a success. We've addressed it in the project assumptions.

One very important note here: we have not specifically talked about forming your project team (we'll discuss that later in this chapter), but you would be remiss to formulate your requirements without additional input from your IT staff as well as from key stakeholders. Users, departmental managers, trainers, and HR representatives should be included in defining functional requirements. Your IT team can then translate them into technical requirements. In addition, you will need these same experts to help you define appropriate policies, procedures, and processes for implementing and maintaining wireless security once project work is complete. Building this important information and feedback into your project plan will help you deliver a project that meets diverse organizational needs.

Functional Requirements

Different people phrase functional requirements differently. How you word them is not nearly as important as that you word them to include what you want your wireless project to include by way of functionality. Therefore, the functional requirements for a wireless security project could include:

1. Address physical security—Monitoring and/or restricting access to company's physical premises and network components.

2. Address network components—Identifying and locating all existing authorized and rogue access points and ad hoc networks. Identifying all existing wireless devices and connection methods. Identifying procedures for locating rogues and how they will be addressed.

3. Develop ability to monitor and detect intrusion via wireless access.

4. Develop ability to monitor and manage wireless data confidentiality, integrity, and access.

5. Develop list of network resources to which users should have access (with the understanding that not all resources need to be accessible via remote or wireless connections).

6. Develop policies and procedures to dictate appropriate/secure use and to educate users about maintaining wireless security.

Technical Requirements

Technical requirements for a wireless security project could include:

1. Physical security—Security guards monitoring/controlling building entry/exit (ensuring proper identification, preventing "tailgating" (when one visitor enters right behind another authorized visitor), requiring visitors to sign in or be escorted, etc.), card key access, locked server rooms, locked doors, cabinets, and drawers in public or easy-to-access locations.

2. Address wireless network components—Based on the data provided earlier in this chapter (Threat Assessment), identify the tools needed to locate wireless components on your network.

3. Identify the technical requirements for an intrusion detection/intrusion prevention (IDS/IPS) system that has the ability to monitor and detect intrusion via wireless access.

4. Identify the technical requirements for encryption, secure connections, and secure access via wireless technologies and via Internet connections accessed through wireless connections in a variety of locations.

5. Identify the technical requirements for securing a variety of wireless devices and policies for the use of such devices.

6. Identify the specific technical requirements for users regarding the use of wireless networks and wireless devices on company

premises and off company premises when connecting to the company network and noncompany networks.

7. Identify the ongoing operational procedures related to maintaining wireless security including frequency and method of scanning, physical inspection practices, and maintaining security on user's wireless devices.

You may have other requirements and your technical specifications should be much more specific. For instance, you should identify which assets (laptops, PDAs) you'll use for identifying all existing authorized and unauthorized access points and ad hoc networks. What operating system are these devices using? Which programs will you use for this activity, which version, where will you get it, what else is needed (other equipment, other programs) to perform this activity and what are the specifications of the program (i.e., what does this program need to do?). In some cases, you may be listing the requirements that are used to evaluate and purchase (or download in the case of freeware) a program. In other cases, you may be listing the technical requirements for the laptop, all software applications, antenna, and so on. This is just one example of the specificity you should strive for in your technical requirements. The seven items in the list are representative of the types of technical requirements, but you will probably have a longer list of technical requirements and your list should be far more specific. Here's an example of the level of specificity for a single elements of the technical specifications that would be desirable:

- Dell Inspiron 3500 laptop with 512KB RAM, 40GB hard disk running Windows XP Professional (Asset tag # 44932)

- Orinoco Classic Gold wireless card

- NetStumbler ver. 0.4.0

In addition, you might also specify a number of other tools you want to use in your wireless security project including (but certainly not limited to):

- NetStumbler, MiniStumbler
- Kismet
- WinSniffer
- ettercap
- L0phtCrack
- LRC
- Share Enumerator Legion 2.1
- Network Management and Control—Hyena, LANBrowser, Solarwinds, SNMPc
- Wireless Protocol Analyzers—Wildpackets Airopeek, AirMagnet, Fluke WaveRunner Wireless Tester, Ethereal, and more
- Operating System Fingerprinting and Port Scanning— LANGuard Network Security Scanner
- Networking Utilities – WS_Ping Propack, NetScan Tools Professional

Technical requirements might also include specific training initiatives to ensure staff is trained on key technologies, assessment methodologies, or wireless network detection and intrusion tools. Since hackers are well trained in these technologies, you should ensure your own staff is also well versed in using these tools so that you can at least level the playing field.

Legal/Compliance Requirements

This is an area where you're going to have to do some serious research, talk with your legal, financial, and HR departments and determine exactly which requirements your company must comply with. As we discussed in Chapter 9, there are a wide variety of laws and regulations, and chances are good if you're the head of your IT department that you're already aware of the particular regulations you need to address. However, it's not a bad idea to do some additional research to be sure you've got your bases covered.

Once you're clear which rules, regulations, and laws apply to your business, you'll need to develop a specific list of requirements. In many cases, these can and should be incorporated into your functional and technical requirements. You may choose to keep track of your compliance requirements within your functional and technical specification by flagging them in some manner such as using COMP: at the beginning of a requirements description or by putting them in one section. Since many of the compliance requirements may overlap regular requirements, you'll need to determine the best method for listing compliance-related requirements. For example, some requirements might be both your own requirements and those needed for compliance. Others might be to satisfy compliance issues only. Do you need to know which is which? Maybe yes, maybe no, you'll have to decide. Regardless of your approach, you should be sure to clearly indicate which items are required for compliance and what those compliance requirements are specifically. This should later be incorporated into task details. For example, suppose in order to be compliant with some particular requirement you must use encryption. The compliance requirement doesn't specify which type of encryption or how it is to be implemented. Therefore, you choose to implement WEP. You'll need to include this in your functional (encryption), technical (128-bit WEP), and compliance (data encryption methods) requirements. You'll need to add one or more tasks to your Work Breakdown Structure (WBS) that implement WEP on your wireless network. You'll need to add testing tasks to ensure that the WEP implementation works as specified and that users can connect wirelessly to the network once WEP is implemented. Then, you'll need tasks in your WBS that also document the implementation of WEP as a compliance requirement and generate whatever documentation is required in order to prove compliance.

Policy Requirements

Policy requirements may fall under functional requirements but there's no rule that you can't create your own category of requirements if it helps ensure you cover all the bases. We'll look at policies in more detail in a later chapter, but for now, we will walk through a few ideas for policies related to wireless security.

> **User policies**—Installation of wireless access points on the company network; use of wireless devices on company premises; use of wireless devices when traveling; appropriate use of unsecured wireless networks when traveling; guidelines for securing confidential data when traveling.

> **IT policies**—Installation of wireless access points on the company network; management and authorization of wireless devices for use on company premises; management and authorization of wireless devices for users who travel; configuration management for company-issued wireless devices; configuration management for noncompany issued wireless devices; procedures for monitoring the presence of wireless networks connected to the corporate network; procedures for monitoring intrusion via the wireless network; emergency response to wireless intrusion event; remediation for response to wireless intrusion event.

Scope

The scope of your wireless security project is based on a number of factors unique to your organization. Your scope statement should identify what *is* and what *is not* part of the project. By defining what is not included, you can be sure that everyone is pretty clear about where this project is headed. Where possible, identify scope using specific, measurable terms. For instance, your scope might include the building located at 123 Main Street but not the manufacturing facility located at 999 South Street since the manufacturing facility does not have a computer network but only standalone manufacturing computers. You might say your scope includes all network segments, all wireless devices including (list all authorized devices). You might say your project includes all devices that run 802.11 or 802.1X but will not address wireless keyboard, mice, overhead projection systems, remote controls for televisions, sound systems or projectors, nor will it address Bluetooth or RFID. Once you get into the swing of things, you should be able to clearly say what is and is not included and this will give you a great idea of how big this project is (and is not).

Schedule

You may not be able to create any sort of meaningful schedule at this point, but that's fine. What you should do at this point is see if there are any external drivers for your schedule such as hard deadlines, legal or compliance deadlines that must be met, funding events, public market events, and so on. Look around to see if there is anything that would require your project be completed by a specified time. If not, you may have a bit more flexibility on your wireless project schedule than you initially thought. You might also be able to develop a high-level understanding of how long this project is likely to take. How long will it take you to inventory all company-issued wireless devices? It probably depends on whether you have a database of devices with asset tags and device owners or not. If you have to walk around to every user and ask what devices they have, what operating system they're running, what type of wireless connection they use, you're going to need more time. This kind of information can be used to generate a first-pass schedule estimate that tells you this project is three months or twelve months long. If you still can't make a first-pass guess, that's fine but be sure to ask yourself (and your team), "What other information would we need to generate a fairly good ballpark estimate?" That way, you can focus on clarifying that data rather than randomly gathering data that gets you no closer to the answer.

After you create your Work Breakdown Structure, you should be able to create a very tight schedule. Once you finalize the WBS, it will be the schedule you have to commit to and manage against. At this juncture, you'll just need a rough idea of timelines, but be careful here. Any estimate you casually toss around now might come back to haunt you later. People have a strange way of remembering the one thing you wish they'd forget and if you say, "I don't know, I think it should just take a couple of months," you'll find that 59 days later someone is asking you for the results of your project. What they didn't hear (or didn't want to hear) is that "it *might* take 60 days and that's once we begin working on project tasks." Be cautious about tossing around estimates and if you're really pressed to give an initial estimate, pack it with as many disclaimers as you can. Later, you will have to (and should) commit to a project schedule but at this juncture, it's not much more than guesswork.

Budget

Just as your schedule may be fuzzy at this juncture, the budget may also be vague at the moment. As with schedule, you need to determine if there are any budgetary constraints specifically tied to your wireless security project budget. It's possible there was recently a new allocation for wireless technology in your firm and you can pull from that budget. It's possible there was recently a budget cut and all budgets were slashed 10 percent, which will trickle down into your IT department. Your choice at that point will likely be to slash all your projects by 10 percent or look at your project list and determine which project(s) should take the hit. In fact, this might be the opportunity you needed to kill a dead project that needed to go away but no one had the nerve to cancel it and reallocate those funds to your wireless security project.

Every company will differ in the way it allocates funds for projects and the way budgets are developed. However, your starting point needs to be your requirements list and your scope because those will dictate how big the project is. Once you understand how large the project is, you can begin to balance schedule, budget, and quality to find the optimal mix for your wireless security project.

As with schedule, once you've developed your WBS and your detailed task list, you should have a very clear sense of how much the project will cost and you should be prepared to defend your budget and manage it. The same perils exist as well. If you toss out a number, you can be sure that will be your top number and it's only going down from there, so avoid giving any financial estimates until you have a better idea of what number is realistic. Many organizations seem to be more tolerant of not knowing an exact budget more so than not knowing an exact schedule. Most companies ask "how long will it take?" before they ask "how much will it cost?" though every company culture is different. If you're pressed for a budget estimate before you have any idea of what it will cost, just say you're working up an estimate and should have one ready by (whenever) but it's too early to provide any estimates. They might not like that answer but it's safer than being held to a randomly generated guess.

Quality

You may have a distinct approach to quality in your wireless security project in mind but if not, you can begin by defining what level of confidence you want in your wireless security. For instance, 100 percent confidence that your wireless network is secure will be costly and time-consuming (not to mention impossible to achieve) and the risks to your network do not support such an iron-clad approach. What if you were 80 percent sure your wireless network was secure, would that be sufficient? It may seem odd to accept less than 100 percent confidence or 100 percent quality but that's not realistic given the time/cost factors involved with that level of quality. Do you want to use military standards for your firm? That's probably over-engineering the solution to a great extent for most companies, so you may choose to implement 80 percent of the DoD standards. You can see that as you begin to look at your approach, you can begin to define quality in meaningful ways.

Keep in mind that the functional and technical requirements also help define quality by the inclusion or exclusion of various requirements. In fact, your technical requirements generally define your initial level of quality and can be used as a great starting place for understanding project quality.

Quality is also supported and developed through proper training. If your team members don't know how to use AirSnort or NetStumbler, there's a good chance that project results will be less than optimal. Identify training needs once you've identified key skills needed (see next section) and be sure that you have the skills and expertise needed to deliver a quality job.

Finally, understand that quality is as much a mindset as a measurement. Keep your team focused on doing their jobs with 100 percent accuracy. If every task is completed as specified, you should have a high-quality result on the other end of your project work. Therefore, quality can be built in to task details (completion criteria are excellent for driving quality in a project) and quality can be built one task at a time. Focus your team on delivering quality and use the tools at your disposal to monitor and measure quality as you move through your project work.

Business Intelligence...

Quality in Technical Projects

Most people don't like to admit there's something they don't know and technical people are probably at the top of that list. Given that very human trait, it's important that you, as the IT security project manager, create an environment where teammates are encouraged to ask questions, to say "I don't know," and to ask for assistance. Security and project quality are both dramatically reduced when someone is stumbling around trying to figure out an answer without asking for help to avoid looking dumb. When time is of the essence, having someone fiddle around with settings or reading the software's documentation or Help file may not be the most productive use of time, especially if there is someone on the team (or externally) that has the answer and could help. Discovery is a wonderful way to learn, but it's not always the most productive use of time when *time* is of the essence. Having a more experienced team member provide answers, assistance, or even impromptu training is more efficient in some instances, and it can happen only when team members feel comfortable saying "I don't know" or "I need some assistance." Pairing subject matter experts with novices can foster a learning environment. Creating an atmosphere of open teamwork will improve the quality of your project and increase everyone's skills along the way.

Once you have defined your initial scope, schedule, budget, and quality, you also need to look at the relative priority of those parameters. What is your least flexible parameter? Which one absolutely must be met? Which parameter is your most flexible, the one that can "give" if things start going wrong? This is critically important to understand before you launch the project so if you're not clear about your least flexible and most flexible parameters, you need to find out now. Some people misunderstand the nature of this discussion and think it's just a way to avoid responsibility for results. Although some might use it that way, it's important to understand that things will change during the course of the project. As the project manager, you need to understand how to prioritize things and how to make the best decisions for the project. Understanding the least and most flexible parameters will provide you the tools you need to make sound decisions without letting you off the hook for delivering results. If you haven't talked with your project sponsor yet or if you haven't clarified the priorities yet, develop your own assessment of priorities based on your current understanding of constraints and then discuss them with your project sponsor. If there's any disagreement or confusion, be sure to follow up with an e-mail clarifying or reiterating the result of the meeting so there's no confusion down the road.

Key Skills Needed

Throughout this book, we've discussed defining the skills needed before you identify the people for your project because you can keep a more open mind about what you need without filtering it through the people issues you might encounter. For your wireless security project, you'll need a variety of skills and we've provided a list to start you off. Keep in mind it may not include everything you need for your wireless security project or it might include things that you don't need; you will have to fine tune this to ensure it meets the unique requirements of your project.

- Configuring wireless components—MAC address filtering, WEP/WPA, RF cell sizing, active and passive scanners

- Integrating wireless access with network access

- Operating systems—Windows Server, Windows XP, Linux, Macintosh, PocketPC, Windows CE

- Monitoring and sweeping for wireless access points, use of discovery protocol

- Intrusion detection configuration and monitoring

- Wireless tools—NetStumbler, MiniStumbler, Kismet, AirSnort, AiroPeek, FakeAP, PERL, VBScript

- Authentication, encryption—RC4, RC5, DES/3DES, AES (FIPS 197)

- Segmentation, DMZs, VLANs—Firewalls, enterprise wireless gateways, enterprise encryption gateways, routers, Layer 3 switch (switch router), VPN, VPN concentrator, SSH2 Server, RADIUS

- Network layer protocols

  - Layer 2 (Data Link layer)—WEP (all variations such as TKIP), 802.1x/EAP (all variations), Enterprise Encryption Gateways, Layer 2 Tunneling Protocol (L2TP)

  - Layer 3 (Network layer)—Point-to-Point Tunneling protocol (PPTP), IP Security (IPSec)

  - Layer 7 (Application layer)—Secure Shell (SSH), Secure Shell Version 2 (SSH2), Novell Directory Services (NDS or eDirectory), Microsoft Active Directory (AD)

- Client configuration and security

- IP Services

- Staging, testing, and equipment installation

- Documentation—Technical (configuration, specifications), operational, and policy documentation

Key Personnel Needed

The list of needed skills is pretty extensive, so your first task, once you've completed the skills needs assessment, is to match those skills to your current team. Identify any gaps and decide whether you need to fill those gaps with training, hiring, or contracting. One way to discern this is by developing a sort of "gap hierarchy" where the gaps are prioritized based on how big or critical they are. For example, if someone on your team is well-versed in operating systems but isn't up to speed on PDA operating systems, then training might be in order. On the other hand, if you have no one on your team well-versed in secure remote communication methods, including authentication and encryption protocols, you may want to contract out for that skill. However, if you determine that you will have an on-going need for that skill set, you may want to get permission to hire another IT person to complement your team's skills or send one of your existing people to extensive training. You'll have to balance your immediate needs against your long-term needs to find the right mix.

When you get into project scheduling, you'll find out where you have resource constraints including double-booking someone for project work based on a particularly unique skill set they may have. This may lead you to train additional IT staff or to hire an outside contractor to fill in those gaps or help you work around those constraints.

This is also a good time to make sure you know who your project sponsor is and what his or her schedule looks like during the estimated duration of the project. We're assuming you've already been in contact with your project sponsor because that is typically how projects are initiated, but if you haven't identified or talked with your project sponsor, there's no time like the present to do so.

Project Processes and Procedures

The processes and procedures you'll need for your wireless security project are probably much the same as other project processes and procedures. Some additional items that might make sense would be:

- Method for reporting and addressing rogue wireless access points and ad hoc networks

- Method for inventorying and tracking existing wireless assets.

- Method for reporting existing wireless security environment including:

    - Wireless devices in use

    - Wireless networks implemented

    - Location and type of wireless access points in use

    - Existing authentication and encryption methods implemented

    - Known security risks or gaps in existing system

- Developing security checklists including list of wireless equipment (already listed), client side software and installations settings, configuration data, and so on, periodic inventory checks, periodic physical security checks of wireless equipment

Project Team

After you've identified needed skills and determined the key personnel for your team, you should begin forming your project team. In addition to the technical skills mentioned earlier in this chapter, you'll also need to be sure to include key stakeholders on your project team, especially during the definition stage (scope, requirements, etc.). Be sure to include user representatives during the definition phase and also when you begin testing your wireless security solutions. If you devise a solution that only the most savvy IT folks can implement, you'll have a cacophony of dissatisfied users pounding on your door (literally or figuratively). Also be sure to include subject matter experts including those that can help craft policies and procedures. Include those who really enjoy working with detail who can monitor, manage, and create your project documentation. If you have a compliance officer or someone who is tasked with monitoring and managing compliance issues, be sure he or she is also included on the project team. Finally, you may need someone from legal or who understands legal issues to help guide you as you define the scope of the project and the functional and/or technical requirements to ensure you've got all your bases covered. One way to be sure you've got the right people on the team is to ask, "What else do I need to know?" and "Who else needs to know about this?" Ask this of yourself, your IT staff, and your initial project team. You can always pare down your project participants but if you miss a key player you'll have to deal with the ramifications, which can include missing a key element for the project or just having to deal with the political fall-out of overlooking someone "important."

Identify project team roles so everyone knows how they fit in and what they should be doing. For complex or lengthy tasks (to be defined later), you may assign leads to work with subteams. Also create a team roster with contact information and be sure to have team members identify any times they'll be unavailable (upcoming scheduled vacations or leave, lengthy training or seminars scheduled, etc.) so you can quickly determine early in the project cycle whether you'll need to bring in more people or find ways to fill gaps.

Project Organization

Everyone has a slightly different way of organizing a project, and we discussed a number of general project organizational ideas earlier in the book, so we won't repeat that here. However you choose to organize your project should include the basics such as defining the project team structure, how things will proceed, when meetings will occur, who has to attend, how project status will be reported, how and where documentation should be stored, and so on. For a security project of this nature, you may want to divide your project team into different groups and have different groups test each other's security solutions in a friendly competition. This might help avoid collusion between team members (leaving back doors open) and it might also help ensure that testing is thorough and comprehensive. As we've mentioned a number of times, there's a danger that testing will test the plan and not test the actual security, so using creative methods to ensure your testing is as thorough as your attackers is an important part of organizing your project.

It is in this phase you should define what type of reporting will be required. One type of reporting for wireless network security that is needed is a list (and map, if possible) of all known, existing wireless access points in the building. This will be updated after the scan takes place once all currently unknown WAPs are also mapped. You'll need to create checklists for network and user wireless device inventories and you'll need to define standard operating procedures for your wireless security project. How are issues tracked and resolved? How are issues escalated? How are reports formatted and to whom are they submitted? All the run-of-the-mill project processes should be defined and modified to meet your project team's needs before proceeding into project work.

Project Work Breakdown Structure

1. Perform wireless network organizational risk assessment

   1.1 Develop list of assets requiring protection

   1.2 Develop list of network assets requiring protection

   1.3 Perform impact analysis

       1.3.1   Cost

       1.3.2   Time

       1.3.3   People

       1.3.4   Legal liability

       1.3.5   Regulatory issues

   1.4 Perform scan for rogue access points or ad hoc networks

2. Perform wireless network vulnerability assessment

   2.1 War dialing

   2.2 NetStumbling

   2.3 Direct access

2.4 MAC address spoofing

2.5 Cloaked access points

2.6 Man-in-the-middle attacks

2.7 Wireless network hijacking

2.8 Encrypted network attack

2.9 RF jamming

3. Define strategy for strengthening wireless security

  3.1 Identify all modem connections and define "modem strategy" (keep or transfer to another connection type)

  3.2 Limit network resource access via wireless connections

  3.3 Define authentication methods to be used

  3.4 Define data security or encryption methods to be used

  3.5 Define changes to policy needed to strengthen security

    3.5.1 IT security policies

    3.5.2 IT operational policies

    3.5.3 User policies

4. Implement strategy for strengthening wireless security

  4.1 Implement strong security on needed modem connections

  4.2 Implement security on all wireless network components

    4.2.1 Implement MAC address filtering

    4.2.2 Suppress SSID broadcasting

    4.2.3 Implement WEP or WPA

    4.2.4 Implement RADIUS (or equivalent)

    4.2.5 Encrypt email

    4.2.6 Use HTTPS, SSH where applicable

    4.2.7 Use secure FTP (SSH2, SSL) where applicable

4.3 Implement security on all wireless user devices

4.3.1 Ensure all user devices operating systems are up-to-date and have all patches installed

4.3.2 Ensure all user devices applications are up-to-date and have all patches installed

4.3.3 Ensure all user devices anti-virus, anti-spyware programs are up-to-date

4.3.4 Ensure all software configurations are secure and correct

4.4 Implement security policies

5. Test security implementation

5.1 Test modem security

5.2 Test wireless network security

5.3 Test wireless user device security

5.4 Test various user security configurations

6. Develop security policies and procedures to support security implementation

6.1 Develop policy regarding scanning for rogue AP and ad hoc networks

6.2 Develop policy and procedure for maintaining wireless security

6.2.1 Develop policies and procedures for maintaining physical perimeter security

6.2.2 Develop policies and procedures for maintaining wireless component security (APs, etc.)

6.2.3 Develop policies and procedures for maintaining wireless device security (laptops, PDAs)

6.2.4 Develop policies and procedures for maintaining user awareness and security skills

6.3. Develop policy and procedure for securing and tracking corporate wireless network components (APs, etc.)

6.4 Develop policy and procedure for securing and tracking users' wireless devices

6.5 Develop policy regarding network resources accessible via wireless connections

6.6 Develop policy regarding user practices for maintaining security with wireless devices

6.7 Develop change management policies regarding maintaining wireless security after project completion

7. Document all security assessments and security implementations

7.1 Document result of assessment

7.2 Document security implementations

7.3 Document operational requirements for maintaining security

7.4 Document all compliance-related materials

Just a quick reminder that you should include task details, which can include (but are not limited to):

- Task name (verb/noun format is preferred)
- Task number (if used)
- Task owner
- Task contributors (working on the project task)
- Description of task
- Duration
- Deadline/due date
- Cost
- Completion criteria
- Resources required

- Dependencies
- Constraints
- Applicable technical or compliance requirements
- Specific task risks, mitigation and triggers (if applicable)

Obviously, the more detail you can add to your tasks, the better everyone will understand exactly what it will take to complete the tasks and the entire project. Using subject matter experts to help complete task details will yield the most detailed and meaningful task details.

Project Risks

Project risks are those things that can (and likely will) go wrong during the course of the project. They are things that you should look for and assess, then plan to avoid or mitigate. This is a great job for all the "naysayers" on your team. You want them to find all the things that could possibly go wrong and challenge them to find a way to avoid those problems. The risks to a wireless security project are going to be unique to each organization and they fall along the lines of typical project risks. Your budget might be at risk, you might risk losing key team members to layoffs or you might not have the technical skills you think you have.

Although we've run through this drill earlier in the book, we'll quickly recap here for convenience. First, brainstorm every risk you and the team can think of. Next, rank the risks in order of criticality and likelihood of occurrence. Criticality should be defined so everyone uses the same ranking system. It could be 1 = Devastating, 5 = Mildly annoying, whatever works for your team. Likelihood should be a similar ranking system where 1 = Extremely likely, 5 = Extremely unlikely (in both ranking systems, there would be similarly defined 2, 3, and 4). Rank each risk according to both scales and then take a look at them. Use a bit of human reasoning and see if the final, ranked list actually reflects reality; if not, adjust the ranking manually to reflect what you all believe is realistic and likely. Next, select a cut-off point and agree to address only the top five or top ten risks. You could spend forever dealing with risks and mitigation strategies but if one of your risks is "The world might come to an end" there's really not much point in planning for that type of risk and you might as well move on.

For each risk identified, devise a strategy to avoid or reduce the risk. In essence, identify your "Plan B" before you need it. Be sure to look at the *risk* of the avoidance or mitigation strategy as well. Again, you could spend all day looking at risks but if you fail to look at the risk of the mitigation strategy, you could easily introduce far worse risk into the mix.

Once you're confident in your risk and mitigation strategies, develop triggers for each risk. In some cases, you may want to develop several triggers for a particular risk. For instance, if one of your risks is that there is a layoff coming and you don't know if your staff will be hit, you might add one trigger for "announcement of departmental layoffs" so that when this is announced, you begin looking at your Plan B option. A second trigger might be when the actual personnel are identified. You might then implement phase 2 of your Plan B option. Finally, when those personnel have left the building, you might implement phase 3 of your Plan B option.

For some risks, you may want to add milestones to your project plan so you can keep an eye out for them. For example, if one of the risks is that the new equipment you order might not be available at the time you need it (perhaps you're implementing a new technology that is just coming to market), you not only have to create Plan B but you also have to know to implement Plan B about two weeks before the equipment should be ordered. Adding milestones for risks helps keep them in the front of your mind so they don't sneak up on you.

Project Constraints and Assumptions

In a wireless security project, your constraints will be similar to other kinds of projects. They are often time, budget, or talent constraints. Although they should be addressed via your project planning activities, they may not be. For example, you may be constrained by pending litigation, by a pending merger or reorganization, or by a pending layoff. Typically, project constraints are external to your project and generally are tied to your macro-environment. List these and determine if any of them constitute a "project killer." If so, you need to circle back with your project sponsor and get clarification as to how to proceed. There's no point in firing up a project that is so constrained from the outset that it has little chance of success.

Assumptions can be thought of as the success factors if you're *assuming* certain conditions will be available during the course of the project. If you delineated success factors in your requirements, you may choose to list them as assumptions here as well. The reason for defining your assumptions is twofold: first, you want to make sure that you're looking at the project with eyes wide open; second, you want to document the assumptions you're making because if any of those things change, it probably will change the outcome of the project. For instance, if you assume that you will be able to schedule time to perform penetration testing and your Vice President of Information Technology comes back to you and says under no circumstances will you perform penetration testing, that may be a major setback to your project plan. If this is listed as an assumption, you can gain agreement from your project sponsor about these assumptions. Then, if things change later, you'll at least have documentation showing that it was listed as an assumption (or success factor), that it was approved by the project sponsor, and that it later changed and had a negative impact on the project outcome.

Project Schedule and Budget

You've created your detailed Work Breakdown Structure and you've developed your task details. At this point, you should be very clear about your project's projected schedule and budget.

The schedule should be defined by placing your tasks in optimal order, then by identifying dependencies. Constraints and conflicts should then be addressed to generate you first real project schedule. Since we're assuming you're familiar with basic project management principles, we won't go into project scheduling techniques. Of course, using a project management software program greatly assists in creating and managing a project schedule, so now would be the time to input project tasks and generate your schedule if you're using a software program. Software programs are also very helpful at identifying the critical path so you can properly manage those key elements.

As for your schedule, once you've delineated all your tasks, you should also be able to generate a real budget based on the cost of project tasks, the cost of labor (if you track labor costs with your projects), and the cost of training and other auxiliary elements.

A quick reminder about both schedule and budget—don't pad them. Make your schedule and budget estimates as tight and accurate as possible, then add a "management reserve" that provides a general buffer against unexpected changes to your schedule or budget. In this way, you'll be able to see more clearly what you planned on doing and what you were actually able to do. If you pad your estimates, you'll never really know what you thought you could accomplish vs. the padded estimate.

Wireless Security Project Outline

1. Perform wireless network organizational risk assessment.

2. Perform wireless network vulnerability assessment.

3. Define strategy for strengthening wireless security.

4. Implement strategy for strengthening wireless security.

5. Test security implementation.

6. Develop security policies and procedures to support security implementation.

7. Document all security assessments and security implementations.

Summary

We've covered a lot of territory in this chapter. We looked at wireless security from end to end starting with auditing wireless security. There are numerous kinds of wireless devices, not all of which you'll need to address in your wireless security plan, but if you are unaware of these device types, you won't know if they pose a threat or not. We also looked at the basics of wireless technology reviewing the 802.11 IEEE standard.

Understanding the threats in the wireless world requires a deep understanding of how attackers work and the tools they use. We reviewed some of the threat types including war dialing, wardriving (NetStumbling or stumbling), and Bluetooth attacks. In order to develop a useful wireless security project plan, you'll need to perform a risk assessment for your organization. By dividing this assessment into people, process, and technology and by looking at confidentiality, integrity, and availability of data, you can develop a holistic view of your company's risk profile. Since you'll always have to balance security, cost, and practicality, you'll need to assess and evaluate your company's risk profile and risk tolerance to determine how much security is needed, reasonable, and feasible.

Understanding what assets you're actually protecting helps you develop a sound wireless security plan. Assets such as customer credit cards, health care information, financial or bank data, employee lists, trade secrets, intellectual property, and R&D data are high on the list of valuable data assets to be protected. In addition, there are network assets that should be protected including usernames, passwords, directory listings, network firewalls, routers, switches, IP addresses, and ports/protocols in use. This is information that intruders often use to gain access to the valuable data assets or to simply create havoc on the network. An impact analysis helps you understand the ramifications of a potential wireless network intrusion. These elements include data loss (confidentiality, integrity, availability), productivity loss, financial loss, as well as the less tangible but very real problems of losing your company's good reputation or losing the trust and confidence of your customers. There are also legal or regulatory implications that must be assessed.

After going through this material, we began walking through the steps needed to create a meaningful wireless security project plan. We identified the problem, the mission or desired outcome, and the solution. The project definition includes identifying the functional requirements that lead, in most cases, to the technical requirements. We also identified other types of requirements that could potentially apply to your wireless security project including legal or compliance requirements and policy requirements. There certainly are some areas of overlap between the wireless project and other IT security projects, including authentication and encryption, that should be tied in to other projects as applicable.

Developing the project scope, initial estimated schedule, budget, and quality were reviewed with an eye toward the unique elements found in a wireless security project. We were then able to define the skills needed for this project. Though your list of skills will differ from the list provided, it got you thinking in the right direction in terms of the specific skills needed for a wireless security project, which differ in some ways from other IT projects. Once your skill set is defined, you're ready to identify the people needed for the project and to begin forming your project team.

With a project team in place, your next major task together is to create the Work Breakdown Structure. It includes all the major and minor tasks needed to secure your wireless network including the assessment, design, and implementation of a security solution and, of course, the documentation of all security changes made.

The risks, assumptions, and constraints are unique to every company and every IT project, so there's no specific information that can be provided that will fit all organizations. Defining these three key elements is critical to project success, so be sure you walk through these steps and clearly articulate these items.

Finally, we provided a quick outline for you to use in developing your wireless security project plan, as a quick recap for you. Throughout this chapter, we've looked at the standard project management methodology with an eye toward developing a sound wireless security project plan. You should have a solid idea of where to start your own wireless security project plan and, utilizing the information in this chapter, you should be able to take it from here.

Solutions Fast Track

Wireless Security Auditing

☑ Intruders and hackers look for the easiest targets first and often will skip over targets that are secured.

☑ There are a growing number of wireless devices and wireless protocols in use in the market today, making wireless security an even more important security project.

☑ It's important to understand types of threats, including war dialing, wardriving, and Bluetooth attacks.

☑ Risk assessment should include the types of assets to be protected. This includes sensitive or confidential data as well as certain network data such as usernames, passwords, or directory structures.

☑ Threat prevention runs the gamut from shutting down modems to implementing MAC address filtering, suppressing SSID broadcasts, and implementing various security measures such as authentication and/or encryption.

☑ An impact analysis should include the cost in time and money of a potential breach as well as the less tangible costs such as loss of reputation, trust, or confidence. It also should include the legal liability of such an intrusion.

Project Parameters

☑ Project parameters begin with defining the project's problem statement, mission, or outcome statement and defining the appropriate solution for the project.

☑ Requirements should be defined early in the project definition stage because they essentially define the scope of your project.

☑ Requirements include functional, technical, legal, and regulatory (compliance) requirements.

☑ Some people include success factors in the requirements since these factors are required for project success. Others include success factors in the assumptions section of the project plan.

☑ Scope, schedule, budget, and quality can be defined after the initial project definition is complete and after the requirements have been clearly delineated.

☑ Key skills can be defined after the technical requirements are defined and the list should be comprehensive.

☑ Key personnel can be matched to the project based on the required skills for the project. If there are any gaps, you can begin planning how to address those gaps including providing training, hiring outside contractors, or creating and hiring a new position.

Project Team

☑ You should have identified key stakeholders early in the definition phase in order to help craft the definition so the project would meet many stakeholder needs.

☑ The project team will be comprised of a variety of different kinds of team members, some of whom may participate only in some phases of project work.

Project Organization

☑ Organizing a wireless security project is fairly standard and should include developing appropriate processes and procedures for your team.

☑ Project status reporting, issues logs, error reports, and more should be developed during this phase.

☑ Be sure to include processes related to regulatory or compliance activities and documentation in your project plan.

Project Work Breakdown Structure

☑ A Work Breakdown Structure for a wireless security project plan was developed outlining the seven major tasks.

☑ Subtasks were defined for many of the tasks; your WBS will be different.

☑ Task details should be developed with attention to detail. The more clearly defined the tasks are, the more clear the project itself becomes. Quality is built into projects through well-defined tasks.

Project Risks and Mitigation Strategies

☑ There are numerous risks to a wireless security project as there are with any IT project.

☑ All risks should be identified then ranked. The ranked list should be shortened to the highest overall risks identified.

☑ Mitigation strategies, risk analysis of the mitigation strategies, and triggers should be identified for all risks.

Project Constraints and Assumptions

☑ Constraints are any elements that may hamper your project's success. These are often found outside of the immediate project environment.

☑ Assumptions are those things you are taking to be true or in existence and upon which your project's success rests. Some use assumptions in place of success factors.

Project Schedule and Budget

☑ Once you've defined your WBS in detail, you should be able to develop a realistic schedule.

☑ If you have project management software available to you, this is a good time to input your tasks and schedule into the program to allow the software to assist you in creating a schedule and identifying the critical path.

☑ Budgets can be developed by adding the cost of all tasks plus any administrative costs or costs that apply across the project that cannot (or should not) be attributed to any one particular task.

☑ Be sure to include the cost of training, compliance, and any other auxiliary project costs.

☑ Avoid padding your estimates. Instead, create accurate estimates then use a "management reserve" to adjust your schedule or budget.

Wireless Security Project Outline

☑ An outline was provided to give you the major steps in your project plan.

☑ You can modify this outline to suit your needs but it can serve as a good starting point for planning your wireless security project.

Chapter 13

IT Operational Security Plan

Solutions in this chapter:

- Operational Security Assessment
- Project Parameters
- Project Team
- Project Organization
- Project Work Breakdown Structure
- Project Risks and Mitigation Strategies
- Project Constraints and Assumptions
- Project Schedule and Budget
- Operational Security Project Outline

☑ Summary

☑ Solutions Fast Track

Introduction

Network security is no longer just a technical issue, it's a business issue. It's no longer just a problem for the IT department to handle, it's an organizational problem. In the past, IT security was viewed as an expense, but slowly, companies are beginning to see it as an investment. It has evolved from an ad hoc activity to one that is planned using proven methodologies. Perhaps the most important shift occurring is that organizations are beginning to move from the reactive "security incident response" mentality to the "organizational resiliency" (thanks to folks at CERT/CC for that phrase). Companies are facing the stark reality that security is no longer just something a few geeky guys do in the dark recesses of the IT department. Corporate executives understand that while network services have moved more toward "utility" services, security has moved toward a more specialized commodity that involves the entire organization.

Operational security is sometimes overlooked or put together in a patchwork fashion. That's unfortunate because all the hard work that went into your IT security projects is pretty much wasted if you don't develop on-going operations that support or enhance security. This is accomplished through your operational security plan. In this chapter, we're going to look at five distinct areas that support security: incident response, corporate and IT policies related to security; disaster recovery (whether a hurricane or a network intrusion), regulatory issues, and configuration management. These are not the most exciting topics to techies, which is probably why they're often neglected. If this topic bores you to tears, find someone on your team who loves policies and procedures and get him or her fired up about this project then hand it over. Whatever you do, don't squander a great opportunity to tighten up security on the front and back end of your technology initiatives.

Operational Security Assessment

As with all security initiatives, it's wise to begin with an assessment of your operational security. We'll continue to use the five topic areas mentioned in the Introduction to guide us through our assessment and our planning activities:

- Incident response
- Security policies
- Disaster recovery
- Regulatory compliance
- Configuration management

The first operational area is obvious – what do you do if there is a security incident? If you don't have a planned response, you're likely to overlook something (or create a bigger problem) in the aftermath of an attack. You and your team may be scrambling to lock the doors and forget that the window is wide open. How you respond to incidents can mean the difference between being down for an hour or a month.

Policies are a part of every organization, whether they're formal or informal, written or practiced. It's important to define policies that support security without creating a convoluted tangle of rules and regulations that only serve to confuse users. Confused users are dangerous users because rather than try to understand what they should and should not do, they'll do whatever they know how to do or whatever is easiest. This type of user behavior neither supports nor enhances security.

We often think of disaster recovery in the context of natural disasters such as fires, floods, earthquakes or hurricanes. However, unnatural disasters include network intrusion, data modification, data falsification or data corruption. In these cases, it's important to have a clear path to recovery. If you recall from Chapter 1, companies that fail to restore lost data within 24 hours of an attack or system failure have a 50 percent chance of going out of business within three years. Those are seriously bad odds, and they don't bode well for IT job security either. Having a viable disaster recovery plan in place may not only save your job but it may well save your company.

Throughout this book, we've discussed regulatory issues that impact your IT security projects. While it's outside the scope of this book to cover all of them in detail, we will take a more in-depth look at some of the issues facing companies in the compliance and regulatory arena so you can determine next steps for your own organization.

Configuration management, though individually called out, is really incorporated into a number of different areas. Configuration management is an important part of maintaining a secure and compliant network environment. It should be incorporated into your response team's security management and proactive services definitions; it should be done through developing policies and procedures for your IT staff's day-to-day operations, and it should be done on a consistent basis and incorporated into disaster recovery plans on a regular basis. Configuration management is a large topic and might be a large enough issue in your organization to warrant its own distinct project plan. You can find additional information on configuration management online. A good place to start is: http://en.wikipedia.org/wiki/Configuration_management#Sites_for_configuration_management.

Business Intelligence…

Risk Assessment Tools

There are many great tools available for performing risk assessments. Here are four you might want to investigate.

Operationally Critical Threat, Analysis, and Vulnerability Evaluations (OCTAVE) A process document that provides an extensive risk assessment format (www.cert.org/octave).

GAO Information Security Risk Assessment Case studies of organizations that implemented risk assessment programs (www.gao.gov/special.pubs/ai99139.pdf).

Continued

RiskWatch Software created that poses a series of questions to
help individuals perform a risk assessment. It also includes modules for
review against the ISO 17799 standard (www.riskwatch.com).
    Consultative, Objective and Bi-functional Risk Analysis A risk
assessment software program that includes questions that map against
the ISO 17799 standard (www.security-risk-analysis.com/index.htm).

Incident response

As we step through the assessment activities, we'll also discuss best practices so that when you're ready to develop your operational security project plan, you'll have the information you need to develop a solid
incident response plan. Before we head into the details, let's take a quick
look at the history of incident response. This will give you a bit of perspective and it's a great (geeky) conversation starter at tech conventions
and high school reunions.

   In 1988, an "Internet worm" hit a lot of computers then connected to
the Internet. While 1988 may seem like the Stone Age of the Internet,
that first attack disabled a large percentage of those 60,000 computers. In
response to that incident, the Computer Emergency Response Team
(CERT) was formed. CERT was chartered to be a single, trusted point of
contact for computer emergency response data; to act as a clearinghouse
for trusted information. In 1995, according to the CERT website, there
were 171 vulnerabilities reported to CERT. In 2005, there were 5,990
vulnerabilities reported. If the remainder of 2006 tracks with first quarter
results, CERT will log over 6,388 reported vulnerabilities. Clearly, we are
on an unfortunate upward trajectory.

   Those 60,000 computers connected to the Internet pale in comparison to the some-200 million hosts now estimated to be connected to the
Internet. It's no surprise, then, that the volume of vulnerabilities reported
has increased significantly. Today, there are numerous resources available to
anyone who wants to form a security response team and there are also
various organizations including the Forum of Incident Response and
Security Teams (FIRST) and the TERENA-sponsored TF-CSIRT, a task

force for the collaboration of incident response teams in Europe. If you're interested in these topics, visit the CERT site at www.cert.org.

Most organizations don't plan for incident response until after they've had their first incident. This leaves most organizations without even basic knowledge about their network status, such as:

- Not knowing if, for how long, or to what degree the network has been breached

- Not knowing what information has been stolen, modified or corrupted by the breach and the criticality/sensitivity of that information

- Not knowing what method(s) the intruder(s) used to gain access to the network

- Not knowing how to stop a breach in progress

- Not knowing who should respond and in what manner

- Not knowing who has the authority to respond

- Not knowing who to contact regarding the breach (executives, legal counsel, law enforcement)

These problems are amplified by companies with offices in multiple locations, whether domestic or international. Without a clearly defined plan in place, you're putting your company's future at risk. Many companies hold mistaken beliefs about forming an incident handling team. The reasons run the gamut, but here are a few common attitudes that get some companies in trouble:

- It's too intimidating; ignore it and it will go away.

- Just take care of problems as they arise.

- Our firewall keeps us safe.

- It's too much money to spend on something as non-strategic as the network.

- Dave's pretty good with computers, he'll handle it.

Clearly, being in a state of denial doesn't fix the problem, so part of your job is to advocate for the creation and support of an incident response team. This should be one of the major components of your IT operational security project plan, so let's take a look at the details of what that type of team should do and how to form one.

Company-Wide Incident Response Teams

Most organizations of any size and geographic distribution found themselves hastily developing interdepartmental response procedures in the spring of 1999. As the *Melissa* virus knocked out the core communication medium, the bridge lines went up and calls went out to IT managers of offices all over the world. United in a single goal, restoring business as usual, companies that previously had no formal incident response planning spontaneously created a corporate incident response team. Most of the development of formal incident response teams came about as a solution to problems they had faced in managing their response to the most recent issue.

The biggest obstacle in the opening hours of March 26, 1999, was the rapid loss of e-mail communication. Initial responses by most messaging groups upon detecting the virus was to shut down Internet mail gateways, leaving internal message transfer agents enabled. However, it quickly became clear that having already entered the internal network and hijacking distribution lists, it was necessary to bring down e-mail entirely. Unfortunately, security administrators were no different than any other users, and relied almost entirely on their e-mail clients' address books for locating contact information for company personnel. With the corporate messaging servers down, initial contact had to be performed through contact spidering, or simply waiting for the phone to ring at the corporate help desk.

There was a common thread in companies that had difficulty getting back online, even after having gotten all the necessary representatives on a conference call. In most of these organizations, despite having all the right contacts available, there was still contention over responsibilities. In some cases, IT teams from remote organizations were reluctant to take the necessary steps to secure their environments, insisting that the central IT group should be responsible for managing matters pertaining to organizational security. In other cases, the messaging group refused to bring up remote sites until those sites could provide documentation showing that all desktops at the site had been updated with the latest anti-virus software. Clearly, when no one is in charge and no plan is in place, chaos reigns.

Each member of an incident response team should have a clearly defined circle of responsibility. These circles should be directly related to the member's position in an organizational chart, with the relevant corporate hierarchies providing the incident response team's chain of command. At the top of the chart, where an organizational diagram would reflect corporate headquarters, sits the CIO, CSO, or Director of Information Security. The chart should continue down in a multi-tier format, with remote offices at the bottom of the chart. For example, the team member from corporate IT who acts as liaison to the distributed retail locations would be responsible for ensuring that the proper steps are being taken at each of the retail locations.

It is important to keep in mind that incident response could require the skills of any of four different specialties: *networking, messaging, desktop,* and *server* support. At each of the upper levels of the hierarchy there should be representatives, preferably subject matter experts, in each specialty. By ensuring that each of these specialties is properly represented on a response team, you should be prepared to deal with any emergency, no matter what aspect of your infrastructure is initially impacted.

Once the team is developed, you have to find a way to *maintain* the team. At one company, the Director of Information Security instituted a plan to run a fire drill twice a year, setting off an alarm and seeing how long it took for all the core team members to join the call. After the call, each of the primary contacts was asked to submit updated contact sheets, since the fire drill frequently identified personnel changes that would have otherwise gone unnoticed. Another company decided to dual-purpose the organizational incident response team as an information security steering committee. Quarterly meetings were held at corporate headquarters and video conferencing was used to allow remote locations to join in. At each meeting, roundtable discussions were held to review the status of various projects and identify any issues that team members were concerned about. To keep the meeting interesting, vendors or industry professionals were invited to give presentations on various topics. By developing and maintaining an incident response team in this way, your organization will be able to take advantage of the best talents and ideas of your entire organization, both during emergencies and normal day-to-day operations. Properly developed and maintained, this team can save your organization both time and money when the next worst-case scenario finds its way into your environment.

Response Team Services

Although we used the term "incident response" in the section heading, we really should use a broader term, *incident handling*, to indicate what the plan should incorporate. We'll also use the term "operational response team" or "response team" (RT) just so we don't step on any toes (some response team names are trademarked). The response team should be a part of the IT team, but it should also include other key stakeholders such as corporate executives, facilities and operations management and others needed to handle security incidents. Figure 13.1 provides a general list of services a response team can provide to an organization.

Figure 13.1 Common Response Team Services

Response Team Services

Security Management	Proactive Services	Reactive Services
⊙ Risk analysis	⊙ Warnings and alerts	⊙ Warnings and alerts
⊙ Trend analysis	⊙ Threat Communication	⊙ Vulnerability handling - Analysis - Response - Coordination
⊙ Disaster planning	⊙ Configuration Mgmt / Maintenance of Security Solutions	
⊙ Education and awareness		⊙ Incident handling - Analysis - Response support - Response on site coordination
⊙ Training	⊙ Security Assessments	
⊙ Product evaluation	⊙ Security Policies and Procedures	
	⊙ Intrusion Detection	⊙ Artifact handling - Analysis - Response - Coordination

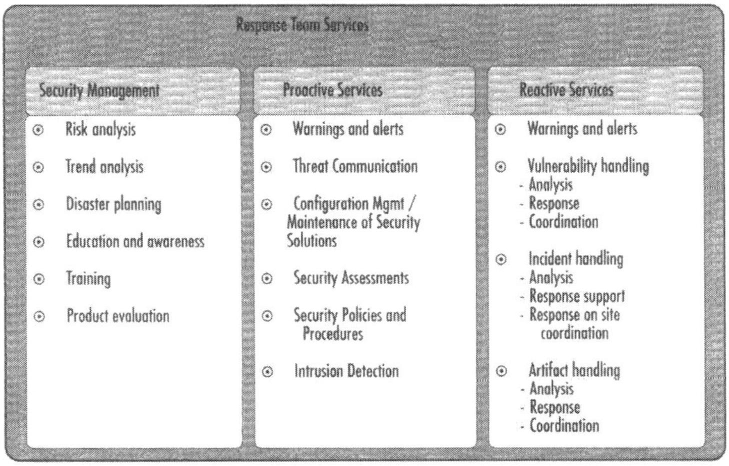

Security management includes performing a risk analysis, which is part of the IT security projects we've discussed throughout this book. Trend analysis can also be part of the security management services. Trend analysis involves looking at network data and analyzing it to search for patterns that occur over time. There's an excellent resource available on trend analysis called *Models of Information Security Trend Analysis* by Tim Shimeall, Ph.D. and Phil Williams, Ph.D. from CERT Analysis Center, Software Engineering Institute, Carnegie Mellon University, Pittsburgh, Penn. It can be found at www.cert.org/archive/pdf/info-security.pdf and is a great reference if you're interested in learning more about the intricacies of trend analysis in the IT security arena. Clearly, someone needs to look at security-related data in log files and elsewhere and try to decipher normal patterns from abnormal patterns that might indicate a problem in progress. Trend analysis might also be part of artifact handling when looking at the trail left by a breach. Disaster planning, which we'll discuss later in this chapter, is another management service the RT can provide. User education is an often overlooked function and assigning this to the RT can keep their skills up-to-date and can provide an extremely useful link back into the user community. In concert with education and awareness, the RT team can provide security training or train-the-trainer programs to ensure that security education is replicated across the enterprise in an effective and efficient manner. User awareness is a critical component of overall network security, and providing consistent, helpful information to users can increase awareness and compliance with security policies and procedures. Finally, the RT can assist in evaluating products for the network. The team might evaluate the security features of a new application or the features of a new security product and how, or even if, it might fit into your overall security strategy.

Proactive services include warnings and alerts about threats and vulnerabilities that exist. This is particularly helpful as part of user awareness and education. If users know that a new phishing scam is asking for usernames and passwords, for example, the RT can alert users and help avoid incidents. Threat communication can include technical information being communicated to executives or IT staff. You can task your RT with

alerting your IT staff to new or developing threats along with recommendations on how to avoid or address vulnerabilities related to these
threats. The team may also be involved with configuring and maintaining
security solutions the company is implementing. Configuration management is an on-going security process that should be incorporated into the
mission of the RT or should be specifically assigned to a senior IT staff
member (or team). Configuration management (CM) ensures that network components are and continue to be properly configured to maintain security. After your security project teams have completed their
work, the maintenance of the network configuration should be clearly
delegated to an individual or team. In many organizations, this is a subset
of the RT. An in-depth look at configuration management is outside the
scope of this book, but there are numerous online resources at your disposal to learn more about configuration management and associated software tools you can utilize to assist in your CM processes. The team may
be tasked with staying up to date on these systems so they provide the
subject matter expertise needed to manage these security solutions at
optimal levels for your organization.

   Reactive services are, of course, the ones you hope you'll never need.
Should your organization have the need for an incident response, a rapid
deployment of your RT can make all the difference between a 'simple'
intrusion and a devastating breach. The reactive services provided by the
RT can include warnings and alerts about threats or intrusions that
appear to be occurring (during initial assessment) or that actually are
occurring (initial response). They can handle vulnerabilities including
analysis, response and coordination. When vendors or other industry
experts announce newly discovered vulnerabilities, you need a team that
can rapidly assess the organization's exposure and respond with recommendations, procedures, patches or monitoring services to address the
specific vulnerability. If an incident does occur, they are typically the first
responders who will analyze the problem, coordinate efforts across the
enterprise to respond to the problem and provide response services on
site, if that's the stated function of the team. In some companies, an RT
deploys to the various company locations to coordinate incident response.

In other companies, the RT is centrally located and provides e-mail and phone support to widely-dispersed IT resources domestically or internationally. Finally, the reactive services include handling what are commonly called "artifacts" in the computer forensics field. It's estimated that over 85 percent of all cybercrimes leave an electronic trail, or an electronic *artifact*. The term artifact is usually used to connote "of human craft or invention," so artifacts of cybercrimes are those electronic trails or footprints left by the intruder. The RT should be trained in finding, analyzing and responding to the artifacts found in the wake of an intrusion attempt or a breach.

Business Intelligence...

Computer Security Incident Response Teams

Computer security incident response teams, or CSIRTS, are teams that not only respond to computer security problems; they should be proactively involved with helping your company avoid computer security threats. There are numerous books, articles, white papers and Websites that provide specific guidance on forming and managing a response team. Our goal in this chapter is not to provide you with a step-by-step guide for forming a team, but in assessing your response capabilities, we will cover the basics of an RT. If you'd like more information on forming a world-class incident response team, check out these websites for starters.

Carnegie Mellon University Software Engineering Institute (CMU SEI)- www.cert.org/csirts/csirt_faq.html

Computer Security Institute - www.gocsi.com/

SANS (SysAdmin, Audit, Network, Security) Institute – www.sans.org

Response Team Assessment

We've briefly covered response team services, so let's turn our attention now to your RT assessment. You'll need to take a look at a number of factors as you look at your company's need for a response team. If you already have a team in place, you need to assess the services provided by the team and whether or not the team is covering all the bases. We've continually talked about the three primary components of all security plans: people, process and technology. A response team interacts with all three of these elements in a variety of ways. We know that IT security comes about as a result of a multi-layer defense strategy that includes:

- Keeping operating systems and applications patched and up to date (technology and process).

- Installing, maintaining and monitoring perimeter defenses (technology and process).

- Reviewing, revising and publishing security policies and procedures (people and process).

- Providing security awareness training to users (people and process).

- Managing incidents (people, process and technology).

Using the model we developed earlier, let's look at your response team's capabilities. There is clearly some overlap in these areas with security activities we've discussed in other chapters.

Security Management Services

Risk analysis, disaster planning, user awareness, training and product evaluation all fall under security management services. We've already discussed risk analysis and risk assessment elsewhere in this book, but this is certainly an area that can be part of the RT's mission, either as part of your corporate IT security initiative or as part of the on-going operations after the security initiative is complete. Security is not a one-shot deal, so you will need to have a team dedicated to on-going security assessment, analysis and planning.

Risk Analysis

We've covered risk analysis and assessment throughout this book, so you should have a clear understanding of what skills are required to perform a thorough risk analysis. If your RT doesn't have the skills needed to confidently perform a risk analysis, you have one of two viable options. The first is to send one or more of your IT staff to intensive training to upgrade and update their skills so they can perform a comprehensive risk analysis. If you don't have staff on board that you believe is capable of this, you might need to look at hiring an outside consultant to perform your risk assessment and analysis for you. However, in the long term, you will need this capability on your team, so you should look both near- and long-term at your options.

Trend Analysis

The CERT document referred to earlier on trend analysis provides an excellent explanation of how trend analysis can help improve network security. Authors Shimeall and Williams state, "In the area of information security, enhanced understanding of trends, patterns, and anomalies could contribute significantly to indicators and warning processes that are a key component of efforts to anticipate, thwart, or mitigate intrusions. It is possible, for example, to extrapolate trends so that defenders have at least some expectation about broad developments that might occur. While this is not foolproof by any means, it can provide some basis for anticipation and lessen surprises." Trend analysis should be part of your response team's security management services so that it can potentially anticipate and monitor troublesome trends and avoid being caught completely off-guard.

Disaster Planning

Disaster planning is part of the security services an RT can provide. The RT can develop a thorough disaster plan that should be part of a larger business continuity planning initiative for your company. If disaster were to strike, how would your company continue daily operations? The answer clearly goes far beyond the functionality of the network and the availability of databases and websites. If possible, avoid taking responsibility for the entire business continuity planning process since IT is just one piece of the puzzle. A business continuity project should be headed up or at least sponsored by a senior level executive, and a business continuity planning project should involve stakeholders from every part of your company — facilities management to operations, finance, HR and IT, to name a few. Disaster planning from a business perspective includes how IT services will be re-established after a disaster. Disaster planning from an IT perspective involves how network services will be restored after a disaster occurs, including natural disasters and network security breaches.

Your assessment should look at your RT's capabilities with regard to disaster planning including the existing disaster plan, the ability to manage and implement a disaster plan after a disaster strikes. We'll cover this in more detail later in this chapter.

Education and Awareness

Although adequately managing your network borders can help to prevent a substantial portion of the external threats to your environment, there are always going to be access points that you simply cannot control. Users who bring their laptops home with them can easily provide a roaming target for autonomous threats such as worms, Trojan horses, and other applications that are forbidden by corporate policy. A software update from a vendor might inadvertently contain the next Code Red, as of yet undetected in an inactive state, waiting for a certain date six months in the future. No matter how locked down your network and perimeter may be, there will always be risks and vulnerabilities that must be addressed. Raising user awareness about security threats, risks and vulnerabilities and educating them about how to avoid or reduce these risks is as important as locking down your borders. Developing effective awareness campaigns should be part of the security management responsibilities of your RT team. A review of educational and awareness activities is part of your RT assessment. Awareness campaigns include awareness of security threats, security best practices as well as awareness of corporate security policies. We'll discuss creating security policies later in this chapter, and the awareness techniques we discuss here also apply to policies you and your team develop to address on-going security practices.

Developing Effective Awareness Campaigns

In order to get the attention of the user base, you'll need to provide incentive to the managers of those groups to help IT get the word out about how to recognize and respond to potential security threats. In order to involve the company's managers in IT security, RT leaders have to make the tasks as simple as possible. When the guidelines are clear and concise and leave no room for interpretation, your chances of maintaining security are much higher. There are many examples of fairly straightforward tasks that can be assigned to managers. For example, the enforcement of acceptable-use policies is one of the most common ways to involve management in information security (though the detection of violations is and probably always will be an IT responsibility).

Company-wide awareness campaigns also leave room for engaging management in your information security posture. Although the IT staff can do a lot to protect users from inadvertently causing harm to the company by implementing technology-based safeguards, in many cases, the users are still the last line of defense. If we could magically teach users to never leave their workstations unsecured and to recognize and delete suspicious e-mail, a considerable portion of major security incidents would never come to fruition. Let's look at three common approaches to disseminating security awareness materials. You can assess whether your RT is taking appropriate measures, given your corporate culture and network structure, to raise and maintain user awareness about IT security through:

- Centralized corporate IT department
- Distributed department campaigning
- Enforcement

Creating Awareness via a Centralized Corporate IT Department

Using this approach, corporate IT assumes responsibility for developing and distributing security awareness campaigns. The problem with this approach is that there is an inherent conflict of interest here. Your IT staff is tasked with keeping the network up and running and at the same time, they are asked to lock down the network to keep it secure. Government best practices (National Security Agency, for example) suggest you keep these two functions completely separate. This is not always possible in small organizations, but if you can separate these out, you'll probably have better results. Your organization may already have produced mouse pads, buttons, or posters that include the help-desk telephone number and instructions to contact this number for any computer issues. Sometimes, this task is handed to the messaging group, and periodic company wide e-mails are distributed including information on what to do if you have computer issues.

Depending on the creative forces behind the campaign, this method can have varying results. Typically, such help-desk awareness promotions are fairly passive in nature. When a user has a problem, he or she looks up the help desk e-mail address or phone number or search for the most recent e-mail to find the number of the help-desk. Communications received from corporate IT are often given the same attention as spam—a cursory glance before moving on to the next e-mail. Part of the reason for this is the nature of the e-mail – many users assume it will be too technical to understand. Let's face it, IT departments are not known for their effective communications styles with users. (If your department excels in this area, you're among the elite).

Even plastering offices with posters or mouse pads can be overlooked; people can become immune to any kind of mass communication today. After all, they've learned to look past banner ads, ignore billboards, mute the TV during commercials and skip entire pages in the newspaper. There are numerous methods of effectively communicating with your user base. You can use humor, rewards and awards (some people might consider this a form of corporate bribery, but if it works, it may cost far less than recovering from a security breach) to get users to pay attention. Look for ways to be creatively entertaining. Ask users to submit humorous IT-related anecdotes and include them in your e-mail distribution. Give small awards to those who submit the selected story. Include a little known fact or an amusing quote – anything to get users to actually read IT e-mail on security. Be sure to make the e-mail readable – leave out jargon and complicated explanations and just make it clear, concise and engaging. If you don't have someone on the RT team that can craft this kind of message, collaborate with your internal communications or PR department for some assistance. In the end, the most challenging obstacle in centralized awareness campaigns is actually getting the attention of the user to ensure the information is read, absorbed and retained.

Creating Awareness via a Distributed Departmental Campaign

In some highly compartmentalized organizations, it may be beneficial to distribute the responsibility for security awareness to individual depart-ments. This approach is useful in that it allows the department to fine-tune the messages to be relayed to the users in a manner more aligned with the users in that area. For example, if global messages are deployed that focus heavily on preventing data theft or inadvertent release of pro-prietary documents, some staff may perceive these e-mails to be irrelevant to them. If they believe the information does not apply to them, they will disregard the e-mail and the information contained within. If a local department is tasked with delivering certain messages, the RT team can work with departments by providing the message and allowing (or requesting) department to tune the message to their department. The upside to this is that the message might be delivered in a manner more appealing to the targeted users. The downside is that your RT will have to be confident that the departments are actually distributing the message. It certainly doesn't help if your organization has pockets of security and pockets of happy-go-lucky ignorant users because their department never passed the message along. If the responsibility is delegated and never exe-cuted, you are in a worse position than if you'd used a centralized IT method of disseminating this information.

In many cases, departmental assistance supplements the centralized security campaign. Issues that can impact users regardless of department are left to IT to manage; more specific concerns such as data privacy and integrity can sometimes be delegated to the organizational groups that require specialized security. The problem is often that departments don't know what to ask and IT doesn't advise. The communication gap at this point becomes the security breach. The response team's charter might include communicating with departmental representatives to identify security needs unique to those areas. This removes the circular problem that often accompanies user security issues – the users don't know the right questions to ask and the IT staff doesn't know what the users need.

The development of such programs will vary greatly from one organization to the next, but as with any interdepartmental initiative, the first task is to enlist the help of the senior management of your department. Once you convince them of the potential benefits of distributing the load of user education, they should be more willing to help you craft a project plan, identify the departments most in need of such programs, and facilitate the interdepartmental communication to get the program off the ground.

Business Intelligence...

USB Sure Is Handy, but Consumer Keys Are Creating a Huge Security Headache

USB makes it extremely convenient for employees to transfer data to portable devices, whether it's for work at home or more sinister purposes. It's not easy to deal with the security headaches this practice creates, but tools are now emerging that allow administrators to know which external devices have been connected to the network, and which files were written to them. Typically this is accomplished with software agents that allow network managers to centrally control USB devices. One approach is to enable the use of company-issued USB drives, while rejecting others. Both SanDisk and Sony have created USB devices that use biometric (fingerprint) technology to secure both a computer (desktop or laptop) and the USB device itself.

Creating Awareness via Enforcement

In a pure enforcement awareness campaign, you count on feedback from automated defense systems to provide awareness back to your user base. A prime example is a content filter scheme that responds to forbidden requests with a customized message designed not only to inform the user that their request has been denied, but also to remind the user that when using corporate resources, their activity is subject to scrutiny. This approach can be quite effective, but there is the potential for this method to backfire.

In many organizations, IT is viewed in any one of several potentially negative ways. The "Enforcer" image usually doesn't foster good will and cooperation between IT and users. If IT takes on an adversarial role, the users are not likely to willingly comply with IT requests or mandates unless they have no other option. In any kind of management relationship, developing the desire to cooperate is always more effective than forcing someone to do so. If users have a dislike or mistrust of the IT department or the RT, they're likely to ignore a virus warning or fail to notify IT of a strange dialog box that popped up after they clicked on a link in an e-mail.

There is an element of psychology involved in designing awareness campaigns. Your task is to provide a balance — effectively conveying what users can do to help minimize the various risks to an organization, reminding them of their responsibilities as a corporate network user, and encouraging them to ask for help when they need it. The threat of repercussions should be saved for the most egregious offenders; if a user has reached the point where he or she needs stronger action, it's probably time to recommend disciplinary action anyway. We'll discuss policies and procedures that will help reinforce (and require) appropriate security procedures later in this chapter. Reminding users of these policies and procedures through awareness campaigns can be helpful since most users glance at policies and procedures during their new hire orientation and never look at them again. Keeping them in front of users in a friendly, useful manner can raise security levels significantly. This job falls to the RT in many companies, assuming a company has a response team.

Make certain that users are aware of what they can do to help protect company resources. If a user in your organization suspected that they might have just released a virus, what should they do? Do they know who to call? More importantly, would they be afraid to call? Your RT's job is to make sure users are aware of their roles and responsibilities in maintaining network security.

Policies

Your IT operations security project plan should include a review of your company's current security policy environment. Once you've completed your review or assessment, you'll need to create a project plan to revise the corporate security policies to help support and enhance network security after your project work is complete. In this section, we'll break down the process into several defined steps, each of which help you to create, review, and enforce the policies you need to secure your corporate network. As we've discussed, current technology can be used to *create* a secure infrastructure, but good policies are necessary to *maintain* it.

Security policies are usually seen as necessary to gain compliance with some higher authority, not as a needed function in network operations. They are often overlooked and undervalued until they are really needed. People, unlike computers, don't follow instructions exactly as told. They have choices, and their choices can put cracks in the security walls. Based on research conducted in 2002, about 78 percent of internally caused security breaches were due to inadequate security policies or users disregarding those policies. The question is: Why weren't security policies put in place if they could have helped to prevent some of these incidents? Part of the answer is that companies may not be aware of just how much security policies can bolster network security.

Founding Principles of a Good Security Policy

A security policy will not solve all your misconfiguration and personnel problems, but it will provide a piece of the puzzle that no other component can provide: structure. Clearly, the goal of information security is to maintain information confidentiality, integrity, and availability (CIA). Security policies are one of the few security tools that help us guard against unknown, unforeseen, future attacks. Policies define what actions need to be taken to maintain secure networks, such as removing inactive users, monitoring firewall activity, and maintaining current, standard server builds. However, proper policies are also not the silver bullet. Policies that are not reviewed, updated, circulated, or enforced will become outdated and ineffectual.

Security policy is one area where management support is critical. Because security policies deal much more with the day-to-day actions of employees, and changes in policy should ideally result in changes in procedures, it is important that security implementers have the backing of management. Effecting procedural change in a corporation where employees are set in their ways can be very difficult, and requires much effort. Before you make an effort to implement any policies, make certain you have specific commitments from management as to their role in your initiative, and the support they will provide.

Security policies should be clear and concise. We've all read policies that sounded like the attorneys had spent three months on it. While there may be some required "legal language" in security policies, the general rule is that they should speak directly to the target audience and provide meaningful information. There are a number of best practices for writing policies; we've included some of them here as a guide for your policy review. Remember, your review of policies should include not only the actual impact of the policy (the do's and don'ts) but the clarity and consistency of the language. If one policy talks about hosts (which, by the way, is something most users don't understand) and another discusses desktop computers, users may be confused. Review your policies for content and style (this is one place where style actually does count). Here are some best practices to consider:

1. Consider the reader.
2. Use consistent naming conventions.
3. Use an easy-to-read writing style.
4. Keep documents current.
5. Balance protection and productivity.
6. Designate policy ownership.

Understanding Current Policy Standards

There are numerous policy standards you can use as reference points for developing your security standards. We'll discuss a few of them here and you can follow up with some independent research to find out what might be most appropriate for your organization.

ISO 17799

One of the most widely accepted and endorsed security policy guidelines in use is the International Organization for Standardization (ISO) 17799:2000. This document was originally the British Standard (BS) 7799, and was submitted to the ISO in late 2000.

There has been some confusion over the ISO 17799 in that you cannot become certified as ISO17799-compliant. When the BS 7799 was originally submitted, BSI declined to include BS 7799-2 for approval, which is a checklist of controls that a company can be audited against. The ISO 17799 is not appropriate to be certified against, and therefore, the ISO has not offered a certification through its registrars. However, if your company has a desire to be certified against the BS 7799-2, which is the closest certification available, you can get more information at BSI's homepage, www.bsi.com.

The ISO17799 can be purchased from BSI for under $200, and it is a worthwhile investment. Though not perfect, it is one of the best we have, and one of the most widely referred-to security documents. It appears to have good traction and is gaining ground, both in the American and international communities, as a solid security standard.

Business Intelligence...

ISO 17799 – Security Management Guidelines

You may be familiar with the International Organization for Standardization (ISO). In 2005, they released a specification, ISO/IEC 17799:2005, which establishes guidelines and general principles for initiating, implementing, maintaining, and improving information security management in an organization. According to the website (www.iso.org), "the objectives outlined provide general guidance on the commonly-accepted goals of information security management. ISO/IEC 17799:2005 contains best practices of control objectives and controls in the following areas of information security management:

- Security policy
- Organization of information security
- Asset management
- Human resources security
- Physical and environmental security
- Communications and operations management
- Access control
- Information systems acquisition, development and maintenance
- Information security incident management
- Business continuity management
- Compliance

The control objectives and controls in ISO/IEC 17799:2005 are intended to be implemented to meet the requirements identified by a risk assessment. ISO/IEC 17799:2005 is intended as a common basis and practical guideline for developing organizational security standards and effective security management practices, and to help build confidence in inter-organizational activities."

SAS70

The Statement on Auditing Standards (SAS) No. 70, Service Organizations, is a tool available to auditing firms and CPAs to conduct an audit of a company that already has implemented an information security program. The SAS70 does not contain a checklist of security controls, but rather allows an auditing firm to issue a statement of how well a company is adhering to their stated information security policy.

If you have already implemented a security policy based on a standard, such as the ISO 17799, the SAS70 may give your information security program additional credibility. Having more accreditation groups stating that your program gets a "pass" grade doesn't necessarily mean you have a more secure program. However, it can help to make customers happy or meet federal or insurance requirements. Remember that the SAS70 is not appropriate for use as a checklist to create an information security policy.

There are three other sets of guidelines that might be of interest to you. They are:

- **Control Objectives for Information and (Related) Technology (CobiT)** A free set of guidelines for information security published by the Information Systems Audit and Control Association (ISACA).

- **ISO 15408/Common Criteria** A technical standard published by the ISO used to support the specification and technical evaluation of IT security features in products.

- **Government Information Security Reform Act (GISRA)** Requires civilian Federal Agencies to examine the adequacy of their information security policies, among other requirements.

Business Intelligence...

Guard Against the Unknown

Imagine if you were able to stop attacks before they started. Imagine if you were able to patch vulnerabilities before they are discovered. Sound impossible? Perhaps not.

If you implement proper information security policies and procedures, you may be able to prevent attacks before they even start. For example, if your policies require you to follow the principle of defense-in-depth, and you have a properly implemented security perimeter around your entire network, you are less likely to suffer an impact from a failure in one component of your network. Another example: If you have proper personnel policies and procedures implemented, such as performing background checks on employees, removing old user accounts held by former employees, and evaluating the threat potential of current employees, you may be less likely to suffer an attack from an insider. With the proper personnel controls in place, you may be able to recognize and mitigate threats from a potentially subversive employee before they take action. You may even be able to recognize them as a threat before they get any ideas and address the problem before it starts.

Creating Corporate Security Policies

Let's begin by stating something obvious, but something easily over-looked. Policies include the written policies in your employee handbook and they also include computer-related methods of managing network security. Both types of policies interact, but they are managed in two distinctly different ways. A written policy can be developed from a software program, replicated throughout the organization and enforced through monitoring user behaviors. A computer policy is developed on the computer, replicated throughout the organization and enforced using hardware and software tools. In this section, we'll discuss both kinds of policies. Let's begin with "written" policies.

First, gather all existing corporate policies that pertain in any way to computer or network security or to security, in general. You want to include general security policies because some may tangentially relate to network security such as policies regarding visitor access or after-hours access to the premises. These kinds of policies clearly impact the overall security of the network and should be included in your scope. The scope for policy review and revision should be "policies that directly or indirectly impact the security of the network, the confidentiality, integrity and availability of the data on the network and the users who use the network." While that's a broad statement, you should start broad and narrow it down later, if needed.

Almost all procedures require technical insight into some area, and many procedures should not be developed without input from experts in those areas. Even areas such as physical security require insight into physical authentication routines, biometrics, and networking and power considerations for physical setting of systems. On the other hand, an exclusive focus on the technical elements may miss some of the people-side issues, which is why you want to have a wide representation of stakeholders participate in these policy review and revision tasks. Figure 13.2 provides a framework, based on the NSA model, of how security policies and procedures should be laid out.

Figure 13.2 Framework for Security Policies

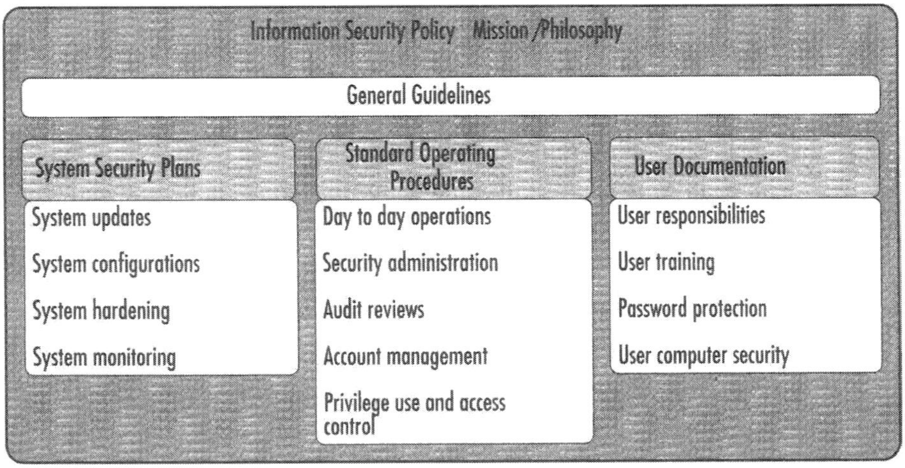

Once you've identified all existing corporate policies that fall within your stated scope, you should categorize them if they are not already categorized. There are numerous resources you can use in creating policies, and if you plan on using a resource (book, manual or software program), you may want to utilize the categories provided. Remember, you may have written computer policies that address these areas. Using the model provided in Figure 13.2, we would say that our written policies fall into the "User Documentation" category and our computer policies fall into the "System Security Plans" category. For example, your written e-mail policy might state that users are not to click on links provided in e-mails from unknown sources. Your computer e-mail policy might prevent users from downloading images in e-mails automatically. Both are e-mail policies; both are implemented in different ways for the same intended effect – network security. We've included a list for your reference, and while it doesn't cover every possible topic, it's pretty extensive.

- Anti-Virus Process
- E-mail Policy
- E-mail Retention
- Encryption Policy
- Information Sensitivity Policy
- Internet DMZ Equipment Policy
- Password Protection Policy
- Remote Access Policy
- Server Security Policy
- Use Policy
- VPN Security Policy
- Wireless Communication Policy

You can also head up to the SANS website for a list found at www.sans.org/resources/policies/#template and download either

Microsoft Word formatted document or Adobe PDF formatted files. These are templates you can use by inserting your company's name in them, so they can be very helpful. You can also review the various security checklists provided by the National Institute of Standards and Technology (NIST) and review the policies required to address all of these various security areas. The checklists can be found at http://csrc.nist.gov/pcig/cig.html.

However, there are four things to keep in mind when using templates.

1. Templates are *one-size-fits-all* and may not be right for your company. You may need to edit them or revise them pretty significantly to make them fit your situation, so don't just do the old "cut-and-paste" and hope for the best. Review, revise and edit until the policy fits your environment.

2. If you do use templates, be sure that they fit your organization's overall tone and approach and that the resulting policies are clear, concise and user-friendly.

3. Be sure that you have the legal right to use the material. You don't want to inadvertently use copyrighted or protected material inappropriately. Most templates indicate how and when they can be legally used and they usually include internal use, but you couldn't sell the templates as your own, for example. Be sure you're in the clear when using templates or language from other sources.

4. Check the final draft with your Human Resources department, your executive team and your legal counsel before finalizing and releasing them. There may be issues about which your team is not aware that should be incorporated into your policies, especially if you use templates that originate outside your organization.

Your policy team should include representatives from legal, human resources, management and IT staff. The security policies should include or address these high level issues:

- Acceptable-use policies

- Permitted activities

- Discipline or repercussions for infractions

- Auditing policies

- Disaster recovery plans

- Reporting hierarchy and escalation paths

- Overall security policy

  - What needs protection and from what type of attack?

  - What methodologies will be utilized for protection?

  - Who is responsible for implementation, monitoring and maintenance?

  - Risk analysis – what is vulnerable and what is the cost if lost/damaged/compromised?

- Growth and service needs projections

- User training and education plans

These documents are necessary for the proper implementation and enforcement of policy after delivery of your overall security plan and your RT may be the team responsible for these activities. One thing should be clear is that these activities should be someone's responsibility, and it should be clearly stated in the job description so that one person is the primary owner of these activities. Otherwise, you risk having no one in charge and that's a sure recipe for failure.

Policy development, like IT security management, is a process. It contains a series of steps that takes the user towards a goal, and no single fix can solve all problems. The following is a process that draws from multiple resources to help security managers develop their policy:

1. **Justification** Formalize a justification for the creation of your security policy. This usually comes from a management directive, hopefully from the Board of Directors. This is your ticket to

create what you need to get your job done. Make certain you have a way to check back with the Board or executive team should it be necessary to get organizational support to complete the task.

2. **Scope** Clearly define the scope of your document — who is covered under your policy and who isn't. Does this apply to all users, to mobile users, or just to Help Desk staff? Does this apply to data centers, to remote offices or to all locations? Does this policy apply to company employees and contractors as well as external vendors? Be as clear and exact here as possible because as with any scope statement, this defines the boundaries. It might also be helpful to define what or who a policy does not cover. If this applies to data centers but not to vendors' data centers, state that clearly. Some topics useful in defining scope are:

- Data centers

- Subsidiaries

- Customer call centers

- Satellite offices

- Business partners

- Professional relationships

- Clients

- Suppliers

- Employees, contractors and vendor staff

- Salaried versus hourly employees

- Executive versus non-executive staff

- IT security staff or management versus IT operational staff

3. **Outline** Compose a rough outline of all the areas you need your policy to cover. If you start here, you'll be able to fill in the blanks as you find sample policies, omit redundancies, and create controls to enforce your policies.

4. **Management support** Management support is different from justification. Justification says "we need this done, and this is why." Management support says "I will help you get this done." This usually comes in the form of support from VPs for smaller organizations, or department managers for larger organizations. Having the support of the Board behind you can make this task much easier.

5. **Areas of responsibility** This is related to the initial scoping you performed, but on a more detailed level. By now you have identified the general areas where you will be responsible for creating a security policy. For example, in your scoping you may have defined that your policy will cover data centers that are directly controlled by your organization, not third parties. You may also have already contacted the manager for the data center and informed them that you will be creating their security policy. If physical security is already covered under a corporate physical security policy, and the data center follows these policies, it may not be necessary to create a second, redundant physical security policy. However, you certainly could integrate the current physical security policy into your document, and include any modifications if necessary, so long as you have permission of the physical security policy coordinator.

6. **Implementation and Enforcement** Once the policy is written, the easy part is over. Distributing it to the rest of your organization, and ensuring it is read and followed, is the hard part. This is one of the most critical steps in developing your policy program. This is where all your work culminates in getting results and is one of the most important reasons to have management support. If you have managed your program properly, there

are many managers, plus the Board, that have supported you in your policy development process. Hopefully you have maintained good relationships with all of them, and they are anticipating the final result of your work. If you write your policies correctly, they will not be an additional burden on your users and there will be less resistance.

7. **Review** Once you have developed and deployed your policy, your job is not yet finished. Changes in regulations, environment, business strategy, structure, or organization, personnel, and technology can all affect the way your policy is interpreted and implemented. Remember that policies should be living documents and the responsibility for maintaining these policies can be delegated to your RT or to a sub-team whose mission is to review, revise and maintain security policies. This is especially true in corporate environments in which you must comply with regulatory or legal standards.

There are also a number of free or commercial policy templates, some of which are listed in this chapter. With the acceptance of the BS 7799 as the ISO 17799, there is a worldwide standard on which you can base your policy creation decisions. However, many policies in existence today were not created using guidelines or templates, but were thrown together in an ad hoc fashion. This is why a policy review should be conducted as part of your IT operational security project – to update and revise policies to create a clear, consistent body of knowledge for the organization.

It's helpful if all policies related to IT security follow the same basic format so that users can quickly read and understand the policies. Creating a template for your policies will make the job of creating policies easier, as well. We've listed the headings that are typically found in security policies, and you can use these to craft your own template. These are based on best practices, and you can select the sections that make sense for your organization.

1. **Policy Name and Overview** Give a brief overview of the policy.

2. **Introduction** Introduce the policy, goals, and why it exists.

3. **Purpose** What is it meant to accomplish, and what risks does it mitigate?

4. **Authority** Who approved this policy?

5. **Policy Ownership** Who is the owner of this policy; who makes changes, and who do I contact with questions?

6. **Scope** Where does this apply to the organization, and who is affected?

7. **Duration** What is the time span of this policy's existence?

8. **Related Documents** What other documents contribute to this policy?

9. **Actual Policy Text** What actual rules will be implemented by procedures?

10. **Roles and responsibilities**

    1. Roles defined and assigned to employees for various classifications.

    2. Responsibilities defined for each role.

11. **Compliance requirements** How do you comply with this policy and what constitutes a violation?

12. **Exceptions to this policy** Those explicitly outside scope.

13. **Enforcement of this policy** How is this policy enforced and what are the consequences for violation?

14. **Revision History** Tracks changes; necessary for handing off to new owners.

Tools

There are a variety of tools available that can help you write your information security policies. These are useful if the policy administrator does not have the time or resources to create an information security document. However, be careful to not place too much trust in the prewritten policies. No policies should be created and deployed if they haven't been reviewed for consistency and checked for conflicts with corporate or government regulations.

Charles Woods has developed a well-regarded compilation of security policies, especially ones that can help you with compliance issues. You can learn more about products that help you develop policies and practices that assist in security and compliance at www.informationshield.com/index.htm.

Another product that you might find useful is PolicyCenter, which helps the policy administrator to create their policies and distribute, track, and enforce them. PolicyCenter uses the templates from Wood's Information Security Policies Made Easy. For more information, see www.pentasafe.com or www.netiq.com/solutions/security/default.asp.

NetIQ offerings allow administrators to create, distribute, and enforce their policies. These features help to create a "living policy" document. For more information, visit www.polivec.com.

Business Intelligence...

Rewriting Your Policies for a Management System

With the advent of automated security policy management systems, there are some things you may want to consider when implementing your information security policy. Do you want to backtrack and implement part of your security policy program using an automated tool? Consider the benefits, but also consider the traps. On one hand, you will be able to monitor continuously for compliance with your security policies, checking everything from patch level to password strength, from access controls to

Continued

intrusion signatures. This can assist you in securing your hosts and network by holding the reigns of policy tight on your network.

However, also consider the switching costs involved once you port your existing policies to the new management system. This will take time and resources, and will probably need to be repeated if you choose to switch to a competing product. In addition, these products are relatively new and untested and may have their own inherent concerns. Finally, these products cover only a specific set of information security policy procedural controls and still require the maintenance of a policy administrator.

Consider the needs of your network and whether you feel you will benefit from the implementation of such a system. If your corporate culture or policies require tight maintenance on compliance with policies in your hosts and networks, either due to heightened threats or government regulation, an automated security policy management system may be appropriate. However, if you think it will add to the security of your network, but you fail to implement additional policies and controls, you are probably leaving a gaping hole in your security policy.

Policy Distribution and Education

Now that we have created our policies, either from templates or tools, we need to implement and enforce them. No matter how wonderful and eloquent a policy may be, if it's not distributed and enforced properly, it is not worth the paper it is printed on.

First, we have to determine the scope of our recipients. It won't make much sense to give our new policies to individuals who don't need to read them, and at the same time it would be a mistake if we missed important personnel. The answer is *not* to distribute all policies to all people in a blanket coverage issuance of our new policies. Instead, you should work with your stakeholders to determine which policies should be distributed to the various segments of the user population.

By discussing this with stakeholders, you can provide a useful IT perspective about security while the stakeholder provides a useful perspective about the user community. Striking this balance will help ensure the policies are not only targeted to the right users but that there are no critical gaps. A few overlaps are better than gaps, but a blanket distribution is almost guaranteed to miss the intended target.

There are numerous creative ways to get users to read and implement policies and security guidelines. As much as you might like to just send them out in a long PDF file or email and then post it on an intranet, that technique is number one on the top of the list of ineffective ways to promulgate security policy.

Instead, make the task palatable. Have department managers discuss policies at staff meetings, post important policies on posters in hallways and break rooms, include the important information in bite-sized chunks in newsletters or interesting e-mails or as screensavers or "message of the day." When you make the communication quick, easy and relevant to the intended audience, you're more likely to get a higher rate of compliance.

Remember, you can simply stand there and be the enforcer, which is only effective when you're standing there, or you can gain compliance through education. It's how good managers manage. By educating your audience in interesting and informative ways, you get higher compliance over a longer term than if you stand there ready to handcuff anyone who disobeys. Get your Human Resources and Training teams involved with educating people on the key policies and find ways to keep these messages in front of users in ways that they won't simply overlook. There are numerous resources you can use to create awareness programs,

Here are two useful links for help in creating an effective awareness program:

- http://csrc.nist.gov/ATE/awareness.html
- www.sans.org/rr/whitepapers/awareness/

Maintaining Corporate Security Policies

Policies must be maintained with constant diligence; otherwise, they will become stale and outdated. The more policies become outdated, the more difficult it is to bring them, and the company, back into compliance. A tool has been released by the Human Firewall Council (www.humanfirewall.org), which allows administrators to evaluate their current security practices against the ISO 17799. It also provides them with a Security Management Index, a ranking of their security management against others in their industry.

As you know, a project is a unique solution to a unique problem, but a process or procedure is developed in response to an on-going need. In this case, you're using a project to develop a process, which is a common outcome of project work. Develop a process for reviewing security policies on a periodic basis. If you are subject to compliance or regulatory requirements, you will absolutely need to have a reliable *process* in place for staying up-to-date. If you are not subject to regulatory constraints, you need to implement a periodic review in order to simply maintain network security. Outdated policies can become a legal liability as much as having no policy in place, so don't assume you can create policies once and be done with it.

If you find this entire endeavor to be a bit unappealing (most IT folks would rather go study DOS commands than deal with policies), find someone on your team that finds this interesting and challenging. Find someone who communicates well and (ideally) is a decent writer and ask them to own the process or the task or to head up the project team. This is a very important part of overall network security and it should get your star players, not your also-ran's. Well-crafted policies delivered in an appealing and usable format will go much further than any firewall ever can. Incorporate solid policy development and management as part of your overall operational security plan.

Disaster Recovery

Disaster recovery is often considered a key component of business continuity planning. However, business continuity planning is broader in scope than disaster planning from an IT perspective. Therefore, it's important that your IT disaster recovery plans include other key stakeholders in the organization. Disaster response planning should be a coordinated effort among various groups within the company. Disaster planning and business continuity planning is a big undertaking and will require a concerted effort on your company's part to develop a coherent plan. A thorough discussion of disaster planning is outside the scope of this chapter, so we'll just cover the basics here. You and your team will need to do additional research to determine the specific elements you'll need to address for your company since every company's disaster and business continuity plans will be different. The basic elements of such a plan should include:

1. Examine and analyze potential threats and vulnerabilities

2. Assess impact of a disruption to normal services

1. Alternative business process handling

2. Customer service backup and recovery

3. Administration, operations, communications and IT

3. Prepare information about existing systems

4. Review involvement of emergency services

5. Initial assessment of potential impact of emergency

6. Mobilizing the recovery teams

7. Notifying employees, families and the media

8. Maintaining suitable records and event logs

You'll need to make sure you cover these key areas:

- Facilities

- Hardware and software

- Communications

- Data files

- Customer services

- User operations

- IT network and communication services

- End-user systems

- Other processing operations

There are a variety of books, training courses and tools available on the Internet that will assist you in creating a business continuity and disaster recovery plan for your organization. While this is not solely the responsibility of the IT department, it's unlikely there is another group in your organization that is, or should be, tasked with this job, so you should consider it the job of IT to head up this planning effort.

The Small Business Administration's website provides a number of guidelines that should be considered in your disaster and recovery planning, though it is by no means exhaustive.

Facilities

1. Develop contingency plans to remain in operation if your office, plant, or store is unusable. Could you operate out of your home or a nearby storefront? Could you quickly transport critical items such as computers, inventory, and equipment? Could you save replaced equipment and reactivate it in an emergency? Could you store inventory, equipment, and supplies off-site? Examine the possibilities, make a plan, and assure that you and your employees know what to do.

2. Keep extras of any hard-to-replace parts or supplies on hand. Store them off-site. If this cannot be done, work with suppliers in advance to assure a secure and adequate supply. Store several days' supply in a place that is not vulnerable to the same disaster as your facility. Be sure to keep this auxiliary supply up-to-date.

3. Make upgrades now that would prevent possible future damage. Strengthening exterior walls, adding a retaining wall or shoring up a creek bank are relatively minor projects in comparison to losing the building to flood waters.

Operations

1. Purchase a backup generator to maintain full operations or critical functions such as refrigeration, lighting, security systems, and computer control in the event of a power failure.

2. Have back-up vendors and shippers in place in case your primary ones are disabled. Set up relationships in advance and maintain them. Place occasional orders so that they regard you as an active customer when you need them.

3. Guard against loss of your customer base by diversifying your product lines, sales locations, or target customers. Make it part of your annual plan to develop new customers, even if your current customer base seems fine. Make the time to do so.

Information and Communications

1. Make backup copies of all critical records such as accounting and employee data, as well as customer lists, production formulas, and inventory. Keep a backup copy of your computer's basic operating system, boot files, and critical software. Store a copy of all vital information on-site and a second in a safe off-site location. Make it a critical part of your routine to regularly back up files.

2. Make pre-arrangements with computer vendors to quickly replace damaged vital hardware. Keep invoices, shipping lists, and other documentation of your system configuration off-site so you can quickly order the correct replacement components. Take care of credit checks, purchase accounts and other vendor requirements in advance so that the vendor can ship replacements immediately.

3. Surge-protect all computer and phone equipment through power and phone lines. A power surge through a telephone line can destroy an entire computer through a connected modem. Invest in a surge protector that has a battery backup to assure that systems keep working through blackouts.

4. Maintain an up-to-date copy of phone numbers, computer and Internet logon codes and passwords, employee phone numbers and other critical information in an accessible location. Develop an employee "telephone tree" to rapidly contact employees in an emergency.

Business Insurance

1. Review your current insurance coverage. Is it enough to get your business back in operation? Will it cover the replacement cost of vital facilities? Make it a regular annual procedure to review and update insurance. Also remember that insurance on mortgaged property probably only covers the lender with nothing left over for you.

2. Be aware of your contents insurance. Does it cover the replacement cost of critical equipment?

3. Know what your insurance does not cover. Most general casualty policies do not cover flood damage. Many require additional riders for windstorm, sewer backup, or earth movement. Consider adding coverage for likely perils, especially flood insurance.

4. Consider business interruption insurance that assists you with operating needs during a period of shutdown. It may help you meet payrolls, pay vendors, and purchase inventory until you are in full operation again. Also be prepared for the extraordinary costs of a disaster such as leasing temporary equipment, restoring lost data, and hiring temporary workers.

5. Don't assume that, just because it never happened before, it never will. Flooding patterns are changed by development: water, which runs off new streets and parking lots, may overwhelm nearby streams and surrounding land. Landslides and sinkholes may develop because of distant earth movement, natural or man-made. The creek by your building may be a tiny, placid stream that has never flooded, but a downpour may change it into a destructive torrent that destroys your building foundation. Plan for the worst.

For more information on small business continuity planning and other small business resources, you can visit the Small Business Administration website at www.sba.gov. You can also find some helpful resources on the Disaster Recovery Journal Website at www.drj.com. The information provided here and supplemented by additional targeted resources should spark thought about what your company will need to recover from a disaster, whether that's a security breach or a hurricane, flood or earthquake.

Be sure you put your plan to the test through simulations and assessments. An untested plan is a big unknown and while you can't always simulate everything that will occur during a disaster, you can anticipate the common scenarios and test your plan. For example, if the corporate network was down, you couldn't use e-mail. How would you communicate? What if the phone systems were also out? You might be able to use cell phones if the land lines were down. Simulating a scenario where power, network and phone communications are down might help you identify gaps in your plan. While you may never know how well you've prepared until you need to implement your plan, recent events such as the Hurricane Katrina disaster response have yielded a lot of new information about how to respond (and how *not* to respond) that you can and should use to reinforce your disaster planning activities.

You will likely want to create a separate project plan for disaster and business continuity planning and work through it as you would any other IT project plan. However, this should be part of the mission and responsibility of your response team.

Regulatory Issues

One of the odd things about regulatory and compliance issues is that meeting these standards does not necessarily make your network or data secure. While that is the intent of these kinds of regulations, they often fall short of their intended effect. In part, that's because lawmakers are not IT security experts, and in part, it's because these are complex issues and it usually takes a few iterations before regulations align with the legitimate operational needs of the business. So, don't be lulled into a false sense of security, thinking that if you are compliant, you are also secure.

Earlier in the book, we discussed the legal implications of many of the regulations facing corporations today. In this chapter, we're going to run through some of these same regulations, but this time with an eye toward operational elements such as creating policies that help you comply. We're providing additional resources, but again, it's important to emphasize that because there are serious consequences to being out of compliance, you should be in close communication with your financial, legal and HR departments during your compliance assessment and implementation work to keep you and your company on the right side of the compliance issue. Also keep in mind that many of these policies and regulations are being updated on a somewhat regular basis, so the links or references might change.

Business Intelligence...

Five Compliance Myths

A white paper released by Symantec entitled "Debunking the Top Five Myths of Compliance" is an interesting read for anyone working on compliance issues in the corporate world. The five myths discussed are:

1. Compliance initiatives don't align with business objectives.
2. Compliance can be solved with a project.
3. Compliance is someone else's problem.
4. IT security is about protecting computers.
5. One security/compliance product can do it all.

The white paper provides a good overview but Myths 1 and 2 are of particular interest. The elements common to all compliance initiatives are those things that align with sound business practices, such as accountability, integrity, custodianship, risk management and standardization. If compliance and security initiatives can be seen as aligned with sound business practices and supporting the long-term success of the company, the perception of compliance-related activities might improve. Granted, there may still be a disconnect between the requirements for compliance and the way your business runs, but seeing compliance as part of sound business practices might help your organization buy into compliance requirements more readily. Myth 2, that compliance can be solved with a project, is also an important take-away. While this book is

Continued

focused on project planning for a variety of security issues, it is clear that operational security, the day-to-day security discussed in this chapter, is how compliance is achieved and maintained. It should be assessed, planned and initially implemented via a project plan, but maintaining compliance requires an on-going commitment with consistent organizational practices in place. This is an important point to understand as you plan your organizational security project so you can be sure the hand-off to daily operations at project completion supports and enhances continued compliance.

The Symantec website has a lot of good information on IT security and compliance, though it naturally is slanted toward their products and solutions. You can find the white paper many places online, but here's one link to it: www.bindview.com/resources/whitepapers/Debunking_WP.pdf (Bindview was acquired by Symantec).

Health Insurance Portability and Accountability Act

The Health Insurance Portability and Accountability Act (HIPAA) was signed into law in 1996. HIPAA came about in response to a need to establish standards for the transfer of patient data among health care providers. This includes health care clearinghouses, health plans, and health care providers who conduct certain financial and administrative transactions electronically. Insurance providers, hospitals, and doctors use a wide array of information systems to store and transfer patient information, and have various claim forms with varying formats, codes, and other details that must be completed for each claim. HIPAA was enacted to simplify the claim process. Privacy and security issues were also addressed in this legislation to protect patient data.

The latest documents including resources to determine if your company must comply with HIPAA standards can be found at www.cms. hhs.gov/HIPAAGenInfo/02_TheHIPAALawandMore.asp#TopOfPage. The guidelines include:

1. **Administrative procedures** Documented practices to establish and enforce security policies

2. **Physical safeguards** Protection of buildings and equipment from natural hazards and intrusions

3. **Technical security services** Processes that protect, control, and monitor information access

4. **Technical security mechanisms** Controls that restrict unauthorized access to data transmitted over a network

There are implementation guides available for purchase at www.wpc-edi.com/hipaa.

By now, you're probably aware of your company's need to be compliant with HIPAA, but if you're new to your job or new to the company, you may want to become more familiar with HIPAA. You might find some useful tips on how to address compliance issues on these Websites.

Gramm-Leach-Bliley Act

On November 12, 1999, President Clinton signed the Financial Modernization Act, commonly known as the Gramm-Leach-Bliley Act (GLBA). GLBA includes provisions to protect consumers' personal financial information held by financial institutions. There are three principal parts to the privacy requirements: the financial Privacy Rule, Safeguards Rule and pretexting provisions.

The Financial Privacy Rule governs the collection and disclosure of customers' personal financial information by financial institutions. It also applies to companies, whether or not they are financial institutions, who receive such information. An overview of the financial privacy requirements is summarized on the Federal Trade Commission website at www.ftc.gov/bcp/conline/pubs/buspubs/glbshort.htm.

The Safeguards Rule requires all financial institutions to design, implement and maintain safeguards to protect customer information. The Safeguards Rule applies not only to financial institutions that collect information from their own customers, but also to financial institutions "such as credit reporting agencies" that receive customer information from other financial institutions.

The Gramm-Leach-Bliley Act also prohibits "pretexting," the use of false pretenses, including fraudulent statements and impersonation, to obtain consumers' personal financial information, such as bank balances. This law also prohibits the knowing solicitation of others to engage in pretexting. The Commission has been active in bringing cases to halt the operations of companies and individuals that allegedly practice pretexting and sell consumers' financial information. For more information, visit www.ftc.gov/privacy/privacyinitiatives/glbact.html.

Sarbanes-Oxley Act

As you know, Sarbanes-Oxley deals with financial information and it applies to companies that deal with a variety of financial types of data. As with HIPAA, if your company is required to be compliant with SOX, you're probably already painfully aware of this fact and have had to deal with it. Your operational IT security plan should review current and updated compliance data and ensure that your operational plans incorporate methods that support or enhance compliance with SOX. Clearly, many of these regulations continue to undergo modification, often to clarify the intent or implementation of a particular aspect of the regulation.

If you want more information on SOX, the University of Cincinnati College of Law has a great Website that gives you some of the details (a link from the Security and Exchange Commission Website), at www.law.uc.edu/CCL/SOact/toc.html. Due to the complexity of these regulations, you should certainly involve your financial and legal experts in discussions about what's needed to become or remain compliant. If your company is currently compliant, your IT security project might look at ways of reducing the burden of maintaining compliance through the use of appropriate technologies and through the revision and enforcement of security policies.

If you want to really dig in and learn more, there's a wealth of information on the SEC's Website at www.sec.gov/index.htm.

Business Intelligence...

SEC Announces Next Steps for Sarbanes-Oxley Implementation to Help Small Companies

Anyone working at a small public company knows the challenges that SOX compliance brought on. In response to several on-going problems, the SEC issued a press release that speaks directly to changes that should relieve some of the burden on small companies.

On May 17, 2006, the Securities and Exchange Commission took a series of actions it intended to take to improve the implementation of the Section 404 internal control requirements of the Sarbanes-Oxley Act of 2002.

The actions the Commission intended to take included issuing SEC guidance for companies and working with the *Public Company Accounting Oversight Board* (PCAOB) on revisions of its internal control auditing standard. These actions are based on extensive analysis and commentary in recent months from investors, companies, auditors, and others. The actions also included SEC inspections of PCAOB efforts to improve Section 404 oversight and a brief further postponement of the Section 404 requirements for the smallest company filers, although ultimately all public companies will be required to comply with the internal control reporting requirements of Section 404.

If you read the press release carefully (follow the link provided below), you'll notice some interesting language such as "we will take a giant step toward 'getting it right'" and "future guidance will be scalable and responsive to their individual circumstances." This language suggests that the SEC knows that compliance is needed but that many smaller companies are struggling to make sense or to implement these regulations. Given the number of companies subject to SOX and the overwhelming complexity of the rules, this is an important acknowledgement from the SEC and should help companies that are struggling to become compliant even after compliance deadlines have passed.

For more information or to read the entire press release, see www.sec.gov/news/press/2006/2006-75.htm

There are numerous other regulations to which your company may have to apply but these are the "big three" compliance headaches for most companies. In order to incorporate these regulations and compliance requirements into your IT operational security project plan, you'll need to be fairly familiar with the requirements, so the first step would become well-versed in these areas.

Many companies sell products they claim help companies become compliant with a variety of regulations. Clearly, some of these claims are true and some are probably not-so-true. However, before you run out and purchase a variety of these products, you should complete your assessment and create a project plan for gaining and maintaining compliance. Taking an ad hoc approach to purchasing and implementing compliance products will leave you with a patchwork of solutions that may do nothing more than drain your IT budget. If you use the steps delineated throughout this book – define the problem, define the desired outcome, look at potential solutions, look at constraints, assumptions and requirements, and select the most appropriate solution – you'll end up with a much more thorough and consistent solution to your security and compliance needs. As the earlier sidebar pointed out, security and compliance cannot be viewed simply as "projects," they must be seen as on-going activities that are woven into the fabric of corporate operations. However, becoming secure and compliant is often best done through a project plan that has the development of on-going processes and procedures to maintain and enhance security as one of its objectives.

Project Parameters

Now that we've looked at the elements of IT operational security including incident response, policies, disaster recovery and regulatory issues, let's define the problem statement, the mission statement and the project's other parameters. Remember that your operational security planning should begin with forming a core project team that can participate in defining the project parameters from the ground up. Once you've defined the basic project requirements and parameters, you can then modify team membership so that you include needed subject matter experts and other key stakeholders for the project.

We're assuming you know how to do the basic project definition tasks, so we will run through these elements rather quickly with an eye on operational security.

Problem

The essential problem is that technology, alone, cannot protect your network. People need to understand what they can, should and must do to maintain that security. Your organization needs to have a plan for how to respond if something does happen – whether that's a security breach or a disaster. If your company is subject to regulations, you must develop processes, procedures and policies that enable you to remain compliant and to maintain security after project work is complete. So, let's pose three potential problem statements you can use as starting points.

> Our firm is looking into expanding, and part of this expansion would include handling consumer credit card data. If we choose to go this route, we will be required to comply with GLBA regulations. The executive team wants to know what it will take (how much time and money) to become compliant so they can make a decision as to whether they want to begin handling consumer credit card data or not. At present, we are not subject to any regulation and we do not know if our organization is even close to being compliant with GLBA regulations.

> Our firm is required to comply with Sarbanes-Oxley, but we are struggling with understanding the rules, regulations and compliance requirements. Since we are a very small firm, the regulatory burden has been significant.

> Our firm has been fortunate not to have experienced a security breach, but we do not have a well-thought out approach to responding to an incident, whether natural or manmade.

Mission/Outcome

Your mission statement, often called an outcome statement, is the flip side of your problem statement and you should be able to come up with an outcome statement pretty easily. We'll continue with the three sample problem statements.

> To provide a clear assessment to management of the time and cost required to become compliant with GLBA regulations so the executive team can make an informed decision about the cost/benefit ratio of the proposed transaction.

> Taking a fresh look at our current practices using a more methodical project management approach will yield a better strategy for us to get closer to becoming and remaining fully compliant with Sarbanes-Oxley now and in the future.

> We will have a clear, concise plan for maintaining security in the event of a security incident, whether natural or man-made. We will know exactly what to do in the event of a problem and will respond in a calm, rational and effective manner.

Solution

We're taking a short cut here because the next step in your process would be to think through all the possible solutions you and your team could come up with and then rank the solutions, identify organizational constraints that would impact solution selection and select a solution. We're assuming you'll do all of that and that you're ready to select your solution. Clearly, the solution must be one that addresses the needs of your particular organization (time, budget, scope) and if needed, the regulatory environment.

Your solution should also encompass the four distinct operational security areas we discussed in this chapter: incident response, policy management, disaster planning and recovery and regulatory compliance. Your solution will form the foundation of your operational security project plan, so we'll assume for our purposes that you are addressing all four areas. The solution statement would look something like this:

> To address these concerns, we will perform an operational risk assessment and form a permanent response team tasked with reviewing, managing and maintaining operational security including incident response, policy management, disaster response and regulatory compliance related to the corporate IT infrastructure and services.

Your solution may vary but the idea is to determine how you will address the problem and the mission or desired/required outcome. You can also develop your three to five top level objectives at this point based on the solution you've identified. We'll expand on these objectives when we create our work breakdown structure later in this chapter.

Scope

As with any project scope statement, you need to define what is and is not included in your project. This scope statement will form the foundation of your Work Breakdown Structure and after you've defined your WBS, you'll come back to your scope statement to see if the two match. If not, you'll have to revise one or the other so that you have consistency throughout your operational security project. Let's look at some of the things that could be included (or excluded) from your scope statement.

- **Incident response** Your operational security plan, at minimum, should include planning for incident response. Best practices dictate forming a response team but if your planning activities suggest a different and more optimal path, incorporate that into your plan.

- **Policy management** Policy management includes the compiling, review, revision and maintenance of all corporate policies related to IT and network security. You may choose to carve this out into a separate project using a different team. Be clear about whether your project includes or excludes policy management. Also define clear boundaries of policy management for project purposes so you know what is included and excluded from your policy management tasks.

- **Disaster response** This is part of business continuity planning (BCP) and while IT plays an ever increasing role in BCP, you may decide to parse out this work. For example, your company may already have BCP teams or projects in place and you may need to prepare your IT portions and insert them into the larger BC plan. Be clear about what your planning activities include and exclude and how this fits into the larger BCP process at your company.

- **Regulatory compliance** Compliance crosses several major corporate "boundaries" and touches legal, financial, HR, training and IT. If your operational security plan includes regulatory compliance, be specific about which regulations you're addressing and how you'll gain and maintain compliance. If this is going to be delegated to a regulatory project team or a team whose mission is to manage regulatory issues, be clear about that as well. Compliance must be maintained once achieved, so your project plan should include on-going operational procedures that support compliance if compliance is part of your project plan.

Cost

Operational security planning costs can include the cost of purchasing tools, equipment and training resources but most of your cost in a project of this nature is going to be time. The majority of tasks in this project involve gathering, reviewing, revising, disseminating, managing and updating data. If you have a specific budget allocated to this project, make note of it here so you can compare it to the costs you calculate after developing your WBS.

Time

Operational security planning is usually not as time-sensitive as other IT security projects may be. Certainly having a trained response team or well-crafted user security policies are important and should be in place, but securing the infrastructure is usually a first step followed by a review and improvement of operational security. Therefore, you may find that your schedule for operational security is longer because it typically is not as time-sensitive. That doesn't mean you can "back burner" it and expect everything will turn out fine. It should be a priority to perform the tasks in this project to maintain the security your team has worked so hard to achieve through the other projects.

Quality

As we've stated throughout the book, quality is as much a state of mind as it is specific measurable results. In your operational security project plan, quality will include statements and measurements in the following areas:

- **Incident response** Your incident response plan should include metrics about response time and time between response and recovery. It could include quality measurements related to how many incidents were detected and prevented, how many incidents were detected and responded to and how well various systems performed.

- **Policy management** Policy management quality is a bit more difficult to quantify. The goal should be to create and manage policies that are as clear, concise and effective as possible. Metrics might include number of policies reviewed and revised, number of security incidents related to user issues before and after policy revision or the number of awareness campaigns or employees trained through the policy management activities.

- **Disaster response** BCP and disaster response quality should strive to be as complete as possible. A high quality plan will touch on all the major points of BCP. This area may be difficult to determine the quality of the plan in advance of actually using the plan so testing portions of the plan through simulations and assessments will be an important part of developing a quality disaster response plan.

- **Regulatory compliance** Compliance is an area where there are sometimes very clear measurements and sometimes vague or conflicting requirements for compliance. As the regulatory environment continues to evolve, especially with regard to computer security, it will be important to use as many quantifiable metrics as possible. Your legal liability may well be based upon quality assessments such as percentage of policies compliant with Statute 123 or the number of transactions that fall inside or outside some particular measurement. If there are specific quality measurements included in the regulatory areas you must comply with, be sure to include those in your quality statements and in your technical requirements.

Remember, too, that you need to assign relative priorities to scope, cost, time and quality so that when you're in the middle of managing your project, you know how to make decisions consistent with the priorities of the project and the organization. Define which parameter is least flexible – the one that should not change — no matter what. Then define which parameter is most flexible – the one that can move around to accommodate the other elements. That's not to say that you shouldn't try to meet all four parameters, but that you need to know the relative importance of these factors so you can work your plan. Things always change in a project, and you simply need to know where to "give" and where to hold firm. Run your decisions by your project sponsor and be sure that he or she agrees with your assessment. If you have a disconnect here, you could end up with a major problem down the road.

Functional Requirements

Your functional requirements describe the things that should be part of the project plan, but they do not describe specifically how those requirements will be implemented. Functional requirements in each of the four areas discussed in this chapter may include:

- **Incident response** Your incident response plan should describe exactly what actions should be done in the event of an incident. How those actions are implemented may be described as part of your functional requirements or they may be part of your technical requirements.

- **Policy management** Policy management functional requirements could include the specific categories of policies your operational security plan will address. Functional requirements in this area could also include specific user or organizational requirements for policy that should be included in the project plan so that you describe the full scope of policies to be addressed.

- **Disaster response** Which disaster response activities should be included in your project? Is this part of a larger BCP or will you be incorporating the basic BCP elements into your operational security plan? Define specifically what you will address within the scope of your operational security project plan.

- **Regulatory compliance** What specific regulations is your company required to comply with and what are the areas of compliance required? If you clearly define these functional requirements, developing methods for meeting compliance requirements will be that much less burdensome.

Technical Requirements

The technical requirements for most IT projects are often the easiest to define, but in the case of operational security requirements, the functional requirements may end up being easier to define. Technical requirements should be developed from your functional requirements and should include details on how you will be required to deliver the functional requirements of the project.

- **Incident response** Your technical requirements should describe how you will respond to an incident. In the technical requirements, you should include tools, technologies and timelines that are required or that will support meeting the functional requirements. If you will use specific tools like sniffer tools or IDS/IPS systems, those should be clearly spec'd out in the technical requirements.

- **Policy management** What are the technical requirements for policy management? They might include specific policy development software tools or they might include the required elements of all IT security policies. The technical requirements provide detail on how you will develop the policies in your organization, so they might also include the methods you'll use to collect, store, archive and manage policy revisions. For example, you might define a document management system for version management as part of your policy management technical requirements. Since policies are typically part of the compliance environment as well, you may need to define specific technologies that will be used to meet policy management requirements for compliance purposes.

- **Disaster response** The technical requirements for disaster response may be quite varied since BCP and disaster response may include partial and full recovery requirements. If your company has multiple geographic locations, your technical specifications will vary from a company that has one location. You might define the amount of power a backup generate will need (or your project plan may include tasks to help you define that), the number of users to be supported in a temporary or alternate work location, the amount of network storage required or the specifications for off-site storage of critical network data.

- **Regulatory compliance** Technical requirements for regulatory compliance vary greatly due to the diverse nature of the compliance environment. Specifications that describe how you will meet functional (and regulatory) requirements may include software specifications, audit cycles, monitoring tools and more.

Legal/Compliance Requirements

There may be legal and compliance requirements that don't fit neatly into functional or technical requirements that you may want to clearly delineate in this section. In addition, even if it overlaps a bit, you may find it helpful to articulate the compliance requirements in a separate section so they can be easily found, referred to and updated as needed. It's wise to take whatever advance steps you can to make your compliance process easier and less burdensome on your entire organization. Keeping compliance requirements separate can also help you distinguish between operational plans that you are choosing to implement to improve security versus those you are required to take by an outside organization that ultimately may, or may not, improve security in your organization.

Success Factors

You may choose to include success factors in your requirements planning or you may choose to include it later in your project assumptions section. In either case, you should clearly articulate what it will take for the project to be a success. If those factors are missing or constrained, your project success is at risk. If the success factors are never articulated, you might fail to realize a key component is missing. Once defined, these can be listed as requirements for the project and can be included in risk management planning as well, since a missing success factor puts the project at risk.

Required Skills

The skills needed for an operational security project plan really run the gamut from technical skills to operational management to communication and writing skills and just about everything in between. We've created a preliminary list from which you can start.

- **Technical skills** Networking, systems (servers, hosts), security components (routers, firewalls), administration, operations, applications, databases.

- **Auditing skills** Thoroughness, attention to detail, understanding of auditing/assessment procedures and best practices, documentation, versioning (document management), and archiving.

- **Planning and coordination skills** The operational security plan touches all parts of the organization so the ability to effectively plan cross-departmental activities and the ability to coordinate across the enterprise are important skills for this type of project. In addition, disaster and continuity planning require strong planning and coordination skills as does developing an incident response team.

- **Writing skills** The ability to clearly articulate polices and procedures, incident response procedures, disaster recovery plans and more requires strong writing skills.

- **Communication skills** An operational security project requires the ability to communicate effectively with a variety of stakeholders across the enterprise. The coordination of incident response or disaster response planning (and implementation) requires strong communication skills as does the promulgation of corporate security policies throughout the company.

Personnel Needed

Your operational security project plan will need people from inside and outside your IT department. After identifying your required skills, you'll need to begin looking for the right resources in your organization to assist in this project. Look across your organization for the right people – don't be myopic and look only at IT staff for help with this project. The more you can reach out and involve people from different areas of your company, the better your organizational security planning process will be. You may still need to head this up and keep in on track but you should certainly include a representative cross-section of your company in this process.

Project Processes and Procedures

Project processes and procedures are those needed to run this specific project. We're assuming you have a whole slew of processes and procedures at your disposal from working on other similar projects. So, let's look at which ones might be unique to an operational security project plan.

First, you'll need cross-functional communication and coordination. Whereas other IT projects teams may have included members from other departments, this project *must* include members from across the organization. Do they all use email? For example, some companies have divisions or sections of their companies that are less technical than others. If you have a manufacturing plant, do all the employees there have access to email or an intranet? If not, then disseminating project update or security policies to them may present a different set of issues. Look across the organization and across your proposed team (we'll cover team composition in the next section) and determine the processes and procedures that might work with this diverse population. If some members of the team use Instant Messaging and other members are not IM-enabled, you may have communication problems.

Second, you'll need to test many of your plans in simulation types of settings. For example, you can run a drill for incident response or disaster response but you won't be able to fully simulate all aspects of an actual problem. Your processes and procedures should address this unique need as well. How are problems with drills or simulations addressed? How should be they be documented or escalated? Certainly, you'll need to have well-thought out change management processes that help you revise your project plan based on results from tests. If you find that your project work or your test results are missing the mark, you'll need to have very solid practices in place to manage the process of implementing feedback and change based on project results.

For compliance and regulatory issues, you most likely have to follow very specific mandatory steps, processes and procedures. These should be included as project procedures so that as you work your way through your project you don't have two sets of procedures to follow. You may choose to incorporate them in a way that makes it clear they are part of the regulatory or compliance process so they can be given the attention needed. You'll also need to define the processes and procedures needed once project work is complete to maintain compliance standards. This is usually accomplished by adding one or more tasks in your project plan regarding on-going operations and project hand-off, as discussed earlier in this book.

Project Team

We've touched on this throughout the chapter because we've talked about the far-reaching nature of an operational security project plan. Once you've defined the functional, technical, and regulatory requirements for the project, you've defined what you need to accomplish in the project. By looking at the specific skills needed to accomplish project work, you've essentially defined who you need. Gathering that team together and coordinating those activities will be your biggest challenge for two reasons. First, you'll be interacting with people from all over your organization and coordinating them can simply be a challenging task. Second, not everyone is going to recognize, accept or respond to the authority of an operational security project manager. This is where executive support becomes vital to project success. If you have one of the top executives in your company supporting you and your project's objectives, you should find more organizational cooperation. If needed, your executive support may also include putting a bit of pressure on unruly or unwilling participants to ensure project success.

Gather your project team together and get them fired up about the project by helping them understand the importance of their work on the project and how it supports and enhances the company's efforts. Make sure you introduce everyone present since there may be people who have never worked together before. In large companies, there very well could be people who've never met or even heard of others before this meeting. Develop a team roster and distribute it to all team members. Define roles and responsibilities so that everyone is clear about how the project will proceed and how they will interact with the team. These are all basic IT project management concepts that are not unique to operational security. However, operational security is likely to pull in people from areas of the organization who may not normally interact closely with IT or who have never been involved with this kind of project. Therefore, it's your job as project manager to pull these folks in, make them feel welcomed and set clear expectations so everyone can work effectively in their assigned roles.

Project Organization

Organizing an operational security project is challenging because it can (and usually is) so wide-reaching in scope. Your typical organizational methods will probably work well but you'll need to coordinate to a greater extent. This type of project lends itself well to creating sub-teams since developing policies is a set of tasks distinctly separate (though related) from forming a disaster response plan. These teams can be coordinated but allowed to work in parallel if the project is well-organized. You may choose to break the four topic areas we've discussed (incident response, policy management, disaster response and compliance) into four sub-projects that roll up into a master plan so that resources, schedules and activities can be effectively coordinated. It's highly likely that you'll have activities that intersect that need to be coordinated. For example, you'll certainly need to coordinate compliance activities with policy development so that the policy team can create the policies and operational procedures needed to maintain compliance on a moving-forward basis. You should also keep an eye on translating all of this work into on-going operational procedures. At the end of your project work, you should have procedures defined that deal with incident response, policy management, disaster response and compliance for day-to-day operations. Once project work is completed, you should have updated policies and procedures for daily operations.

Project Work Breakdown Structure

Creating a work breakdown structure begins with your top level objectives. If you haven't defined those top level objectives yet, you can do so now. Ideally, you should define three to five top level objectives, though in some cases you might reasonably come up with six or seven. Too many and you've gone into too much detail too early, too few and you may be overlooking something or may not fully understand your project. Since we've been working with four project elements, let's use those as our four objectives. If your project is not going to cover these four areas, you can modify your project's WBS as needed.

1. Develop Incident Response Plan

    1.1 Assess incident response risk

    1.2 Develop incident response plan

        1.2.1 Develop network incident response plans

        1.2.2 Develop communication incident response plans

        1.2.3 Develop Web incident response plans

        1.2.4 Develop perimeter incident response plans

        1.2.5 Develop server and host incident response plans

        1.2.6 Develop infrastructure component (wireless, routers, DHCP, etc.) incident response plans

    1.3 Develop incident response team

        1.3.1 Develop incident response skills requirements

        1.3.2 Develop incident response operational procedures and processes

        1.3.3 Define incident response legal and regulatory requirements

        1.3.4 Define incident response documentation requirements

1.3.5 Define incident response reporting and escalation requirements

1.4 Develop incident response notification plan

1.4.1 Define notification process for local management

1.4.2 Define notification process for corporate IT management

1.4.3 Define notification process for regional or global management

1.4.4 Define notification process for local law enforcement action

1.4.5 Define notification process for national law enforcement (FBI, Homeland Security) action

1.5 Develop plan testing methodology

1.6 Develop plan test schedule

1.7 Develop plan maintenance schedule

1.8 Develop on-going team training processes

2. Develop Policy Management System

2.1 Review current policies

2.1.1 Review current policy management practices

2.1.2 Develop procedures for categorizing and assessing security policies

2.1.3 Develop policy management assessment and summary

2.2 Develop list of current policies

2.2.1 Inventory all applicable policies

2.2.1.1 Name of policy

2.2.1.2 Date of policy

2.2.1.3 Category or topic of policy

2.2.1.4 Scope of policy

2.2.1.5 Exclusions to policy

2.2.1.6 Owner of policy

2.2.2 Organize policies by category

2.3 Identify policy gaps

2.3.1 Identify gaps in policy by topic area

2.3.2 Identify gaps in policy by last update (i.e. a policy written in 1997 is more at risk than a policy written in 2005).

2.3.3 Identify gaps in policy by business area

2.3.4 Identify gaps in policy based on compliance areas

2.3.5 Develop gap analysis summary and action plan

2.4 Develop, revise and update policies based on Task 2.3.5

2.5 Conduct policy review prior to release

2.6 Release updated policies

2.7 Develop policy management/maintenance plans

3. Disaster Planning

3.1 Examine and analyze potential threats and vulnerabilities

3.1.1 Assess facilities vulnerabilities

3.1.2 Assess hardware and software vulnerabilities

3.1.3 Assess communications vulnerabilities

3.1.4 Assess data files vulnerabilities (confidentiality, integrity, availability)

3.1.5 Assess customer services vulnerabilities

3.1.6 Assess user operations vulnerabilities

3.1.7 Assess IT network and communication services (remote access, email) vulnerabilities

3.1.8 Assess end-user systems vulnerabilities

3.1.9 Assess other processing operations vulnerabilities

3.2 Assess impact of a disruption to normal services

3.2.1 Identify alternative business process handling

3.2.2 Identify customer service backup and recovery

3.2.3 Administration, operations, communications and IT

3.2.4 Identify compliance issues related to disaster management

3.3 Prepare information about existing systems

3.4 Review involvement of emergency services

3.5 Prepare initial assessment of potential impact of emergency

3.6 Define processes and procedures for mobilizing the recovery teams

3.7 Define processes and procedures for notifying employees, families and the media

3.8 Define processes and procedures for maintaining suitable records and event logs

4. Regulatory Compliance

4.1 Identify regulations that apply to organization

4.2 Identify specific compliance requirements

4.2.1 Identify required administrative procedures

4.2.2 Identify required physical safeguards

4.2.3 Identify technical security services required

4.2.4 Identify technical security mechanisms required

4.2. Identify policies and procedures required to gain compliance

4.3 Implement changes required for compliance

4.4 Identify policies and procedures required to maintain compliance

4.5 Implement policies and procedures required to maintain compliance

4.6 Identify procedures for reporting non-compliance

    4.6.1 Identify procedures for reporting non-compliance to company management

    4.6.2 Identify procedures for reporting non-compliance to regulatory bodies

    4.6.3 Identify procedures for emergency response to non-compliance

    4.6.4 Identify procedures for non-emergency response to non-compliance

4.7 Identify legal requirements for reporting and documentation

4.8 Identify requirements for on-going compliance audits

4.9 Identify requirements for on-going compliance maintenance activities

Remember to check your scope against your functional, technical and regulatory requirements and make sure everything syncs up. This is one place that scope begins to creep out of control and ensuring that your requirements are reflected in your WBS and that the WBS reflects your requirements is a great checkpoint in your project planning process. Also, if anything has changed (or even if it hasn't), this is also a good time to sit down with your project sponsor and review the project before project work begins. If any changes need to occur, now's the time to make them.

Task details are developed after your WBS. Remember the basics. Tasks should have one and only one owner, though others may contribute to task work. Task details help drive quality, so be sure to have subject matter experts assist in developing task details, especially completion criteria. Note any dependencies, constraints or requirements associated with tasks so you can build them into your project schedule and budget. Identify how long a task will take (duration allotted) and how much you expect it to cost. Some projects work with hard costs only and do not track direct project labor. Other companies want people to keep timesheets to track time against specific projects. This is especially true in consulting firms, but your firm may also require this level of tracking.

Project Risks and Mitigation Strategies

The risks to an operational security plan are as varied as the tasks within the plan. Let's break it down based on the four high level objectives and we can walk through a few of the possible risks. You and your project team should sit down, identify the risks and rank them based on their likelihood of occurring and the criticality of such an occurrence. Then, you can choose how far down the prioritized list to go in your planning session. For each risk, develop a mitigation strategy that includes potential ways to avoid the risk altogether or ways to reduce the impact of the risk should it end up occurring. Finally, be sure to include triggers so you know when you'll implement your mitigation plan. If appropriate, you should also look at potential risks your alternative strategies may inject into your project plan. In some cases, you may find that you'd rather deal with a particular risk, should it occur, than to implement a more flawed "Plan B."

Incident response

Remember, risk planning is not the risk that an incident will occur but the risk that something will impact our incident response project plan. What are the things that could put that project segment at risk? Things like a corporate re-organization, acquisition or spin-off certainly would impact your project. Staff layoffs could decimate your response team; budget cutbacks could impact your team's ability to remain current on threats and vulnerabilities. Budget cutbacks could also put equipment (hardware, software) purchases at risk. Changes in the legal or compliance markets could imperil your incident response project plan as well.

Policy management

Changes in the management structure or philosophy of the company could certainly put a policy management project at risk. Another potential risk to this part of the project is the other corporate-wide disruptions including re-organizations, acquisitions, spin-offs that would impact the scope of the project. Layoffs could impact your ability to complete the project. Changes in the legal or regulatory environment could certainly put a project of this nature at risk. The project could also be delayed by changes in technology, so the project should be coordinated with any major infrastructure changes such as the implementation of a wireless network, the upgrading of remote access technologies or the introduction of new authentication technologies, to name a few.

Disaster planning

You disaster planning is also subject to the same macro-level considerations as the previous two topics covered. Changes to various infrastructure components such as the introduction of a new facility or the closing of an older one that was providing data services or backup functions could impact your disaster planning project. You and your team should look closely at what could impact your disaster planning and address these because when it's all said and done, you need a solid disaster recovery plan in place. You need to test that plan and keep it up-to-date so that if a disaster strikes, you have some reasonable path to follow. Budget cuts, layoffs and other organizational change can dramatically impact your disaster readiness, so you should give this area of risk mitigation serious attention.

Regulatory/compliance

The biggest risks to this section of your project plan involve things generally outside of your control whether that's changes to the language or intent of the regulations or lack of clarity about requirements for compliance. This is an area where you should involve executives and legal

www.syngress.com

counsel, if appropriate, to ensure you've covered the potential risks and understand the intricacies of this environment.

Project Constraints and Assumptions

Utilize this section of your project plan to list any known constraints to your project as well as any assumptions under which you're operating. Constraints are usually restrictions impacting your project as a whole such as resource limitations or constraints imposed by other corporate initiatives or directives. Constraints could also come from the legal or regulatory environment, so be sure to look at these as well.

Assumptions are critical to include in your project plan because with every project, we make certain assumptions about the environment that will be in place when we commence project work. Examples of assumptions include staffing levels, expertise on your IT project team or the timing of other key events. While it's sometimes hard to see exactly what we're assuming to be true about a situation, work with your project team to identify these assumptions and document them in your project plan. Run them by your project sponsor to be sure they're acceptable assumptions. If you assume that the company will proceed with purchasing and implementing an IDS or IPS system and it doesn't, your incident response plan could change significantly. If you're assuming your company will remain at its current size and number of locations, list that since any change could impact all areas of your operational security plan.

Project Schedule and Budget

At this point, you should have all the data you need to develop a preliminary schedule and budget based on the information defined in your WBS. You'll need to enter your WBS into a project management software tool if you want to use automated scheduling features (highly recommended). You'll need to look at resource constraints as well as dependencies. In this project, you may have four sub-teams performing project work but there may be overlap. It's conceivable (perhaps likely) that you'll have the same or overlapping resources on your policy management section and on your compliance section because these two areas are so closely connected. You may also have the same or an overlapping group of people working on your incident response section and your disaster planning section. Be sure you account for overlapping resource conflicts in your schedule. You also need to identify dependencies for the project. These will probably have common characteristics the four sections. For example, your policy group's timing will depend on the timelines of the incident response team, the disaster recovery team and the compliance team because policies cross all those boundaries. Look for these areas and be sure that your schedule accommodates these. Once you've loaded in your dependencies, check your critical path. If all (or none) of your tasks are on the critical path, something's wrong and you'll need to go back through your schedule to see what's going on.

Each task contains details regarding cost, so you should also be able create a realistic budget for your project at this point. Both schedule and budget should be reviewed with your project sponsor and signed off on. If there are any problems, resolve them now before project work begins.

One final note on project budgets – you will need to have on-going activities to support network security. Your project plan should include an assessment of the on-going activities and costs the company will incur to maintain security. This is typically less than the cost of going through another full-blown security assessment. Including information about the cost of on-going security operations at the end of your project, as part of project close-out can help you budget moving forward.

IT Operational Security Project Outline

1. Develop Incident Response Plan

    1.1 Assess incident response risk

    1.2 Develop incident response plan

    1.3 Develop incident response team

    1.4 Develop incident response notification plan

1.5 Develop plan testing methodology

1.6 Develop plan test schedule

1.7 Develop plan maintenance schedule

1.8 Develop on-going team training processes

2. Develop Policy Management System

2.1 Review current policies

2.2 Develop list of current policies

2.3 Identify policy gap

2.4 Develop, revise and update policies based on Task 2.3.5

2.5 Conduct policy review prior to release

2.6 Release updated policies

2.7 Develop policy management/maintenance plans

3. Disaster Planning

3.1 Examine and analyze potential threats and vulnerabilities

3.2 Assess impact of a disruption to normal services

3.3 Prepare information about existing systems

3.4 Review involvement of emergency services

3.5 Prepare initial assessment of potential impact of emergency

3.6 Define processes and procedures for mobilizing the recovery teams

3.7 Define processes and procedures for notifying employees, families and the media

3.8 Define processes and procedures for maintaining suitable records and event logs

4. Regulatory Compliance

4.1 Identify regulations that apply to organization

4.2. Identify policies and procedures required to gain compliance

4.3 Implement changes required for compliance

4.4 Identify policies and procedures required to maintain compliance

4.5 Implement policies and procedures required to maintain compliance

4.6 Identify procedures for reporting non-compliance

4.7 Identify legal requirements for reporting and documentation

4.8 Identify requirements for on-going compliance audits

4.9 Identify requirements for on-going compliance maintenance activities

Summary

You can secure your network using hardware and software but if you don't develop operational plans to maintain that security, you still have significant risk to your network. Operational security involves developing incident response teams that can address three major areas of security: security management, proactive services and reactive services. Your response team planning project (or sub-project) should address these areas and provide on-going support for network security. The work of the response team overlaps other areas of the organization and including key stakeholders in the response team's planning and implementation will help provide a more comprehensive approach to incident management.

Policies and procedures are vital to on-going security operations. The IT staff will need updated policies and procedures for managing day-to-day security and users will need updated policies and procedures to help them do their part to maintain a safe and secure network environment. Most companies have policies and procedures related to network and computer security but they are often implemented in a haphazard or lax manner, resulting in security lapses. Since a large number of internal security breaches are the result of someone intentionally or unintentionally disregarding security policies, this is an area that will bolster network security significantly. Review and revise policies then make sure they're kept up-to-date and that users are well aware of them. Using targeted education and awareness campaigns, you can be sure your users have the tools they need to help maintain a secure computing environment.

Disaster planning is the subject of entire books, so we only covered the basics in this chapter. However, you should be aware that disaster planning and recovery are part of the larger business continuity planning function. As such, your project team should include stakeholders from every corner of the organization. In some companies, the IT staff heads up BC planning because so much of the work involves ensuring network services become quickly available after a disaster. In other companies, IT staff participates as part of a corporate project team to perform overall BC planning that incorporates IT plans.

Regulations regarding confidentiality and privacy have proliferated in recent years and almost every IT staff has to deal with some sort of regulations. While this can be an onerous task, working within a consistent methodology such as IT project management can make the task more manageable. Failure to comply with regulations can be costly in some cases; in other cases, it can be the cause of serious legal action. To avoid these problems, be sure to understand your company's compliance issues and seek expert advice as you move toward compliance. Some regulatory agencies have provided very clear guidelines; other guidelines are vague or contradictory. Addressing these issues within an IT project management framework can help you support and defend your position and ultimately get you close to achieving and maintaining compliance.

All four of these areas have overlapping segments and taking an integrated approach to operational security will help you avoid gaps that can be created by looking at these areas as individual projects. Operational security project plans are often developed and implemented in parallel or subsequent to other IT security project plans because they provide the framework for maintaining IT security once achieved. This critical step should be undertaken with the same attention to security and detail as every other IT security project plan and should be the final piece of the puzzle in maintaining a secure environment. Network and IT security is a never-ending job, but putting solid operational plans in place will help reduce the burden by building in practices and procedures that support and enhance IT security.

Solutions Fast Track

Operational Security Assessment

☑ Operational security planning and implementation helps support and enhance network security through addressing the on-going security needs of the organization.

☑ These on-going needs can be broken down into five main areas: Incident response, security policies, disaster recovery, regulatory compliance and configuration management

☑ Incident response is typically managed through the creation of a response team.

☑ The response team's mission can be broken down into three areas: security management services, proactive services and reactive services. Together, these three areas address the on-going security services needed to maintain a secure network environment.

☑ Most companies have policies related to network security including IT operational procedures or policies and user policies.

☑ Policies that are not current are a liability to network security because they may require or advise users to take actions that are no longer appropriate or that cause confusion.

☑ Policies should be written in a clear, concise and easy-to-understand manner that enables the intended audience to quickly and easily understand what is required to maintain security.

☑ Awareness campaigns are an important part of promulgating security policies. Raising user awareness about security issues, especially in an environment where security threats change everyday, can mean the difference between an attempted intrusion and a successful one.

☑ Disaster planning is part of the larger business continuity planning process.

☑ Disaster planning is often part of the mission of the response team and there may be overlap in these planning processes.

☑ Disaster planning should include facilities, operations, IT operations and business functions.

☑ The regulatory environment is constantly changing and you may need outside expertise or legal counsel to assist in your compliance planning.

☑ Using a project management methodology will help in gaining and maintaining compliance.

☑ Be sure to build compliance requirements into your project plan so that you can use your project plan as a means toward compliance.

Project Parameters

☑ Executive support is essential to the success of all projects, but even more so to IT operational projects that span the organization.

☑ Define your functional and technical requirements with an eye toward compliance issues to reduce your challenges in this area.

Project Team

☑ Be sure to create a cross-functional team for your operational security. There are often issues outside of the IT department that should be taken into consideration during the planning phase.

☑ An operational security project requires slightly different skills than a purely technical project. These included the ability to perform organizational audits, to develop policies and procedures and to create consistent, clear and useable documentation.

Project Organization

☑ An operational security plan requires a bit more cross-departmental coordination due to the wide reaching nature of operations.

☑ Some operational security planning can be done in parallel with other project work; other planning must be done only at the conclusion of other project work. Identify areas where working in parallel is feasible (and desirable) to avoid working at cross-purposes.

Project Work Breakdown Structure

☑ Your Work Breakdown Structure development should begin with developing the high level objectives of the project.

☑ The four high level objectives for your operational security project plan include incident response, policy management, disaster planning and regulatory compliance.

☑ Task details should be developed by subject matter experts.

☑ Task details should include compliance or regulatory requirements so that when project work is complete, the bulk of the compliance work has been completed as well.

Project Risks and Mitigation Strategies

☑ Every project has risks that must be addressed. When working on an operational security project plan, your risks are often related to the wider organizational environment.

☑ In some cases, mitigating your risks can cause more operational problems than the risk itself. After identifying operational security risks, determine whether your "Plan B" introduces more risk than the original action.

Project Constraints and Assumptions

☑ Constraints limit your ability to complete project work. Constraints are external to the project itself and have to do with the organizational environment in which the project is being managed.

☑ Listing assumptions is critical for project success because if any of the elements you're assuming to be true or present changes, your entire project is at risk.

☑ In an operational security project plan, constraints and assumptions can be related to corporate-wide actions such as acquisitions, divestitures, joint ventures and other business relationships.

☑ Operational security plans are also impacted by impending hiring or layoff plans. Disruptions to your corporate-wide operational security project team can derail even the best project plans.

Project Schedule and Budget

☑ The schedule for your operational security project plan requires coordination across a variety of functional areas.

☑ Some operational security components can be done in parallel with other activities. In some cases, the operational security planning must be done only at the completion of other project (typically more technical projects) so that security can be maintained on a going-forward basis.

☑ The budget for an operational security budget often is more heavily weighted toward labor costs than expenditures for tools, technology or equipment.

☑ Be sure your project budget can later be translated into a budget to support on-going security operations.

Index

Syngress: *The Definition of a Serious Security Library*

Syn·gress (sin‑gres): *noun, sing.* Freedom from risk or danger; safety. See *security*.

Printed in Great Britain
by Amazon

59259083R00364